FLORENTINE NEW TOWNS

DAVID FRIEDMAN

FLORENTINE NEW TOWNS

URBAN DESIGN IN THE LATE MIDDLE AGES

The Architectural History Foundation
New York, New York

The MIT Press
Cambridge, Massachusetts, and London, England

© 1988 by the Architectural History Foundation and the Massachusetts Institute of
Technology
Printed in the United States of America

Friedman, David, 1943 Aug. 15-
    Florentine new towns: urban design in the late Middle Ages/David Friedman.
    p. cm. — (Architectural History Foundation books; 12)
  (American monograph series)
    Bibliography: p. 352
    Includes index.
    ISBN 0-262-06113-9
    1. New towns — Italy — Florence Region.   2. Cities and towns, Medieval — Italy —
Florence Region.   3. City planning — Italy — Florence Region. I. Title. II. Series.
III. Series: American monograph series (Architectural History Foundation (New York,
N.Y.))
    NA9053.N4F75 1988   88-6289
    711′.4′094551 — dc19   CIP

David Friedman is Associate Professor of History in the Architecture Department at the
Massachusetts Institute of Technology

Photographs not otherwise credited are the author's. Similarly, uncredited plans and
drawings were prepared for him. Except where noted, the plans of Italian towns are
based on the most recent cadastral surveys of the Ufficio Tecnico Erariale.

Designed by William Rueter

Publication of this book has been aided by a grant from the Millard Meiss Publication
Fund of the College Art Association of America. [MM]

TO ANN

CONTENTS

ACKNOWLEDGMENTS

THE MODEL for my treatment of the urban environment as a subject of art historical inquiry is Wolfgang Braunfels's *Mittelalterliche Stadtbaukunst in der Toskana*. Like Braunfels, I embrace the ideas that officials in charge of the physical fabric of late medieval Italian cities pursued aesthetic as well as practical goals and that the environments they created were intended to serve political interests or, as Braunfels might have put it, represent cultural values. Braunfels himself did not give much significance to the new towns but fortunately a predecessor, Maina Richter, did. Her article, "Die 'Terra murata' im Florentinischen Gebiet," anticipates my work in relating the towns to Florentine territorial policy and her extensive archival research was the point of departure for my own. In his *Arte e urbanistica in Toscana, 1000 – 1315*, Enrico Guidoni defined a new way of looking at town plans to which my own geometric interpretation is indebted. If I have succeeded in advancing the discussion of new towns and medieval urbanism, much of the credit belongs to James Ackerman who both as teacher and colleague has supported this project and encouraged its approach.

In the early years of my work I benefited greatly from Howard Saalman's interest in new towns. The comradeship of fellow students in the Florentine Archives, particularly John Najemy and Humphrey Butters, was of inestimable value. So, too, was the guidance of Gino Corti who also corrected my transcriptions of documents for this publication. In later years my colleagues at the University of Pennsylvania and the Massachusetts Institute of Technology, particularly Henry Millon and Stanford Anderson, expanded my critical horizons and tamed my wilder fantasies.

Villa I Tatti, the Harvard University Center for Italian Renaissance Studies, through its directors Myron Gilmore and Craig Smyth, and the Institute for Advanced Study, where Irving and Marilyn Lavin took members under their wing, provided stimulating environments in which to work. The staffs of the Archivio di Stato, the Bibliotheca Nazionale Centrale, the Kunsthistorisches Institut, and, especially, Villa I Tatti in Florence, and of the mayors' offices of Scarperia, San Giovanni, and Castelfranco have all provided generous and valued assistance.

Financial support that enabled me to work on this project came from the University of Pennsylvania, the Massachusetts Institute of Technology, the American Council of Learned Societies, the National Endowment for the Humanities, and the Institute for Advanced Study, Princeton.

Nicholas Adams of Lehigh University helped me to accomplish a major restructuring of the manuscript with great insight and tact. Victoria Newhouse of the Architectural History Foundation, and the copy editor, Barbara Anderman, struggled to bring clarity to the text and, where they could, to give it grace. Moira Duggan created the index. Richard Rainville, Howard Averback, and Judith Randolph prepared the manuscript. Donna Harris and Stephen Baker designed and executed the plans. The printing skills of Janet de Jesus brought the photographs to life. My heartfelt thanks to all.

My greatest debt is to Ann Gabhart who sustained me when the demands of this project were heaviest and to whom, with gratitude and love, I dedicate it.

FLORENTINE NEW TOWNS

INTRODUCTION

S AN GIOVANNI is a big, bustling town at the center of the upper Arno valley. It lies on flat land between the gravel flood plain of the river and the tracks of the state rail line, along a road that, since the thirteenth century, has linked Florence with Rome. This road serves as the spine of a very special system of streets. Unlike the surrounding villages in the Chianti region to the west and in the Apennines to the east, whose precipitous, hillside sites induce an irregular pattern of curving or climbing roadways, San Giovanni is shaped by streets that are straight, run parallel to one another, and intersect cross streets at right angles. Men, not topography, established their form.

The view down any of the principal thoroughfares (Fig. 1) extends the length of the town. Facades line both sides of each street, and only cross streets interrupt the continuous parallel enclosure, introducing accents of light and increased traffic at regular intervals. The prospect down any road was once closed by the defensive wall (this has now been replaced by other structures), which circled the settlement. Movement on any of the principal streets leads to the center of the town, where a large rectangular piazza stretches from one side of the urban complex to the other. In the middle of the piazza, to the west of the main street, stands the town hall. San Giovanni, the church of the town's first convent, dominates the space to the east; the parish church of San Lorenzo and the oratory of the town's miraculous Madonna frame the square to the west. The piazza is the daily meeting place for the townspeople, the site of the weekly market and of holiday celebrations.

The regularity of San Giovanni's plan is the product of the town's

1 San Giovanni. Main street, view from the southeast.

origin. San Giovanni was a founded or new town, created in 1299. It is one of a thousand such towns that more than doubled the number of European urban centers between the early twelfth and the mid-fourteenth centuries. Sponsored by such political authorities as the Holy Roman emperors and the kings of France as well as local counts, abbeys, and city governments, founded towns adapted the land to new conditions. They accommodated a growing international trade, provided regional centers where previously there had been only small agricultural villages, pioneered undeveloped areas, and secured contested territory. Settlers were drawn from the vicinity or relocated from great distances. Government was established by the town's founder, whose agents administered justice and collected taxes. Many of these settlements prospered. Lübeck in Germany, Montauban in France, Salisbury in England, and Alessandria in Italy are all medieval new towns.

When new towns were placed on open sites, their founders were called on to plan the physical layout as well as to organize economic and political activity. Planning could be limited to the surveying of a single street and a few house lots or it could extend to the design of a complex urban composition. Formally ambitious schemes were rare. One successful plan, reproduced without concern for the special conditions of the site, could serve many projects. Type, not invention, dominates the formal history of the new towns. In the great majority of cases the significance of the towns is best appreciated by geographers, economists, and historians of law, military events, and local history. On a few occasions, however, the planning process was the focus of a broad cultural and artistic debate. The plans produced under these special circumstances include some of the greatest works of western urbanism.

The present book examines the most obvious and best documented case of this kind. Its subject is a group of five towns founded by the city of Florence between 1299 and 1350. San Giovanni is one of them; the others are Castelfranco di Sopra, Terranuova, Scarperia, and Firenzuola. The documentation for the unrealized plan for Giglio Fiorentino adds further information. The towns preserve their medieval plans relatively well. In the best of them there is a grandness of conception and an attention to detail that raises orthogonal planning to the level of art.

In the Florentine new towns the discipline of straight lines and right angles is rigorously enforced; it is, however, only the medium for expressing more sophisticated formal ideas. Symmetry dominates the plans. The main street is one axis of composition; a line drawn perpendicular to it, through the middle of a central square, is a second. A large number of parts of the plans conform to the magnetic field of these lines, from the arrangement of building lots around the square to the configuration of the town's defenses. The variety of size and shape of the elements integrated into San Giovanni's orthogonal matrix is extraordinary. Long blocks oriented parallel to the axis of the main street are made to fit comfortably with a square of extended proportions perpendicular to them. In contrast to the mechanical repetition of like units that is sometimes held up as the paradigm of medieval new-town planning, the complexity of Florentine designs distinguishes them as the most accomplished urban projects of their age.

The Florentine new towns were works of art in the literal sense that their designers were artists. We do not know this about any other medieval new-town project. In part this is the result of the surviving documentation. For most new towns only the official acts of foundation are preserved. These documents assign authority and grant legal privilege; they say almost nothing about design and construction. The Florentine archives preserve both this and another level of record; in addition to legislative documents, the deliberations and financial accounts of planning committees and builders chronicle the city's activities as a founder of towns. The daily records identify the designers of the new towns as mason-architects from the circle of builders active in the city's public projects. Careful examination of the plans reveals their contribution. In an age in which geometry was considered the essence of art, the indispensable theoretical base for all design, the geometrically generated proportions of the new-town plans are a sure sign of the participation of professionals in the design process.

The new towns were built to serve Florence. They were fortresses in newly acquired territory, markets that collected produce for the city, and centers of loyal population. They became administrative capitals of the expanded Florentine state and the main resting places on routes that brought people and merchandise from all over Europe. The towns represented Florence, both to its new subjects and to travelers; their very names proclaimed their allegiance to the city. San Giovanni was the name of the city's patron saint; Firenzuola and Giglio Fiorentino borrowed Florence's own name. The towns tied the land to the capital by presenting models of urban life to the rural population. The public institutions of the new towns were copies of Florentine examples. Through them the residents of the settlements assimilated city ways and integrated themselves into the life of the state. By the fifteenth century men from the new towns were making important contributions to events within the city.

The Florence that the new towns represented was itself a recent

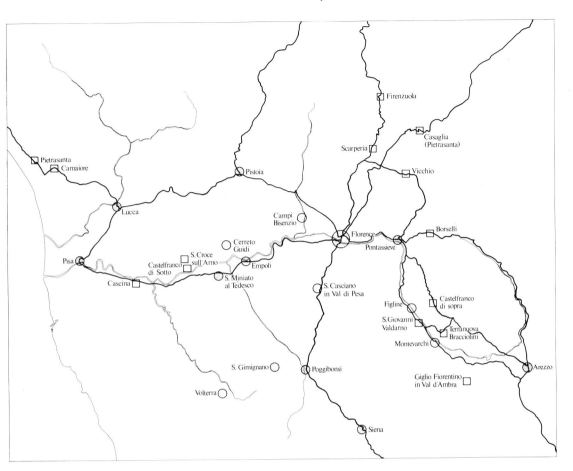

2 Tuscany. Squares represent founded towns, circles are towns expanded by the Florentines, shaded circles are cities.

creation. A merchant regime came to power in the city in 1282 with the expansion of public authority as one of its principal goals. This political idea had many implications for the physical character of the city. The government took control of the urban environment in a way that no previous regime had. It passed the first law of eminent domain since antiquity and embarked on an ambitious program of reconstruction and expansion. The new cathedral, the monumental town hall, numerous churches, and the circuit of walls that increased the size of the city five fold were all projects undertaken by the merchant commune.

The plan of the city underwent a major transformation in this period.

From a townscape of isolated neighborhoods shot through with back alleys accessible only to the people who inhabited them and dominated by the urban castles of the powerful extended families of the nobility, the government attempted to remake the city into a spatially unified whole. Straight, wide streets were the primary instruments of change. The new roadways rationalized the city's space and improved hygiene. More important, they established a system of public space protected by the new merchant regime that tied all the areas of the city together. Roadways replaced the courts at the center of private precincts as the focus of architectural design. The street system converged on the center of town, where the great buildings that served the whole community were prominently sited.

This architectural vision has had a lasting effect on all western urban design. The great cities of modern Europe have monumental cores and comprehensive systems of public thoroughfares. Squares and streets provide the sites for building; architecture looks outward with elaborate facades. The late Middle Ages pioneered this urban structure but even in Florence the rebuilding of the environment was never completed. A long history of habitation marked the city in ways that had little to do with the new values. Even the ambitious government of the priors could not completely transform a city whose origins reached back to antiquity. To appreciate the most comprehensive schemes of the merchant commune we must look to the new towns. At San Giovanni and the other towns, Florentine planners not only represented the capital city, they perfected it. These were the ideal cities of the merchant commune. Thus, a study of the new towns is a study of Florence itself.

Florence's new towns were located in the countryside, 30 to 50 kilometers north and east of the city (Fig. 2). The most important projects were conceived in clusters, with the upper Arno valley the first area targeted for development. In 1285 the Florentines discussed the creation of one or two towns there (Document 1); when they went ahead with the project in 1299, the foundation document called for three towns (Document 2). The immediate results of this initiative were the towns of San Giovanni and Castelfranco di Sopra.[1] San Giovanni (Figs. 3 – 10; see Fig. 1) is located between the towns of Figline and Montevarchi, on land that until the thirteenth century had been marsh.[2] Earlier settlements and an older road lie on the gently rolling plateau to the northeast of the riverbed. Castelfranco (Figs. 11 – 15) was sited there, about 6.5 kilometers from San Giovanni. A third town was built in 1337, when the residents of twelve villages southwest of

3 San Giovanni. From the cadastral plan, nineteenth century (ASF, uncataloged).

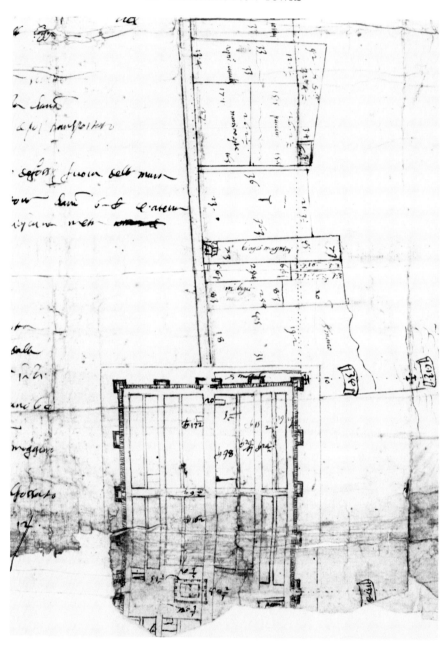

4 San Giovanni. Sixteenth century (ASF, *Piante dei Capitani di parte*, cartone XVIII, no. 28. Text in Document 22).

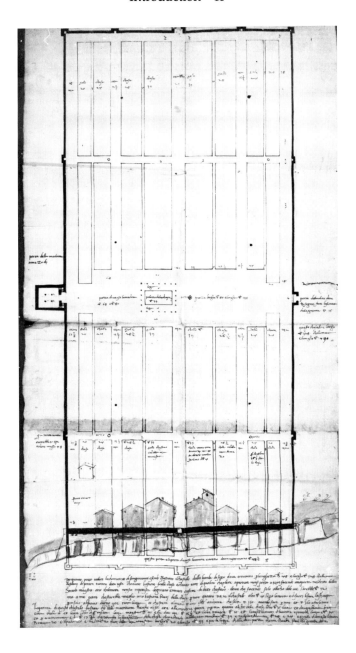

5 Piero della Zucca, drawing of San Giovanni, 10 March 1553 (ASF, *Cinque conser-vatori del contado*, 258, fol. 602 bis. Text in Document 23).

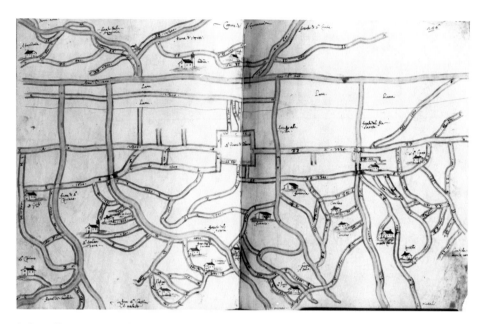

6 San Giovanni and surroundings (ASF, *Capitani di parte,* numeri neri 121, fols. 227v – 228r).

7 Giorgio Vasari and Giovanni Stradano, *Allegory of San Giovanni Valdarno,* detail, 1563 – 1565. Palazzo Vecchio, Florence, Salone dei Cinquecento (Photograph: Soprintendenza alle Gallerie, Florence).

8 San Giovanni. Central square with the Palazzo Pretorio and the church of San Lorenzo, seen from oratory of Santa Maria delle Grazie.

9 San Giovanni. Central square with the church of San Giovanni, seen from the Palazzo Pretorio.

10 San Giovanni. Alley behind lots facing onto the main street.

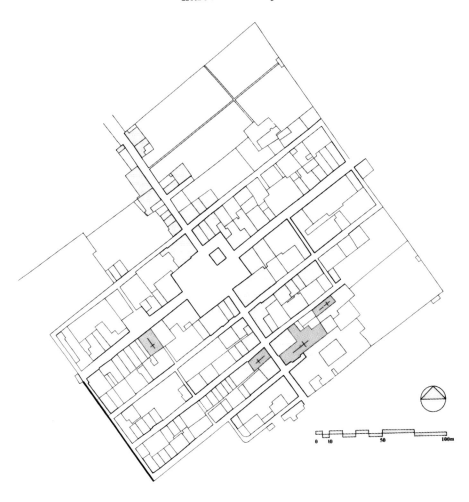

11 Castelfranco. From the cadastral plan, nineteenth century (ASF, uncataloged).

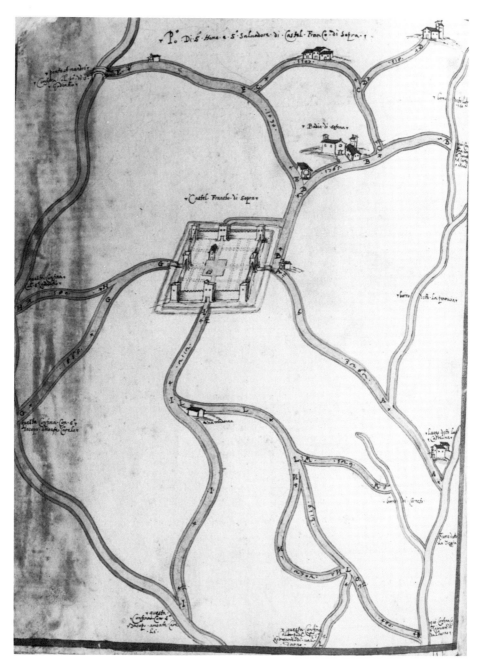

12 Castelfranco and surroundings (ASF, *Piante dei capitani di parte*, piante dei popoli e strade, 121/I, fol. 253v).

13 Castelfranco. Central square, view from the south.

14 Castelfranco. Southwest gate.

15 Castelfranco. Road inside the town wall.

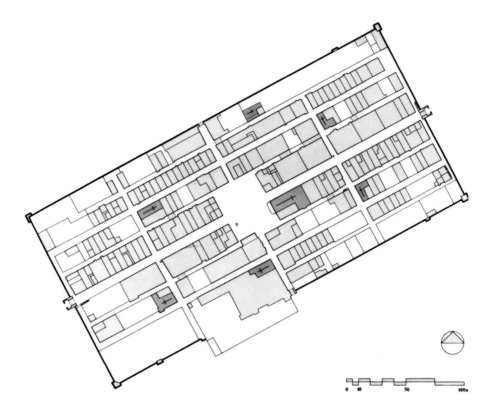

16 Terranuova. From the cadastral plan, nineteenth century (Ufficio Tecnico Erariale, Arezzo).

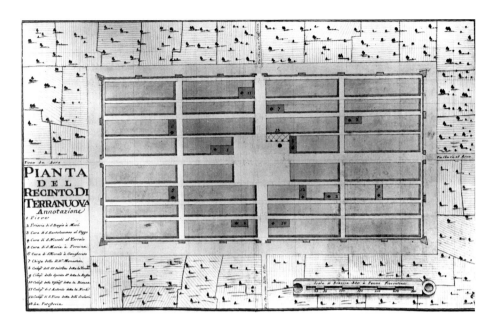

17 Terranuova, 1779 (Biblioteca Nazionale, Florence, *Manoscritti*, A.1.13, fol. 34).

18 Terranuova. Central square, view from the northwest.

19 Terranuova. Main cross street, view from the northwest.

20 Terranuova. Residential street in the southeast quarter.

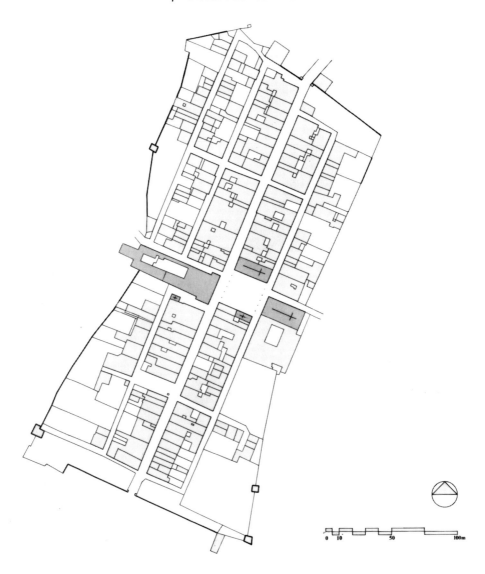

21 Scarperia. From the cadastral plan, nineteenth century (ASF, uncataloged).

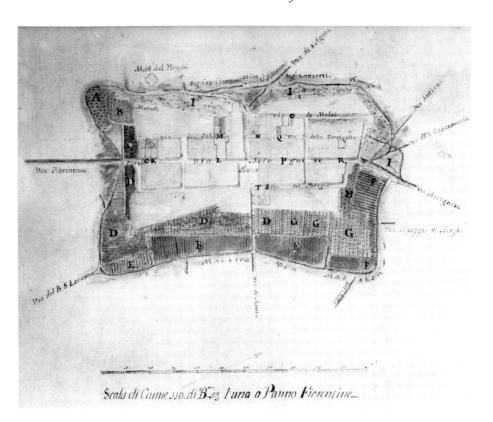

22 Scarperia, after 1776 (ASF, *Conventi soppressi,* 136, 143/I, no. 23. Text in Document 24).

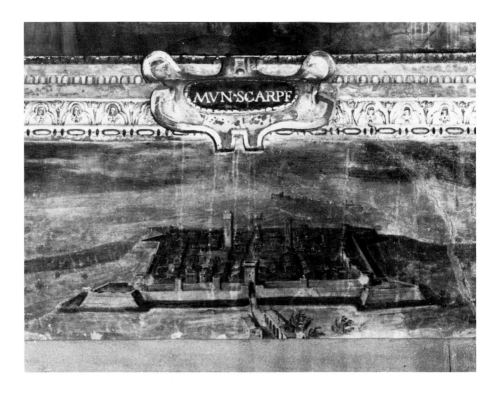

23 Giovanni Stradano, *Scarperia*, 1556 – 1559. Palazzo Vecchio, Florence, Sala Cosimo I.

24 Scarperia. Main street, view from the south (Photograph: Alinari 10093).

25 Scarperia. Central square, looking toward San Barnaba.

26 Scarperia. Central square, looking toward the Palazzo Vicarile.

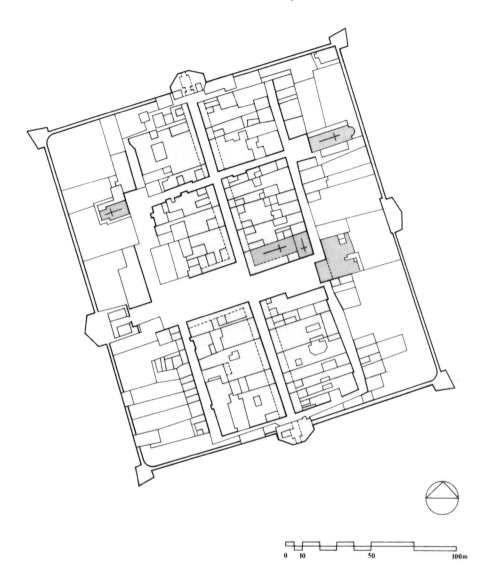

27 Firenzuola. From the cadastral plan, nineteenth century (ASF, uncataloged).

28 Firenzuola. Central square (G. Carli. *Firenzuola,* 1981).

Castelfranco petitioned the Florentine *Signoria* for protection (Document 16). Designated Castel Santa Maria by the Florentines, the town came to be known as Terranuova, and is now known as Terranuova Bracciolini after its native son, Poggio Bracciolini, chancellor of the Florentine republic between 1453 and 1459 (Figs. 16 – 20).[3]

The Apennine mountains north of Florence are the site of the city's second system of new towns. In 1306 the *Signoria* proclaimed its intention to found two towns straddling the Apennine watershed (Document 3). The town nearer the city, officially named Castel San Barnaba but known as Scarperia after the earlier title of the site, was begun immediately (Figs. 21 – 26).[4] It is located in the Mugello region, about 4 kilometers north of the Sieve river, on a flat spur of land that rises gradually north toward the mountain ridge and a pass now called the Giogo di Scarperia. The second town, designated in the foundation document as "ultra alpes," was not begun until 1332 (Document 13).[5] It lies on the valley floor below the Giogo and was given the name Firenzuola (Figs. 27, 28). Because of its position at the farthest reaches of Florentine controlled territory, Firenzuola was constantly overrun by the city's enemies. Burned in 1342 and 1351,[6] it was not completed until the 1370s, and then on a significantly reduced scale.[7]

In 1350 Florence planned another town of the same type as the five that have survived. It was to have been called Giglio Fiorentino and was slated for a site in the Val d'Ambra, an upland valley to the southeast of the upper Arno valley, toward Arezzo. No settlement or construction was generated by this effort, but before the project died a governmental town building committee — the *Ufficiali delle Castella* — prepared a full description of the scheme, in which everything from immigration schedules to street plans and building codes for houses was discussed. The documentation for this project (Documents 17 – 21) provides a uniquely detailed picture of the early stages of a new town project (Fig. 29).[8]

At the time that it was building the five new towns and planning the Giglio Fiorentino project, the Florentine government was involved in a number of other town building efforts. Most like the new towns were two projects for settlements atop mountain passes at the border of Florence's territory. One, called Pietrasanta, was the city's first effort to establish a new town (Document 1). In the summer of 1284 Florence purchased the land for the project, north of the Apennine watershed, on the road between Borgo San Lorenzo in the Mugello region and Faenza in the Po valley. The mountain site exposed the settlers to attack both by the city's enemies and by the forces of nature. The town survives only in a village

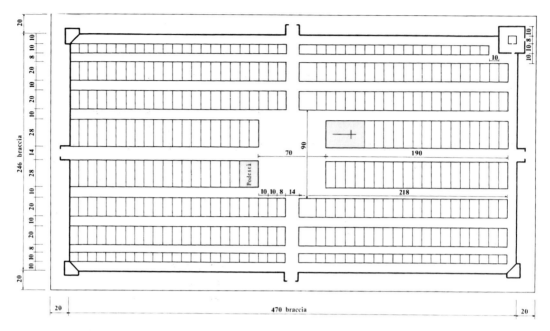

29 Giglio Fiorentino. Reconstruction of the plan (ASF *Uff. Cast., Rocche,* 1, fols. 15v – 18r, 19 May 1350. Text and translation in Document 19).

bearing the name Casaglia which provides no clues to the original plan.[9] In 1329, the Florentine government conceived a similar project for a site at the top of the Consuma pass, between Pontassieve on the Arno and the Casentino region to the east; it is known only from the document proclaiming its foundation (Document 12). Both this town and Pietrasanta were intended as markets to encourage the importation of grain and as colonies that would develop abandoned land. In both regards they are unlike the Florentine new towns sited nearer the city on lower ground. These were to be real frontier towns, Florentine outposts that could not have become the centers of thriving local economies. The scheme to populate Pietrasanta with settlers from Florence — and to give out farmland in addition to building sites in the town — was unique in the city's conception of new towns and would have insured the settlement's separation from its neighbors. The failure of these schemes demonstrates the experimental nature of the new-town formula and the limits of its potential.

A very different sort of project — one that would hardly be considered town building were it not for the subsequent histories of the sites —

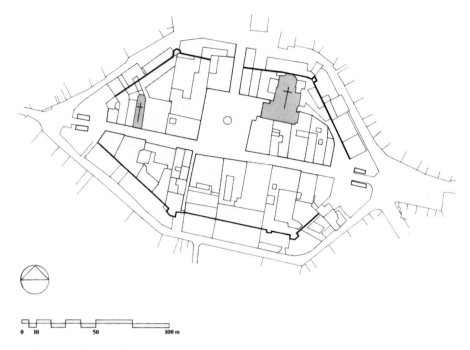

30 Vicchio. Fortified between 1365 and the end of the 1370s. From the cadastral plan, nineteenth century (ASF, uncataloged).

engaged the Florentines sporadically throughout the fourteenth century. In 1300 three villages in the neighborhood of Empoli in the lower Arno valley petitioned the Florentine government for permission to build fortifications to which they could retreat for protection in time of war.[10] A petition from another rural group, dated 1309, solicited both the city's permission and its expert advice for a hilltop retreat at Vicchio in the Mugello.[11] This latter project was taken up again in 1324 and, once more, in 1365.[12] Between 1365 and the end of the 1370s a hexagonal circuit of stone fortifications was built at Vicchio, "so that the people of the surrounding countryside can retreat to it and defend themselves" (Fig. 30).[13] While a few residents of the surrounding villages were required to build houses within the walls, none was asked to move there. The need for protection and defense also prompted the Florentines to build fortifications at Pontassieve, at the confluence of the Sieve and Arno rivers (Fig. 31), between 1356 and the late 1370s.[14]

In the second half of the fourteenth century, a period of demographic

31 Pontassieve. Fortified between 1356 and the late 1370s; streets surveyed in 1382. From the cadastral plan, nineteenth century (ASF, uncataloged).

32 Figline. Expanded and refortified between 1353 and the early 1370s.

33 San Casciano. Expanded and refortified between 1354 and 1358.

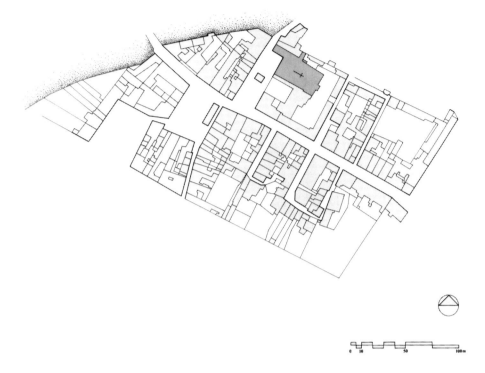

34 Campi. Received a market field, a residential area, and new walls between 1376 and 1389.

crisis created by the plague of 1348, the Florentines did not attempt to found any new settlements. Much of the Tuscan territory had already been pacified and urbanized by this time. Town building was restricted to the expansion and improvement of existing facilities. Pontassieve became a permanent settlement in this period. In 1382, well after the fortifications were completed, the land inside the walls was surveyed into a system of streets and squares.[15] Twelve years later the town received market privileges in order to promote immigration.[16] Further upstream in the Valdarno, the thirteenth-century settlement at Figline (Fig. 32) was expanded and refortified between 1353 and the early 1370s.[17] In the Val di Pesa, south of Florence, the town of San Casciano (Fig. 33) was similarly enlarged, refortified, and internally restructured between 1354 and 1358.[18] Campi (Fig. 34), just south of Prato in the lower Valdarno, was given a market field, a residential area laid out orthogonally, and a new set of walls between 1376 and 1389.[19]

All of these projects, in their goals and in their form, were different from the five new towns and the Giglio Fiorentino project. They were less ambitious and more constrained. Yet work on enlargement, like work on the empty defenses used as retreats by neighboring villagers, involved many of the same tasks required of new-town construction. The documents connected with these projects and the environments that survive teach us a great deal about Florentine town building in the fourteenth century. The evidence of these projects, like that of towns built by governments other than that of Florence, is used in this study to illuminate the history of the new towns.

CHAPTER 1

POLICY

THE PROSPERITY OF FLORENCE was dependent on the city's control of the neighboring countryside. As a source of food for its citizens, raw materials for its artisans, soldiers for its armies, tax revenue, and population itself, the city's territories were indispensable. Like other Italian communes, Florence had not always possessed this resource. The *comitatus*, or land tied to the urban centers of antiquity, passed out of the control of cities during the period of Longobard rule (568 – 774), and it was not until the twelfth century that the newly powerful communes began the reconquest of what was then called the *contado*. The cities' first goal was to extend political dominion to the diocesan boundary. Later, the more powerful of them began to acquire territory at the expense of neighboring towns. Florence was among the most expansive. In 1295 Pistoia came under the city's domination; in 1337, Arezzo; in 1351, Prato; in 1354, San Gimignano; in 1406, Pisa; in 1472, Volterra; and in 1559, Siena, the city's last great prize (see Fig. 2).

These successes came relatively late in the history of the Florentine commune. The victories on which the material prosperity of the city was based occurred earlier and closer to home. The government's rivals were not foreign powers but the great barons—the Guidi, the Uberti, the Ubaldini—who had ruled the lands immediately outside the city's walls since the period of the Ottonian emperors. To guarantee the safety of its trade routes and its access to the produce that fed its citizens, the communal government had to bring these noblemen under its authority. The valley of the Arno above and below the city, the Chianti hills to the south, and the valley of the Mugello in the Apennines were the first targets of Florentine expansion into the countryside.

The conquest of the *contado* demanded the best efforts of the Florentines for over a century. The city acquired single pieces of property and entire towns and their territories. Military campaigns produced some gains, but more was obtained by treaty and purchase than by strength of arms. The government forced the barons into the city's orbit by granting them citizenship and demanding that they establish a residence within the walls. Securing their loyalty, however, was not easily accomplished and retaining control of the newly acquired land proved to be as hard as winning it. Florence's citizen armies were not adequate for the task. Castles provided a more effective and permanent defense and in the late Middle Ages the Florentines built, repaired, and manned many of them. These fortifications differed little from those of the barons'. They were located where they could dominate the landscape, and their residential facilities were limited to the requirements of a small garrison.

At the close of the thirteenth century the city initiated a new strategy for stabilizing the military and political situation in the countryside. The policy required the rural population to move from the villages in which their families had lived for generations as subjects of the feudal barons to newly created towns sponsored and controlled by Florence. The immigrants were freed from their ties to the land and the lords. They swore loyalty to the city, were liable for its taxes, and became part of the Florentine defense of the region. The new towns were large by the standards of the countryside. While the villages from which the settlers came were seldom larger than fifty households, the new towns were planned for between three and five hundred families or as many as twenty-five hundred people. Organized into a militia, the immigrants manned the walls of the towns, giving Florence a permanent military presence in the newly conquered lands.

The role of the new towns in opposing the barons and strengthening Florentine control of the countryside is not a question of historical interpretation; it is explicit in all the documents of their early history. When, in the summer of 1285, the topic of founding towns in the upper Arno valley was introduced to the councils of the Florentine government for the first time, the ensuing debate pitted the interests of the city's merchant patriciate against those of the nobility. The *capitano del popolo*, the Florentine officer directly responsible to the merchants and artisans of the city, proposed the town foundation idea "to frustrate the schemes of the exiled citizens" (Document 1). The Ghibelline families, who had been banned from the city following the defeat of Conradin in 1268, were not present to defend themselves, but their cause found champions among nobles in the Guelph faction. In the debate merchants, artisans, and some noblemen spoke in favor of the establishment of new towns; only knights, who shared the exiles' interests, opposed the proposition. Despite a compromise solution that would have left the settlements unfortified, the new-town idea was shelved for almost fifteen years.

When the project was taken up again at the end of the thirteenth century, the political situation in Florence was very different. The Ordinances of Justice of 1293 had dramatically reduced the power of the nobility in city affairs. The establishment of new towns now received the full support of the citizen councils, and government documents described the role of the towns in conquering the countryside and opposing the power of the nobility. The *Provvisione* of 1299 declared the city's intention to build towns in the upper Arno Valley "in order to increase and better to preserve the honor and the jurisdiction of the commune of Florence" (Document 2). The purpose of founding Scarperia and Firenzuola, in 1306, was "to crush the arrogance of the Ubaldini and others of the Mugello and the land beyond the Apennines, who have rebelled against the commune and populace of Florence and built the castle of Monteaccianico and others elsewhere, and who wage war and no longer have God before their eyes, and who do not remember that they were born part of the commune of Florence." The towns were built to "totally destroy their resources" (Document 3).

The military strength of the new towns derived in large part from the concentration of people. The Florentine army, never more than a temporary levy of citizens supplemented by mercenaries hired for a few months at a time, provided a garrison of only a few soldiers.[1] In an emergency the local militia was the first source of troops. This body was also under Florentine control; though led by the town's officers, it was periodically inspected by city officials. The militia at Scarperia, for example, was reviewed in January 1367 and each of its members told that he had personally to arm himself with a helmet, a buckler, a lance, and a knife or sword. In addition, fifty of the militiamen were to be equipped with cuirasses. The mayor and the rector of the town were given the further responsibilities of procuring bombards and slings for the communal arsenal and of replenishing the public grain stock.[2] In wartime the strength of the militia could be supplemented by Florentine troops. The new towns were particularly well designed to accommodate a large number of temporary occupants. When Scarperia was under siege in 1351, more than five hundred Florentine soldiers were packed inside its walls.[3] In 1359 the town was reported to have a capacity of four hundred cavalry. No other site in the Mugello could take more than half that number, although other towns, notably Borgo San Lorenzo which was registered for two hundred, were larger in size.[4]

New towns facilitated the defense not only of people but also of property. While people might be able to move quickly to a safe place, they could not bring with them their homes or, more important, the grain in their storehouses. Food supplies were a significant factor in fourteenth-century warfare; a military campaign consisted as much of damaging the enemy's countryside as of pitched battles or sieges of towns. The description of the Florentine campaign of 1290 against Arezzo by the merchant and chronicler Giovanni Villani (c. 1275 – 1348) talks of a limited victory, even though the city was not taken, because the Florentine army camped for twenty-nine days before the walls of Arezzo "and pillaged the countryside from head to toe. For six miles around Arezzo not one vine, one tree, nor a stalk of wheat remained." On the way home the army passed through the Casentino region "laying waste to the lands of Count Guido Novello."[5] The only defenses against such tactics were armed warehouses, as provided by the new towns. In time of war the Florentine officials issued strict orders to the residents of weaker towns, enjoining them to bring their produce to specifically designated fortresses.[6]

Systematically carried out, such a policy also provided an offensive strategy against an attacker. Medieval armies depended heavily on the land for their supplies; if an enemy could be denied resources it could be driven from the field, even if it had not been defeated in battle. Matteo Villani, who continued his brother's chronicle, describes such a situation during the invasion of Florentine territory in 1351 by the forces of Giovanni Visconti. The Milanese army of five thousand German mercenaries, two thousand knights, and six thousand foot soldiers was "not well provided with foodstuffs and hoped to supply itself with goods from the Florentine *contado*." The troops had some successes at first, taking Campi and the neighboring towns, but soon they had used up this stock and, being unable to receive supplies from Bologna, were forced to withdraw from the Arno valley without ever engaging the weaker Florentine forces in battle.[7]

Another incident in the Visconti war illustrates how strong a new town's military position could be. After quitting the area immediately around Florence, the Visconti army moved north into the Mugello region where, after a few minor skirmishes, it laid siege to Scarperia. The camp of 13,000 Milanese soldiers completely surrounded the new town. Inside Scarperia there was only the local militia, no more than 400 men,[8] and 500

Florentine soldiers, commanded by the city's captain of the Mugello, the German mercenary Jacopo di Fiore. The siege lasted for sixty-one days and included three separate, full-scale attacks supported by catapults, movable archery towers, and sappers. Yet despite the tremendous strength of the Visconti army and the temporary nature of the town's wall, Scarperia could not be taken.[9]

It was not by chance that the Visconti army chose to attack Scarperia. This new town had a special military importance. Giovanni Villani says that it was founded as a bulwark against the Ubaldini.[10] In 1348, when Florence renewed its attack on the Apennine feudatories, Scarperia was the center of operations.[11] Other Florentine-controlled towns were nearer the battlefield, but Scarperia was selected as the site of the warehouse for the army's munitions and food supplies.[12] The carpenters and blacksmiths who built Florence's war machines were also located there.[13] Some indication of the town's importance is given by the correspondence of the Florentine war committee. Of the sixty-six letters sent by the committee to all its correspondents between May and September 1350, sixteen went to Scarperia while only twelve were addressed to the army in the field.[14] In 1351, as the Visconti army descended into the Mugello, but before its generals had committed their forces to a single strategy, it was to Scarperia that Florence sent its available troops. In the years following the Visconti war, Florence officially recognized the military preeminence of Scarperia by installing the Florentine vicar for the Mugello there.[15] In the fifteenth century three of the new towns, Scarperia, San Giovanni, and Firenzuola, served as the capitals of administrative subdivisions of the Florentine state.[16]

In the fourteenth century, communication and exchange depended almost exclusively on roads and the new towns were closely tied to this statewide, government supported system. From the time of the first deliberations of the Florentine councils, protection of roads was considered one of the primary functions of the new towns. When one of the city's officers argued against the foundation of towns in the Arno Valley, he suggested as an alternative that "certain [already existing] communities be made responsible for the safety of the roads" (Document 1). Fifteen years later San Giovanni was built astride the main road between Florence and Arezzo (and ultimately Rome), and Castelfranco beside the older route to the same destination on the adjacent plateau.

The towns, of course, profited considerably from their location. Pietrasanta and the settlement on the Consuma pass were planned almost exclusively in relation to the roads from the Romagna and the Casentino regions, which would bring produce to the towns' markets. Even when a settlement had only a local market, road traffic could be of benefit. Providing services to travelers was one of the main economic activities of at least three of the new foundations. Scarperia and Firenzuola housed more members of the Florentine hostellers' guild than any other towns between Florence and Bologna.[17] From the traveler's point of view, the ever-present danger of attack made the protection of the towns very welcome. The complementary nature of road and town sometimes even meant that the two were planned and constructed as part of the same project.

Until 1306, when the foundation of Scarperia and Firenzuola was declared, the route between Florence and the north ran for a considerable distance through land controlled by the Ubaldini barons.[18] Despite its victory over the clan in 1306, Florence had to fight these feudatories again in 1342, in 1348, and in 1351.[19] City officials seem to have had no illusions about their power over the Ubaldini. To ensure reliable communications with Bologna they decided to lay a new route to the east of the Ubaldini strongholds on land where, with the aid of two new towns, they could hope to keep a permanent presence (Fig. 35).

Work on the project began simultaneously with both the destruction of the Ubaldini castle that had dominated the Bologna road and the foundation of Scarperia about five kilometers away.[20] At first the old road was simply diverted to run through the new town,[21] but the location of Scarperia — on a spur of land that rises to the Apennine ridge below the pass now called the Giogo di Scarperia — reveals that the city had already decided to build the new route.

A first indication of the road's completion appears in the 1330s. In 1332 Firenzuola was laid out on the other side of the Apennine crest. Its street plan, like that of Scarperia, is oriented toward the new pass. The gate facing in that direction is called, in the documents of that year, "ianua florentina," while the street that leads to it, the main street of the town, "runs on a straight line toward Florence and toward Bologna" (Document 13). The older road lay a number of kilometers to the west, but the gate of the new town that was to face west is called, simply, "ianua S. Maria." The route of the new road was more fully mapped out in 1334, when the hostellers' guild of Florence listed the towns of Ponzalla, Rifredo, and Casa Nuova, all points on the Scarperia – Firenzuola road as it exists today, in the administrative section "della strada di San Gallo verso San Piero a Sieve" (and Bologna).[22] The first recorded use of the road was in 1342, when the Florentine army, in an attempt to raise the Ubaldini siege of

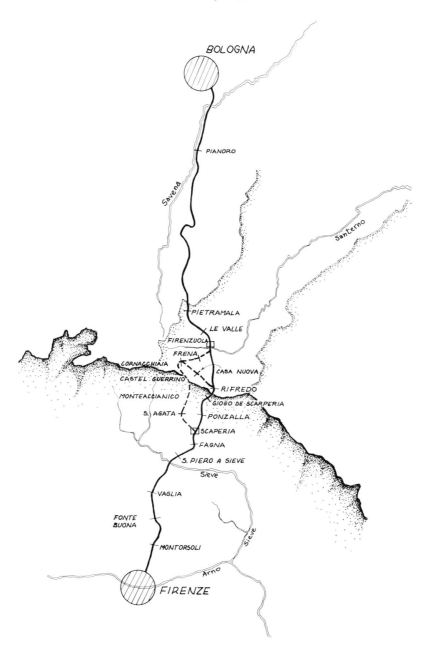

35 Roads across the Apennines in the area of Scarperia and Firenzuola. Fourteenth century.

Firenzuola, was defeated on the march from Florence at Rifredo.[23] In the early fifteenth century, when the new road was in common use, the route between Florence and Bologna ran as follows: Florence, Uccelatoio, Vaglia, Tagliaferro, San Piero a Sieve, Scarperia, Uomo Morto, Giogo, Rifredo, Firenzuola, Le Valle, Pianoro, Bologna.[24] The overnight stops on this journey were almost inevitably made at one or the other or both of the new towns.

The most distinctive feature of the founding of new towns — the feature that distinguishes these towns from Florence's other town building projects and had such a dramatic impact on the surrounding countryside — was the resettlement of population that accompanied each of the foundations. The new-town residents were for the most part people whom the city had only recently brought under its control, guaranteeing them freedom from feudal obligations. Members of the nobility were excluded from the settlements and could not own land or buildings within a mile of them or hold any public office. The Florentines saw the redistribution of the population as essential to their new-town effort. Scarperia "liberated the subjects of the Ubaldini so that [the castle of] Monteaccianico could never be rebuilt;"[25] Terranuova was populated by the villagers of the counts of Battifolle "to deprive" the counts "of their following and authority forever";[26] San Giovanni and Castelfranco di Sopra grew at the expense of the nobles of the Valdarno,[27] and the population of Firenzuola was composed of residents from villages that had once belonged to the Ubaldini.[28] Only a small number of the settlers seem to have come to the towns on their own initiative. New citizens were for the most part selected by Florentine officials who, when they could, relocated complete villages to gain the greatest strategic and political advantage.

The recruiting of settlers for Scarperia illustrates this. The founding of the town coincided with the declaration of war against the Ubaldini and the siege of their castle at Monteaccianico (Document 3). As usual, a Florentine official was given the power to select the new town's settlers. His patent of authority, granted a few months after the foundation act, contains a list of twenty-seven villages from the neighborhood surrounding the site — including the "populus de Monte Accianico," the village connected with the main Ubaldini castle — and the instructions "to place in the [new] community the following congregations, that is, villages or populi" (Document 4). To ensure that his orders were enforced and that the villages did not fall back into the hands of the Ubaldini, the official was given the power to destroy the places from which he had drawn the settlers. Monteaccianico, the main Ubaldini stronghold, was thus destroyed and its population moved into Scarperia. In a petition to the Florentine *Signoria* of 1354, the residents of Scarperia clearly state their origins as vassals of the Ubaldini. "The men of this town are for the most part the descendants of people who lived under the yolk of the Ubaldini at Monteaccianico and elsewhere. They were liberated by the *popolo* and *comune* of Florence and sent to reside in the town of Scarperia, built by the *popolo* and *comune* of Florence, where they lived, and intend to continue to live, faithfully and obediently under the domination of the aforesaid *popolo* and *comune* and the *parte guelfe.*"[29]

The relocation of population also had a decisive effect on legal claims to land. Evidence from the Val d'Ambra region illustrates this. In January 1350 Florence received the villages of Cappanole, Castiglione Alberti, Pieve a Prisciano, Montelucci, Cacciano, Cornia, San Lorentino, and Badia Agnano from the Benedictine abbey of Agnano. Within a month of signing the treaty, in which it promised to "defend and preserve" the abbey's villages, the city took the first steps toward the foundation of a new town, Giglio Fiorentino, that would require destruction of the villages and relocation of their population. One of the most important incentives for the proposed change was the uncertain state of the titles to the towns and land.

In the document by which he ceded the possessions of his abbey to Florence, the abbot of Agnano, Basileus, explained his decision by the fact that "for a long time this monastery with its possessions and its subjects has been invaded, usurped and held by certain magnates of the area who are also enemies of Florence. To such an extent has the abbey been bothered that it is not able peacefully to have or hold its possessions and goods, or its subjects." With Florentine support it hopes "freely to have and receive the fruit and income of its possessions and goods" (Document 17). Indeed, if an eighteenth-century commentator was right when he said that the abbey once controlled twenty-four towns,[30] the seven that it was able to hand over to Florence represent quite a depletion of its estate.

The abbey's chief enemy was the Ubertini clan whose head, Buoso degli Ubertini, was the bishop of Arezzo. On two occasions, in 1340 and 1350, the abbot and bishop had to refer their differences to papal adjudication.[31] A special provision in the abbey's treaty with Florence stipulated that if the city should ever cede its possessions in the Val d'Ambra to the bishop of Arezzo, the towns and property that had belonged to the abbey would be excepted.

The difficulties between the two parties were long-standing and seem to have resulted from the Ubertinis' role in founding the abbey of Agnano.[32] Because the Ubertini considered the abbey part of their patrimony, they made donations of land to it without the land ever passing out of their control. Thus San Pancrazio, which was given to the abbey in 1262 by the four sons of Count Guido Ubertini, was immediately placed by the abbot under the administration of the vicar of the bishop of Arezzo at a time when both he and the bishop were Ubertini.[33] The town seemed so little to have changed lords, it was listed with other towns belonging to the Ubertini in a reaffirmation of the family charter by Corrado II in 1268.[34] Given this intermix of claims, it is easy to imagine that friction developed between the abbey and its benefactors when the abbot acted independently of them. In fact, the Ubertini had a strong claim to at least three of the villages ceded by Basileus to Florence.[35]

In the fourteenth century a legal claim to territory was formulated in terms of towns, or *comuni,* and their *curia,* the land surrounding them, which was owned by the inhabitants of the towns or by the lord of the *comune.* Land that Florence had bought from the Tarlati nobles in the lower Val d'Ambra in 1337 was defined as "the towns and the *curia,* territory, and district of the aforesaid fortified towns, *comunes* and villages."[36] The abbey of Agnano's land was described the same way (Document 17), as was the territory in the *Provvisione* for the foundation of Giglio Fiorentino (Document 18). Had the Florentines succeeded in relocating the population of the Val d'Ambra towns and razing the buildings on the old sites, they would have destroyed the territorial units by which the Ubertini could have made their claims. Even the parish organization would have been upset: of the six churches that existed in the area, not counting the church at the monastery of Agnano,[37] only one, the church of San Piero at Pieve a Prisciano, was to have been reestablished in the new settlement. Presumably the possessions of the destroyed churches would have gone to San Piero in Giglio Fiorentino. The difficulties of prosecuting a claim for properties whose parts were integrated into a wholly different context can well be imagined. As the power in control of the *de facto* situation, Florence could only expect to benefit from the confusion.

The reorganization of the Val d'Ambra would have weakened, too, the position of the abbey of Agnano. Under the old system, to the extent that the monks were able to make it work, the population was led by the abbey and directed the profits from the territory to the abbey's coffers. The new system was to be entirely out of the monks' control. All decisions for the organization and construction of Giglio Fiorentino were made by Florentine officials who consulted only with representatives of the villages. No monks were included in any of the planning or governing committees; they were not even to participate in the religious organization of the town. There was to be no dedication, either of the church or of any of the town gates, to commemorate the abbey's relationship with the inhabitants. The abbey was not just excluded, it was humiliated. A short sentence after the description of the proposed new town ordered that the campanile of the abbey be lowered (Document 19). This was the same action Florentine governments in the period of the Guelph and Ghibelline wars of the mid-thirteenth century had taken against their enemies. Then, too, it was meant to weaken and embarrass the owner of the tower.

CHAPTER 2

PLANS

THE PLANS OF FLORENTINE NEW TOWNS form a distinctive family of orthogonal designs. They share essential qualities, despite diverse physical circumstances and the evolution of new-town planning during the fourteenth century. All the plans address a common set of problems and conform to the same planning principles. The new towns had as their first task the collection of a loyal population and the creation of a strong defensive position. They were all connected to Florence by a road, granted market privileges, and assigned an administrative role in the new Florentine territorial state. The balance between these functions varied from town to town. At Scarperia and Firenzuola the military situation was unusually perilous; Terranuova's character was heavily influenced by the fragmentation of its population; San Giovanni was the capital of the vicarate of the entire upper Valdarno; and Castelfranco was the center only for the league of villages in its immediate vicinity. These circumstances had a significant influence on the way the towns developed. Today each settlement has its own distinct character; at the moment of foundation, however, the plans were much less varied.

Assigned the task of selecting a site, Florentine town builders consistently chose flat ground. Hilltop locations and steep slopes were used for fortified retreats, but never for the new towns. Whether on the valley floor or on an upland plateau, only the most regular terrain would do. If nature had imperfections, Florentine officers ordered earth-moving operations to correct them. On the resulting standardized ground, the new towns conformed to a single basic pattern with two variations, both of which appear in the foundations of 1299. San Giovanni's plan, with its extended central square, was reused at Scarperia and Firenzuola. The plan of Castelfranco, whose distinctive feature is a square with proportions of 9:7, served as the inspiration for the plans of Terranuova and Giglio Fiorentino.

Orthogonality is the basis of Florentine new-town design, as it is for all of the most ambitious planning schemes of the Middle Ages. Fourteenth-century city dwellers considered straight streets beautiful and a public ornament; town planners combined them in parallel and perpendicular relationships, however, for practical reasons. In the Middle Ages it is only on an orthogonally articulated plane that the precise location of a point could be known. Orthogonality facilitated the coordination of the parts of a composition and simplified the calculation of area. Only in the Renaissance did surveyors develop the techniques that allowed them to construct mathematically accurate maps of irregular geographic and urban forms. Before that time the space of the natural world was measured approximately. In the late Middle Ages, comprehensive urban design was possible only with the aid of the simple and consistent rules of orthogonality.

A comparison of two early-fourteenth-century "maps" illustrates the value of orthogonality to the urban environment. One is the anonymous plan of Rome of about 1320, from the *Chronologia Magna* of Paulinus Venetus (Fig. 36). The other, a drawing in the *Capitoli* of the Sienese state councils, dated 4 April 1306, shows a small town called Talamone, on the coast of the Sienese state (Fig. 37).[1] Both documents combine building elevations and street plans; neither of them is based on a geometric survey.

The view of Rome is the more accomplished of the two. The building elevations are rich in detail that identifies the city's monuments. The drawing employs an ink wash to represent the hills of the city, and introduces energetic figures in the fields northeast of the Castel Sant'Angelo. The streets, however, are represented with minimal accuracy. Only those approaching the bridge to the Vatican are individualized enough to be identifiable, and even they are represented with a regularity that makes them look like the straight streets with which this area was redeveloped in the sixteenth and nineteenth centuries, rather than the crooked Via dei Pellegrini and Via Papale that were the main streets of the medieval city.

The Talamone drawing reproduces the forms of the town much more closely. The town gates, the church, and the fortresses (shown in elevation), are all in place, if not in proportion. The streets and blocks of the drawing—except for those at the top of the sheet which do not exist in the modern town—can all be matched with existing features. The scale of the Talamone drawing—much larger than that of the Rome plan—in part explains its greater precision; a more significant factor, however, is the

36 Rome, ca. 1320 (Paulinus Venetus, *Chronologia Magna*. Biblioteca Nazionale Marciana, Venice).

nature of Talamone's street system (Fig. 38).

Talamone was a founded town, laid out on an orthogonal plan. The plan is easily described using the three geometric concepts of straight, parallel, and perpendicular. The drawing is not to scale—it did without accurate dimensions—but it gives, nonetheless, a fairly reliable picture of the town. The infinitely more complex forms of the Roman streets are not so easily schematized; in the fourteenth century this meant that they could not be reproduced.

Just how basic the idea of orthogonality was to Florentine thinking about new towns is revealed in an extraordinary document in which the officers of a Florentine government agency, the *Ufficiali delle Castella*, describe the project of Giglio Fiorentino (Document 19). The language of this extended account is striking. The authors refer to a series of streets that run in one direction and other streets with a different orientation. They describe a four-sided wall that encloses the site and list row after row of house lots. Dimensions are given for everything, including the 70-by-90-*braccia* (40.9 by 52.6 meters)[2] central square. Nowhere, however, does the document define the spatial relationship of one element to another. It is impossible to reconstruct the Giglio plan without assuming that elements which are "next to" (as the text has it) one another are also parallel, and that the elements that cross—or the sides of a wall that meet—do so at right angles. That these definitions were omitted can only be explained by the fact that they were considered unnecessary. The concept of orthogonality was so basic, so essential to any rational physical scheme, that to use it—literally—went without saying.

The description of Giglio Fiorentino illustrates that size was the town planners' first concern. There were many practical reasons why it was important. The amount of land to be acquired, and therefore the total cost, depended on the project's size, as did the number of immigrants the new settlement could accommodate. In providing dimensions, the planners also fixed the line of the town's defenses. This had a fundamental effect on the town's design. The ditches and palisades that the founders built and that succeeding generations reinforced with stone structures were essential to the open character of the plan. Without this defensive outline the continuous street system and the generous central square, features that were so important to a new-town plan, would have been impossible. The houses of the first settlers would have been huddled together for protection, and this first cell would surely have left its mark on the fully developed street system. The houses themselves might have formed the defensive barrier, as do the thick, windowless rear walls of a circle of houses in many Tuscan villages. Agnano, one of the communities that was to have

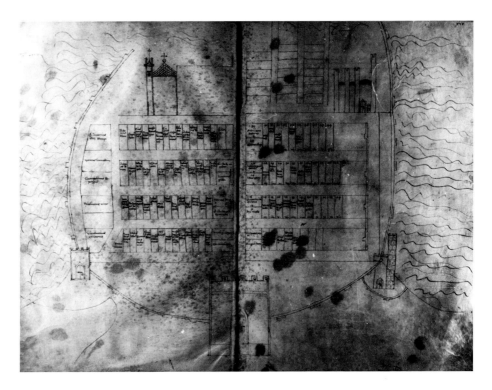

37 Talamone, 1306 (Archivio di Stato di Siena, *Capitoli*, 3). South at top of sheet.

been relocated at Giglio Fiorentino, preserves this arrangement (Figs. 39 – 41). Its heavily battered external wall is the circumference of a circle of houses that face onto a central open place in front of the conventual church that was the seed of the settlement. The only street within the village is formed by a row of houses built along one side of the "square."

Over the centuries the population of Florentine new towns grew, but future immigration was not a primary consideration of the city's settlement scheme. The towns were intended for a particular group of settlers, and the plans showed no provisions for physical growth. The wall that defended a new community also confined it. Any expansion beyond the defenses had little in common with the layout of the original plan. At first suburbs grew along the roads from the town gates. In the nineteenth and twentieth centuries the pattern of expansion has responded to the requirements of garden villas and tall apartment blocks. San Giovanni and Scarperia, the most flourishing of the new towns today, offer the best examples.

0   10   50   100 m

38 Talamone.

Finite size and fixed shape were uncommon in medieval new towns. The twelfth-century town of Bern, which expanded in three smoothly seamed stages along the axis of the town's broad market street (Fig. 42), was characteristic of the flexibility of most medieval plans. Towns founded after 1255 by the administration of Alphonse de Poitiers in the county of Toulouse were laid out according to an open-ended survey system. Sainte-Foy-la-Grande on the Dordogne river and Montréal in the

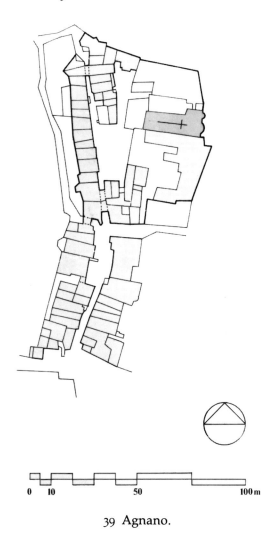

0   10   50   100 m

39 Agnano.

present-day department of Gers, both dating from the first year of Alphonse's town building campaign, are good examples of this town type
(Figs. 43, 44). The formal theme of these plans is based on two pairs of
parallel streets oriented at right angles to one another. The square space
enclosed by their intersection was the market, where inauguration ceremonies, including the raising of a staff with the founder's coat of arms,
took place. In the years immediately following the foundation of towns of
this kind sometimes only the sides of the square were inhabited but as the
town grew the four streets structured further development. Along one

40 Agnano. View of borgo.

axis, the distance between the two streets—the width of the market—
established the amount of space between all the parallel streets. Along the
other axis a larger interval dictated the size of the rectangular blocks that
most efficiently accommodated the town's row houses. This system could
be infinitely enlarged. In both Sainte-Foy and Montréal the streets and
blocks multiplied in good order, but expansion has now pushed the market place, still the functional center of the community, to one side of the
inhabited area.

   Such asymmetry had no place in the Florentine concept of new-town
design. Unforeseen circumstances could force the city's officials to ap-
prove construction that unbalanced a new-town plan, as was the case in
Scarperia, but no town was designed as anything other than an essentially
symmetrical composition. The principal axis of symmetry of every plan
was a section of the main road that ran through the site. As the town's
main street, the road determined the orientation of the blocks and of the
majority of the town's remaining streets and alleys. The description of
Giglio Fiorentino conveys the importance of the idea of symmetry around

41 Agnano. View of external wall and escarpment.

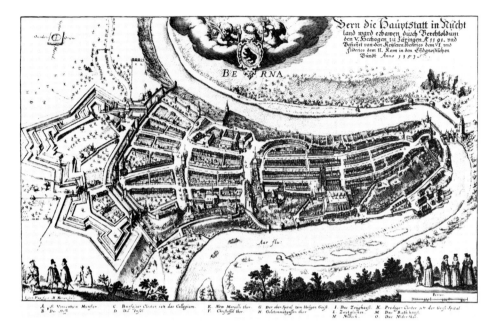

42 Bern. Founded 1190 by Duke Berthold V of Zähringen (Matthaeus Merian, *Topographia Helvetiae, Rhaetiae et Valesiae*, 1642).

the main street. The description lists Giglio's streets, and the lots abutting them, in an orderly way, beginning at the town's edge and working toward the main street. It then gives the depth of the lots on the main street and the width of the main street itself, and concludes by saying that "in the other part of the town, houses and streets shall be made as designated above," i.e., symmetrically (Document 19).

As the axis of symmetry, the *via maestra* received special treatment and influenced the plan of a new town in a number of ways. It was the widest in the town and, as at Giglio, the houses along its sides had to observe special architectural requirements. Its orientation was the orientation of the town. All the Florentine plans were rectangular: the early designs (San Giovanni and Scarperia) had proportions of about $2\frac{1}{2}:1$, the later ones (Firenzuola, Terranuova, Giglio) slightly less than $2:1$. Even Castelfranco, which was almost square, had one axis longer than the other. There, too, the axis of the main street dominated.

Midway along the main street of a new town and at the middle of the area enclosed by its defensive perimeter, there was a public piazza. In some of the towns this space was approximately square, in some it was

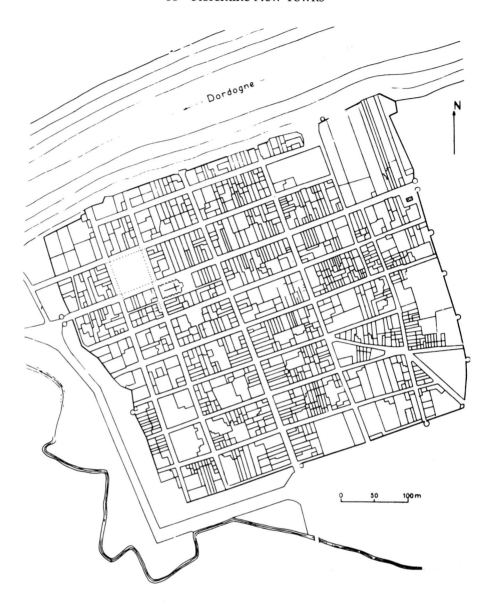

43 Sainte-Foy-la-Grande. Founded in 1255 by Alphonse de Poitiers, count of Toulouse and brother of Louis IX of France (P. Lavedan and J. Hugueney, *L'Urbanisme au Moyen Age*, 1974).

44 Montréal. Founded in 1255 by Alphonse de Poitiers (P. Lavedan and J. Hugueney, *L'Urbanisme au Moyen Age*, 1974).

rectangular, but in every case it was the focus of the plan and the center of public life. The position of the square was fixed by a cross axis that stretched between the gates in the middle of the town's long walls. The cross axis sometimes took the form of a street, sometimes the square itself extended almost the entire distance between the walls. In either case this axis generated a secondary symmetry. Few streets and no blocks of house lots were oriented with the cross axis, but the arrangement of elements on one side of it mirrored the arrangement on the other, echoing the rigorous symmetry around the axis of the town's main street.

The two axes that fixed the position of the square also divided the towns into four quarters. These quarters were the residential areas and were densely packed with houses on lots from 10 to 12 *braccia* (5.84 to 7 meters) wide and 10 to 38 *braccia* (5.84 to 22.2 meters) deep. The center of each quarter, except in the Giglio Fiorentino plan, was marked by a secondary intersection, and the streets that defined these crossings combined to make a circle around the center of town. The wall of the town reflected the same idea, wrapping itself tightly around the settlement.

All the elements of a new-town plan were closely integrated in the Florentine designs. Conceived as finite objects, the towns were laid out symmetrically and with a powerful central element. These are designs that are subject to the same formal laws as single buildings and this, in the context of medieval urban design practice, is their most distinctive characteristic.

The first building activity at the site of a Florentine new town was to establish a defensive perimeter. The demand for speed precluded the use

45 Terranuova. Town wall.

of stone; ditches (20 *braccia* [11.7 meters] wide and 10 *braccia* [5.84 meters] deep at Giglio Fiorentino) and wooden palisades had to suffice at first. Only later, at the financial convenience of the settlers, were they replaced by permanent structures.

The amount of time that elapsed before walls were built varied greatly from settlement to settlement. At Terranuova, which was founded in 1337, the wall was completed between 1350 and 1364 (Fig. 45).[3] At Firenzuola, contracts for the construction of permanent defenses were drawn up three and five years after the town's foundation, in 1335 and 1338, yet in 1351 the town was still not fully walled, and in 1371 the defenses had to be remade.[4] At Scarperia, despite its military importance, palisades still formed the major part of the defenses in 1370, sixty-four years after construction of the town had begun.[5]

At Firenzuola, according to the contracts of 1335 and 1338, the stone walls were 20 *braccia* (11.7 meters) high and 2 *braccia* (1.17 meters) thick. They were faced with coursed stone and filled with a cement and aggregate core. The merlons were brick. The gates of the town were originally 26 *braccia* (15.18 meters) tall, but at least one of them was increased to a height of 32 *braccia* (18.69 meters) because of a nearby hill.[6] Sixteen towers were planned to reinforce the defenses. At Terranuova and at San Giovanni there were to be twenty-four such towers, each rising 15 *braccia* (8.76 meters) above the top of the walls.[7]

The cost of the fortifications was shared by the government of Florence, the residents of the new town (who were often freed from taxes while they paid for especially costly work), and residents of the villages in the neighborhood of the town, who might benefit from the military protection of the new fortress. At Giglio Fiorentino the ditches around the town were to have been excavated by the local league of villages, the gates built at Florentine expense, and the rest of the defenses put up by the residents of the new town, who were exempted from Florentine taxes for ten years. For the project at Firenzuola two types of contracts survive. One was between Florentine officials and Florentine masons for the construction of the gates and 25 *braccia* (14.6 meters) of wall on either side of each gate. The other held the commune at Firenzuola and local builders responsible for the construction of the remainder of the defensive circuit. The local work was to have been modeled after the sections of wall built by the Florentines.[8]

For the efficient operation of the defenses, new-town designs had to include a space, free of buildings, immediately inside the walls. This zone may be seen in the early plans of San Giovanni (see Figs. 6, 7); it is described in the Giglio Fiorentino foundation documents (Documents 19,

20), mentioned in the fifteenth-century statutes of Scarperia,[9] and is still partly visible at Castelfranco. A plaque, now under the loggia of the Palazzo Pretorio at San Giovanni but once probably attached to the wall of the town, gives the width of the military zone as 20 *braccia* (11.7 meters).[10] The space at Giglio Fiorentino was to be 10 *braccia* (5.84 meters) wide, and the one at Terranuova, while only 7 to 8 *braccia* (4.1 to 4.7 meters) along the shorter eastern and western walls, was originally about 12 *braccia* (7 meters) along the more extended northern and southern perimeters. Though the measurements varied considerably, in each case the perimeter road was one of the widest in the town, to allow troops to move freely around the defenses during an attack.

The perimeter road represented an important achievement for Florentine town planners. Such roads, though little used, had long been considered ideal for military purposes, but they were vulnerable to usurpation by private construction. The government of Siena resigned itself to the encroachment on this space, and in its city statutes of 1262 required that houses along the wall be fitted with merlons. In the fourteenth century the Sienese government levied a tax on houses that used the town wall for support, and demanded a minimum window height to preserve the wall's military strength.[11] The Florentines asserted governmental authority more firmly when they built the city's new wall in 1285. They established public roads 16 *braccia* (9.3 meters) wide both inside and outside the wall, and wrote and enforced a law prohibiting the kind of abusive construction that had been normal in the city up until that time.[12]

The most vulnerable parts of any town defense system were the gates. The towers that rose above the entryways to the Florentine settlements were the largest and tallest on the wall (see Fig. 14). The machicolated galleries at their summits provided platforms from which an attacker could be fired on; barbicans on the bridges over the ditch created a first barrier to an assault.

Defense was also enhanced by the settlers' ability to keep the gates under surveillance from a single point in the town. At Scarperia a tower was built at the intersection of the two main streets to improve the vantage point of the guards. This direct connection between the center of town and the gates also facilitated the reinforcement of the perimeter. Similar direct access could strengthen intermediary towers; at San Giovanni every street ended at a tower, inside which were the stairs that gave access to the battlements.

One feature of the defense system had only a limited connection with the town. This was the keep, or *cassero*, an independent enceinte fortified toward both the countryside and the town. Giglio Fiorentino, in 1350, was the only Florentine town whose earliest plans included a keep. It consisted of a tower 40 *braccia* (23.3 meters) high set at a corner of the town wall. It was surrounded by a wall 10 *braccia* (5.84 meters) from its base and by a ditch facing both the countryside and the town. This special enclosure measured only 33 square meters, and its accommodations included just three rooms within the tower and a well. Doors toward the countryside and into the town permitted the defenders to attack and to receive reinforcements from either direction. Within twelve years of the planning of Giglio Fiorentino, two other towns were reinforced with keeps: Scarperia, between 1355 and 1360, and Firenzuola in 1362.[13] The most elaborate of all the Florentine keeps was the castle at Scarperia (Figs. 46, 47). It not only contained quarters for the regular garrison and for temporary reinforcements, it was also the residence of the Florentine official in the town. A single building could fulfill these diverse functions because of its unique location within the plan. Most Florentine keeps, like the one the city built at San Gimignano after receiving dominion over that town in 1353 (Fig. 48), lay at the edge of the area defended by the town walls, separate from the residential sections. The keep at Scarperia abutted the town wall and had its own heavily fortified gate to the countryside, but thanks to Scarperia's extended rectangular plan, it also faced onto the town's main square. On the town side, behind a monumental facade, the keep contained the rooms of the Florentine official.

Although keeps or citadels were imposed on towns and cities throughout history in order to control rebellious populations, the rash of keep building in the Florentine new towns between 1350 and 1360 seems to be explained by a change in fortification theory coupled with an attempt to reinforce the towns' defenses. It does not appear to be a sign of any deterioration in the relationship between Florence and the new-town residents. The keep at Giglio Fiorentino was placed on the side of town opposite the Ubertini castle of Montuoti, the direction from which the city's feudal enemies were most likely to attack. The keeps at Scarperia and Firenzuola were built in response to the Visconti war of 1351, which demonstrated to the city's officials both the military importance of these towns and the incompleteness of their defenses. But the town walls and the keeps did not defend quite the same thing. The tower at Giglio Fiorentino, for example, could not have acted as a retreat for all the members of the community. Indeed, if the citizens had been forced to draw back to such a stronghold much of what they were fighting to protect, their houses and possessions, would already have been lost. Florence, however, had an additional concern. Even if the town fell, the city still wanted its soldiers to maintain their presence at this strategic spot in its territory.

46 Scarperia. Palazzo Vicarile (Photograph: Alinari 10091).

47 Scarperia. Courtyard of the Palazzo Vicarile.

48 San Gimignano (E. Detti, G.F. Di Pietro, and G. Fanelli, *Città murate e sviluppo contemporaneo*, 1968).

A town's walls were not only its defense but also its face to the rest of the world. Church and town-hall towers might punctuate the skyline to mark especially important public buildings, but it was the walls, and particularly the gates astride the road leading into the town, that dominated the visitor's attention. At first sight the walls indicated military strength. They may also have bespoken the town's unity and its separation from the surrounding land. What they signified above all was the town's political ties.

The very form of the new-town gates made a recognizable reference to the gates of the mother city. In a regional landscape in which the most prominent cities employed distinctive types of gates—from the broad, thin, brick towers of Siena to the polychrome double tower compositions of Lucca—the tall, stone-faced single towers crowned by aggressively projecting machicolations were unmistakably Florentine.

The decorative enrichment of the gates also made the towns' associations clear. In the big cities of Italy a wide range of figural images appeared on the facades of gates; lions, patron saints, and the Virgin Mary were the most common of them. Not infrequently these images developed a reputation for miraculous powers. The Madonna painted over the western gate at San Giovanni was such a picture. The Madonna's following was so great that the oratory, begun in the late fifteenth century to shelter the image, was eventually enlarged so that it blocked the gate.[14] The initial decoration of new-town gates, however, was with coats of arms. At Firenzuola, the gate dating from 1335 was to bear the arms of the communes of Firenzuola and Florence. A year later the contract for another gate in the town stipulated that the lily of the Florentine commune, as well as the arms of the church and those of Robert of Anjou, king of Naples and lord of Florence, were to be immured on the gate's exterior facade.[15] At Giglio Fiorentino the arms of the town consisted of a blue *giglio*, or lily, on a yellow ground (but for the colors, the arms of the commune of Florence) flanked by small shields with the arms of the Florentine *popolo* and *comune*. Though artistically modest, such coats of arms made an unambiguous statement.

The requirements of defense did not dominate the planning of the new towns despite the fact that military issues were of great concern to the Florentines. Although discussion of fortifications takes up more space in the surviving documents than any other aspect of town planning, and fortification was the largest expense of any project, a system of defense was understood to serve the community, and not vice versa. The plan of San Giovanni (see Figs. 3 – 6) offers the most vivid demonstration of Florentine priorities. This early new town was the only one in which the towers that reinforced the town wall were coordinated with the street plan and every street ended in a tower. The binding of streets and towers confronted the planners of San Giovanni with a difficult decision. The intervals between streets and between towers were determined according to very different considerations. The distance between streets varied according to lot sizes and the length of blocks, while the distance between towers, determined by the range of weapons and a desire to optimize access to all parts of the wall, was ideally always the same.[16] The conflict between these requirements led to the abandonment, in later Florentine plans, of the coordination attempted at San Giovanni, but when faced with irreconcilable alternatives Florentine planners responded to civilian concerns. At San Giovanni it is the intervals between towers, not between streets, that are modified.

The preeminent form-giving element of a Florentine new town was the section of intercity road that ran between the two main gates (see Figs. 1, 24). This road brought life to the community and its importance is reflected in its generous width and its central position. The property that bordered the main street was the most valuable in the town, being immediately in the path of arriving travelers. The town statutes reinforced this advantage by limiting the ability of merchants and hostelers to advertise their services. In a regulation that began, "That no one may enrich himself at the cost of others, but rather be content with that which naturally comes his way," the hostelers, wine sellers, and merchants of Scarperia were prohibited from approaching any passerby to solicit trade.[17] Even when the conversation was initiated by the prospective customer, the vendor could not step more than 2 *braccia* (1.17 meters) from the door of his place of business to respond. Specifically prohibited was the practice of sending scouts to solicit customers on the main street or at the town's gates. All of this was particularly disadvantageous to those who did not have their establishments in plain view of the traveler.

It is understandable, then, that one of the goals of the Florentine planners was to give frontage on the main street to as many of the settlers as possible. Contemporary housing practice suggested the way to do this. The base unit of new-town design was the row house. The lots that accommodated these modest structures were rectangular, with their short sides fronting onto the street. Frontage was determined by the width of a single room. Larger houses attained their greater space by increased depth and additional stories, not, in the fourteenth century at least, by extended frontage. Neighboring structures abutted one another, combining to form long blocks that were interrupted only infrequently by cross streets.

While neither the row house nor the extended block was an innovation of new-town planners, the close coordination of the rows of lots and the street plan had not been frequently applied elsewhere. In Florence, especially in the areas closest to the last circle of walls (Fig. 49), the streets were so far apart that the buildings lining them consumed a very small part of the available ground. The remaining area functioned as garden and farmland or, occasionally, as a work area, until new streets were developed to open up this internal frontier. In the new towns these hidden spaces were eliminated. The streets were only as far from one another as the depth of the house lots between them.

There were two basic arrangements of lots and blocks in the Florentine new towns. The first occurred in all the new towns planned through 1332, thus, in San Giovanni, Scarperia, Firenzuola, and Castelfranco. Its primary characteristic was the back-to-back placement of the rows of house lots and their separation by narrow alleyways. At San Giovanni (see Figs. 3 – 5) the alleys behind the main street were 4 *braccia* (2.4 meters) wide and those between the third and fourth rows of houses 3 *braccia* (1.75 meters)

49 Florence (F. Fantozzi, *Pianta geometrica di Firenze*, 1843).

wide. The limited width of the alleys reflected their secondary importance in the town. The alleys were considered so minor in comparison with the town's other streets that they were not even protected by the same regulations. At Firenzuola a decree of the founding officials (Document 15) kept the main streets clear of bridges between facing buildings, and although there is no record of them, similar laws must have existed in the other towns, since bridges and a whole range of other obstructions are nowhere to be seen. By contrast, the alleys at San Giovanni were so built over that today they resemble tunnels more than open-air passages (see Fig. 10). They did, however, provide access to the backs of the properties and some air and light for the rooms at the rear. At Castelfranco, Scarperia, and Firenzuola the alleys were considerably narrower. At Castelfranco (see Fig. 11), the space between the backs of buildings was about half a meter. Reduced to this size the "alleys" were no more than property dividers, air shafts, and sewers.[18]

The reduction of the alleys to this vestigial condition was followed by a major change in the organization of the house lots. At Terranuova the alleys were replaced by service streets 8 *braccia* (4.7 meters) wide, giving each lot a double exposure (see Fig. 16). The service streets were wide enough to provide convenient access to the rear and, perhaps most important, as much light and air for the back half of the house as for the front.

Whether arranged back-to-back or standing free at front and back, the lots in all the Florentine new towns were combined in long rows that ran parallel with the main street. The Florentine planners never chose to orient the blocks at right angles to the main streets, as was done, for example, at Talamone (see Fig. 37). The central axis dominated the Florentine compositions. Most of the city's new towns were between 2 and 2.5 times longer than they were wide; there were never more than five cross streets in a town, while nine streets on the long axis was common. The cross axes fell at the center of town, at its outermost limits, and at the points roughly midway between them. The purpose of these streets was to provide communication; in most cases the houses that flanked them did not face onto them. This arrangement must be regarded as the heritage of older towns of the area, which were also located on main roads. Compared to them, the cross communications of the new towns were extremely good. At Montevarchi (Fig. 50), on the same Florence – Arezzo road as San Giovanni, the only way to get from one street of the town to another was through narrow alleys or from the perimeter of the town, where all the streets curved together to exit from the same two gates.

The predominance of the long axis in the layout of new-town street grids is particularly noticeable in the description of Giglio Fiorentino (Document 19). When all the streets of the town were named there was mention of only one cross street, the one at the town's center, and when the total number of streets was given as nine, even that one cross street was omitted. The quarter-point cross streets and the military streets at the perimeter of the town (these, at least, must surely have been intended) were all overlooked.

The scarcity of cross streets in the Giglio Fiorentino scheme would have created huge blocks. Although Giglio was to be the smallest of the Florentine new towns, its blocks, at 228 *braccia* (133 meters), were longer than those at either San Giovanni (almost twice as large a town) or Terranuova.

50 Montevarchi. Founded between 1217 and 1254 by the Guidi counts (E. Detti,
G.F. Di Pietro, and G. Fanelli, *Città murate e sviluppo contemporaneo*, 1968).

How did the designers decide on these dimensions? What proportions
would the plan have had? The width of the town was fixed by the depth of
the eight rows of lots that were standard in the new towns, and by the
width of the intervening streets. At Giglio the sum of these dimensions
was 240 *braccia* (140 meters). The length, we are told, was 470 *braccia* (274.5
meters). Thus Giglio, like the other Florentine towns founded after 1330,
had proportions of roughly 2 : 1. But formal considerations could not have
been the only factor in determining the town's length. The number of

building lots the *Ufficiali delle Castella* thought would be needed must also have been a compelling consideration.

The planners of Giglio Fiorentino had a fairly good idea of how many families would settle in the new town. The population was to consist almost entirely of people from the eight newly acquired villages in the Val d'Ambra. Only as an afterthought were immigrants from outside Florentine territory invited. Because agricultural land was not distributed to the settlers of the Florentine new towns, the Giglio project would not have attracted many farmers to the area. The few outsiders who might have been interested in the new community more likely depended on a craft or trade for the large part of their livelihood. Unfortunately, we have no information about these people.

The population of the eight villages in the Val d'Ambra can be roughly calculated from the documents ratifying the treaty between the abbey of Agnano and the city government. Between 3 and 10 April 1350, the inhabitants of each village were convened and, swearing themselves to be at least two-thirds of the population of the community, agreed to the conditions of the treaty.[19] At Cornia 42 men were registered, at Cacciano 31, at Montelucci 23, at Pieve a Prisciano 33, at Castiglione Alberti 34, at San Lorentino (including the men of Cappanole) 15, and at Badia Agnano 43 men, for a total of 221 signatories.

Any attempt to calculate from these figures the number of building lots required in the new town involves many variables. If we take 221 as the number of males and then subtract, for each town, the names that repeat, on the assumption that they belonged to persons in the same family who lived together (in Cornia there were 11 men sharing 5 last names, at Cacciano 10 shared 4, at Montelucci 8 shared 3, at Pieve a Prisciano 12 shared 5, at Castiglione Alberti 13 shared 6, at San Lorentino 6 shared 2, and at Badia Agnano 17 shared 7), only 176 lots were necessary. If we assume, however, that the 221 constituted only two-thirds of the male population and that each man had his own family, the town would have needed 330 lots. We cannot know where, between these two extremes, the actual number fell. Neither, perhaps, could the officials charged with planning the new town. Certainly there was no census or even, at that time, a tax role that might have provided more accurate information. A safe strategy would have been to plan for the largest likely number and fill the unused lots with outsiders. Indeed, this seems to be the course taken by the officials, because the town plan provided for between 320 and 351 building lots.[20]

There were three lot sizes in the Giglio Fiorentino project. The main-street lots were the largest at 28 by 10 *braccia* (16.4 by 5.84 meters), those of the middle blocks were 20 by 10 *braccia* (11.7 by 5.84 meters), and the smallest were the lots 10 *braccia* square, near the wall. The 10 *braccia* width was standard in most of the new towns; only the depth varied. The deepest lots were in the center of the town. As many as four decreasing lot sizes were possible from the main street to the perimeter of the settlement. At Terranuova, for example, the lots on the main street were about 30 *braccia* (17.5 meters) deep, those on the next streets about 25.5 *braccia* (14.9 meters), about 20 *braccia* (11.7 meters), and, originally, about 16 *braccia* (9.3 meters), respectively.

The grading of lots had an obvious economic logic. Business opportunity was greater on the main street and the larger lots provided the space needed to take advantage of it. The main street properties were surely given to the richer immigrants. Whoever lived in them needed the capital to exploit the site and to afford the special class of building required there.[21] The arrangement also solved what must have been a delicate social problem. It is likely that the richer immigrants possessed larger and more advantageously sited homes in the old villages. Unless the new-town planners wanted to change this village hierarchy—and we have no evidence that they did—they were obliged to recreate the physical conditions that would allow for these social distinctions. The varying quality of the lots allowed the more important immigrants to receive special treatment. For the Giglio Fiorentino project, of which there is the most information, the committee responsible for the distribution of lots was made up of representatives from the villages concerned, as well as Florentine officials. Together they could identify and differentiate among the immigrants and distribute the lots so as to satisfy the largest number of people.

In the back-to-back block system of the early new towns, distinctions between streets were inevitable. Since no houses faced onto the alleys, both sides of the streets between the first and second sets of blocks had houses and workshops opening onto them. These streets—at San Giovanni (see Fig. 5) they were 15 *braccia* (8.76 meters) wide—were different from both the heavily traveled main street, with its inns and shops, and the broad, quiet military streets adjacent to the town wall. They were the center of the towns' residential neighborhoods. In 1337, with the introduction of the freestanding block in the plan of Terranuova (see Fig. 16), double-loaded streets were no longer unavoidable. Since the houses could face in one of two directions, it was possible for planners to balance the orientation of the houses evenly over the plan. Each street could be bordered by the fronts of houses on one side and by the backs of houses on the other. The planners of Terranuova chose to ignore this opportunity, repeating, instead, the traditional arrangement. Streets 8 *braccia* (4.7 meters) wide were treated like the alleys at San Giovanni. No houses faced onto them and, like the alleys at San Giovanni, they were extensively covered with bridges and other construction. As always, a few streets — at Terranuova the streets two back from the main street — accommodated most of the town's residential activity.

Only the project for Giglio Fiorentino (Document 19; see Fig. 29) realized the potential of the Terranuova plan to diffuse the town's activities over the whole street system. The *Ufficiali delle Castella* fixed the width of the main street of Giglio at 14 *braccia* (8.2 meters) and the depth of the lots abutting it at 28 *braccia* (16.4 meters) deep. The street behind these lots was 10 *braccia* (5.84 meters) wide and the next row of lots 20 *braccia* (11.7 meters) deep; the next street and set of lots had these same dimensions. There was then a street 8 *braccia* (4.7 meters) wide, lots 10 *braccia* deep, and finally the military road of 10 *braccia* width. The document does not record the orientation of the lots; the widths of the streets, however, provide clues. At Terranuova the main street measured 14 *braccia*, the residential streets 10 *braccia*, and the service roads 8 *braccia*. If we assume that streets with the same role were assigned identical widths in both projects, then in the Giglio plan only the third street back from the main street was defined as a service street. If no houses faced onto it, those on its outer side faced the military road and those on its inner side faced a 10 *braccia* street toward the center of town. The houses at the center of the plan were oriented to the *via maestra*. They turned their backs on a 10 *braccia* street which, had it been treated like the other 10 *braccia* streets in the plan, would have received the fronts of the lots on its outer side. As a result no street except the *via maestra* was double-loaded.

Another peculiarity of the Giglio plan was the elimination of most of the town's cross streets. Of the five cross streets normal to a Florentine plan, Giglio preserved only the one at the middle of the town. Minor intersections, in other new towns, were associated with significant social activities and were important for the neighborhoods. At San Giovanni a well once stood at or near each of these intersections (see Fig. 5); at Terranuova they were the sites of churches (see Fig. 16).

The only large, open space in a Florentine new town was the piazza located at the intersection of the two axes of the plan, at the center of the area enclosed by the circuit of the town walls. The *palazzo* of the Florentine official, the town hall, the town's main church,[22] the oratories of the oldest confraternities, and the town's first convents were placed around, and in one case within, this central square. On its open ground religious festivals and public ceremonies were celebrated. The Florentine official took his oath of office in the square, and the population assembled to hear a reading of the town's statutes there.[23] At Firenzuola town residents made public announcements in the square to clear real estate titles,[24] and were obliged to gather there to celebrate the feast day of Florence's patron saint.[25]

The central squares of the new towns as they now survive are strongly marked by these solemn uses. Their large scale and the public buildings that surround them give the squares a ceremonial character that seems appropriate to the formalities of church and state. The mundane functions of town life, however, also took place on this open ground. The most regular and significant of these activities was the market.

All the new towns were endowed with market privileges. At Giglio Fiorentino the market was established in the very document of foundation. Pietrasanta/Casaglia, the town on the Consuma pass, was conceived, explicitly, as a market for the purchase of grain (Document 1). Record of the market at Scarperia survives from within five years of the establishment of the town.[26] The most lively market was the weekly one, attended by farmers, artisans, and traders both from within and beyond the community. The towns actively sought to attract business, removing legal obstacles to participation by granting immunity to debtors and litigants in civil cases on market day.[27] Trading itself was closely regulated. Town law defined both the time and the place of business, established fines for trading that took place before the sound of the bell that opened the market, and stipulated that all goods had to be brought to the market place (presumably to be taxed) before they could be exchanged. At Castelfranco, whose town statutes provide the clearest picture of market practice, a committee of four officials regulated the market's activity. They were present on market day and were empowered to represent Castelfranco in the Florentine courts to protect the market's privileges and the commune's "honor."[28] In addition to the weekly market, town officials permitted daily trading in perishable produce. At Castelfranco "grocers who bring fruit and vegetables and things to eat are permitted to come [to the marketplace] every day without incurring any fine."[29] Similarly, in Scarperia, meat could be sold daily at a special booth next to the palace of the Florentine official.[30]

The site of the markets was not the same in every town. The oldest towns seem to have used the central square. Again, the evidence is clearest for Castelfranco. An addition to the town statutes dated 1409, changing the day of Castelfranco's market in the hope of encouraging more activity, began: "That there shall be a market every Wednesday on the square at

Castelfranco."[31] By the fifteenth century many of the new towns were holding their weekly market on a market field, or *mercatale*, outside the town walls. The oldest surviving statutes of Scarperia and Firenzuola (from the early part of the fifteenth century) noted this, but also gave some indication that the *mercatale* may not have been the market's original location.[32] The statutes of Firenzuola acknowledged that the market was still held in town on some occasions and proclaimed the government's intention to reform this practice. Scarperia's statutes mentioned booths on the square for the sale of meat. Similar structures must have been much more common sixty years earlier, in 1341, when some of them had to be cleared away for celebration of the feast day of the town's patron saint.[33]

Almost all the new towns founded in Europe since the ninth century used their central square as a market place. This can be seen in the bastides of southwestern France, in the German colonial towns in eastern Europe, and in the settlements in Swabia, Bavaria, and Austria, which represent the most numerous, the most carefully planned, and the most influential new-town schemes of the later Middle Ages. The Florentine conception of the square as the center of ceremony is unusual. If it was not part of the original Florentine new-town idea, the city's planners did commit themselves to it before the end of their activity as founders of towns. The evidence from Firenzuola and Scarperia shows they thought of the central square in this way by the early decades of the fifteenth century. The foundation document for Giglio Fiorentino pushes the date of their acceptance of the idea back to the middle of the fourteenth century. At the same time as the Florentines were expanding the space dedicated to public assembly in front of their own town hall, the Palazzo dei Signori, their new-town planners explicitly placed the market in the last of the city's foundations "outside of the town" (Document 19). The square at Giglio was reserved for the palace of the Florentine official, the loggia for ceremonial events connected with it, and the church of the new parish. This design marks a turning point in the Florentine attitude toward the central squares of the new towns. From 1350 forward the squares are increasingly treated as monumental spaces. The market was moved outside of the town to make way for buildings of a new scale and quality and functions associated with the administration and representation of the Florentine state.

There were two types of central square in the Florentine new towns. They were not developmentally related but rather represent reactions to two different situations. Both appeared in the first Florentine projects, one at San Giovanni, the other at Castelfranco. At San Giovanni, where the heavy Florence – Arezzo traffic could be expected to break up any square placed astride the main road, the planners gave the piazza a rectangular format (248 by 80 *braccia* [145 by 46.7 meters] according to a fifteenth-century plan) and oriented its long axis transversely to the road (see Figs. 3, 8, 9). Thanks to this arrangement the road did not destroy the usefulness of the square but only divided it into two separate areas. Each of these was large enough to turn its back on the road and was formally more coherent than the long, thin shape of the total open space in the center of the town. Placement of the town hall between the two areas officially recognized their separateness. The rectangular piazza and the entire system of the San Giovanni plan were reproduced at Scarperia and Firenzuola, which were on the busy Florence – Bologna road.

In designing Castelfranco the planning officials did not have to worry about the traffic on the town's main street. The road carried traffic only between the valley floor and the old—and in the fourteenth century largely superseded—Florence – Arezzo road that twisted across the slope of the gentle mountain called the Pratomagno a few hundred meters uphill from the town. The piazza at Castelfranco measures approximately forty by fifty meters (and perhaps originally sixty),[34] with streets entering it in the middle of each side (see Figs. 12, 13). The designers did not consider the roads disruptive. Though now bisected twice, the space preserves its coherence as a single unit. This type of square was repeated at Terranuova and in the Giglio Fiorentino project. Those towns did not have a square format like Castelfranco, but they did share with the early town the low rate of traffic on the roads on which they were sited.

The squares at both Terranuova (see Figs. 16, 18) and Giglio Fiorentino (see Fig. 29) were 70 by 90 *braccia* (40.8 by 52.5 meters), approximately the same size as the square at Castelfranco. They were, however, more regular than the early square and incorporated two important changes. First, they were reoriented by ninety degrees. Their long axis ran perpendicular to the axis of the main street, rather than being congruent with it as at Castelfranco. Second, the corners of the piazzas were opened up by streets 8 and 10 *braccia* (4.7 and 5.8 meters) wide, which replaced the drainage space between the backs of houses at Castelfranco. This change ventilated the squares; they became more accessible and less confined. The new streets also reinforced the square's compositional ties to the rest of the plan. The size of the square and the dimensions of the streets and blocks at the center of the design were one. The streets that represented the axes of symmetry of the whole plan were the axes, too, of the square.

The regularity of the piazza was only the most prominent evidence of the formal rigor that set the Florentine new towns apart from all other contemporary urban plans. The fixed overall dimensions, the double symmetry generated by the two perpendicular axes, the nonserial nature of the blocks and streets, the perfect centrality of the main square site, the repetition of the motif of intersection at critical points throughout the plan, and the synchronization of the systems of circulation and defense were all equally rare qualities in the fourteenth century; their coordination in a single composition was a unique achievement. Fixed dimensions created an opportunity that the Florentine planners did not fail to exploit. The application of a system of diminishing block depths and the establishment of neighborhood centers in the middle of each quarter were possible only in a town of finite size. The area within the walls was understood as a field of composition, like the surface inside the frame of an altar panel or the ground to be covered by a building. The arrangement of the streets, square, and building lots responded not just to the requirements of utility and regularity but also to those of formal design. In contrast to the open-ended systems of Bern and Sainte-Foy-la-Grande, the Florentine towns were complete at the moment of their foundation; they asked only to be filled with the families designated for relocation inside their walls.

CHAPTER 3

MODELS

THE TRADITION OF TOWN FOUNDATION in western Europe stretches back to antiquity. From the eighth through the fifth century B.C. Sicily and southern Italy were colonized by immigrants from the Greek homeland, who lived in founded towns at the center of new city-states. Half a millennium later, Rome expanded its empire by creating territories inhabited and administered from newly made urban centers. Throughout the Middle Ages, in Great Britain and on the continent, notably in the southwest of France and in eastern Europe, conquest and development of land was accomplished by the *ex novo* creation of towns.

Many of these settlements were laid out on orthogonal plans. Greek Agrigento, Roman Trier, and the thirteenth-century Sainte-Foy-la-Grande were all based on straight streets that intersected at right angles. Beyond this, however, the towns were very little alike. Their streets had different widths and were arranged in different patterns. Their blocks were sized and proportioned differently to suit different building types. Their public spaces took many shapes and related in different ways to the rest of the plan. Orthogonal planning has successfully accommodated the urban life of widely divergent civilizations precisely because it offers so many options.

As latecomers to the foundation of towns, the Florentines could look to earlier projects for instruction. There were precedents for the collection of populations, the establishment of markets and parishes, and the organization of town and provincial governments, as there were for the design of town plans. Each plan element—squares, street systems, lot patterns—had been developed in many alternative forms. As their designs show, the

51 Stefano Buonsignori, plan of the center of Florence, 1584, in the edition of Giovanni Giacomo de Rossi, 1660 (Harvard College Map Room).

Florentine town builders knew and used a wide range of this information.

The colonies of antiquity are sometimes cited as the ultimate source for medieval orthogonal designs. This interpretation seems especially compelling in the case of towns founded by a former Roman colony, as Florence itself was (Fig. 51). In fact, the plans of most ancient urban sites survived to the fourteenth century in a confusing state of preservation. The changes that swept the Arno valley in the early Middle Ages, for example, had obliterated most of Florence's first-century plan.[1] Literary

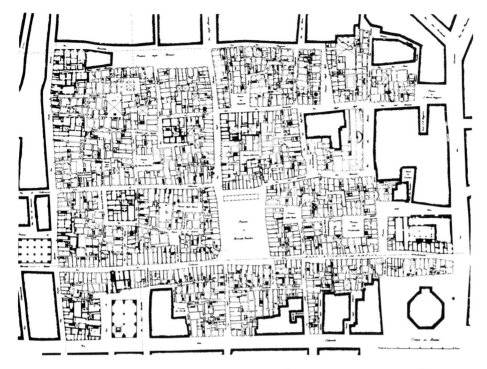

52 A. Ruffoni, plan of the center of Florence, after 1888 (G. Fanelli, *Architettura e città*, 1973).

sources contained a minimal amount of useful information about physical planning but they did succeed in firing the imagination of medieval planners.[2] The foundation of Vittoria, the ill-fated town with which Frederick II hoped to replace the city of Parma, began at a moment selected by court astrologers with a ceremony in which the emperor traced the perimeter of the site with a plow in imitation of the ancient ritual of cutting the *sulcus*.[3]

In the late Middle Ages the ancient origin of Florence, if not the city's exact history, was common knowledge. Giovanni Villani attributed the city's foundation to Julius Caesar in 70 B.C.[4] Proof of its antiquity, Villani asserted, was buried just under the surface. When they dug, he wrote, Florentines would find the paving of the Roman streets. From these excavations and the ruins of the ancient aqueduct it would be possible to know the location but not, Villani admitted, the exact size or form of the ancient city. Villani correctly believed that the colony's forum was at the site of the *mercato vecchio*, where, he said, the church of Santa Maria in Campidoglio preserved the toponym, but he also quoted his contemporaries who located the public square of the ancient city between the Bargello and the Palazzo della Signoria. Villani had a few fanciful ideas of his own. He believed that a strong fortress was a prominent feature of the forum, and that the amphitheater whose foundations defined an oval pattern of streets in the area west of the Piazza Santa Croce was an assembly hall used for political debates. He called this the *parlascio*.[5] For Villani, Roman Florentia was a conceptual rather than a physical reality. Its streets and buildings were buried in the earth, proof of Florence's origin, yet largely unknowable. It was Roman town-foundation policy that Villani felt he understood best. According to him, Florentia was founded after the Romans had destroyed the city of Fiesole "to insure that Fiesole could not be rebuilt." It was populated with those of the conquered people who accepted Roman rule, as well as by Roman citizens, and was considered a simulacrum of the mother city, "la piccola Roma." All of this was closer to the reality of the Florentine new towns than it was to Roman history. Villani spun a story that ennobled fourteenth-century Florentine policy by giving it an ancient model.

While Villani was unsure about how much of Roman Florentia survived the Barbarian invasions, he was confident in his understanding of the city refounded by Charlemagne.[6] He knew the circuit of its walls, the locations of its palaces, the names of its streets, its bridges, and even something about its sewers. This Christian city, with its many churches dedicated and positioned "al modo di Roma," was, for Villani, the seed from which fourteenth-century Florence had grown. It was centralized and symmetrical. Four major gates were arranged "almost in a cross." The city was divided into quarters and at its center was the *mercato vecchio*.

It is this abstraction that may have influenced fourteenth-century new-town planners. They rightfully chose to disregard surviving details of the Roman city as inappropriate to the economic and architectural needs of the medieval urban environment. The blocks of Roman Florentia, sixty meters square, met the requirements of single-story buildings like the Roman *domus* that opened onto interior courts, but could accommodate only awkwardly the tall, narrow, street-oriented row houses of late medieval usage. The many alleys and semiprivate open spaces that today cut through the surviving blocks of Florence's ancient center are the best evidence of the plan's incompatibility with medieval building requirements (Fig. 52). In their failure to stress and therefore to maximize frontage on the main street, Roman plans ran counter to medieval practice. The many intersections wasted the frontage, and the blocks facing the main street were no larger than those on the town's periphery. Even the central-

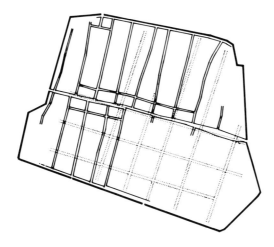

53 Winchester. Dotted lines show the plan of the Roman town; solid lines show the plan of the town founded by Alfred the Great in the late ninth century (after M. Biddle and D. Hill, "Late Saxon Planned Towns," 1971).

ity that Villani emphasized as a quality of Roman Florence was not the centrality of medieval plans. The intersection of the ancient city's two main streets was only roughly in the center of the plan. The site of the forum was similarly eccentric. Occupying one corner of the intersection, it lay outside the flow of traffic, not astride it.

By the early fourteenth century the plan of Florence had developed a further defect. The medieval community sat rather uneasily on the grid of the Roman town. The open space that had been the forum was still bustling with activity as a market but it was devoid of monumental buildings. The centers of public life now lay on the eastern periphery: the cathedral in the north, the town hall in the south. This Florence could serve even less well than Villani's imaginary Roman or Carolingian city as a model for the new towns.

New-town planning had moved away from the model of the Roman colonies at least four hundred years before the foundation of the Florentine towns. A dramatic illustration of this break is offered by the plan of Winchester, England (Fig. 53).[7] Originally the colony of Venta Belgarum, the site had lost its Roman street grid by the fifth century. Only the town wall and the street that ran between its east and west gates survived into the Middle Ages. Because of the site's defenses, Alfred the Great, King of Wessex, chose it for his new capital at the end of the ninth century. In the planning of the refounded town only the old main street maintained its position; nothing else of the Roman grid — based on blocks 135 meters square — was reconstructed. The medieval plan, preserved in the modern city, was made up of two kinds of rectangular blocks. The first lay on either side of the High Street and had its long axis parallel with the main road. Behind these blocks, and separated from them by a back street, were blocks that were arranged with their long axis perpendicular to the main street, extending uninterrupted to the town wall. Houses faced the streets that bordered these 80-meter-deep blocks on either side. The blocks on the main street, on the other hand, had a depth of only 31 meters and supported a single file of houses facing onto the High Street where the town market was held. The varied size and orientation of the blocks of medieval Winchester destroyed the homogeneity of the classical plan. In its place there was a focus, in this case on a main street, which was primarily functional but also formal, and was characteristic, in one way or another, of most of the new-town designs for the next one thousand years.

The use of blocks of extended dimensions in patterns of simple, rough symmetry is visible wherever orthogonal planning occurs in medieval Europe. Examples are the excavated ninth-century trading centers of Emden and Hamburg in northern Germany, and plans of early agricultural settlements in southwestern France, such as Nogaro (founded in 1060 by the archbishop of Auch) and Saint Nicolas de la Grave (founded in 1135 by the abbey of Moissac).[8]

It is from these origins that medieval new-town planning developed, and by the end of the thirteenth century many hundreds of towns had been planned and planted. The men in charge of the San Giovanni and Castelfranco projects were far more likely to have looked to these contemporary designs than to the remnants of the thirteen-hundred-year-old plan of Florence's city center. To do so they would not have had to search far beyond the borders of Florentine territory. The city's ally in the Arno valley, the Guelph city of Lucca, was engaged in the same effort to expand her territorial holdings as was Florence. In the middle of the thirteenth century Lucca turned to a new-town strategy. Her towns, like the Florentine towns that followed them, began as resettlement sites for the serfs of the city's baronial rivals[9] and grew into capitals of the Lucchese territorial state.[10] They, too, were on important roads, served military functions, and became the economic centers of the surrounding countryside.

Camaiore (Figs. 54, 55) and Pietrasanta (Figs. 56, 57), a different town from the Florentine foundation by the same name now called Casaglia, are the most conspicuous Lucchese new towns. Both were founded in 1255,

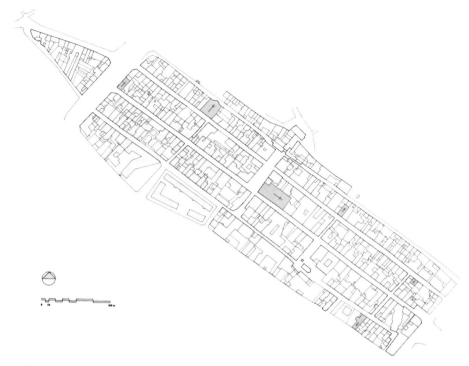

54 Camaiore. Founded by the city of Lucca in 1255. From the cadastral plan, nineteenth century (Ufficio Tecnico Erariale, Lucca).

55 Camaiore. Central square, view from the north.

56 Pietrasanta. Founded in 1255 by the city of Lucca. From the cadastral plan, nineteenth century (Ufficio Tecnico Erariale, Lucca).

57 Pietrasanta. Central square, view from the southwest.

immediately following a victory by the city over the barons of Versiglia, along the Tyrrhenian coast. The towns were laid out on the same plan, but of the two Pietrasanta is the more perfectly realized and the better preserved. Aside from a group of extra blocks appended to the northeast flank of the town and a military installation on an adjacent hill, the settlement is arranged according to strict symmetry and orthogonality.

The core of Pietrasanta is a rectangle approximately 147 by 558 meters. It is structured around a street 6.5 meters wide — a section of the road from Lucca to Genoa — that runs the entire length of the town's long axis. On either side of the main street are blocks made up of two rows of lots placed back to back. Like all the elements of this plan, the dimensions of the lots vary considerably from one place to another, but in general the lots of 19.75 meters that face onto the main street are about a meter deeper than those facing onto the back streets. The back streets themselves have the same width as the central street and are flanked on their outer sides by another row of lots 18.75 meters deep. The lateral development of the plan is completed by roads also 6.5 meters wide, now largely built over, between the third row of houses and the wall of the town.

Cross-communication at Pietrasanta was provided by the military road at the perimeter of the plan and by streets three meters wide that divided the rows of lots at the midpoint between the central square and the town wall. The plan's most prominent transverse element was the central square, which was about twenty-five meters wide and extended from one side of the town to the other. It hosted the Palazzo Pretorio (the seat of the Lucchese official in Pietrasanta), the main church (in this case the seat of a bishopric), an Augustinian convent, and, from 1324, a fortress adjacent to the southwest gate of the town.

This Lucchese design was almost certainly the inspiration for the plan of San Giovanni. The dominance of the long axis, the double-loaded streets, the quartering of the plan, and the creation, with the minor cross axes, of a focal point within each quarter are important characteristics of both designs. But it is the extended piazza, oriented at right angles to the main axis of the plan, that is the most striking formal idea of both designs and the most telling point of comparison between them. Pietrasanta and Camaiore, San Giovanni and its progeny at Scarperia and Firenzuola are almost the only new towns in Italy to use it.[11]

The originality of the Pietrasanta plan lies in its integration of the forceful but unwieldy extended piazza into a coordinated orthogonal design. Credit for the invention of both the piazza form and its transverse arrangement belongs to the town builders of the German-speaking lands closest to Italy. The characteristic public space of new towns in southern Germany, in Switzerland, and in Austria is a wide market street. It appears in some of the earliest examples of monumental city planning of the Middle Ages. The approach to the cathedral at Speyer, created by the Salian emperors in the first half of the eleventh century, is a market street 650 meters long and 20 to 25 meters wide. A similar street, also used as a market, informed the first plan of Freiburg im Breisgau, founded in 1119 by the dukes of Zähringen. At Villingen (Figs. 58, 59) and Rottweil, foundations traditionally associated with the Zähringer dukes and which date to the 1120s, two market streets intersect at the center of the plan, forming what is referred to as a *Strassenkreuz* system. Recent opinion holds that the plan was the result of enlargements that took place after the extinction of the Zähringer line in 1218, when the towns had passed under the rule of Hohenstaufen king Frederick II. The best argument for dating the plans, since the documents remain inconclusive, is the relative abundance of *Strassenkreuz* plans in the thirteenth century and the scarcity of them in the twelfth. Only Villingen and Rottweil might be dated to the earlier period, but there are a number of similar towns in Swabia founded in the thirteenth century by members of the lower nobility under the influence of

58 Villingen. Founded in the 1120s by the dukes of Zähringen; expanded in the thirteenth century (Plan: Cord Meckseper).

59 Villingen. Central intersection, view from southeast.

Frederick's town planners.[12] Among these is Kenzingen (Fig. 60), founded by Rudolph II of Üsenberg in 1249. Here the two axes of the cross are distinguished by different widths. The wider of the two axes is the shorter; the width of the longer is more like that of a conventional street. It defines the town's rectangular proportions and establishes the axis to which the plan's secondary streets conform. Other *Strassenkreuz* plans were laid out for the Wittelsbach dukes of Bavaria — who were connected to the Hohenstaufen by political obligation and ties of marriage — at Landau on the Isar (1224), Kelheim (about 1231), Deggendorf (shortly after 1242), and Neustadt on the Danube (between 1260 and 1270) (Figs. 61, 62).[13]

The empire's eastern crown lands produced town plans similar to those in Swabia and Bavaria, but development here followed a different course. The extended market street that was the basis of early new-town design in Austria was often the only major element of the plan. Other streets, if they existed at all, were dwarfed by the market. In the course of the later Middle Ages the marketplace evolved toward more measured forms. An intermediate stage with proportions ranging from 12:1 to 6:1, is called by modern scholars the *Strassenplatz*. By the late twelfth century there appeared the *Rechteckplatz*, whose proportions were between 4:1 and 3:2.[14] The market square that belonged to the mid-thirteenth century expansion of Linz

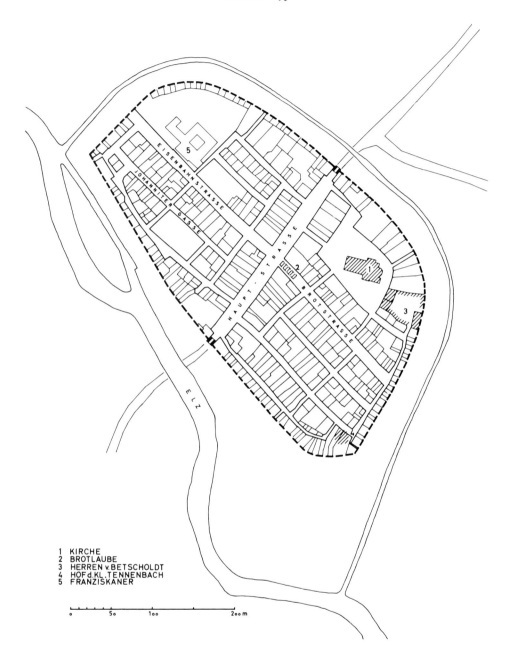

1 KIRCHE
2 BROTLAUBE
3 HERREN v.BETSCHOLDT
4 HOF d.KL.TENNENBACH
5 FRANZISKANER

60 Kenzingen. Founded in 1249 by Rudolph II of Üsenberg (Plan: Cord Meckseper).

61 Neustadt on the Danube. Founded between 1260 and 1270 by the Wittelsbach dukes of Bavaria (E. Leiwehr, *Marktplätze in Südostbayern*, 1976).

62 Neustadt on the Danube. Main street, view from the north.

today measures 60 by 190 meters; the square in the thirteenth-century *Burgerstadt* of St. Polton in lower Austria measures 45 by 140 meters.[15] Unlike the market street and the *Strassenplatz*, these rectangular squares were integrated into compositions in which the system of secondary streets played as important a part as the square. Towns that used the *Rechteckplatz* in a way that is even closer to its use in Tuscany are found in and around Carinthia.

Located in the southwestern part of modern Austria, Carinthia was ruled by the Hohenstaufen from 1237 until the 1250s, through Conrad IV, Frederick II's son, king of Styria, Austria, and Carinthia. The region's importance in the Middle Ages derived from the roads that passed through it: from Vienna in the east and Salzburg and Bavaria in the north, routes descended through Carinthia to Udine and Venice by the Pontebba pass. The towns similar to the Tuscan settlements are located on these roads.

In the first half of the thirteenth century Bernhard, duke of Carinthia, used the foundation of towns and the enlargement and fortification of

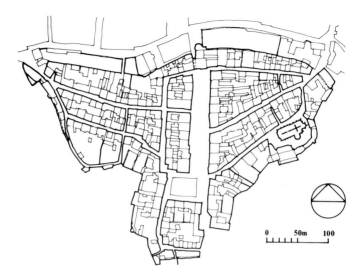

63 Völkermarkt. Founded between 1231 and 1240 by Bernhard, duke of Carinthia.

64 Völkermarkt. Central square, view from the south.

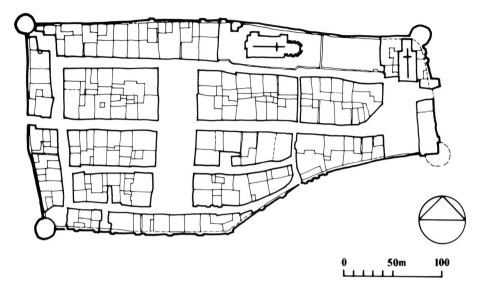

0   50m   100

65 Radstadt. Founded in the last quarter of the thirteenth century.

older settlements to secure his authority in the area. St. Veit an der Glan, with a history of settlement that goes back to antiquity, and Klagenfurt, the modern provincial capital, were both established as walled cities and have *Strassenkreuz* plans like Villingen and Rottweil.

At Völkermarkt (Figs. 63, 64), near the site of a trading place known from the early twelfth century, Bernhard built a new, walled market between 1231 and 1240.[16] The main feature of the town is a rectangular square about 40 meters wide and 180 long to which, on the south side, an 80-by-50-meter square was appended, reflecting the presence of a market of Jewish merchants. The long axis of the combined markets is oriented in the direction of the river Drave in the valley south of the town, where, in 1218, Bernhard had built a bridge to facilitate the transport of iron and lead to the market. The street system of Völkermarkt runs across the axis of the square, with three streets radiating from the eastern entrance of the town and two parallel streets extending to the west. Though irregular, this plan, like the Swabian and Bavarian examples, is formed by the intersection of two equally important axes: one is defined by the combined markets, the other by the streets accommodating the town's residential development.

What the Völkermarkt plan would have looked like had it been realized in more strictly orthogonal terms is illustrated by a town in the mountains north of Carinthia, on the Salzburg branch of the Pontebba road. Radstadt

(Fig. 65) was founded in the last quarter of the thirteenth century on a rise in the floor of an upland valley just below the most difficult passage in the traverse of the Tauern mountains. Its central square measures about 50 by 160 meters and lies crosswise to the main road. Despite an even number of streets, one roadway assumed a central position and the plan developed along streets parallel with this axis. The secular public buildings, now of eighteenth-century construction, lie on the square between the main street and the parallel street to the north. The early-fourteenth-century parish church is located on this northern street, at some remove from the square, like the churches of many of the German towns.

A plan similar to that of Radstadt — with an extended square perpendicular to the system of the streets — can be found south of Carinthia, again on the Pontebba road, in what is now Italian territory. Gloizio di Mels, viscount of the dukes of Carinthia and vassal of the patriarch of Aquileia, established a new town at Venzone (Fig. 66), next to an older settlement. This occurred some time between 1252, when a market was installed at this narrow site in the valley of the Tagliamento, and 1258, when the fortifications were begun.[17] The location of the older settlement is marked by the *duomo*, partly rebuilt by Gloizio. It lies immediately south of the new town, which is dominated by a rectangular piazza and includes a number of very loosely arranged streets. The streets are not quite parallel, and are spaced at such distance that great gardens survive behind the houses. Nevertheless, the street system conforms to the Völkermarkt pattern. The axis of the Pontebba road dominates. The central street is flanked by residential streets and the only consistent cross axis is formed by the square and the street that, in the thirteenth century, continued it to the east.[18] The intersection of the square and the main street is dominated by a town hall built in the late fourteenth century.[19]

The transverse-piazza scheme of thirteenth-century German new-town planning could have come to Tuscany in a number of ways. Though the distance between the two areas was great, connections between them were considerable. Today most of the towns discussed are of minor importance, but in the late Middle Ages they hosted markets that were as active as all but the largest in Europe. Like the Florentine new towns, the German foundations were on major roads and would have been familiar to many Tuscan travelers. Venzone was undoubtedly the best-known. On the Pontebba road south of the Alpine watershed and on the Italian side of a toll barrier established by the lords of Venzone, the town was an important place for the exchange of goods. Trading houses from all over Italy

66 Venzone. Enlarged between 1252 and 1258 by Gloizio di Mels, viscount of the dukes of Carinthia.

had factors resident in Venzone; Florentine merchants were there from at least the late thirteenth century.[20]

An intimate knowledge of the German town plans probably depended on the experience of builders and surveyors and they, too, had contact with the north. If the practice of other Italian cities can serve as a guide, it was the building professionals connected with the cathedral workshop at Lucca that designed the plan of Pietrasanta.[21] The most important of the builders at Lucca came from northern Italy. Guido Bigarelli da Como, who was also the designer and carver of the baptismal font at Pisa, worked at Lucca cathedral in the period of the building of the new towns.[22] Giannino di Bono, also "da Como," was active at Lucca cathedral from as early as 1256 and was the master "operis tecti et companilis" there in 1274.[23] The most prominent of the builders at the cathedral was "Lombardus quondam Guidi," who appears in the cathedral documents from 1238 to 1259 and is called there "operarius et magister Sancti Martini."[24] Lombardo was also a sculptor and in his work for the cathedral his northern origins are clear. The scenes attributed to him from the life of Saint Martin and Saint Regulus and the figures of the months of the year on the cathedral porch show full knowledge of the contemporary style of Lombard sculpture, particularly of the late reliefs by Benedetto Antelami for the baptistery at Parma. Guidobono Bigarelli, "quondam magister Lanfranchus," is one more figure active at the cathedral. Evidence of his activity in the north is documented in the form of a bequest, in 1258, to the *opera* of San Vergilio at Trento in the Alto Adige where, it seems, he had worked.[25]

Along with commercial and professional ties, there was also a political connection between Lucca and the areas immediately north of the Alps that helps explain the presence of the transverse-piazza plan in Tuscany. About twenty miles from Lucca, at the castle of San Miniato al Tedesco in the lower Arno valley, was the seat of the imperial vicar of Tuscany. The fortifications of the castle were renewed by Frederick II's builders between 1217 and 1221[26] and another castle, at Prato, was constructed by them in the 1230s or the 1240s.[27] Lucca's relationship with the empire in this period was surprisingly cordial. Despite the staunch Guelph politics of the commune, its unwavering alliance with Florence, and the almost unrelieved state of war with Ghibelline Pisa and the local magnates, there were regular and mutually advantageous contacts between Lucca and Frederick. When the emperor was in Tuscany in 1239 the Lucchese government received him with great festivities and even contributed one of its citizens to his service as imperial vicar of the Garfagnana. It was Lucca's desire to control this mountain area north of the city that motivated the accommodation with

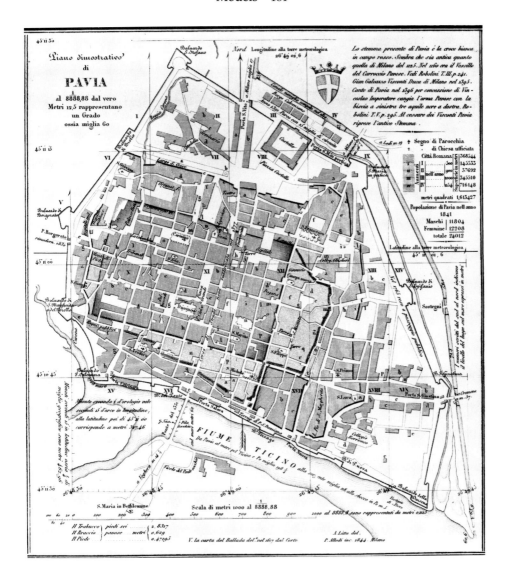

67 Pavia, *Tavola Storica de Pavia*, "Piano dimostrativo de Pavia," Milan, 1844.
The Piazza Grande at the center of the town was mentioned for the first time in
1393 (Map Division, The New York Public Library, Astor, Lenox and Tilden
Foundations).

the emperor. The effort was rewarded in 1248 when, despite nominal support for the claims of the barons who were his vassals, the emperor placed the area, as a feudal appanage, in Lucca's hands.[28]

Besides Pietrasanta, San Giovanni, and Venzone, two other Italian cities had extended rectangular piazzas. Both were intimately connected with the empire. Pavia (Fig. 67) had been a seat of court since the time of the Lombard kingdom and an imperial residence under Charlemagne and the German emperors. The plan of the city was restructured in the late fourteenth century by Galeazzo II and his son Gian Galeazzo Visconti, heads of the most powerful imperially aligned family in late-medieval Italy. The Visconti were intermarried with German princely families. They held, from 1294, the imperial vicarate of Milan, and in 1395 became hereditary princes of the empire. Changes in the plan of Pavia, which was originally a Roman colony on an orthogonal street system, were made in connection with the construction of the large Visconti palace at the edge of the town. The most prominent part of the restructuring was the insertion of a large open square in front of the town hall. First mentioned in 1393, the rectangular piazza, with proportions of about 4:1, was probably carved out of the fabric of the city twelve to eighteen years earlier. Streets established the termini of the square at both its north and south ends; the center of the piazza was crossed by the main east – west street of the Roman plan.[29]

The model for the Piazza Grande in Pavia was probably the Piazza Erbe in Verona (Fig. 68). The form of the Piazza Erbe is only partly medieval; in a large and more regular configuration its space is that of the forum of the Roman colony from which the city descends. The present square, which is bowed on its long sides and has proportions of roughly 4:1 or 5:1, lies immediately to the south of the main east – west street of both the ancient and medieval plan, the present-day Corso Borsari, and astride the street from the ancient Porta Leoni in the south. A street of Roman origin that bisected the square across its long axis took on a new importance in the Middle Ages with the construction of the commune's public buildings. In 1193 the Palazzo del Comune was begun on the southeast side of the intersection. At the beginning of the fourteenth century the Casa dei Mercanti was built opposite it, on the southwest side. From the thirteenth through the fifteenth century the eastern arm of the cross street received additional buildings of the government bureaucracy as well as the equestrian tombs of the Scaliger lords of the city in the adjacent churchyard of Santa Maria Antica.

The Piazza Erbe could have exerted an influence in Pavia because Verona itself had such an important place in the political and physical

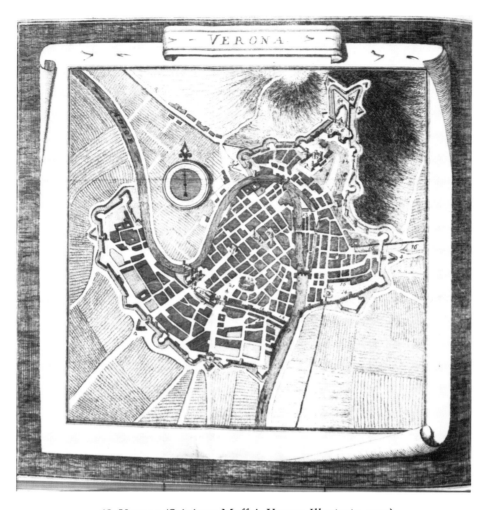

68 Verona (Scipione Maffei, *Verona Illustrata*, 1771).

geography of imperial Italy. As of 1232, when Ezzelino da Romano established his rule in Verona with the assistance of imperial troops, the city had
been a strong supporter of the Ghibelline cause. Ezzelino became a close
confederate of Frederick II, taking the emperor's natural daughter as his
wife in 1238, and giving his own niece in marriage to Frederick's bastard
son, Enzo, king of Sardinia, shortly before the young Hohenstaufen's
capture by the Bolognese in 1249. Ezzelino was the political leader who
enforced imperial policy in northern Italy, and on a number of occasions
Verona played host to Frederick II and other visitors from the court.[30]

69 Borgomanero. Founded in the early thirteenth century by the city of Novara.

70 Borgomanero. Central square, view from the south.

Verona's control of the road to Germany through the Brenner pass made the city the key to the empire's hopes in Italy. For Bavarians, Saxons, and Tiroleans, as well as the residents of upper and lower Austria, Verona was the gateway to Italy. It was not only the first truly Italian city that they encountered after the passage through the Alps, it was also a Roman city. The considerable architectural remains of the ancient past — the great amphitheater, the city gates, and even the bridge that allowed travelers to cross the Adige river — displayed the city's history. The street plan may have made as great an impression as the monuments. The Piazza Erbe, an extended market square similar to those in Germany, would have struck German visitors with its finite proportions and may have had a role in the evolution of the *Strassenplatz* into the *Rechteckplatz* in the thirteenth century.[31]

The Piazza Erbe and other rectangular market squares of Roman origin, like the combined Piazza dei Signori-Piazza Erbe of Vicenza, bear an obvious resemblance to the squares of Pietrasanta and San Giovanni. The encroachment that these *fora* suffered in the course of the Middle Ages gave them the same extended proportions as their counterparts in the Tuscan new towns. Like the Tuscan squares they were located at the center of town, hosted important public buildings, and supported market activity. However, the fact that the piazza is the only element that the plans of Verona and Vicenza share with the Tuscan towns argues against their role as a model. The German plans offer the example not just of a single detail but of an entire composition. With their extended square, the dominance of the axis of the central street, the transverse relationship of street and square, the arrangement of secondary streets around the main axis, and the division of the plan into quarters, they establish the plan type to which the Tuscan towns belong.

The foundation of San Giovanni represents only half of the Florentine new-town activity of 1299; the nearby town of Castelfranco was established in the same year in very different conditions. The site of Castelfranco was a physically restricted, upland plain and the road that ran through the middle of the town was not a busy one. Whether for these or other reasons, the plan of the town was not that of San Giovanni. The two intersecting streets at its center were of roughly the same length (approximately 240 and 270 meters), and the piazza that was laid out around the intersection was itself almost square (approximately 40 by 50 meters).

None of the sources of the San Giovanni plan have much relevance for Castelfranco. There are no Lucchese towns like it and, of the German lands, only Austria offers any possible model. Wiener Neustadt, a town founded by the Babenberg dukes in 1194, had a centralized piazza formed around the intersection of the two streets that led to the town gates. The town that most closely parallels Castelfranco is Borgomanero (Figs. 69, 70), founded by the Po valley comune of Novara in the first third of the thirteenth century.[32] The plan of Borgomanero had as its axis the road from Novara north into the mountains. On either side of this were four, sometimes six, rows of irregular lots laid out back-to-back, about 61 and 33 meters deep. The main street was crossed by another street of equal width (today measuring 11.25 meters) at the center of the town, and around this intersection a piazza was carved out with proportions of approximately 3:5 (30 by 53 meters). As in the piazza at Castelfranco, the long axis of the square ran parallel to the main street and the intersecting street divided the square into unequal parts. These segments are today 16.5 and 25.5 meters deep; the equivalent sections at Castelfranco are about 17 and 28 meters deep.[33]

The Borgomanero square was irregular in yet another way. At Castelfranco the square was closely integrated into the rest of the town's plan (see Fig. 11). Its width was fixed by the width of the main street plus the

71 Massa Lombarda.

depth of the lots along its sides; its length, discounting the width of the cross street, was an even multiple of the standard lot width. The open space was definable in terms of the units of the plan, the streets and building lots, and its position respected their integrity. At Borgomanero the square intruded on the plan. The boundaries of the properties shown on the twentieth-century tax map of the town have no relation to the outline of the square. The rear property line of lots on the main street regularly lies farther from the street than do the east and west edges of the piazza, and some lots are even wrapped around two sides of the square.

The informality of this arrangement suggests a possible genesis of the Borgomanero type of square. A number of northern Italian new towns, like Fossano, Massa Lombarda (Fig. 71), or Villanova d'Asti, have squares that look like incomplete versions of the Borgomanero type. Of the four

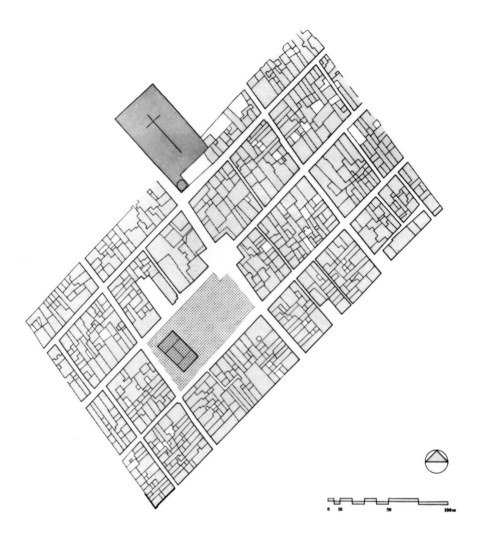

72 Villarreal. Founded by James I of Aragon, who granted the town a charter in 1274 (after J. M. Doñate, *La Torre Mocha*, 1977).

73   Villarreal. Central square, view from the south.

quadrants surrounding the central intersection, only three, two, or even one is cleared. The squares seem to have been created by the carving out of space from the adjacent blocks in piecemeal fashion. A rationalization of this process may have led to the first centralized square design at Borgo-manero.[34]

The way in which the Borgomanero plan traveled to Tuscany can be imagined more easily than could the route of the south German plan. Neither politics nor geography presented an obstacle. Like Florence, Novara was an independent Guelph city and the exchange of artistic ideas, at least between Tuscany and the Po valley in general, is an accepted historical phenomenon. This, however, does not explain specifically how the plan was transmitted to Florence. Another offspring of the Borgomanero plan gives the best insight into that process.

Villarreal (Figs. 72, 73), was founded by James I of Aragon in newly conquered lands on the Mediterranean coast north of Valencia. The town was granted a charter in 1274.[35] Its plan had the form of a slightly oblique parallelogram.[36] The main street ran parallel to the coast and had back streets on either side of it that were crossed by a street at the town's center;

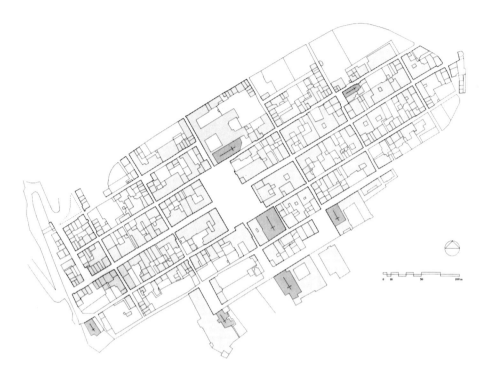

74 Cittaducale. Founded in 1309 by Charles II of Naples.

other cross streets were placed midway between this central cross street
and the ends of the town. Astride the central intersection was the piazza,
now measuring approximately 27 by 30 meters, its perimeter opened by
streets at the center of each face and closed at the corners. It was surrounded by porticos with pointed masonry arches of a type that could
have been built between the fourteenth and sixteenth centuries.[37]

Villarreal was unique among Spanish medieval town foundations.
While others were orthogonally planned, none had the symmetry that is
characteristic of both plan and piazza at Villarreal. It immediately appears
likely that the design was imported, but a survey of new-town plans from
the neighboring area of colonized southwestern France yields no examples with similar axial symmetry and central focus nor with the specific
form of Villarreal's piazza. James I himself provided the best clue to the
plan's origin. In the chronicle that bears his name, James wrote about a
military engineer who had served him in the siege of Mallorca in 1229 and
who during the campaign of 1254 offered a plan of attack on the town of

75 Cittaducale. Central square, view from the northeast.

Burianna, four miles from the site of Villarreal.[38] The engineer's name was Nicolosa and he came from the town of Albenga on the Ligurian coast northwest of Genoa. Master Nicolosa was still in the service of the Aragonese crown in June 1280, when he built a wooden bridge at Belaguer for James's son, Peter III. Given what appears to be his regular position with the court, Nicolosa was possibly the one who prepared the plan for Villarreal, using a design that he knew from his early experience in Italy.[39]

Nicolosa stands in a long line of northern Italian builders active in eastern Spain in the Middle Ages.[40] His presence substantiates the most satisfactory hypothesis about the transmission of planning ideas across large distances. Despite the interest of government officials and of merchants in the form of towns, neither group was qualified to deal with the compositional and dimensional issues involved in creating a complex urban design. By contrast, builders learned survey techniques and developed sensitivity to design as the basic skills of their profession. This expertise, coupled with the builders' mobility, explains better than anything else how the plan of Borgomanero or of Venzone came to Tuscany.

Florentines did not lose contact with the European tradition of new-town design after their accomplishments in the planning of San Giovanni and Castelfranco. When, in 1337, the city's planners prepared a design for Terranuova, they again looked abroad for ideas. The new plan borrowed forms from both of the early Florentine designs — Castelfranco's square and the street system from San Giovanni — but in the Terranuova plan these features were altered in two ways. At Castelfranco, Borgomanero, and Villarreal, the longer axis of the square coincided with the axis of the main street of the town; the square at Terranuova was laid across that street like the much longer square at San Giovanni. Also, at Terranuova the corners of the square were open. The major streets still intercepted the centers of each side of the square, but now the first back streets also communicated with it. The very existence of these streets, an expanded form of the alleys that had separated the rows of lots in the preceding towns, was a third novelty of the Terranuova plan.

Two of the innovations of the Terranuova plan appear in the town of Cittaducale (Figs. 74, 75), located on what in the early fourteenth century was the border between the kingdom of Naples and the papal state, between the cities of Rieti and L'Aquila. Cittaducale was founded in 1309 by Florence's Guelph ally Charles II, king of Naples, and his son Robert, then duke of Calabria, to defend the frontier and the local population and as a source of revenue for the crown.[41] About 550 meters long and 160 meters wide, the town has as its long axis a center street 8 meters wide. This is flanked by two blocks 34 meters deep, plus some secondary development beyond these. The back streets that separate the blocks are 4 to 5 meters wide; the six streets that cross the main axis are a little narrower, about 4 meters wide. The square at the center of the plan measures 84 by 44 meters (on the north side of the square) or 55 meters (on the south side). The square sits astride the main axis of the plan. It extends 38 meters on either side of the central street, and is intersected at the center of its short faces by the main cross street of the plan. As at Terranuova, the corners of the square are opened by two of the back streets that run parallel with the main street.

The one new feature of the Terranuova plan that did not appear at Cittaducale was the freestanding lot row. The expansion of the narrow alleys of San Giovanni and the air shafts of Castelfranco to full-sized streets made a tremendous difference in both the impression of spaciousness at Terranuova and in the amount of light accessible to householders. Florentine planners may have experienced the advantages of freestanding lot rows at Talamone, the Sienese foundation of 1306 (see Figs. 37, 38), where the blocks were about 11 or 12 meters deep and the standard lot width, as shown in the 1306 drawing, was about 6 meters.

The influence of distant models is visible in all the founded towns in Tuscany. Pietrasanta and Camaiore begin to document the frequency of this influence outside Florentine territory. Two other towns, one in the

76 Castelfranco di Sotto. Founded before 1262 or after 1284 by the city of Lucca (?)
From the cadastral plan, nineteenth century (Ufficio Tecnico Erariale, Lucca).

lower Arno valley, the other near Arezzo, enlarge the picture. The first of
these is Castelfranco di Sotto (Fig. 76), located twenty-five kilometers from
Lucca on the Arno below San Miniato al Tedesco. The origins of Castelfranco are uncertain. Emmanuel Repetti, the nineteenth-century historical
geographer of Tuscany, said that the town was built during the Guelph-
Ghibelline wars of the 1260s by the inhabitants of four nearby villages.[42]
But the plan of Castelfranco is too sophisticated to have been designed by

the residents of small rural villages. It seems probable that, like the villagers who joined together to petition Florence for the foundation of Terranuova in 1337, these local inhabitants turned to a larger authority in the area for assistance. We know that the town was taken in 1262 by Count Guido Novello, in 1266 by Pisa, and in 1268 by Lucca. Its church, dedicated to Saint Peter, was built "from the ground up" in 1284 with the aid of the bishop of Lucca. Giovanni Villani attributed the foundation to Lucca.[43]

The plan of Castelfranco di Sotto, like the plan of so many Italian new towns, was based on the intersection of two main streets and the division of the town into equal quarters. The main streets were of about equal length, and the perimeter of the town was almost square, with a gate marking the center of each face. The main streets were precisely surveyed. Four secondary streets ran parallel with each of them. The northwest – southeast streets succeeded one another at regular intervals, two on either side of the main axis. The streets that run northeast – southwest were less evenly distributed. On the north side of the town the first secondary street lay at the same distance from the main street as all the northwest – southeast streets lay from one another. The next street to the north, however, was separated from the first by almost twice that distance. On the town's south side the first northeast – southwest street was about one and one half times as far from the main northwest – southeast axis as its counterpart on the north side. It was about the same distance to the southern limit of the town.

The block pattern that results from this distribution of the secondary streets was unique in Italy. Immediately to the north of the street that ran between the east and west gates of the town was a file of almost perfectly square blocks. Three parallel files of blocks all had different proportions but were all rectangular. Thus, despite its characteristically Italian central axes, the plan was asymmetrical. Its most striking feature, the row of square blocks, lay to one side of the central axis without an answering file on the other side.

While the combination of square and oblong blocks produced a conflict in the design of this Italian town, the same forms were almost inevitable features of the new towns that followed the double intersection scheme, represented by the plan of Sainte-Foy-la-Grande (see Fig. 43).[44]

The sophistication of the Castelfranco design leaves no doubt as to its dependence on earlier plans. In both Germany and France the development of the double intersection plan can be traced through a number of preliminary stages; in Tuscany no such preparatory designs exist. The inconsistency of the Castelfranco plan also confirms its non-Tuscan origin. Its centrality conformed to a requirement of Tuscan planning but

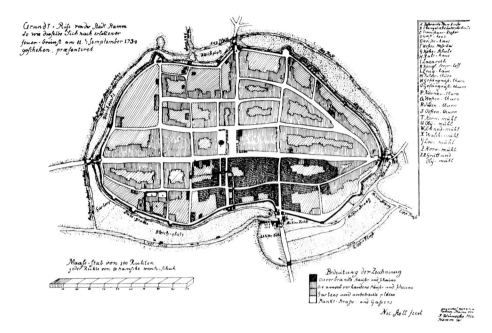

77 Hamm. Founded in 1226 by Count Adolf von der Mark (H. Offenberg and
J. Lappe, *Stadt Hamm*, 1936).

contradicted the essential nature of the double intersection scheme. The
French and German towns built on this pattern rarely, and then only by
chance, had a strong center.

Equally foreign to Italian practice was the plan of the new town of
Montevarchi in the upper Arno valley. This market settlement was
founded between 1217 and 1254 by the Guidi,[45] counts palatinate who,
according to legend, were descended from German barons who came to
Italy with Otto I.[46] The town was laid out at the foot of a hilltop castle long
held by these powerful feudatories, about ten kilometers from the future
location of San Giovanni. The thirteenth-century Montevarchi (see Fig.
50) was laid out around a central street paralleled on both sides by back
streets. The square with the church of San Lorenzo lay to the east of the
main thoroughfare, at the center of the town. Communication across the
axis of the main street was limited. Two squares connected one of the back
streets with the main street, but alleys alone cross the entire width of the
plan. The back streets curved gently at each end to connect with the main
street only at its two extremities. This was unusual in Italian town planning but, like the elongated transverse square, was common north of the
Alps. The *spindelform* plan, as it is called because of its similarity to a

weaver's bobbin, appeared in towns that had transversely laid squares, such as Brunswick Altstadt and Freienstein.[47] Hamm (Fig. 77), in the state of North Rhine-Westphalia, founded by Count Adolf von der Mark in 1226, had a plan that was almost identical to that of Montevarchi.[48]

European new towns everywhere provide examples of plans that are borrowed from earlier foundations. In southwestern France, in the second half of the thirteenth century, representatives of the kings of France founded scores of towns based on the double intersection scheme. In southern Germany, Switzerland, and Austria, the idea of a wide market street or of an extended rectangular square lay at the heart of the planning of settlements spread across hundreds of miles. Isolated examples of sophisticated plan types argue for borrowing rather than independent invention. That Villarreal in Spain and Castelfranco di Sotto and Montevarchi in Tuscany had no kin among their neighbors poses questions about their origins, but their refinement is even more puzzling. These were not experimental efforts; they benefited from an evolutionary process that took place elsewhere.

The Florentines had access to a wide spectrum of medieval new-town design and they borrowed from it eclectically. Florentine plans reveal a debt to Lucca (and through Lucca to southern Germany), to Lombardy, to Siena, and to the house of Anjou, but they followed no source exactly. Of all the towns, San Giovanni was most faithful to its model, Pietrasanta, yet even here it was only the plan type that was reproduced. Proportions and the hierarchy among the elements of the plan were significantly different. Elsewhere in Europe models were reproduced less critically. Grenade-sur-Garonne (see Fig. 82) in the county of Toulouse, for all its refinement, was more faithful to its model, Sainte-Foy-le-Grande (see Fig. 43), than were any of the Florentine towns to theirs.

The Florentines demonstrated their disposition to variety and invention in their first towns. While the plans of San Giovanni and Castelfranco di Sopra conformed to the same basic principles of design, their essential elements — the piazza and the overall outline of the town — were fundamentally different. When later planners set out foundations, they interpreted these two great models freely. Even the administrative official who produced the plan of Scarperia from the plan of San Giovanni made significant changes. Later towns, notably Terranuova and Giglio Fiorentino, reveal a substantial rethinking of basic design issues and an ongoing attention to the most recent achievements of European new-town builders.

CHAPTER 4

GEOMETRY

KNOWLEDGE of a wide spectrum of European new-town design seems only to have inspired Florentine planners to originality. Their own contribution was so fundamental that it is more accurate to say that they transformed the medieval tradition than that they summed it up. The decision on which the most important aspects of their achievement was based was the one to give their settlements finite dimensions. The act of laying out the full defensive perimeter of a town at the moment of its foundation had many implications for urban design. It was responsible for the openness of the plans and the continuity of streets across the towns, and it left the houses free to develop without consideration of defense. The quartering of a plan, the strong definition of its center and its symmetry, and the close coordination of all its parts—from lots, to blocks, to street intervals, to the position of the wall itself—were only possible because the layouts did not try to accommodate population growth or expansion of the street system.

The fixed size and shape of the Florentine new towns reveal an attitude toward city planning that is more characteristic of the Renaissance than of the Middle Ages. It was in the Renaissance that, for the first time since antiquity, the task of building cities was claimed as part of the discipline of architecture. In *De Re Aedificatoria* Leone Baptista Alberti presented the common ground between architecture and city planning as a simple equation: "If the philosophers are correct . . . the city is like a large house and the house, in turn, like a city."[1] In Alberti's view the organization and integration of the parts of a composition were the architect's first responsibility and the first quality of any design project.[2] For Alberti the city was subject to the same considerations: "The principal ornament of a city is the orderly arrangement of streets, squares, and buildings according to their dignity and their function."[3]

Other fifteenth-century writers characterized their concept of the architectural nature of the city plan with vivid metaphors. The human analogy, which lent authority to all aspects of the architecture of Francesco di Giorgio, also informed his discussions of cities: a drawing from the treatise on architecture and engineering that he wrote in the last decades of the fifteenth century juxtaposed a male figure and the outline of a city, equating the human head with the command center of the town's defenses, hands and feet with the bastions at the corners of the wall, the viscera with the market place, and the heart with the parish church.[4] For Filarete it was the fixed perimeter of the city that most forcefully established it as an architectural object. The star shape that resulted from the superimposition of two equal squares gave his plan of Sforzinda a distinctive outline and a clear character.[5] The town plans proposed by Filarete, Francesco di Giorgio, and the theoreticians and town builders of the sixteenth century placed a premium on centrality, symmetry, and fixed proportions, all of which were essential aspects of the fourteenth-century Florentine new-town plans.

In the late Middle Ages, the theoretical base of architecture was geometry. Geometry determined proportion and fixed position. Large-scale issues of plan and elevation depended on it no less than did the definition of the smallest detail. Even the rudimentary structural calculations of medieval building were based on the authority of geometry.[6] The premise was always the same: regular geometric figures and the dimensional values that derived from them were rational, strong, and aesthetically pleasing. They resolved the practical problems of setting out a design, and brought conceptual as well as formal unity to a project. Drawings from the thirteenth through the sixteenth century reveal the complexity with which a master mason could manipulate the figures of his geometric constructions and the ubiquity of geometry's applications.[7] In the Gothic period, in theory at least, design meant geometry.

For Villard de Honnecourt, whose early-thirteenth-century *Sketchbook* is the first source for much of our knowledge of Gothic design theory, the relationship between design and geometry was unquestioned. His text begins: "In this book you will find good advice concerning the proper technique of masonry and devices of carpentry. You will also find the technique of drawing—the forms—just as the art of geometry requires and teaches it."[8] That geometry was not merely an aid in drafting but the essence of design itself is even more explicitly the message in an introductory text that preceded an account of the customs and regulations of the mason's craft in England in about 1400: "There is no artifice nor handicraft that is wrought by man's hand but is wrought by geometry."[9] Even the masons' great "secret," revealed in print in 1486 by Mathes Roriczer, a master from the lodge in Regensburg, turned out to be geometric in nature.[10] Roriczer showed how the plan and elevation of a Gothic design were unified by geometry. Using a pinnacle to illustrate this universal principle of Gothic architecture, he rotated its square plan to generate a series of dimensions that define the rising structure. The rotated square — the most common construction of medieval architectural geometry — appeared in Villard's *Sketchbook*,[11] as well as in Vitruvius and Plato.[12] In the debate about the design of Milan cathedral, which left a unique record of design values in Europe at the turn of the fifteenth century, geometry again played a critical part. Master builders called from Germany and France to work in Milan were described as "virtuosi industriosi et expertissimi viri, artis scilicet geometrie."[13] The local masons were much less accomplished geometricians, using geometric figures casually, sometimes even referring to geometry only after the fact, to rationalize a decision made for other, less theoretical reasons.[14] At various times in the history of the Milan cathedral project, however, local masons championed a nave section based on an equilateral triangle and, later, a crossing that they claimed "corresponds to a rectangle according to the demands of geometry."[15] In an atmosphere so bitter that northern and local masters refused to acknowledge almost any common principles, only the validity of geometry was accepted by both sides.

The plans of the Florentine new towns were structured by geometry. This is a claim that the physical evidence justifies but for which there is no written or graphic documentation. This is not an uncommon situation even among the works of Gothic masons most commited to geometry. With only modern plans of the towns to work with, however, the historian must proceed with caution. To establish the connection between geometry and the designs his analysis must satisfy two requirements. The first is historical. The geometry must be one that the fourteenth-century Florentine planners can reasonably be expected to have known. A geometry and a design may conform merely by coincidence, but more frequently when a modern geometry fits an old design it is because of a relationship between the new geometry and an old one. For the historian it is important to know the original geometric form. The specific geometric figure and the operations and the tools used to generate it all teach valuable lessons about the finished design.

The second requirement is conformity: geometry must mark a series of significant points in a design with a high degree of accuracy. Many factors can obscure the geometric base of an architectural plan that has survived only in its constructed form. Craftsmen may introduce an error when a design is set out to full scale; the settling of the fabric or partial rebuilding will further distort the intended dimensions. When the design is of a town, these problems become even more severe. Size exaggerates survey errors and the constant repair required by the modest building stock that fills most of a street plan has a cumulative and irreversibly distorting effect. Nonetheless, when the physical evidence of the town is the historian's only source, close tolerances between the values generated by a proposed geometry and the surviving dimensions are essential. Even accurately measured plans are inadequate when the scale is that of a city. Meaningful results are achieved only when numerical values generated by geometry are calculated and compared to measurements taken on the site.[16]

It is the formal sophistication of the Florentine plans that first excites curiosity about the role of geometry in their design. The plans' orthogonality, centrality, and symmetry belong to a world of design that, in the late Middle Ages, was dominated by geometry. At San Giovanni and Terranuova geometry first reveals itself in the sizes of the properties distributed to the immigrants for their houses. All of the lots have the same width; they differ from one another only in the distance to which they extend back from the street. In both towns the deepest lots face onto the main street and the three rows of blocks that succeed the first block get progressively shallower as they approach the town wall. The diminution of lot sizes is partly explained by the effort to accommodate social distinctions among the immigrants and as a response to varying real-estate values within the town, but neither factor explains the need for four property sizes. It is hard to imagine, in these rural communities, a social order so sophisticated that it would distinguish four levels of residents. Nor are there really four different kinds of properties. While the circumstances of the lots on the main street and those on the road by the wall are, indeed quite different, little distinction can be made between the two blocks that lie between them. The houses of the inner of these two blocks may be physically closer to the center of town than those in the outer row, but in functional terms, because the houses of both rows are entered from the same street, there is no difference. In the simpler of the new-town plans the number of lot sizes was reduced. At Scarperia the depth of the lots on the main street — 13 to 16.6 meters — is the one exception to the depth of the lots elsewhere in the plan — about 11 meters. At Giglio Fiorentino, lots

16.4 meters deep face onto the main street, and lots 5.8 meters deep face onto the street along the wall, while two rows of lots 11.6 meters deep lie between them. Compared with these relatively simple arrangements, the four depths of the lots at San Giovanni, which a sixteenth-century map gives as the equivalent of 22.8 meters, 16.4 meters, 14 meters, and 11.7 meters, seem unnecessarily complex. Because the town's practical requirements do not explain the series, one is justified in asking whether the progression may have a formal logic.

Any attempt to understand the relationship among dimensions in a city plan is hindered by approximate measurements. The same unit of the design, measured at different points in the town, varies by as much as five percent. The depth of the central blocks at San Giovanni, for example, can be measured today as 22.5 meters and also as 23.6 meters. In the new towns no single dimension can be taken as exactly the one intended in the design; workable figures are possible, however, by averaging a number of measurements.

At San Giovanni the significant junctures in the plan are not the divisions between the individual rows of lots but the edges of the blocks into which they are grouped, two rows of lots with an alley between (see Fig. 3). Like the rows of lots, the blocks diminish in depth from the axis of the main street to the town wall. An average of the measurements taken in four places gives a depth of 42.7 meters for the first block and 27.5 for the second. Stated in another way, the outer edge of the first block lies, on average, 48.3 meters from the middle of the main street (42.7 meters plus one half the width of the main street) and the outer edge of the second block 84 meters (the first block plus the width of the residential street plus the depth of the second block) from that same imaginary line.

In the search for a system of proportions that might have generated these dimensions, the methods of geometric control known to have been used by medieval builders provide no solution. The relation of the sides of a square to its diagonal ($1 : \sqrt{2} \approx 1 : 1.414$), of the short side of a $2 : 1$ rectangle to its diagonal ($1 : \sqrt{5} \approx 1 : 2.236$), of the sides of an equilateral triangle to its altitude ($2\sqrt{3} \approx 1 : .866$), of one integer in a Fibonacci series to the next ($1 : 1.618$) — none of these, and none of the other traditional constructions, give intervals like those that appear in the new-town plans.[17] Indeed at Terranuova, where five dimensions are organized proportionally, the intervals are irregular. If they are controlled by a consistent system, whether geometric or mathematical, it must be a system that produces a series of values from which only some were chosen.

Only trigonometry is capable of producing a series that includes the

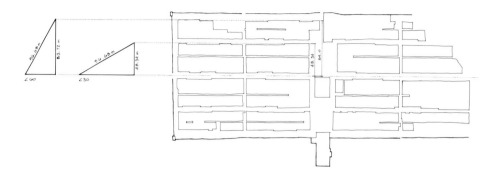

78 San Giovanni. Plan and geometry.

values of 48.34 and 84 meters which we find at San Giovanni (Fig. 78). A right-angle triangle with a side of 48.34 meters has a hypotenuse of 96.68 meters when the angle opposite the 48.34-meter side measures 30 degrees (hypotenuse equals the side divided by the sine of the opposite angle: 96.68 = 48.34/.5). The same hypotenuse produces a side of 83.72 meters when the angle is 60 degrees (sine of the opposite angle multiplied by the hypotenuse: .866 × 96.68 = 83.72). The discrepancy between these geometric values and the averages of the San Giovanni measurements is less than one-third of one percent.[18]

The same geometry informs Terranuova, founded thirty-eight years after San Giovanni, but its influence is much more extensive (Fig. 79). At Terranuova, for the first time, the unifying dimension, called a hypotenuse in my description, appears in its own right, identified with an element of the plan. It measures the distance from the center of the main square, along the main street, to the end of the first block. The dimension is 83.4 meters; twice that figure is the distance from the center of the main square to the town wall. The controlling triangles form a series graded by fifteen-degree changes in the size of their angles. In the first triangle the side opposite the fifteen-degree angle has a length of 21.58 meters; this measurement establishes the size of a strip within the plan that contains half the width of the main street and the width of the first row of blocks. The average of the measurements of this strip taken on the ground at Terranuova is 21.9 meters. The second triangle, with an angle of thirty degrees, has a side of 41.7 meters; this defines a segment of the plan that includes the first strip plus the first back street and the width of the second block. The outer side of the second block measures, on average, 41.6 meters from the center of the main street. The third triangle, which has a forty-five-

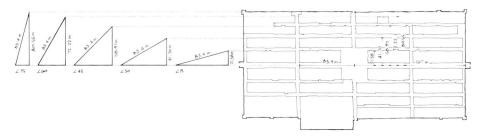

79 Terranuova. Plan and geometry.

degree angle, has a side of 58.97 meters; this measurement allows for the main residential street and the block on its far side as well as the strip encompassed by the second triangle. The outer limit of the third row of blocks measures, on average, 59.32 meters from the center of the main street. The fourth triangle has a sixty-degree angle and a side of 72.22 meters; this segment incorporates another street and the outer row of blocks.[19] The outer edge of this row lies 73.3 meters from the axis of the plan. The fifth and final triangle, with an angle of seventy-five degrees, has a side of 80.55 meters. The inner edge of the town's 85-centimeter-thick wall lies, on average, 80.3 meters from the central axis.

Florentine designers did not establish the proportions of their new-town plans by constructing the triangles of the foregoing analysis. The triangles describe only the finished product; to reconstruct the conceptual framework of the design or the technical process by which it was executed one must look beyond, or in this case behind, such methods of calculation. Modern trigonometry, based on tables of values and mathematical formulae, is abstract; the origin of trigonometry, however, is in the geometric measurement of the circle.

Sine functions have been known since antiquity. The earliest discussion of them is preserved in Ptolemy's *Almagest*. Ptolemy presented sine functions as a table of chords, that is, straight lines connecting points on the circumference of a circle, and expressed them in terms of the arc rather than the related angle. The relationship between chords and sines is completely regular: the chord of an arc is equal to twice the sine of half the arc. Ptolemy provided an extended geometrical demonstration of how chords are computed. He also summarized the results of his constructions in a table that is not unlike a modern sine table. It gave the chords for 360 arcs, at intervals of 0.5 degree, from 0 to 180 degrees.

In the first book of the *Almagest*, Ptolemy stated his wish "to demonstrate the whole topic [of chords] geometrically once and for all,"[20] since the chords were the basis of all calculation in his comprehensive exposition of mathematical astronomy. It is as an astronomical treatise that the *Almagest* preserved its authority throughout the Middle Ages and Renaissance. In the ninth century it was translated into Arabic and in 1175 from Arabic into Latin. Thirty-two medieval manuscripts of Gherard of Cremona's Latin text survive. The best medieval scholarship on astronomy was written in Arabic, but by the end of the twelfth century much of it was available in Latin. An important example is the Toledan tables, prepared in Spain in the late eleventh century and containing a full table of chords.[21]

The end of the thirteenth century saw a renewal of interest in sine geometry. In about 1272 the Toledan tables were recalculated by astronomers at the court of Alfonso X of Castile as part of a translation program that made earlier astronomical texts available in Spanish. The *Libros del Saber de Astronomía* contain many works by the eleventh-century astronomer al-Zarquali, including the description of an instrument of his invention called the *saphaea*, which included a geometrical scale to calculate sines.[22] By 1320 the Alphonsine tables were known in Paris and from there they were spread in Latin translation throughout Europe. John of Murs, who worked on the Alphonsine tables in Paris with John of Lignères and John of Saxony in the 1320s and 1330s, prepared a short treatise on the calculation of sine values which included a geometric sine scale like the one on al-Zarquali's *saphaea*.[23]

Sophisticated scholarship of this kind served a limited audience. Only the most educated men in Europe ever saw, let alone made good use of, the *Almagest* or the other astronomical texts that included a table of chords or sines. There is, however, no reason to exclude Florentines from the small circle of interested scholars. A treatise on the *saphaea* written by John of Lignères in Paris in 1327, one of the earliest Latin works to make use of the Alphonsine tables, was dedicated to Robert of Florence (Roberto de' Bardi), a scholar who became chancellor of the University of Paris in 1339. In 1327 a copy of the work was taken to Marsiglio of Padua in Milan. Even the *Libros del Saber* were available to the Florentines, thanks to an Italian-language translation commissioned in 1341 by the Florentine Guerrucio di Cione Federighi, an agent of the Bardi banking and trading company.[24]

Astronomy represents only one of the medieval applications of trigonometry. Treatises on astronomical instruments contained exercises in the trigonometric measurement of terrestrial dimensions. The standard problem for teaching the tangent function, for example, asked the student to calculate the height of a distant tower by constructing a right angle whose base was the distance between the observer and the tower and whose angles were measured with a sighting instrument. There existed, too, a purely theoretical literature, but those treatises are even rarer than the astronomical ones.[25] A much wider diffusion of geometric knowledge was achieved through a category of texts called *Practical Geometries.*[26] Derived from the tradition of the Roman *agri mensores* and enriched with the geometry of Boethius and Gerbert of Aurillac and extracts from Euclid, the Practical Geometries served as textbooks of basic geometry for a general, literate public. The quality of these works, as well as their content, varied dramatically. All of them used examples from applied geometry, most frequently problems of land survey, but none of them was so closely tied to the literal content of these examples that it could be considered a manual for craftsmen. At the upper level of the spectrum were the treatises in Latin written by university scholars; they contained the most sophisticated mathematics and the most extensive demonstrations of theorems. It is this body of work that includes discussion of the sine function. The *Liber Embadorum* of Abraham bar Hiyya ha-Nisi, known as Savasorda, written in Barcelona or Provence in 1116 and translated into Latin by Plato of Tivoli in 1145, contains a table of twenty-eight chords and instruction for their application, ostensibly, to the measurement of fields.[27]

The broadest treatment of chords belongs to the most sophisticated of all the medieval Practical Geometries, the *Practica Geometriae* of Leonardo Fibonacci, written in Pisa in 1220 or 1221.[28] Fibonacci's text exhibits the greatest tension between the practical application of geometry and its theoretical exposition. The author's preface distinguishes the book's two audiences — those who "would work following geometric demonstrations and those who would proceed following common usage, or, as it were, lay custom."[29] Lay custom could be extremely primitive. Fibonacci's own elegant geometric proofs cannot have meant anything to the "agri mensores" of his ludicrous examples of common survey practice. But there is a body of information in the *Practica Geometriae,* which consists of the formulae resulting from the geometric proofs, that could have found some application among enlightened practitioners. The table of chords belongs to this part of the work. That the table was included in the abridged versions of the *Practica* translated into Italian in the late Middle Ages attests to its usefulness.[30]

Fibonacci gives a geometric proof of his theory of chords that is no less complete than Ptolemy's own. Indeed some of Fibonacci's operations come directly from the *Almagest* and he readily acknowledges his source.[31]

The treatment of chords belongs to the third distinction or chapter, in which the author discusses the measurement of fields. In a section that begins, "Si . . . campum semicircularem metiri desideras," Fibonacci demonstrates how to derive chords from their arcs. He begins with a semicircle, proceeds with smaller arcs, and then gives the operations that, by the division of known quantities, produce the relationships between successively smaller arcs and chords. Having completed his geometrical proof, Fibonacci provides a table of the relationships between arcs and chords for a circle whose diameter is 42 *pertiche* (about 122.5 meters; in Pisa and Florence a *pertica* was 2.918 meters). It will be used, he says, by those who wish to work according to geometry rather than the "vulgar" (and, one supposes, standard) technique of measuring arc and chord with a rope and stakes "which you will place around the curve of the arc so that the rope will not deviate from the circumference of the circle."[32] He gives a formula for calculating the values of arc and chord for circles whose diameter is other than 42 *pertiche*, and another formula for interpolating the chords of arcs and the arcs of chords that lie between the values given in the tables. This latter formula is also given a geometric demonstration. Fibonacci introduces his proof with this theorem: if two arcs of the same circle are unequal, the proportion of the larger arc to its chord will be greater than the proportion of the smaller arc to its chord. He gives the example of the semicircle, which in a circle 42 *pertiche* in diameter has an arc of 66 *pertiche*, or a proportion of arc to chord of 11:7, and an arc that subsumes one sixth of the circumference, which has a relation to its chord of 22:21. Thus Fibonacci's text, like the *Liber Embadorum* and the *Almagest* before it, explicates the most distinctive proportional characteristic of sines: that the relationship among terms is inconstant. In a series of three sines generated by regular intervals of arc (say 30, 60, and 90 degrees) the proportion between the first and the second sine will be different from the proportion between the second and the third.

Fibonacci's table of chords (Fig. 80) contains 66 entries, corresponding to the 66 *pertiche* of the circumference of a semicircle whose diameter is 42 *pertiche*. Savasorda's table had 28 entries, Ptolemy's 360. Each chord refers to two arcs, which are listed with it, one smaller than a semicircle, one larger. The table lists integral units of arc and gives the dimensions of the resulting chords in *pertiche*, *pedes* (6 to a *pertica*), *uncie* (18 to a *pes*), and *punti* (20 to an *uncia*). With 66 entries, each arc is 2.727 degrees larger (or smaller) than its predecessor.

The form of Fibonacci's chord table has important implications for the relationship between the *Practica Geometriae* and the planning of the

.DIS.

ut inequaliū si non fuerit dyametri ideo duos arcus ante ipas cordas ordinaui ut insequentibus tabulis ostenditur.

Arcus gruū	Arcus gruū	Corde gruū	Ax pedes	c uū unc	M puntū		Arco gruū	Arcus gruū	Corde gruū	Ax pedes	c y unc	M puntū
1	131	0	4	17	17		34	98	30	2	6	17
2	130	1	4	17	12		35	97	31	0	8	5
3	129	2	4	17	4		36	96	31	4	8	7
4	128	2	4	17	2		37	95	32	2	5	19
5	127	4	4	12	10		38	94	33	0	1	9
6	126	5	6	16	7		39	93	34	3	13	0
7	125	6	5	14	5		40	92	35	1	4	19
8	124	7	5	12	9		41	91	35	4	12	10
9	123	8	5	8	16		42	90	36	2	0	0
10	122	9	5	7	8		43	89	36	5	2	5
11	121	10	5	4	2		44	88	37	2	4	6
12	120	11	4	17	18		45	87	37	5	2	2
13	119	12	4	13	6		46	86	38	1	17	15
14	118	13	4	7	16		47	85	38	4	12	13
15	117	14	4	1	0		48	84	38	1	4	0
16	116	15	3	11	18		49	83	39	3	11	15
17	115	16	3	2	12		50	82	39	5	17	2
18	114	17	3	12	8		51	81	40	5	2	1
19	113	18	2	0	15		52	80	40	4	2	10
20	112	19	1	8	12		53	79	40	0	0	11
21	111	20	0	13	18		54	78	40	1	14	5
22	110	21	0	0	0		55	77	41	3	7	8
23	109	21	5	2	16		56	76	41	4	16	2
24	108	22	4	4	5		57	75	41	0	4	12
25	107	23	3	4	8		58	74	41	1	8	1
26	106	24	2	2	2		59	73	41	2	9	0
27	105	25	1	0	6		60	72	41	3	7	14
28	104	25	5	16	2		61	71	41	4	9	2
29	103	26	4	8	0		62	70	41	4	15	10
30	102	27	3	0	2		63	69	41	5	6	9
31	101	28	1	9	7		64	68	41	5	12	17
32	100	28	5	16	4		65	67	41	5	16	14
33	99	29	4	2	9		66	66	42	0	0	0

80 Leonardo Fibonacci, table of chords from *Practica Geometriae* (Bibliotheca Apostolica Vaticana, Urb. Lat. 292, fol. 58v).

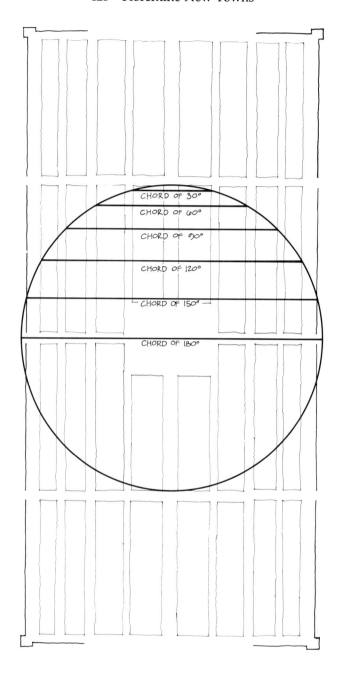

81 Chords and plan of Terranuova.

Florentine towns. The number 66 is divisible by 2, 6, 11, 22, and 33. Of these, 11 has the advantage of formal regularity. Doubled, it produces 22, tripled, 33, and so on until, multiplied by 6, it generates the full 66 units of Fibonacci's division of a semicircle. The angles corresponding to these chords are, of course, also regular. Eleven *pertiche* of arc equals 30 degrees, 22 equals 60 degrees, 33 equals 90 degrees, 44 equals 120 degrees, 55 equals 150 degrees, and 66 equals 180. When these chords are converted into sine values the values are those of the angles of 15, 30, 45, 60, 75, and 90 degrees that define the proportions of the San Giovanni and Terranuova plans. Or stated another way—and this is probably the way the Florentine town builders thought of it—the length of the chords of Fibonacci's 11-*pertiche* units of arc matches the distance between the outer edges of corresponding units situated on either side of the main axis of the new-town plan (Fig. 81).

The connection between the *Practica Geometriae* and the proportions of the Florentine new towns raises a number of questions about the design and execution of the new-town plans. Fibonacci's chord table offers the best solution to the problem of how new-town plans with geometrically determined proportions were set out at the site. With the aid of the table the towns could be laid out with a line or rod and the simple instruments for measuring right angles that we know medieval surveyors used. The chord table eliminates the need to speculate about instruments that measured angles in the horizontal plan—there is almost no evidence of such equipment until the fifteenth century—or about the full-scale construction of circles and chords with ropes or chains.[33] The surveyor had only to lay down a base line, the future axis of the town's main street, and a line perpendicular to it. Measuring out the chords of eleven, twenty-two, thirty-three, forty-four, and fifty-five units of arc—adjusted for an appropriately sized circle using the formula provided by Fibonacci—he fixed the limits of the five units on either side of the town. Survey lines set out from these points on the perpendicular axis, parallel with the base line, completed the construction of the plan's geometric skeleton.

Any *agri mensore*, no matter how "vulgar" his technique, could perform these operations. But who worked out the proportions? Who established the first real dimension—the distance between the far sides of the first blocks—and calculated the size of the circle, given that this dimension represented the chord of an arc one-twelfth the circle's circumference? Who then projected the chords of arcs $\frac{22}{66}$, $\frac{44}{66}$, and $\frac{55}{66}$ of the circumference, to establish the remaining dimensions? The answer is given by Fibonacci himself: "those who wish to solve surveying problems according to the science of geometry."[34] If there were few surveyors who carried out their professional activities in this way, there were a considerable number of men who had learned the basic mathematical skills necessary to execute the computations of Fibonacci's formulae and who knew at least some of the geometry involved. According to Villani in 1338 between one thousand and twelve hundred students were enrolled in the *scuole dell'abbaco* in Florence, where instruction in mathematics and geometry extended over three or four years. Both the businessmen and bureaucrats who were members of the Florentine new-town committees and the clerks and master masons employed by them would have had this basic education. Some of them, like the Guerruccio di Cione Federighi who commissioned the translation of the *Libros del Saber,* may have taken a special interest in Fibonacci's *Geometriae.* Indeed, it is for the scientific dilettante that the book seems to have been written. In any case, many of the committeemen would have known parts of the work, along with Fibonacci's *Liber abaci* of 1202, from their early schooling.[35] Failing all else, a new-town committee could have hired a mathematician, perhaps one of the teachers at the *scuole dell'abbaco,* to execute Fibonacci's calculations. Intervention of this kind was sought by the cathedral authorities of Milan, who in 1391 invited the "discreto viro Gabriele Stornalocho de Placentia experto in arte geometriae" to solve the problem of translating the proportions of a geometrically derived design into units of common measurement.[36] Though the new-town plans presented the same sort of problem, they were made infinitely simpler by Fibonacci's formulae.

If Fibonacci's chord table may explain how the Florentine new-town plans were implemented, it does not explain who was responsible for the idea of applying the geometry to the designs. Of the people involved in planning the towns, those whose professional background would have made them most familiar with the *Practica Geometriae* are the least likely to have come up with the idea. The table in which Fibonacci presents sine values has no formal implications. Its context — the measurement of crescent-shaped fields — in no way suggests the use of sines and chords in new-town plans. The step between the tables and the plans is a giant one: the tables provide only the numbers; physical relationships appear for the first time in the plans.

The application of abstractly determined dimensions to a configuration of physical shapes was, of course, the business of the professional designer. Even the most familiar of architectural geometries, the rotated square, is not itself visible in Gothic designs. Only the values generated by

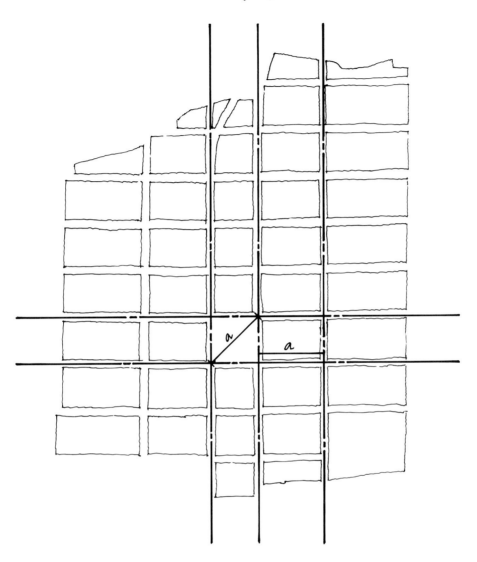

82 Grenade-sur-Garonne. Plan and geometry.

the rotation survive in the monuments. The treatises of Mathes Roriczer, Hanns Schmuttermayer, and Lorenz Lechler clearly show the separateness of the geometric operations that define proportions from the physical form of the design itself.[37] The designer had to know not only how to generate proportions but also how to apply them. Apprenticeship taught both. Work on one job gave the designer useful experience for the next and new designs were generated within the context of well-established tradition. It is precisely the absence of this experience that makes the application of sine geometry to the Florentine plans both so enigmatic and so exciting.[38]

The only medieval new-town plan other than those designed by the Florentines that has so far yielded to geometric analysis is that of Grenade-sur-Garonne (Fig. 82). A project of the same decade as the first of the Florentine new towns, it was founded by Eustache de Beaumarchais, the seneschal of the king of France for the county of Toulouse. The plan of Grenade is a late version of the town type developed by planners in Alphonse de Poitiers's administration around the year 1255. Like its prototype, Sainte-Foy-la-Grande, Grenade has a row of square blocks lined up with its market square and rectangular blocks everywhere else. According to François Boucher, who identified the interrelated proportions of the plan, the length of the rectangular blocks at Grenade is determined by a geometric system. In his analysis, the long side of the inner rows of these blocks is fixed by the distance between the opposite corners of the square blocks, the diagonal of the square; the long side of the outer rows of rectangular blocks is fixed by the diagonal of the inner rectangular blocks. Measurements taken at the site reveal that it was not the dimensions of the blocks that were controlled by geometry, but the position of the survey lines by which the town was laid out. Although no longer visible on the ground, these lines can be reconstructed by assuming that the streets followed them and were laid out astride them—that is, with their edges equidistant from a survey line. The distance between the pairs of primary survey lines, the axes that define the size of the central file of square blocks, is 64 meters. The diagonal of a square 64 meters on a side is 90.5 meters. The distance between the main axes and the first secondary axes is 90.4 meters.[39]

The geometry of Grenade is, of course, the system of rotation described by Villard de Honnecourt in his *Sketchbook* and in the treatises of Roriczer and the other late-Gothic masons. The application of this system at Grenade is significant only because it appears for the first time in connection with the plan of a town. The character of the geometry and the shape of the forms that it generates are otherwise quite familiar. The sine geometry of the Florentine new towns, on the other hand, is unique. There is no tradition of its application to design before the planning of these towns and no demonstrable instances of its use for almost two centuries afterward. How, then, were the Florentine new-town committees and their employees able to visualize its application to the plan of an orthogonal town?

Two potential sources of inspiration were available. Both were geometric patterns based on the circle and both were concerned with the rationalization of space at a large scale. One was the Portolan chart, a type of mariner's map of the Mediterranean, the Black Sea, and the European waters of the Atlantic whose first examples belong to the thirteenth century; the other was the astrolabe, the foremost instrument of medieval science. Neither can have been a direct model. In the case of the chart, sinical qualities appear by coincidence only, and in the case of the astrolabe the technical application of sines may not have been widely understood in fourteenth-century Florence. But these limitations are less important than the visual image the two objects present. Because the patterns that appear on the charts and the astrolabes place sines and chords within the setting of the circle, the proportional qualities of the series are immediately visible. In them the sines themselves become lines with a spatial relationship to one another. The point that is the center of the circle takes on the role of organizer. It defines the place, on the page or on the land, where the system begins. The diameter that it creates fixes the orientation of the sine lines. By means of the circle, sine values are presented as figural geometry. In the language of the medieval craftsmanship, the sine pattern *was* the design of the town. Its center defined the point of intersection of the town's main streets; the sine lines fixed the edges of the residential blocks.

Dante, Petrarch, and Giovanni Villani all seem to have been familiar with Portolan charts.[40] The maps were based on written descriptions of the coasts and sea lanes — the Portolan proper — which had been collected since antiquity. Their medieval form was greatly influenced by the development of the magnetic compass in the twelfth century.[41] While the Portolan recorded distances and topographical information, the compass was able to measure bearing. The combination of these types of information was sufficient to construct the charts. These were not based on a system of coordinates or an absolutely consistent scale; nonetheless, they were a valuable aid to navigation. The earliest surviving example of a Portolan

83 Carta Pisana. Mid to late thirteenth century (Bibliothèque Nationale, Paris, Cartes et Plans, Reg. Ge B 1118).

chart is the Carta Pisana (Fig. 83); it was produced in the northwestern corner of the Mediterranean region, probably in Pisa, in the third quarter of the thirteenth century.[42] It represents European waters, especially those that were most frequently traveled, with reasonable accuracy. Subsequent editions, while closely tied to the early prototypes, contained improvements and Portolan charts remained in use until the seventeenth century.

The most characteristic feature of a Portolan chart is the pattern of radiating lines that forms a web over most of its surface. In the Carta Pisana the pattern was a linear form of the wind rose that served as the face of the fully developed magnetic compass. The center of the pattern is a point from which sixteen lines, representing the eight major winds and the related half-winds, radiate at regular intervals. These lines are inscribed in a circle and at each of the sixteen points at which a radius intersects the circle the fourth part of a thirty-two-point compass rose fans out to connect that point with nine others around the circumference of the circle. The purpose of the web was to mark orientation. In at least one case this web was laid down before the chart was drawn, and would have served as an aid to the draftsman as he recorded the length and bearing of a particular section of the coast. The navigator used the rhumb lines, as they are called, to identify the compass heading between his point of

84 Frontispiece, Petrus Vesconte, *Cartae Nauticae*, 1318 (Österreichische Nationalbibliothek, Vienna, N. B.16.816 CR).

departure and his destination. The pattern of intersecting compass roses was also an emblem of the mapmaker's science. The earliest surviving atlas of Portolan charts, the Petrus Vesconte volume of 1318, used the pattern, without any underlying geographical elements, as the frontispiece of the work (Fig. 84).[43]

Within the web of intersecting compass roses are many sets of parallel lines. Each diameter of the circle has four lines that are parallel to it; these

85 Astrolabe. Signed Ahmad and Muhammed, sons of Ibrahim. A.H. 374 or 394 [A.D. 984/5 or 1003/4] (Museum of the History of Science, Oxford, 1C 3).

86 Astrolabe. Reverse side.

lines define the edges of the quarter-roses and perhaps for that reason have a special graphic weight. Because the quarter-roses are distributed at equal intervals around the circumference of the circle, the lines measure increasingly narrow layers of space. The result is a visual display of proportional values that is very suggestive of the configuration adopted for the new-town plans.[44]

The system of proportional measurements implicit in the compass rose of the Portolan chart is explicitly the subject of a geometric scale connected with the planispheric astrolabe.[45] The astrolabe (Fig. 85) is a two-dimensional representation of the celestial sphere and a computing device with which the medieval astronomer calculated the movements of the heavens. The instrument allowed him to work out the position of the sun and the principal stars, to find his latitude and the direction of true north, and to tell time. An astrolabe is circular and portable, measuring between five and eighteen inches in diameter. It is constructed from a series of superposed, concentric discs. On the front, or face, a disc so extensively perforated that it is called the rete, or net, marks the fixed stars and the ecliptic; it rotates on top of a stereographic projection of the celestial sphere at any given latitude. The astronomer made his calculation by adjusting the position of the stars over the system of coordinates that mapped celestial space.

One way of using the astrolabe required measuring the elevation of heavenly bodies above the horizon. An instrument for taking observations was provided on the back of the astrolabe. It consisted of a sighting rule — an alidade the length of the disc's diameter and pivoted at its center — and a scale of degrees around the circumference of the disc. The interior of the disc accommodated a variety of scales and among them was invariably one that measured trigonometric values. It could be used during observation or, with the alidade, as a trigonometric calculator.

The two most common trigonometric scales of the astrolabe were the shadow square, which measured values of tangent and cotangent by constructing similar triangles, and the sine scale. The sine scale appears on the earliest known astrolabes, including a Persian astrolabe that is dated by inscription to A.D. 984 (Fig. 86). In this instrument the perimeter of the entire upper half of the disc is divided into five-degree units. In the left quadrant, each one of these markings is the point of departure for a line that runs parallel to the horizontal diameter of the astrolabe disc. It is here, with the use of a scale engraved on the rotating alidade, that the astronomer read the sine value of an altitude that he had observed, or calculated the sine of a known angle. The sine scale is precisely the geometry of the Florentine new towns.

The astrolabe and the simpler instrument called the quadrant, which was derived from it, were known in Latin-speaking Europe from as early as the eleventh century.[46] Throughout the Middle Ages treatises were produced on these instruments in both Arabic and Latin. In hardly any of the Latin texts, including the translations from Arabic, was there a discussion of the geometric sine scale,[47] and no astrolabe explicitly for use in Christian Europe incorporated one. The instruments for Christians, which for both cultural and scientific reasons had a very different role from their counterparts in the Islamic world, employed only the shadow square.[48]

The fact that the scales and functions of the astrolabe were not fully understood in the Christian world did not, however, restrict the instrument's fame there. It was used by European astrologers as well as scientists and, by the thirteenth century, there were many others beside them interested in the effects of the stars on human events. The Church accepted this kind of inquiry and some members of the clergy even practiced it.[49] According to Dante, the Church asked only that astrologers acknowledge that God ruled the stars and that Man was free to transcend his destiny.[50] Occasionally an intransigent practitioner went too far and was dealt with by the Inquisition. In 1327 Cecco d'Ascoli, astrologer of the duke of Calabria, was executed in Florence for asserting the primacy of astrological determination, even for the events of the life of Christ.[51] In day-to-day matters, however, the importance of the stars was widely held. Villani explains the causes of the flood of 1333 in Florence in a prolix discussion of theology and astrology entitled "About a great debate in Florence: whether the flood came because of the judgement of God or from natural [i.e. astrological] causes."[52] Even new-town policy was influenced by the science: Villani tells us that the foundation date of Firenzuola was set by astrologers.[53]

A figure as important to the fateful events of life as the astrologer/astronomer naturally found representation in the arts. Adelard of Bath described the figure of Astrology, the seventh of the Liberal Arts, like this: "She appears, surrounded by shining splendor, her body all eyes. In her right hand she holds a quadrant, in her left, an astrolabe."[54] A late-fourteenth-century fresco in Ferrara represents Astronomy in just this form.[55] Closer in time and place to Florence's new towns is the marble relief executed between 1334 and 1343 in one of the hexagonal panels on the base of the campanile of Florence cathedral (Fig. 87). It represents Gionitus, the fourth son of Noah and, according to the thirteenth-century poet and chancellor of the Florentine commune, Brunetto Latini, the first student of astronomy;[56] a concave disc emblazoned with the signs of the zodiac surrounds the figure at work in his study. Gionitus was an orthodox astronomer compared to Cecco d'Ascoli. Outside the rim of sky above Gionitus, overseeing the motion of the stars and blessing the scholar's inquiry, is the figure of God surrounded by a host of angels. Within this ordered environment Gionitus refers to a text that lies across his lap and operates a quadrant. A three-dimensional model of the universe sits on his desk.[57]

The connection of the astrolabe and quadrant with men who, according to Petrarch, were charlatans ignorant even of the procedures of their own pseudoscience suggests another way by which the sine scale could have been known in Florence. If many astrologers had no need, or ability, to make the calculations of which the instrument was capable, then any astrolabe, whether or not it functioned at European latitudes and was inscribed with Latin characters, would have been sufficient to its purpose since any astrolabe identified the Doctor of Astrology.[58]

The instruments may also have appealed to the scientific dilettante. One recent scholarly opinion holds that astrolabes were never accurate enough to provide scientifically useful measurements.[59] According to this interpretation, their true value lay in their ability to represent the contemporary theory of the universe in a tangible form. The owners of these rare objects may have been men similar to the princes of later ages, like the sixteenth- and seventeenth-century Medici, whose libraries and study rooms included devices that demonstrated (as opposed to measured) natural phenomena. Other collectors may have been fascinated with the objects themselves, the elegance of their mechanisms and the beauty of their elaborate engraving. To this day, in Persia and India, astrolabe-like objects are produced for the sole purpose of satisfying this market. Perhaps some of the Muslim astrolabes presently in European collections, like the twelfth-century Moorish astrolabe with sine scales from the collection of Principe Don Tommaso Corsini, now in the Museo di Storia della Scienza in Florence,[60] came to Christian Europe in the later Middle Ages to serve in one of these nonscientific capacities.

Even if the Tuscans were unable to apply the astrolabe's sine scale to trigonometric calculations, the scale still had an important role to play in the formation of new-town plans. Just as it matters little that the rhumb lines of the Portolan chart were only coincidentally sine lines, so the essential value of the astrolabe's sine scale for the town planner was not

87 Andrea Pisano, *Gionitus* or *Astronomy*, 1334 – 1343. Cathedral campanile, Florence (Photograph: Alinari 2005).

mathematical. Fibonacci's chord table provided the means for working out the dimensions of the plans; what the Portolan chart and the sine scale could contribute was a formal model. With their aid we can begin to imagine how proportions which were derived from this advanced form of mathematics found their way into the language of design.

The idea that a sine pattern and a chord table could, together, provide the skeleton of a design is very different from the most widely accepted interpretation of the medieval planning process—that it was based on constructive geometry. The proportions of the sine scale and of the new towns can, of course, be generated geometrically; Enrico Guidoni, the first to recognize the proportional structure of the San Giovanni, Castelfranco, and Terranuova plans, arrived at his conclusions in this way.[61] Guidoni described the proportions as the product of "rotated" polygons: hexagons at San Giovanni and Castelfranco, dodecagons at Terranuova. The polygons could easily have been constructed through operations well known in medieval geometry.[62] The researcher's problem is not to show how the polygons were constructed, but to establish that the next step—the one that extracts sinical proportions from these figures—was in fact taken in the Middle Ages. The rotation of geometric figures that Guidoni describes is not the quadrature of Villard de Honnecourt and of later medieval masons. The two systems generate proportions in very different ways. The proportional series of quadrature, with its constant relationship among terms (for example, $1:\sqrt{2}$ for inscribed squares), comes from the reduction of the size of the figures as they are rotated on their common center and inscribed one within the other. In Guidoni's system rotation is irrelevant to the generation of proportions, which derive, instead, from the distance of the angles of the polygons from an imaginary diameter. It is a system that is unknown among medieval masons. No architectural drawing deals with anything like this form of geometry. In the late Middle Ages only the theory of chords that descends from Ptolemy in the work of Savasorda and Fibonacci, the representation of sines on the astrolabe, and the chordlike pattern on the Portolan chart bear any relation to the geometry of the new towns. The available evidence allows only one conclusion. The sinical proportions of the Florentine new-town plans represent a departure from established architectural practice. They seem to originate outside the arts, in the world of science and practical geometry.[63]

The use of geometry to govern proportions in urban planning is documented for the first time in Renaissance architectural drawings. One of the earliest of these images is closely related to the kind of geometry that

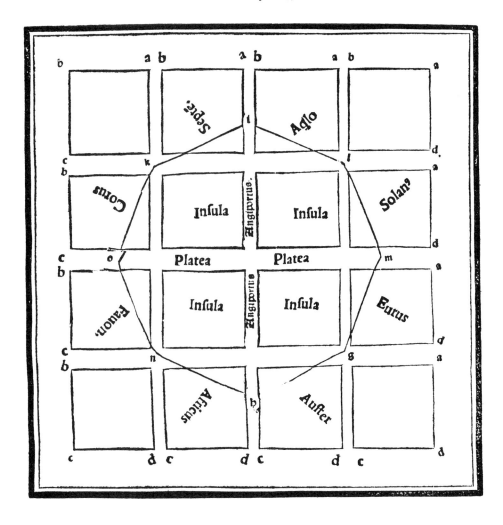

88 Fra Giocondo, wind rose and the street system from Vitruvius, *De Architectura,*
1511 (reproduced by permission of the Houghton Library, Harvard University).

defines the fourteenth-century Florentine towns. Fra Giocondo's edition of Vitruvius, dated 1511, includes an illustration of a famous passage (Book I, Chap. VI, 6 – 8) in which the ancient author describes a method for orienting a city plan so that none of the streets face the major points of the compass, from which the strongest winds were thought to blow (Fig. 88). Fra Giocondo's woodcut shows an orthogonal street system made of sixteen square blocks divided horizontally by wide streets, labelled *platea*, and vertically by narrow ones labelled *angiportus*. Superposed on the plan is the geometric figure of an octagon, each side of which represents one of the winds; none of the sides is parallel to any of the streets.

Fra Giocondo's image adds a detail that does not come from Vitruvius. His wind rose is fully contained within the square of the plan's sixteen blocks and it in turn encloses the four blocks at the center of the plan. Four angles of the octagon coincide with the intersections that fix the boundaries of those blocks. The geometric figure coordinates with the streets, the size of the blocks, and the size of the town. While this is precisely the way geometry appears to control the plans at San Giovanni, Castelfranco, and Terranuova, the wind rose described by Vitruvius had no such purpose.[64] In 1567 Palladio and Daniele Barbaro followed Fra Giocondo, using the octagon of Vitruvius's wind rose not just to orient, but also to order an ancient city plan.[65]

Sine geometry proper made its way into the architectural literature by 1545, with the publication of the first book of Sebastiano Serlio's *Architectura*, which was dedicated to geometry. It presented a number of exercises based on the trigonometric properties of circles. One page explains a method for constructing the curve of a depressed arch (Fig. 89). Two concentric semicircles are divided into fifteen-degree arcs; lines are then dropped from each interval of the larger semicircle and other lines, parallel with the shared diameter, are constructed from the intervals of the smaller semicircle. The points of intersection of the two sets of lines establish the coordinates of the new curve. On the following pages Serlio illustrates designs for vases composed with the same geometric rules. Here the chords not only define the extended curves of the vessel, they also fix the proportions of its parts and the position of the moldings that articulate the form.

Serlio's text allows historians to be certain that, by 1545, the geometry of sines and chords was among the compositional tools of Italian designers. The discovery of a contemporary town plan whose dimensions conformed to this system of proportion would be taken as evidence of the dissemination of sines. The claim that sines played a role in the design of towns

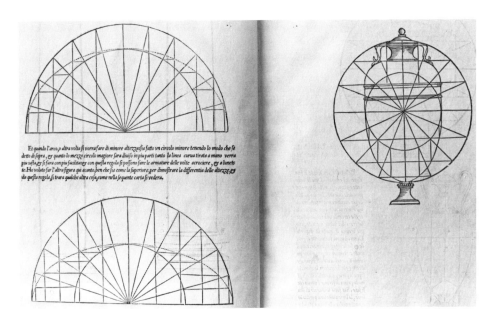

Et quando l'arco,ò altra volta fi vorra fare di minore altezza,fia fatto vn circolo minore tenendo lo modo che fe
detto di fopra, et quanto lo mezzo circolo magiore fera diuifo in piu parti tanto la linea curua tirata a mano verra
piu vefla,et fi fara con piu facilitate et con quefla regola fi poffono fare le armature delle volte a crociere, et a lunetti
te.Ho voluto far l'altra figura qui a canto,ben che fia come la fuperiore,per dimoftrare la differentia delle altezze,et
sla quefla regola,fi traua qualche altra cofa,come nella fequente carta fi vedera.

89 Sine exercises from *Il primo libro d'architettura di M. Sebastiano Serlio Bolognese,* 1551 (fols. 10v – 11r).

would not be challenged. The problem of proof in the case of the plans of the Florentine new towns is not really very different. Fibonacci's *Practica Geometriae* assures us of knowledge of the theory of chords in late medieval Tuscany. The sine scale of the astrolabe and the wind rose of the Portolan chart provide graphic models. The geometry of the new-town plans may be unique in medieval urban design but it has a well-established context elsewhere in the world of the Florentine town builders.

The geometric proportions of a new-town plan are not visible at the site. At San Giovanni the long central square cuts across the plan, exposing the graduated depth of the blocks, but the full sequence of proportions cannot be seen from any single vantage point. A geometric pattern is even less readily observed at Terranuova, where the proportional system determines many more dimensions than at San Giovanni and the central square intersects only one block. In both towns the narrow cross streets provide a better place to check proportions. Here, at least, they can easily be paced off. Only one proportional composition within the Florentine new-town plans allows a visitor to see all its elements simultaneously. This is the central square. Characteristically, even here, the design is not immediately apparent to the eye.

The central square at Terranuova measures 53 by 41 meters, the approximate equivalent of 90 by 70 *braccia* (see Fig. 16). These dimensions must have held a fascination for Florentine town builders, since 90 by 70 *braccia* is about the size of the square at Castelfranco and exactly the dimensions of the square proposed for the Giglio Fiorentino project. The numbers themselves had authority. According to Leon Battista Alberti, seven and nine were especially beloved by God and celebrated in Nature.[66]

The perimeter of the piazza at Terranuova scans as follows. At the center of the square's southwest and northeast sides is the main street 8.15 meters wide. Flanking it are building facades 17.8 meters wide (the ends of the blocks that face onto the main street) and two secondary streets 4.7 meters wide. The other two faces of the square are similarly arranged with the cross street 5.86 meters wide at the center and the houses of the second row of blocks on either side. Though each block extends 81 meters to the first intersection, only 17.6 meters of this length lies on the perimeter of the square. Translated into *braccia,* the perimeter of the square has these dimensions: a main street of 14 *braccia,* a facade of 30⅓ *braccia,* a street 8 *braccia* wide, a section of the second row of houses 30 *braccia* wide, the cross street of 10 *braccia,* a section of houses 30 *braccia* wide, a street of 8 *braccia,* a facade of 30⅓ *braccia,* the 14-*braccia* main street, and so on around the other half of the square. Despite its proportions of 7 : 9, the square has nearly equal sides, each defined by a central street that is flanked by facades 30 *braccia* wide.

This symmetry can best be appreciated in the mind's eye. Any visitor to the square will see more than the 30 *braccia* of housing on either side of the cross street. There is no position that does not command an oblique view into the back streets, beyond the nominal corner of the square. This visual fact does not appear to have concerned the Florentine designers, however, who repeated this symmetry and the corner solution of the square in their project for Giglio Fiorentino (see Fig. 29). The latter was conceived thirteen years after the construction of Terranuova had given a full-scale demonstration of the consequences of this kind of design.

The difference between the square of Terranuova and that of Giglio Fiorentino is only the redistribution of a few *braccia* of space among the streets and facades that occupy the 90-by-70-*braccia* perimeter. The base dimension of the Giglio Fiorentino design, the width of the main street, is unchanged from the Terranuova model at 14 *braccia.* The width of the building lots on either side of it, however, has been reduced to 28 *braccia,* with the extra 2 *braccia* going to the service streets at the corners of the square. On the 70-*braccia* side of the square, the cross street has also been enlarged. Instead of 10 *braccia*, its width is 14 *braccia*. The extra *braccia* were taken, 2 each, from the length of the adjacent block of which only 28 *braccia* face onto the plaza. Again there is an attempt to make the two sides of the square appear equal. Now, a 2:1 proportion between solids and voids dominates the composition, and in fact extends throughout the plan. The relationship between the width of the main street and the depth of the lots that face onto it is 2:1; so is the relationship between the width of the four residential streets (10 *braccia*) and the depth of the lots to which they give access (20 *braccia*), between the depth (20 *braccia*) and the width (10 *braccia*) of these most numerous lots, between the depth of the smallest lots (10 *braccia*) and the mid-sized ones, and, approximately, between the length (470 *braccia*, or 274.5 meters) and the width (246 *braccia*, or 143.7 meters) of the town.

The changes to the square at Giglio and to the dimensions of its blocks reflect the abandonment of the comprehensive system of geometric proportions based on sines and chords that dominated the designs of the best of the earlier Florentine new-town plans. The desire to keep dimensions under formal control survived, but the scheme of the planners of 1350 is much simpler. Instead of the series of proportions of the sine scale, a single relationship dominates. The 2:1 proportion of the Giglio plan is part of a trend in Florentine design in the mid-fourteenth century. Its most prominent manifestation is in the design of the city's cathedral. The proposal for an enlarged tribune, submitted between 1365 and 1367 by the committee of "goldsmiths and painters," inserted a drum between the piers and vault of the earlier design. According to the consultants for the project, the new design made the building more beautiful, more honorable, and "più magnificha." The fourteenth-century chronicler Marchione di Coppo Stefani noted that it also gave the space below the great vault proportions — between height and width — of 2:1.[67]

The proportion of 2:1 is of a very different kind from its predecessors in the new towns. It is mathematical rather than geometric, more characteristic of Renaissance than of Gothic design. But modular and even musical proportioning (2:1 is, of course, the octave) had been employed in the Middle Ages, and its use at Giglio ignores visual issues just as the earlier geometric systems had. At the beginning of the fifteenth century, in order to make a clear visual presentation of his design, Brunelleschi would choose proportions that seem rudimentary compared to the system of sine values that measure the best of new-town designs. The man who laid out the plan of Giglio Fiorentino moved only halfway toward the Renaissance formulation. He rejected the erudite geometric sequence of the sine scale and chord table in favor of the forcefulness of a single, simple proportion. He applied it, however, with the same abstract sense of form that had characterized Florentine new-town design since the plan of San Giovanni.

CHAPTER 5

PLANNERS

ORTHOGONAL STREET SYSTEMS testify to the careful planning that preceded the settlement of hundreds of medieval new-town sites. In very few cases, however, can one point with any certainty to the identity or even the professional character of the men who prepared the designs. The more important the surviving documents, the less they tell about the design. In the most ceremonial papers — the acts of foundation and the charters of liberties to the settlers — the physical details of the new towns, when mentioned at all, are presented as decisions of the founder himself. The tradition of the lord's personal responsibility for his works was a venerable one, and was evident in the first new-town document of the post antique period. In this charter, dated 1120, for the foundation of Freiburg im Breisgau, it is the Zähringer duke Conrad himself who, in the language of the document, "set in place" the market town and "distributed" the building lots.[1]

Even when a prince delegated the authority for a foundation, the persons named in the documents are administrative, not technical, assistants. The three men Edward I of England appointed in 1283 "to plan and assess the new town of Yhamme [New Winchelsea] . . . to plan and give directions for streets and lanes necessary for two churches . . . to assign and to deliver to the barons competent places according to the requirements of their state, and to provide and give directions concerning harbours and all other things necessary for the town" were Stephen de Pencestre, Gregory de Rokesle, and Henry le Waleys, government officials and businessmen.[2] The French royal foundations offer the example of the notary Pons Maynard who in 1255 was empowered "to establish the charter and the consuls of the town and trace the streets, blocks, and lots and to assign them" at Montréal in the Agenais.[3]

German documents present a different sort of administrator with planning authority. When Count Adolf III of Schauenberg spoke in the late twelfth century of his "novum castrum [Hamburg] per Wiradum in areas distributum," the planner of the new town is the man who led its settlement. He appears at the end of the century as one of the consuls of the new city and his descendants are counted among the city's patrician class.[4] The participatory and entrepreneurial nature of this kind of administration is characteristic of many German new-town projects. The founding *promotores* had a financial stake in their town's success; having bought the land from the lord who lent his protection to the project, they expected to realize their profit from the resale of properties to settlers.[5] The office of mayor and the monopoly on milling grain were among the lucrative perquisites they retained. In cases in which the initiative for the new town came from the nobility, an administrative representative *(locator)* had charge of the project. Once the town was in operation he might become its bailiff *(Stadtvogt)*, as did Herborg von Raven, the administrator of the Neubrandenburg project of 1248 for the margrave of Pomerania.[6]

Whether French, German, or English, the ceremonial documents identify only men with legal responsibility for the planning of new towns. If the project enjoyed the specialized services of a surveyor or a professional drawn from the building trades, such an assistant was not listed in the official record. The evidence from Florence is quite different. The archives of the town founding committees that were appointed to act for the government go beyond legislative documentation to preserve contracts and accounts of expenses. Part of the information contained in this daily record is the identity of the new-town planners.

The administration by Florence of new-town projects evolved as the city gained experience. The records for the first towns are of the usual, formal sort; where they reveal anything about the organization of the projects, they are tentative, and give the impression that the system for building towns was experimental. At San Giovanni and Castelfranco di Sopra the priors nominally retained direct control over all aspects of the enterprise. The foundation document (Document 2) specifies financial, military, and political issues for which they were responsible. It also assigns to them the obligation to establish the "latitudine et longitudine . . . modo et forma" of the towns, their defenses, public buildings, houses, and any other facility deemed appropriate. Much of the work could be delegated: the foundation legislation provided for the appointment of administrative officers "rectores seu offitiales," to oversee the project. By April 1300 a committee of two officers was established "to oversee and expedite the *castra* that are being built from nothing."[7] The men selected by the priors were Cioni di Ser Rugierini Minerbetti, who was replaced because of illness by Ser Petraccolo dall'Ancisa, the notary of the committee, and Segna Buene. We know from his name that Cioni was a member of one of the city's distinguished families, but town building administrator was also an appropriate position for a notary, a man of some education and of middle station in the society of the city. Because Ser Petraccolo was the father of Petrarch, we also know a little about his political activity as a White Guelph and his exile from the city in 1302. The "rectores" were citizens serving a term on one of the government committees. If they had a special skill, it was administrative. According to the foundation document of 1299, the officials were to assess the land appropriated for the towns, organize the labor of the immigrants, and tax them for the construction costs. Compared to their counterparts at the later projects, these officials had only limited powers. They were given no responsibility for the plan; it is possible that the priors fulfilled this duty themselves. More probably, the priors dealt with it by exercising the privilege they reserved for themselves in the foundation document "to grant special powers as they shall see fit to whomever and for whatever purpose they wish."

The character of the Florentine records changed in the second quarter of the fourteenth century with the formation of autonomous committees devoted to town building. The first project administered by a town building committee was that of Firenzuola.[8] In 1332 six citizens received "all the powers of the priors and gonfaloniere"[9] so that, compared to either the "rectores" of the San Giovanni project or the military officer who administered the pacification of the Mugello and the foundation of Scarperia in 1306 (Document 4), the committee was relatively independent of the *Signoria*. It was also fairly stable. Like those who sat on the citizen committees that administered other aspects of Florentine governmental business, the six members of the Firenzuola committee, one from each of the *sestiere* of the city, served six-month terms and were succeeded by new committeemen named by the *Signoria*. The documents that tell us so much about the activities of these committees must have greatly aided the orderly transmission of information from one administration to another.[10]

Constituted to deal exclusively with the pacification of the northern Apennine region and the founding of the new town at its center, the

Firenzuola committee was soon given charge of other Florentine town building ventures. The project to build a town on the road to the Casentino, which was begun by the city in 1329 (Document 12), was put into the committee's hands on 5 May 1332. The officials were given permission to spend one thousand lire on the town (the same as they had to spend on the Firenzuola project) for "ditches and palisades and the other expenses of constructing and completing the town." They were awarded the same authority for this project as they had been for the "terra ultre alpes" (Firenzuola).[11] The enlargement and fortification of the town of Cerretto Guidi in the lower Arno valley, a project begun with its own building committee, was put into the hands of the Firenzuola committee in 1338.[12] By 1339 Terranuova, which had originally been provided with its own six-man committee (Document 16), was also administered by the *offitiales alpium*, as the Firenzuola committee was known.[13]

In the mid-fourteenth century Florentine town building — although not specifically the foundation of towns — was at its peak. Administration of the many projects was almost exclusively in the hands of individually constituted committees, each of which was responsible for one or at most two projects. The fortification and enlargement of San Casciano in the hills south of the city on the road to Siena, begun in the late summer and early fall of 1354,[14] was guided by a committee of eight Florentine citizens. In the upper Arno valley Figline,[15] from 1353, and Pontassieve,[16] from 1356, were rebuilt under the control of another eight-man committee. In the central Mugello valley, east of Scarperia, Vicchio was refortified by a committee of four Florentine citizens on the authority of a *Provvisione* of 11 February 1364 / 5.[17] Toward the end of the century town building slackened. In the 1380s, the maintenance of all the new and enlarged towns as well as the completion of those projects still under way and the preservation of the records of the old committees passed to a single government agency, the *Ufficiali delle Castella*.[18]

The office of the *Castella* had been formed at mid-century as custodian of the fortifications in the Florentine countryside.[19] It carried out this responsibility until 1419, when the office was suspended and its responsibilities passed to other parts of the city's bureaucracy.[20] The full range of the *Castella*'s business is not itemized, but its officers appear in the surviving documentation awarding contracts for the improvement of fortresses,[21] appointing men to oversee construction work on the walls of a dependent town,[22] ordering provisions for the city's castles, and appointing military officers to command them.[23] It was also the *Ufficiali delle Castella* who appear to have been the recipients of numerous reports on the condition of the defenses of Florentine towns.[24]

Although custodial work made up the bulk of the *Castella*'s activity, the officers were also concerned with a few town building projects. Two of them, the expansion of the towns of Campi and Pontassieve, fell into their hands in the 1380s, because of the extinction of the *ad hoc* committees that had begun the work. Other projects included a new town in the area northwest of Arezzo, of which nothing more than the proposed site is known,[25] and the project for Giglio Fiorentino.

The men who served on the new-town committees and in the office of the *Castella* had no professional training as builders, surveyors, or designers. Their only qualification was to be part of the section of the Florentine population that participated in city government. Their activity on the town building committees was a civic obligation like many others they fulfilled. Their work required only occasional meetings and their obligation was usually only for six months. The four-member Vicchio committee of 1365, for example, included men who belonged to the Calimala, the Lana, and the Cambio guilds of the city's merchant community.[26] One of them, Nofrio Johanis domine Lapi Arnolfi, served a second term, but that was the limit of his involvement in town foundation work.[27]

The best-known town founder is Giovanni Gherardo Lanfredini, one of the two officers in charge of founding Giglio Fiorentino. The Lanfredini were a family of magnate origin.[28] Giovanni's father held the office of prior in 1334 and was *gonfaloniere* in 1338.[29] Giovanni himself improved his position in Florentine society by marrying well. He was in business as early as 1332 and was a member of the Bardi banking and trading company at the time of its failure in 1345. He served the city in a wide range of positions. In 1342, 1346, and 1351 he was a prior and in 1347 he led the government as *gonfaloniere.* In 1349 he was one of the commissioners who organized the incorporation of San Gimignano and Colle di Val d'Elsa into the Florentine state. Two years later he was vicar of the Val di Nebule[30] and during the period of the Visconti threat in the early 1350s, presumably as a responsibility connected with his status as a magnate, he raised and equipped a body of soldiers to help defend Florentine territory. In 1353 he served as the city's ambassador to Perugia[31] and to the court of the Emperor Charles IV in Treviso and Udine, where he negotiated a treaty for which he was knighted by the government. In 1359 he received the honorary title of Syndic of the Commune.

This was a distinguished record of service. The selection of Giovanni for the mission to the emperor demonstrates the high regard in which he was held by his fellow citizens. His skills as administrator, judge, soldier, diplomat, and politician led him to the highest level of the city's government. It is some indication of the importance attributed to the work of town foundation and of maintaining the city's defenses that Giovanni should have served in the *Castella* as well as in these other posts. As was typical, he did not serve in the *Castella* more than once.

The pattern of limited new-town service placed the Florentine committeemen at a disadvantage compared to their counterparts in northern Europe. Many of these town founders had experience in a number of projects. Henry Le Waleys, in addition to his work at New Winchelsea, participated in the "colloquium" called by Edward I in 1297 to consider a new town at Berwick on Tweed.[32] Pons Maynard administered the foundation of Castillones as well as that of Montréal in France.[33] From numerous examples it appears that the profession of *locator* in Germany was one in which generations of families of the lower nobility specialized.[34]

The inexperience of the Florentine committeemen and the sophistication of the town plans they dealt with presents a paradox that we can understand only by recognizing the limits of the committeemen's responsibility. It was the duty of the citizens who served on the town building agencies to define and to protect Florentine interests in all aspects of the projects. They cannot, however, have been expected either to initiate all the ideas that went into the creation of the towns or to execute their decisions. The great contribution of the documents preserved in the archives of the *Ufficiali delle Castella* is that they reveal how the agencies worked and what kind of assistants they employed. From them we learn about the longevity of the salaried staff: in the face of the regular rotation of nonspecialized committeemen, it was the staff that lent experience and continuity to the administration of the projects.

Our best picture of the operation of a Florentine town building committee is in the records of the project to fortify the hilltop retreat of Vicchio in the central Mugello valley (see Fig. 30). Work was begun on the site in 1324;[35] stone defenses were erected in the three-year period beginning in 1365.[36] Throughout the fourteenth century Vicchio was more important as a retreat for local residents than as a permanent settlement. It probably never included more than twenty-five houses during this period and did not receive its own parish until the nineteenth century.[37] In May 1368 there was, however, at least one street and a square within the walls, and a building that served as the seat of a league of villages faced the square.[38]

The Vicchio committee had the assistance of a number of salaried as well as contractual workers. Some of the former were paid on a per diem basis. These included the *nuntio,* who traveled for the committee in the countryside, first to invite masons to participate in the project and later to demand payment of money owed the project by towns of the Vicchio league.[39] He was paid one florin for each day he was on the road. The committee's lawyer was also paid irregularly for consultation.[40] Members of the staff with greater responsibilities received a monthly salary. The salary of the *camerarius,* or treasurer, who collected money from the towns and disbursed it, on the instructions of the committee, to those who worked on the project, was two florins a month.[41] The notary who kept the records of the committee's deliberations and the project's expenses was paid the same amount.[42]

The committee had another employee, Bacino Cambiuzzi, "magistrum et capudmagistrum et proveditorem constructionem dicte terre Vichii," the chief master and overseer of the works. He received the grand salary of thirty lire, about fifteen florins, a month[43] and held his position for the entire three-year period covered by the committee's record.[44] This was not Bacino's first contact with a Florentine town building project. In 1345 he appeared as the head of a company of masons who were paid by the linear foot for construction of the castle at Buggiano.[45] At Vicchio, twenty years later, Bacino was in a very different position. He was no longer a contractor to the government committee but its salaried employee, and some of his work, the part he did as "provedittore," did not even have much to do with building. He facilitated all aspects of the project. He acted as host to the members of the committee when they visited the site;[46] he gave money, later to be reimbursed by the committee, to other employees for their traveling expenses; he paid the committee's lawyers; and he supplied writing materials for the treasurer and the notary.[47] He bought wine for the workers who came from neighboring towns to dig the ditches and foundations of the new defenses[48] and paid them their daily wages.

Bacino was also the committee's architectural advisor. He appears by name as a witness to the contacts for the construction of the gates and walls of Vicchio and by title as the authority for the design of a number of details that are not fixed in the contracts.[49] In matters that had to do primarily with money or policy and were easily understood by a layman —such as the final decision to finish the walls at fourteen or sixteen *braccia*—the approval of the officials was also required. More technical issues, like the design of a machicolated gallery, the *capomaestro* alone decided. Together with the officials and an outside expert, it was also the *capomaestro* who approved the quality of the completed work.

Construction at the Florentine sites was directed by men from a variety of professional backgrounds. In contrast to Bacino Cambiuzzi, the builder turned administrator at Vicchio, was Matteus, the knight in charge of the Scarperia project (Document 4), a government official turned town designer. The Firenzuola committee hired an overseer whose competence lay somewhere in between. Their man was "prudent and experienced" (perhaps in new-town matters) but was not a builder.[50] In the earliest of the Florentine projects, the abortive attempt to found a town on the pass between Borgo San Lorenzo in the Mugello and Faenza, Bacino's technical and administrative responsibilities were divided between two men. "Tinaccio building master and surveyor and Banducio Rustichi" (whose professional skill was not specific enough to name) are styled the "overseers of the work at the castle of Pietra sancta."[51] The same division of responsibilities occurs in the more detailed record of the administration of the Pontassieve project of 1357. "Francesco pieri del buono civi flor" served as the "sollicitator" or executive officer of the work at a salary of seven florins a month.[52] His partner, the "capomagistro dicti operis et laborerem constructionem dicti castri," was "Taddeo Ristori magistro." Taddeo was paid six florins a month.[53] The pairing of a builder and an administrator was characteristic of many of the new-town projects. It was also the way in which the large workshop at the city's cathedral was organized.[54]

Bacino Cambiuzzi's extensive responsibilities for both the design and administrative details of a town building project were not unique. In 1356 at San Casciano, where the city's eight-man committee employed a large body of assistants including a treasurer, a notary, a *nuntio*, procurement officers for building materials, and an officer to check the quality of the construction, the highest paid employee was Giovanni di Lapo Ghini, elected by the committee "in capud magistrum ordinatorem et sollicitatorem laborerii dicti castri Sancti Casciani." He received twenty soldi, or one lira, for every day he worked at the site.[55] The form of his pay and his title as "sollicitator" tell us that Giovanni served as an overseer, but as "magister ordinatoris" he was something more. According to the committee's records, a house located "near the Porta Fiorentino in a place where a ditch and a road are to go" had to be destroyed so that the town could be completed "secundum ordinem et modum traditum."[56] "Ordinare" is the act of physical planning. The testimony of these documents is that Giovanni's responsibilities included the design of defenses and streets.

The man given this unique undertaking was not an anonymous mason like Bacino Cambiuzzi, but a figure associated with the most prestigious architectural projects of his day. Giovanni di Lapo Ghini appears as early as 15 July 1355 as an advisor at Florence cathedral.[57] In 1358 he offered designs for the marble facing of the cathedral and in 1359, with Francesco

Talenti, he became *capomaestro* at that project, building the first four piers of the nave and later, in 1362, vaulting them.[58] In 1359 and 1360 he was also the builder of the palace of the Mercanzia, the Florentine merchants' court, adjacent to the Palazzo della Signoria.[59]

Giovanni was not the only mason-architect who had worked on the cathedral project and was also employed by the city's town building agencies. Often these highly skilled men were hired by the city as advisors for short periods of time and paid a daily wage. In 1358 Giovanni Gherardini (an advisor to the *capomaestri* of the cathedral in 1366) and Benci Cioni (from 1377 to 1382 *capomaestro* at the Loggia della Signoria, a project administered by the cathedral *opera*) visited the Pontassieve site twice, for periods of three and four days. They accompanied members of the Pontassieve committee and two surveyors to review the work on the town's defenses.[60] They received an honorarium of about $\frac{2}{3}$ lira a day,[61] while Taddeo Ristori, the *capomaestro* of the Pontassieve project who was later (1377 – 78) to assist Benci and Simone di Francesco Talenti at the Loggia della Signoria,[62] had a salary of twelve lire a month. In 1382 Lorenzo di Filippo, who was then *capomaestro* at the cathedral and the Loggia della Signoria,[63] made a two-day trip to San Casciano for the *Ufficiali delle Castella*,[64] for which he was paid four lire.

Like the town building committees and the cathedral *opera*, the *Ufficiali delle Castella* retained its own *capomaestro*. Lorenzo di Filippo's companion at San Casciano was Gattoli Buoni, who was paid thirty lire a month by the *Ufficiali* "in capud magistro dicto offitio."[65] Gattoli also accompanied the officers of the *Castella* in their tours of inspection. Surviving documents record trips of fifteen days and two days in addition to the two-day trip to San Casciano. Gattoli does not seem to have had ongoing responsibility for any one site. He may have earned most of his salary by giving advice at the meetings of the full committee of the *Castella*, which took place in Florence. The work of one of his successors, Francesco Ducci, who was recorded in the office of *capomaestro* of the *Castella* in 1402,[66] indicates the range of duties required of the office's chief building advisor. Francesco is mentioned by name as having received one thousand lire to pay for lime used in the construction of a section of the walls of Firenzuola. He also appears by title in a contract between the *Castella* and two masons to rebuild part of the town's walls. There he was the person from whom the builders had to get instruction for anchoring the corbels of the machicolated gallery. By implication, it was also he who prepared the specifications for the structures described in the contract.[67] Francesco was paid a daily rate (of two lire) rather than the traditional monthly salary. Like

Gattoli he appeared as the *Castella's capomaestro* at a number of towns.[68] Although they did not regularly supervise any single site, Gattoli and Francesco, when accompanying the *Castella's* special advisors, provided continuity of technical direction. They exercised the authority of *capomaestro* when paying out money to meet the committee's contractual obligations and when making design decisions.

Another builder who appeared as an advisor to the *Ufficiali delle Castella* was the master Neri Fioravanti. At the time of his connection with the *Castella*, Neri had already worked on a number of government projects. With his associate, Benci Cioni, he was responsible for revaulting the great chamber of the Palazzo del Podestà between 1340 and 1345,[69] and for beginning work on the church of Santi Anna opposite Orsanmichele in 1349.[70] Neri was also active at the cathedral. In a contract of January 1351 he appeared at the head of a company of stone carvers who cut the marble revetment of the triforium of the campanile.[71] He is best known for his association with the group of masters and painters who proposed, between 1365 and 1367, a new, more ambitious design for the cathedral's tribune.[72]

In late June and early July 1350 Neri traveled with Giovanni Gherardo Lanfredini and Bernardo di Piero degli Strozzi, officers of the *Castella*, in the Val d'Ambra. In entries made at Uzzano, Lanciolina, Cennina, and Civitella, Giovanni and Bernardo awarded contracts for reinforcement of the defense of those towns "with the advice of Neri Fioravanti maestro."[73] Although Neri is nowhere called the *capomaestro* of the *Castella*—that title is recorded for the first time with Gattoli Buoni in 1382—he may nevertheless have had a similar, continuous relationship with the government agency. In August 1353, more than three years after his first recorded connection with the newly formed agency, he spoke in a government council meeting "per offitio Castrorum."[74] It was in 1350, during the January-to-July term of office, that the *Ufficiali delle Castella* established the plan of Giglio Fiorentino.[75]

The documents of the Florentine town building committees give a new picture of the town planning process in the late Middle Ages. They take us behind the official acts of foundation and allow us to know with certainty that the political figures named in them were not solely responsible for the physical design of the settlements. They record the presence of architectural professionals at the town building sites, as advisors, supervisors, administrators, official representatives of the government, and planners. The documents are detailed and important, but they are not a complete

record of Florentine town building activity. Indeed, there is least information for the three towns in the Valdarno, which include the earliest foundations and the most accomplished new-town plans. A discussion of the
authorship of these important designs must focus on the towns themselves. What the committee documents contribute to this discussion is a
new context. They establish the fact that, in some cases at least, professional design skills were used to prepare new-town plans. Thanks to the
documents the question is no longer whether new towns benefited from
the attention of professional designers but, rather, which towns did and
which did not. Fortunately, the answer does not depend on a subjective
assessment of design quality. A comparison of the plans of Scarperia (see
Fig. 21) and Giglio Fiorentino (see Fig. 29) establishes something approaching objective criteria. The two are similar in that both are orthogonal designs prepared for unoccupied sites and are heavily dependent on
earlier plans. They depart only slightly from their models but the kind of
changes that were made are of two very different kinds. Because a government official designed Scarperia and a professional designer participated
in the planning of Giglio, the comparison reveals something important
about the nature of the professional contribution.

Two documents discuss the planning of Scarperia. In the first, the
foundation charter of April 1306 (Document 3), written while the city's
armies were laying siege to the castle of the barons which dominated the
Scarperia area, an administrative team of two men was given charge of the
new-town project. Its powers were extensive and included command of a
body of soldiers to keep the peace in this war-torn area. The two men were
to assess the property to be taken for the town and to select its settlers.
They were also to establish the streets, squares, and churches of the new
settlement and to oversee construction of the gates and bridges of the
defensive perimeter. In the second document, dated three months later,
"dominus Matteus judex, magister de Egimo [?], offitialis et capitanus"
was appointed to this same administrative office (Document 4). This figure
with a legal, administrative, and military portfolio was likewise made
responsible for the town's physical organization. He was expressly empowered to determine the size of the town, to grade its site, and to lay out
its streets, walls, and bridges.

Like the plan for Firenzuola made twenty-six years later (see Fig. 27),
Matteus's scheme for Scarperia was based on the 1299 design of San
Giovanni (see Fig. 3). Being a Florentine town, Scarperia is laid out around
the axis of its main street, its housing is developed in rows of lots parallel
with that axis, and its plan is focused on a central square and divided into

quarters by a central cross axis. Scarperia is particularly like San Giovanni in the back-to-back arrangement of its residential blocks and in the presence of narrow strips of land, used as alleys or sewers, to divide the blocks. Originally it also shared the most distinctive feature of the San Giovanni plan, an extended rectangular piazza that stretched across the main street from one side of the town to the other. The piazza was obliterated by the construction, begun by 1355 and completed by 1360,[76] of a castle to house the Florentine garrison and to accommodate the city's vicar for the Mugello. This structure occupied the entire western half of the square (Fig. 91; see Fig 26). For almost fifty years, however, Scarperia's unusual piazza would have signaled that the town plan derived from that of its predecessor in the Arno valley.

In adapting the San Giovanni plan for reuse at the Mugello site, Matteus was obliged to make a change in scale. San Giovanni is the largest of the Florentine new towns, originally measuring about 460 by 189 meters. Matteus expected a much smaller immigration to Scarperia and the town he laid out has a length of about 317 meters and a width that varies from 137 to 178 meters. All the elements of the San Giovanni plan were reduced at Scarperia. The largest lot is 16.5 meters deep, while the largest at San Giovanni extends 23.6 meters; the width of Scarperia's main street is 7.5 meters, San Giovanni's is 11.2 meters. The reduction in size made exact duplication impossible. At Scarperia, for example, San Giovanni's 1.75- and 2.4-meter-wide alleys were reduced to sewers so narrow that all trace of them has disappeared from the modern map. The impossibility of exact duplication was also liberating; because he could not reproduce the plan of San Giovanni, Matteus was free to invent many details. Preserving those aspects of the plan that were essential to its typological identity — the orthogonal street system, the transverse piazza, and the back-to-back block system — he dealt freely with the details that contributed to the formal elegance of the model. The difference is apparent at first glance. While the wall at San Giovanni conforms to the shape of the town within, Scarperia's defenses respond to the topography of the site. The town, which sits on a wide plateau, is pushed up against a steep escarpment to exploit the defensive advantages of the grade. The irregular line of the natural formation pinches the middle of the plan and expands the sides facing Florence and Bologna. The irregularity of this perimeter, which has a kind of organic symmetry, affects the interior by creating a good deal of ungridable ground between the street system and the walls.

What separates Scarperia most distinctly from its model are its proportions. The town square, because it did not originally have the closed

90 Scarperia. SS. Jacopo e Filippo.

corners of its prototype or the freestanding building at its center, was a deep space without clear definition. The house lots, too, conform to no system of measure. The diminution of lot depths that subtly orders the dimensions of the San Giovanni plan is absent at Scarperia. The houses on the main street have one size and those everywhere else another. The geometry of chord and arc does not fit this plan and we must assume that it played no part in generating the design.

Matteus treated his duties pragmatically. When he exchanged the regularity of San Giovanni's plan for a stronger defensive position for Scarperia, and when he excised the geometry that gave San Giovanni its special character, he consistently leaned toward practical rather than formal considerations. The destruction of the original square was possible only because of this kind of attitude. The proportions of the square and the symmetry of the plan were no more compelling considerations for the Florentine vicar in 1355 than they had been for Matteus in 1307.

The *Ufficiali delle Castella*, advised by Neri Fioravanti, produced a very different sort of plan for Giglio Fiorentino (see Fig. 29). It, too, is a simplified version of a model, in this case the 1337 plan of Terranuova. Here, however, simplicity is part of a new aesthetic. Removal of the secondary intersections that gave focus to the neighborhoods of Terranuova, and banishment of the market to a field outside the walls simplified the town's organization without compromising its formal coherence. The defensive perimeter, for example, retained its rigid orthogonality and close connection to the street plan. The central square was set out with extreme formality, with civil and religious institutions facing each other across its open space. At 70 by 90 *braccia* the overall dimensions of the square remained the same as those of Terranuova and the elements that defined the alternation of solids and voids around its perimeter were even more formally arranged. Clear 2:1 proportions replaced the subtle relationships arrived at by Fibonacci's table of chords. The changes reinforced the unity of the plan and the dominance of its center, producing a strong, simplified composition.

The transformation of the Terranuova plan at Giglio Fiorentino, the creation of one sophisticated composition out of another, is the achievement of a designer. Neither Giovanni Gherardo Lanfredini nor Bernardo Strozzi, officers of the *Castella* in the spring and summer of 1350, were capable of it. More likely the architect Neri Fioravanti deserves the credit. The simplified forms of the Giglio plan reflect the power and scale of his greatest achievements: the rebuilding and vaulting of the main hall of the Bargello in two gigantic square bays and the model for the enlarged tribune of Florence cathedral that he proposed between 1365 and 1367 as a member of the committee of goldsmiths and painters and that gave the building its present 2:1 proportions.

Judging by the examples of San Giovanni and Scarperia, Terranuova and Giglio, new-town planning began with the selection of a model, no matter who was in charge. How the source was treated, though, varied. Matteus acknowledged only some of the elements of the San Giovanni plan. Using it as a model, he dismantled it. He saw it typologically and adapted it according to pragmatic considerations, omitting certain features, such as a system of proportions, whose only justification was formal. His single new idea about physical organization — the bow-tie-like symmetry of the defensive perimeter — was intuitive and undisciplined, if not merely chance. The plan prepared for Giglio Fiorentino had a different relation to its source. It treated the layout of Terranuova with sympathy and understanding. It preserved the elements which defined that type of plan; it respected and promoted tradition. It also acknowledged the formal elements of the Terranuova layout — the street system was integrated with the defensive perimeter, and there was a system of clearly defined measurements throughout. The designer of Giglio Fiorentino understood his model well enough to reinterpret it. He rejected the complexity of the Terranuova plan in favor of 2:1 proportions overall and a single center, thereby challenging and changing the basic aesthetic of Florentine medieval orthogonal planning.

Giglio Fiorentino was not the first site at which formal design became part of Florentine new-town planning. While sharing Giglio Fiorentino's regularity and cohesiveness, the plans of San Giovanni, Castelfranco, and Terranuova surpass that of Giglio Fiorentino in complexity and sophistication of composition. The planners of the earlier towns were pioneers in a way that Neri Fioravanti and his colleagues did not choose to be. Their projects established the Florentine new-town type by synthesizing planning ideas from widely scattered sources and subjecting them for the first time to a rigorous formalist discipline. This was an accomplishment of the highest order, requiring great technical skill and invention. It seems sure that the priors exercised their option "to grant special powers as they shall see fit to whomever and for whatever purpose they wish" by attaching professional designers to the staffs of the early new-town projects.

In the absence of documents we can only speculate about the identity of the men who made the early Florentine plans so satisfying formally. Knowledge of the later towns, however, suggests where they might be found. Many of the most important architectural employees of the town building agencies—Giovanni di Lapo Ghini, the *capomaestro* "ordinatorem et sollicitatorem" at San Casciano, Taddeo Ristori, the *capomaestro* at Pontassieve, the advisors Benci Cioni, Giovanni Gherardini, Lorenzo di Filippo, and Neri Fioravanti—had in common a connection with the architectural workshop at Florence cathedral. They appeared as stone cutters, contractors, and also as the directors, *capomaestri*, of this gigantic project. There is, however, no systematic or official connection between the workshop and the new towns until 1382, when Lorenzo di Filippo, then *capomaestro* at the cathedral, toured the *contado* for the *Ufficiali delle Castella*. In fact, the *opera* is not known to have taken on any public-work projects other than the cathedral until 1368 when the *Signoria* charged it with completing the city's walls.[77]

Well before this rather late date, the administration of the cathedral project, and thus the architectural workshop, had become a public rather than an episcopal agency. From the very beginning of the project, in 1294, the city's representatives had directed the work alongside representatives of the bishop and of the cathedral canons. As the city gradually came to dominate the project's finances, so its representatives controlled decisions pertaining to it. In 1321 five of the city's guilds, in rotating terms of one year, took over exclusive administration of the *opera* for the *Signoria*.[78] From the beginning of work, the post of head of the workshop was of concern to the public authorities. For the "magnificent and visible beginning" of the cathedral, Arnolfo di Cambio, the new church's first master, was rewarded by the city government with life exemption from military duty and taxes.[79] One of Arnolfo's successors, the painter Giotto, was even more clearly an employee of the city. His call to office came directly from the *Signoria*, which was concerned "that the projects which are under way, or need to be undertaken, in the city of Florence by the commune of Florence proceed honorably and decorously." His position is described as "master and governor of the fabric and *opera* of the church of Santa Reparata and of the construction and completion of the walls of the city of Florence and of the fortresses of the city and of other projects which may be said to pertain to the work of any magistracy of the commune."[80] Along with the breadth of the new master's responsibility is the provision that his salary be paid by the commune with money allocated for any of its projects, not just for the cathedral.

If either Arnolfo or Giotto participated in any city project other than the cathedral, it is not identified by contemporary sources. The tradition of the cathedral *capomaestro* serving as a kind of ad hoc master of public works is, however, extensively documented in other cities. At Bologna, between 1245 and 1267, "Magister Albertus de laborerio Sancti Petri" was *capo-maestro* at the cathedral and technical advisor to the government committee responsible for the city's streets. He was concerned with wells, cisterns, sewers, and regulation of the river Reno, and was in charge of quarrying the stone for the city wall and building the commune's bell tower.[81] In the next century Antonio di Vicenzo worked on Bologna's city wall, its castles in the *contado*, the Loggia della Mercanzia, the Palazzo della Società dei Notai, and the Palazzo del Podestà before he was named *capomaestro* of the civic church of San Petronio in 1390. He continued in similar activities, like the construction of the mills at Castel Bolognese, after this appointment.[82] When Lando di Pietro was called to be *capomaestro* of Siena cathedral in 1338, he was praised not just for his skill as a builder of churches but also for his expertise in those things that pertained to the construction of "palaces and of town halls and streets and bridges and fountains and other works of the commune."[83] Indeed, only four years before, he had designed the walls of the Sienese new town at Castelfranco Paganico.[84] His work was expected to be so evenly divided between the cathedral and the commune's other projects that the government and the *opera* shared equally the responsibility for his two hundred lire annual salary. Lorenzo Maitani, who was made *capomaestro* at Orvieto cathedral in 1310, promised, in addition to his work on the church, "to review the bridges and other constructions of the commune and of special persons and to consult on things to be built." In 1327, when the hall of the commune and the city wall were repaired, Lorenzo was given charge of the work.[85]

In all these instances it was the *capomaestri*, not the office of the cathedral *opera*, who undertook supervision of the commune's other works. Before the institutional liaison established in 1368 in Florence, each public project had its own administrative organization. Construction of the churches of Santa Croce and Santo Spirito, of the city walls — even, originally, of the Loggia della Signoria — had individual citizen committees to oversee the work, as did the projects to build the towns of the countryside. Each committee had its own administrative staff, and each probably also employed its own architectural supervisors to direct daily progress of the work. What the documents about Lorenzo Maitani, Lando di Pietro, and Giotto claim is that the man who headed the builders at the cathedral could also have some responsibility, perhaps advisory, for other projects in which his employer, the commune, was involved. The documents of the town building agencies, as discussed earlier, tell essentially the same story.

What, then, does all this reveal about the identity of the professional designers who in 1299 made such an important contribution to the planning of San Giovanni and Castelfranco, or about the man who in 1337 worked on the plan at Terranuova? Vasari offers the heroic interpretation. According to the *Lives*, Arnolfo di Cambio "prepared the plan[s of San Giovanni and Castelfranco] . . . and gave such general satisfaction . . . that he was awarded the citizenship of Florence."[86] However cautious we must be about Vasari's accuracy on this historical issue, we are obliged to acknowledge, through his work, the sixteenth-century reputation of the towns. For Vasari, the new-town projects were important enough to command the participation of architects, and of sufficiently high quality to be attributed to the best designers of the age.

A conclusion based on surviving evidence must stop short of identifying individuals. However, the documentation in the Florentine archives and the sites as they survive go a long way toward establishing the new towns in an art-historical context. The admirable town plans of San Giovanni, Castelfranco, and Terranuova are the result of a cooperative effort between two types of contributors: members of government named in the official acts of foundation and professional designers recorded in the documents of the town building committees. The heart of the Florentine political establishment actively participated in planning the new-town projects. Heads of the government oversaw the first projects; respected members of the guild regime manned the committees that took over this custodianship in the 1330s. The committees were involved in many issues of state embodied in Florentine new-town policy: they selected sites and settlers; decided on markets, roads, tax freedoms, and defensive goals. They did not, however, presume to do the technical work of laying out the town any more than they would, themselves, have built the town walls. For these specialized tasks professional designers were employed, introducing a level of formal sophistication that the town plans would not otherwise have had.

CHAPTER 6

COLONIES

A NEW-TOWN PROJECT came to life with the collection of a population. Settlers were drawn from villages surrounding the new-town site and men and women who had been ruled by the feudal nobility became Florentine subjects. Citizens of the city rejoiced at this; contemporary chronicles praised the towns for "dismantling the following and the authority" of the nobility.[1] For the Florentine town builders, however, relocation was only the first step toward securing this human resource for the city. The new towns could not operate as prisons; their success depended on the support and cooperation of the settlers. Before immigrants could be considered model subjects, their ties to the villages of their birth and to friends of a lifetime had to be weakened or broken, and bonds of loyalty and mutual concern had to be established with new neighbors. The future of the settlers lay in the larger world of the new town, and the community as a whole had to accept the leadership of Florence over a wide range of its activities.

Building a unified community with strong ties to Florence was a more delicate task than was the military and political effort that led up to the foundation of a town, but the Florentines were not without resources. During the early years of the new towns they bought the loyalty of the settlers through the terms of immigration and enforced allegiance with the threat of military action. By the fifteenth century, however, the bonds uniting the city and the towns were social and cultural as much as political. The new towns took in country rustics that Italian city dwellers of the fourteenth century would have considered little better than animals.[2] They came from villages with populations of less than fifty families, from exclusively rural economies, and had had little contact with the world outside the mountains in which they lived. In the course of a few generations the new towns transformed them into a people much like the Florentines themselves. The geographer and mathematician Agnolo da Scarperia, the painter Masaccio from San Giovanni, and Poggio Bracciolini, chancellor of the Florentine republic, from Terranuova, are only the most dramatic examples of new-town men who went to the city and excelled at careers that were possible only in urban cultures. At the same time city dwellers bought land in the area of the towns: a century earlier they would have considered these places dangerous wilderness.[3]

The political purpose of the new towns was served by a settlement policy that was highly structured. The Florentines did not plan to fill their foundations with families who came to the sites of their own free will. The government's aim, expressed in instructions to the Florentine agent at Scarperia in 1306 (Document 4) and in the outline of the Giglio Fiorentino project of 1350 (Documents 19, 20), was to move entire populations from individual villages.

The plan to use the village as the unit of resettlement, while often imperfectly carried out, had a strong influence on the layout of the towns. The residents of the villages were not only taken as a group but were settled that way as well. This kind of block relocation was common in founded towns. At Alessandria in Piedmont, in the twelfth century, seven communes came together to form the city under the auspices of the first Lombard League. Each maintained its own customs, elected representatives to the city government, and had its own church.[4] Cuneo, also in Piedmont,[5] and L'Aquila in the Abruzzi,[6] founded in 1198 and 1254 respectively, had similar arrangements. In these towns only the churches, scattered evenly across the plans, indicate the separate territories of the immigrating villages. Characteristically, the Florentine plans make this demographic structure much more regular.

In the Florentine towns residential neighborhoods formed around the streets one block removed from the main thoroughfare. In most of the towns houses faced onto these streets from both sides, doubling the activity that took place there. The plans further articulated the residential areas by quartering the space within the defenses. Within each quarter the intersection of a residential street and a secondary cross street defined a focal point that offers a valuable clue about settlement patterns in the towns. At San Giovanni the intersections within the quarters were the sites of neighborhood wells, supplementing the town well on the central square (see Fig. 5). At Terranuova each intersection was the site of a church (see Fig. 17).

Terranuova was founded after twelve villages in the upper Arno valley petitioned the government of Florence to build a town in their area in which they could live in safety from the local barons (Document 16). The new town's population was made up of residents from these villages, but only the names of churches indicate the origin of the new settlers. Three of the churches in the town repeat the dedications and site names of churches in the petitioning villages.[7] At Scarperia the names of the quarters, which were also the town's administrative subdivisions, repeat the names of the patron saints of important villages that contributed settlers.[8] The unevenness of this town's development — in 1356 its most populous quarter accommodated 104 families while its smallest hosted only 32 — may have been a result of the Florentine policy of village relocation. A similar case of uneven growth is visible in the plan of Castelfranco di Sopra (see Fig. 11) and seems inexplicable if the immigrants had been placed only according to the economic desirability of the house lots.

The preservation of longstanding units of population in the new towns contradicted the ultimate goals of Florentine policy. Just how seriously the parochial character of the residential quarters compromised the unity of the towns is demonstrated by the history of the church at Terranuova. At the time of the town's foundation the main church, to the extent that there was one, stood at the center of the town's west quarter. This was San Biagio ai Mori, which had probably served the area before the town was sited. The town had no common parish and the central square hosted only a small oratory. The church located in the square today, called Santa Maria di Piazza after Castel Santa Maria, the official name of the town, was not established until the fifteenth century.[9]

This fragmentation existed during the early years of many of the new towns. The evidence from Scarperia (see Fig. 21) is more dramatic. There, as late as 1408, the residential quarters were so fiercely divided that the settlers fought one another along neighborhood lines. The Florentine *Signoria* had to intervene, writing to the city's official at Scarperia about the crisis.[10]

The division of the new towns into quarters was attractive to Florentine town builders for many reasons. One of these was familiarity. The quarters reflected the structure of their own city, which had six internal precincts before 1343 and four after that. These divisions had an impact on many aspects of public life in Florence: taxes were levied, armies raised, justice administered, and government officers selected by precinct. With the change from *sestieri* to *quartieri*, the number of priors decreased from twelve to eight. The authority of the precincts extended into the countryside, each quarter taking administrative responsibility for the territory beyond its section of the city wall. The demography of the precinct re-flected this. Immigrants to the city moved to the section of town nearest their place of origin, finding there fellow countrymen who helped to establish them in the capital.[11] Thus the Florentines, too, had experienced the advantages of finding old friends in new places. By allowing the villagers to move into the new towns with their circle of neighbors, the planners may have hoped to make the transition less daunting and win support for their experiment.

Whatever the city's original approach to the quartering of the new towns, experience taught its officials caution. The *Signoria*'s solution to the disturbances at Scarperia was to eliminate the quarters and to organize the town "as a single body."[12] Long before this, with the planning of Giglio Fiorentino in 1350, the Florentines had recognized the advantage of a unified community and modified their new-town scheme to eliminate any trace of the settlers' origins (see Fig. 29).

The design of Giglio Fiorentino was directly descended from that of Terranuova, its immediate predecessor. It departed from its model, how-ever, in every detail that had to do with the settlement of the immigrant population. Giglio was to have only one church which, sited on the central square, would have served all the residents of the town. Like the parish church at one of the villages whose residents were to be relocated into the new town, it would have been dedicated to Saint Peter. The other six villages were not represented in any of the nomenclature of the new town and did not feature in the names of the gates (quarters, as such, are never mentioned). The residential area of the town was divided into four equal sections, but the plan adjustments at Terranuova that gave the quarters focus and independent, formal identities disappeared at Giglio. A succes-sion of roadways with house fronts on a single side replaced the double-loaded residential streets. The cross streets that defined the neighborhood centers were deleted. The Giglio plan had only one center, which seems to reflect a new urgency in eradicating the traces of the old order. Despite the failure of the project, Giglio's was the first town scheme based on a policy that increasingly dominated the Florentine new-town effort. Having suc-ceeded in wresting the rural population from the control of the feuda-tories, the Florentines turned their attention to consolidating the new communities and strengthening the bonds of these new centers with the city.[13]

The families called upon to emigrate to the Florentine towns seem, on the whole, to have welcomed the invitation and given the projects their support. Their cooperation was not won by immediate material gain. Florence offered an initial five to ten years of tax freedom, but the savings from these abatements were offset by the cost of building houses and defenses. Except at Pietrasanta, an early project on a desolate site, the city never distributed farmland to the settlers. At San Giovanni and at Castelfranco in the fertile Valdarno, the immigrants were responsible for the cost of acquiring the land on which the towns were laid out (Document 2). At Scarperia the city was more generous; settlers were given their lots without payment and they received a full ten years of tax freedom. But these were special terms, dictated by the precarious situation in the Mugello in 1306. Settlers at Scarperia were wise to fear the counterattack of the nobles whose temporary defeat by the city had produced the occasion for the town's foundation. Florence responded to their concerns by accepting responsibility for the property they declared on the tax roles, offering to repay twice its value if it was damaged by an enemy attack (Document 7). Despite the danger, Florentine officials were able to move enough people to Scarperia to establish a viable settlement within a short time of the foundation. Florentine military strength in the area gave the settlers little choice. At the time the city declared the foundation of Scarperia, its armies captured and destroyed the Ubaldini castle at Monteaccianico, the central stronghold of the feudatories who dominated the Mugello.

At Scarperia and Firenzuola the Florentines could offer settlers a special inducement. Unlike the Arno valley towns of San Giovanni and Castelfranco, whose populations had been under Florentine control before they were relocated to new towns, the Apennine towns drew their populations from villages only recently won from the feudatories. For these settlers relocation was accompanied by a dramatic change in their civil condition; Florence freed its new Apennine subjects from serfdom. The Florentine law of 1289 that prohibited the sale of peasants in Florentine territory was an early landmark in the extension of basic liberties to a large segment of the rural population. The law began with the moral assertion that "liberty derives from one's self, not others,"[14] but its attack on the central institution of the old order in the countryside obviously had a partisan motivation as well. As islands of nonfeudal relationships in the countryside, all new towns implemented this policy, but the foundation documents for Scarperia and Firenzuola addressed it directly. Like similar documents for other towns, they exclude magnates from the area of the foundation. In the case of Scarperia and Firenzuola, however, the city also proclaimed the freedom of immigrants who spent a decade in either one of the towns. In the eyes of Florentine law new-town residents "and their descendants" were "free and absolved from any obligations of servitude or loyalty or homage or service or tax and from any other duty no matter what conditions may have existed in the past" (Document 3).

While there could be an initial resistance to moving—as the postponement of relocation deadlines in the Giglio Fiorentino documents and the ultimate failure of that project suggest—once immigrants were settled in the Florentine towns they soon found common cause with their new masters. The Florentine documents may exaggerate when they characterize the desire of the immigrants to Terranuova to recover their "liberty" and to "return to their wonted obedience to the city of Florence like a child at the breast of its pious mother" (Document 16), but there is evidence that the new situation worked to the advantage of both the city and the settlers.

In 1338, just eighteen months after the formation of the Terranuova community, the city's new subjects attacked a neighboring village still controlled by the Guidi magnates. Florence reacted to preserve order. Government officials scolded the Terranuovan residents and commanded them to pay eight thousand florins compensation, but they also allowed them to keep the village and its lands which, according to Giovanni Villani, were worth twice that amount.[15] Villani, predictably, paints a picture of innocent Florentine subjects protecting themselves against fractious neighbors. At the same time, however, he cannot resist praising the Terranuovans for their expansion of the borders of the Florentine state.

When new-town residents had to decide between their old lords and the Florentines, they sided with the city. The residents of Scarperia were presented with this choice in January 1352. The circumstances were not propitious for the Florentines. The new-town residents had just been involved in a brawl with the city's garrison in which a number of townsmen had been killed. Thinking that they might take advantage of the town's mood, the Ubaldini, from whose subjects the new-town population had been drawn, infiltrated the town's defenses and attempted, in a confusing midnight scene, to incite the population against the Florentine soldiers. In Matteo Villani's account, the townsmen uncovered the deception, rejected the alliance with the Ubaldini, and came to the aid of the Florentine forces.[16]

Confrontations with enemies beyond the town walls helped to establish a sense of common cause between the settlers and their Florentine protectors. The main burden of unifying the towns and strengthening their ties with the mother city, however, fell to the town's own institutions. Government and church acted as focal points for community identity and group action and taught the townspeople Florentine ways.

Government in the new towns had two branches. A town council represented the local population. Composed of *penonieri,* delegates from the quarters, and *gonfalonieri,* senior officers, it was responsible for supervising the town's market and overseeing trade, for outfitting and training the citizen militia, and for maintaining the town wall and roads and streets within the township. It hired professional assistants, appointed citizen committees, and, occasionally, dealt directly with the Florentine government. The branch of government that represented Florentine interests in the new towns was headed by an officer called a *podestà.* He was a citizen of Florence appointed by the *Signoria* to serve a six-month term. The *podestà* was a judge, a soldier, and a policeman, and he brought with him a small staff of soldiers and clerks. He maintained regular contact with Florence but was also closely associated with the town council. He attended the meetings of the council, and the councilmen, in turn, reviewed his conduct in office for the Florentine government.[17]

The form of new-town government was Florentine. The council and *gonfalonieri* reproduced the pattern of offices held by citizens in the city, and a *podestà* was the chief legal and administrative officer in both places. In neither city nor town was the *podestà* a local resident, but whereas the Florentine *podestà* was an appointee of the citizens, in the new towns he was chosen by outsiders and represented their authority. Despite such differences, however, sovereign city and subject town administered public affairs in a similar manner. Townsmen were ruled by written law and the form of their statutes was based on Florentine precedent. They participated in public debate on local issues and competed in a political process that awarded the honor of office and the responsibility of making decisions. Knowing only feudal law and the rudimentary political structures of their native villages, the immigrants to the new towns needed the experience of local government to bridge the gap between their rural past and their future with the city.

Along with the institutions of government, the church provided Florentine town builders with the best access to the settlers' social habits. The intimacy of the spiritual relationship and the preeminence of church and altar in the public environment offered opportunities which the town planners were well equipped to exploit. The Florentines considered the foundation of churches at the earliest stage in the creation of a settlement. At Giglio Fiorentino the church on the central square was as much a part of the new-town scheme as the street plan itself, and at Firenzuola there is evidence that the city was even prepared to fund construction of the place of worship (Document 14).

Construction was not, however, the difficult part of establishing a church in a new town. The building itself was of limited value if its clergy did not have the authority to administer the sacraments and control church affairs. These were the privileges of a parish church, but the town builders were not empowered to award parish status. Even the bishop, who had the authority, was limited in his freedom to accommodate city officials by a venerable parish system that, long before the fourteenth century, had assigned all of the Tuscan countryside.

The easiest solution, used by the city whenever possible, was to circumvent the system by relocating a parish church from one of the immigrating villages. Some variation of this strategy provided San Giovanni, Castelfranco, Terranuova, and Giglio Fiorentino with churches. When relocation was impossible, the issue of the church could become the focus of a confrontation between the new town and the old order. This occurred at Scarperia, where the determined resistance of the parish prompted a particularly energetic response from the city. The open conflict produced unique written documentation; a rich body of ecclesiastical papers expresses the commitment of the city and of the town.

The first church at Scarperia, dedicated to San Iacopo and San Filippo, was established at the time of the town's foundation. This church was not, however, an independent institution. The settlement site stood within the confines of a long-established parish whose church, Santa Maria di Fagna, was located only one mile south of the new town center. The prior and canons of Fagna took charge of the church at Scarperia and retained their offices for almost sixty years. Tension between the two institutions must have been considerable. Fagna was an Ubaldini establishment. The baronial family had been lords in the parish for centuries and the Fagna church preserved vivid signs of their patronage. The building's greatest monument was the tomb of Cardinal Ottaviano de'Ubaldini. Ottaviano, who died in 1272, had been bishop of Bologna, the cardinal protector of the Camaldese order, and the papal legate for Italy.[18] In the Mugello he attempted to consolidate the family holdings by purchasing towns and enlarging and strengthening the castle of Monteaccianico. The Florentine army's destruction of Monteaccianico and the relocation of its population in the new town was the story of Scarperia's foundation. The fact that a priest and a body of canons tied by tradition to the Ubaldini continued to minister to the spiritual life of the new community was not merely ironic, it may have been intolerable.

According to a petition from the town's residents in 1364, the Fagna clergy paid minimal attention to the congregation at Santi Iacopo e Filippo.

In that document they ask the bishop of Florence for permission to engage their own priest, one who would live in the town and minister exclusively to its needs (Document 9). The petition was granted, but the conditions of the document made clear the strong claim of the old parish. In order to get their own priest, who remained dependent on Fagna and could not baptize, the residents of Scarperia had to pay the canons of the old church a special fee of forty-five florins and guarantee that they would retain their estate within the town. Thus a new endowment had to be created for the local church. In return for these concessions Santi Iacopo e Filippo received as its ecclesiastical territory the area inside the town's defenses.

However modest and dearly bought, these first privileges marked the turning point for the church at Scarperia. Within eleven years, in 1375, Santi Iacopo e Filippo was granted the right to baptize and become a fully independent parish, and when the church's new status was pronounced, the confines of the parish were also expanded outside the town's walls. All of the territory as far north as the Apennine watershed was given to Santi Iacopo e Filippo (Document 10). Although the new parish had been carved from the territory of the parish at Fagna, no additional tribute was exacted from the residents of the new town. This time the bishop expressly defended the church at Scarperia against the claims of the Fagna clergy. At last the church at Scarperia truly belonged to the town. The effort that it cost the residents and their Florentine patrons is some measure of the importance the city government ascribed to this endeavor. The creation of the parish was a landmark in the establishment of the community and, by extension, in the success of Florentine territorial policy.[19]

In the sixty years before Scarperia gained an independent parish — years of prosperity in which the settlers became increasingly attached to Florence — the town was not without the ministrations of a local church. Between 1324 and 1326 the Augustinian order founded a convent in the town.[20] Although the foundation had papal authority, its location was hotly contested by the clergy at Fagna.[21] The case was heard by the *guardiano* of the Franciscan order in Florence, but final settlement of the affair in favor of the Augustinians may have been a foregone conclusion.[22]

The Augustinian establishment was tailor-made to satisfy Florentine requirements. Independent of the parish system that gave Fagna a stranglehold on Santi Iacopo e Filippo, the conventual church was allied with Florence through the convent at Santo Spirito. The Florentine government may well have promoted its establishment. A seventeenth-century account in the Augustinian archives says that the Florentines gave at least their permission (Document 11), but the convent's dedication suggests a

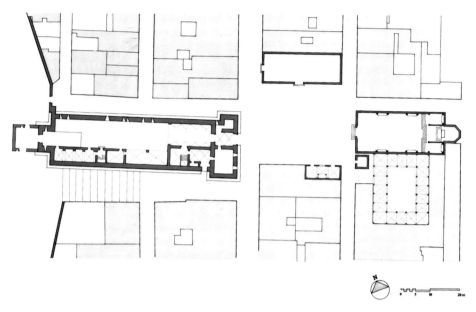

91 Scarperia. Plan of the square.

closer connection. The establishment was called San Barnaba, repeating the official name of the town, Castel San Barnaba. More concrete evidence of a formal tie between the convent and the city appears in the fifteenth century. In 1439 the council of the Florentine province that was administered from Scarperia reconfirmed the church of San Barnaba as the place where the vicar of the province took his oath of office.[23] The convent was also well integrated with the town. Gifts document local devotion as early as the middle of the fourteenth century.[24] Indeed, San Barnaba was as much a product of the townsmen as of the Augustinian order of the city — five of the seven brothers who participated in the convent's foundation were from local families (Document 11).

The parochial church of Santi Iacopo e Filippo and the conventual church of San Barnaba (Figs. 91, 92; see Fig. 90) sit next to one another on Scarperia's main square (see Fig. 25). Matteus, the Florentine official in charge of the foundation, sited the parochial church on the north side of the square, facing the town's main street. San Barnaba, which had to be fitted onto the plan after almost two decades of building, was inserted at the eastern end of the square, encroaching on its space. Today the two buildings appear similar. They are both wood-roofed, aisleless halls. San

92 Scarperia. Central square, seen from the east.

Barnaba measures 14.3 by 35.3 meters; Santi Iacopo e Filippo 10.5 by 27 meters. They are buildings of limited architectural distinction that nonetheless command considerable attention within the square. Their size, in itself, is impressive. They must have towered over early-fourteenth-century houses, which were not likely to have boasted more than two stories and a total height of 6 meters. Their form, too, separates them from their neighbors. Tall central doors and broad unfenestrated side walls present an aspect very different from the openings of the abutting buildings. Gabled roofs would have separated the churches from the line of flat eaves that capped the domestic structures. At ground level, steps projecting into the street mark a significant deviation from the norm established for private building. They indicate that the church floor lay at a higher level than the ground floors of the houses and also that the church was privileged because it could usurp public space. According to town statutes, no individual could occupy even a few feet of the space outside his front door for more than a few days or weeks. The churches of Santi Iacopo e Filippo and San Barnaba threw their stone risers onto public land as a permanent marker of their position on the plan and their stature within the community.

While distinguishing itself by advancing on the main street, Santi Iacopo e Filippo achieved a similar result by retreating from the square. The original assignment of land to the church seems to have been six lots, three on the main street, three on the back streets of the block on the northeast side of the square. The total area of the grant was 15.5 by 27 meters. While the full length of the property was used, conforming the church to the block, five meters of its width were left vacant. The area reverted to the square from which, today, it is indistinguishable. Before the facades of the houses to its right and left were screened by the construction of the Florentine castle and the church of San Barnaba, this setback would have broken the continuity between the church and its neighbors. This same simple device was used by some modestly sized churches in Florence. San Barnaba on the Via Guelfa and San Michele Visdomini on the Via dei Servi are both located at the intersections of long streets with important cross streets. Their plain facades lie 5 to 7 meters behind the fronts of their neighbors, creating a visual caesura and a small church parvis to shelter the church door from street traffic.

The site assigned to San Barnaba gave it an important role in the townscape both inside and outside the walls. From its position at the foot of the square the church turned its facade to the most active space in the town. Unlike Santi Iacopo e Filippo which, by conforming to the orientation of

93 *Saint Francis Driving the Devils from Arezzo,* early fourteenth century. Upper church of St. Francis, Assisi (Photograph: Anderson/Alinari 15355).

the house lots, had an ambiguous relation to the square, San Barnaba provided a prominent backdrop for all public events that took place there. At the same time the church occupied a section of the perimeter of the plan. The east end of the church stood so close to the town's defenses that at least once, in 1360, it had to be rebuilt when they were.[25] It may even have played a role, as many churches did, in the town's fortifications.[26]

Church apses were a valued feature of the view of the townscape seen from the countryside. The churches of great cities had towers and cupolas to signal their presence in the urban landscape; in more modest places the tall church apse, especially if it was near the town wall, could serve the same function. An early-fourteenth-century fresco from the upper church of Saint Francis at Assisi (Fig. 93) demonstrates the fourteenth-century reading of this architectural image. The subject of the fresco is Saint Francis driving the devils from the city of Arezzo. The walled city on its hillside site occupies the right-hand side of the picture. Many buildings are visible, both private and public, but there is no church. Saint Francis approaches the gate of the city from the left; he gestures and the devils flee. Francis's power is explained by a huge church building at his side. Shown in isolation, the church is to be added to the city to represent the community's new-found piety. Indeed, it already shows its characteristic townscape view: we see only its east end.

The extent to which the east end of churches was built to proclaim the godliness of a community is hard to gauge. At least one case is indisputable. The exterior of the choir that Nicola Pisano added to the cathedral of Massa Marittima (Fig. 94) is richly decorated with tall gables and elaborate carving. It is, however, almost invisible from within the city. The facade of the church faces the city's handsome public square; the apse rises high above the town wall. It looks out over the valley and dominates the road that climbs up from the sea to enter the town at the nearby main gate. From the point of view of the visitor, it is the most prominent monument in the townscape.

In its modest way, San Barnaba in Scarperia is the same. Santi Iacopo e Filippo's internal position on the plan and its lack of any tall feature hide it from the countryside. San Barnaba stands prominently on the town's east side, visible from far across the plain. Its apse and, after 1474, its bell tower[27] would have symbolized the protection of the church.

In the early years of the settlement at Scarperia, when Santi Iacopo e Filippo was dispiritedly officiated by the prior at Fagna, San Barnaba must have been invaluable to the community for the spiritual care and friendly

94 Massa Marittima. Cathedral from outside the city wall (Photograph: Alinari 21806).

gathering place that it provided. The most visible program that the friars sponsored to engage the residents in the convent's activities was a religious and moral society of laymen. Dedicated to the Nativity of the Virgin, the confraternity came to be known as the *Compagnia di Piazza,* from the site of the oratory adjacent to the convent, on the south side of the town square. It was founded in 1327[28] and received official episcopal sanction in 1364, the same year that the Florentine bishop awarded the townsmen the right to maintain their own priest at Santi Iacopo e Filippo.[29]

Our direct knowledge of the Company in the first one hundred and fifty years of its existence is sketchy. In the mid-sixteenth century, however, a set of statutes gives a full description of its activities. At that date it was, like many other organizations in the cities of the late Middle Ages and Renaissance, composed of men who had banded together to undertake activities to promote the salvation of their souls. Prayers for the dead were the heart of its efforts. At the death of each member the officers arranged obsequies "in order that [the deceased's] work in the Company shall not have been in vain."[30]

The Company's "work" was religious, moral, and charitable. Religious exercises consisted only of confessing and taking communion once a year, and participating in the memorial masses for the Company's dead, celebrated on the first Sunday of every month. Morality was addressed in a code of behavior. Members were expected to forswear gaming, profanity, and personal grudges.[31] Charitable work established the *Compagnia di Piazza'*s central position in the community at Scarperia. The organization maintained a full schedule of social services for the benefit of its membership and their fellow townsmen. A bequest of 1348 provided income to support the society's distribution of bread.[32] By the mid-sixteenth century it maintained a grain storage hall, located on the second story of the San Barnaba cloister.[33] A hospice outside the town's northern gate was maintained and administered as early as the fourteenth century by the Company.[34] Another hospice, located on the town's market field and already in existence in 1320,[35] passed into the Company's care sometime before the end of the fifteenth century. Both establishments served pilgrims traveling to Rome, the town's orphans, and the sick. Whatever medical treatment was available in these hospices, or in Scarperia in general, seems to have been provided by one of the brothers of San Barnaba. By the sixteenth century the Company was also giving alms in the form of money. Its six elected officials had discretion over amounts up to six soldi; larger bequests were available with the approval of the Company's council of thirty. The council also made annual awards to supplement the dowries of the town's young women;[36] it established an endowment to support a schoolmaster[37] and made contributions to the town's two churches.[38]

The membership of the *Compagnia di Piazza* in the fourteenth century constituted only a small percentage of the new town's population. In 1353, in a period when 234 families resided in Scarperia,[39] the Company's total voting body was, at most, forty-two men.[40] Coming from a broad range of economic levels, the forty-two were, however, a fair representation of the community as a whole. In the mid-century tax lists half the members were assessed in the middle and upper categories while the other half had only modest estates. Only women and those men who declared themselves to be without any property were absent from the Company's roles. The geographic distribution of the membership was similarly even. The brothers came from every neighborhood and the number from each quarter was very roughly in proportion to its population.[41] The membership did not represent a provincial patriciate. It was not dominated by a few families or by the residents of one neighborhood. It was, instead, a cross section of the population that came together at Scarperia. Within twenty-five years of its foundation the *Compagnia di Piazza* had created for its members the kind of society that the Florentines aspired to for the new town as a whole. Tied to one another by the bonds of ritual fraternity, the brothers traded, if only for limited periods of each month, their old social identities for a new one defined by the Company.

In Florence, lay brotherhoods like the Company were models for the population of the larger community, promoting unity and peace.[42] In a city in which networks of patronage, essential for both business and politics, made neighborhood and family associations very powerful, the confraternities offered one of the most effective and widely available opportunities for heads of households to broaden their circle of contacts. Confraternities like the Company of the Virgin of Orsanmichele drew members from all parts of the city (and, in this case, from the countryside as well), binding them with ties of fraternal love and obligation into a society that transcended the geographic and class boundaries that affected most of daily life. This was an invaluable service to the commune. The confraternities served the city by preaching peace among the often bellicose factions of its population. The flagellant Company of Santa Maria del Carmine was founded in 1431 for "the salvation and peace of our city and of every citizen."[43] As early as the thirteenth century the Orsanmichele Company sponsored a weekly mass at which the members prayed to "God to conserve and maintain in true peace and unity our city and the members of our company."[44] The Company itself was to be the seed of this unity. Its

behavior was intended as a model for the community at large. The thirteenth-century statutes of the Company of San Gilio order the members
"to comport themselves honestly, and to love one another. And when we
are found together we should honor and aid each other in a spirit of
friendship so that other persons observing us will make a good example of
us."[45]

The *Compagnia di Piazza* was well positioned to exercise this kind of
influence at Scarperia. Not only were its members tied to all segments of
the population, they were also men of responsibility: twenty-four of the
twenty-eight brothers named in 1353 were heads of households and at
least two of them served on the town council in this period.[46] The Company itself gained status from its distribution of charity, which was treated
as a form of patronage, and also from its role as the guardian of the much
adored Madonna on the altar of the Company's oratory.

The oratory from which the *Compagnia di Piazza* took its name made an
invaluable contribution to the role that the Company played in Scarperia.
The oratory had a physical prominence that was unusual among confraternal meeting places. Its site, adjacent to the conventual church and
opposite the parochial one, put it at the center of community life. For the
most part confraternities were housed more modestly. A residential building, or the sacristy of a church, or rooms within a convent cloister and an
altar in the nearby church represent the more common seats of lay brotherhoods. The ambitions of the Scarperia Company exceeded any of these
arrangements. With a remarkable show of power the young Company
was able to acquire the site best suited to its needs, despite the fact that a
substantial residential structure was already situated there,[47] and to build
an oratory of architectural splendor unmatched elsewhere in the town.

The building that served as the oratory of the *Compagnia di Piazza* until
the Company's suppression in 1784 is, today, a three-story structure on a
rectangular plan, measuring 11 by 5 meters (Fig. 95; see Figs. 25, 91). The two
upper stories are now broken up into three rooms each, but the ground
floor remains undivided. This, the oratory proper, is covered by three bays
of rib vaults. Under the center vault, attached to the back wall, is a gabled
baldachin within which a full-length image of the Virgin presides over the
Company's altar. One of the oratory's long sides, and its major facade,
faces the square. The wall is opened by doors at either end and a large
arched window at its center. The window is screened by an iron grate and
can be closed by wooden shutters. When the shutters are open, the window allows an almost unobstructed view of the baldachin, the altar, and
the Virgin directly behind it (Fig. 96).

95 Scarperia. Oratory of the *Compagnia di Piazza,* from the square.

96 Scarperia. Oratory of the *Compagnia di Piazza,* interior.

97 Oratory of the *Compagnia di Piazza* in the fourteenth century. Reconstruction.

In 1353 the Company assembled "under the loggia and the tabernacle of the Society."[48] That structure survives in the present building but it has been significantly changed. The oratory of 1353, although it was at least five meters tall, had only a single story. It was not until 1484 that the roof of the oratory was raised "because it was as low as the vaults."[49] The addition of a second and maybe a third story brought the accommodations of the *Compagnia di Piazza* up to the standards of the Florentine confraternities. The *Confraternita del Bigallo,* for example, had a street-level oratory, built between 1352 and 1361, which supported a hall for business meetings on the second floor.[50] It is to this period of enlargement in the fifteenth century that the architectural detail of the facade belongs. The door and window frames of the ground and second story are in the style of the Renaissance, their proportions and profiles those of the Florentine architecture of the later fifteenth century. On the inside of the oratory, however, there is no doubt that we are in the presence of the structures cited in 1353. The vaults are particularly distinctive. Their flat curve, thick transverse arches and octagonal ribs, and, along the rear wall, the prismatic corbels from which they spring are familiar in Florentine Dominican conventual architecture of the early fourteenth century.[51] The most prominent element inside the oratory is a baldachin, or "tabernachulo," that occupies the middle of the back wall. It is a groin-vaulted canopy of conspicuously large size, supported by two freestanding and two attached twisted columns.[52]

If the vaults and the baldachin in the oratory building at Scarperia almost surely belong to the complex that was mentioned in 1353, one element of that description is strikingly absent. The present oratory is not a loggia. Of its four sides, the two abutting adjacent properties and one on the side street must always have been closed. The side facing the square is now also defined by a wall, but this was not always the case. Immured within the late-fifteenth-century masonry are two slim octagonal piers. They have tall pedestals, simple prismatic bases, and foliate capitals, like their counterparts in the Dominican aisled halls, and from them spring the ribs of the vault of the loggia.

Situated within a loggia, the oratory would have had a significant impact on the square in front of it (Fig. 97). Although its roof was originally "as low as the vaults," the oratory was the height of a two-story house, and its architecture was cast on the monumental scale of the adjacent churches. The arches dominated the loggia's face to the square. Each was 5 meters high at its crown and 3.5 meters wide. The surrounding architectural frame was minimal: the faceted *pietra serena* piers were too slender to make a strong visual barrier between the openings, while the eaves of the low shed roof shaded the shallow spandrels. Only a step or two separated the Company's sanctuary from the public space of the piazza.

In this setting the tabernacle, and the altar of the Virgin that it enshrined, took on a special character. The covered space of the loggia was only part of the Company's ceremonial complex. It was the stage on which the members performed their services for the community; the square itself served as the auditorium. The tabernacle and altar, placed on the long wall of the rectangular sanctuary, were oriented toward the square and scaled to it. The altar complex was a focus of attention whether services were being celebrated or not. The architectural setting heightened that effect considerably. Seen from the square, the altar and the image of the Virgin were twice framed: by the tabernacle and also by the vaults of the oratory itself.

The loggia of the *Compagnia di Piazza* is unlike other fourteenth-century confraternal oratories. Even those housed in open-walled buildings, like the oratories of the Orsanmichele and Bigallo companies in Florence, of the Company of the Stecchata in Pisa, or of the Company of the Rosaio in Lucca, still provided space for worshippers under their roofs. Although it may have been possible to build the oratory at Scarperia as a loggia only because of this tradition, the immediate architectural model for the design comes from a building type generally used for very different purposes.

In the fourteenth century the loggia was part of the architecture of private families and governmental bodies. It was a ceremonial place for hearing cases of law or for signing documents.[53] Secular loggie took a variety of forms. They could have one, two, three, or more bays. They could be vaulted, or not. What they had in common was a configuration that allowed events taking place within them to be visible from a space outside. Often they had the same stagelike orientation as the loggia of the *Compagnia di Piazza.* The Loggia dei Priori, the ceremonial shelter adjacent to the Florentine town hall, was just such a structure. A more modest example is the loggia in front of the government palace in Certaldo, a town which, like Scarperia, was a Florentine provincial capital.

Every Florentine new town was required to have a loggia for use by the city's officer. In the description of Giglio Fiorentino the fittings of the central square are listed as a church, a well, and the "casa del commune" with a loggia "in which the official of the town for the commune of Florence resides [*stia*]" (Document 19). At San Giovanni the loggia was probably located on the open ground floor of the Palazzo Comunale. The nineteenth-century cadastral maps of Terranuova and Firenzuola both show a loggia projecting into the street from the town hall (see Figs. 16, 27). The statutes of Castelfranco di Sopra, dating to 1394, twice mention a loggia that is used for public functions.[54] Scarperia, too, had a public loggia. The statutes of 1423 of the league of towns centered at Scarperia required all the residents to participate in funeral services for their fellows and to assemble after the ceremonies in the loggia.[55] Elsewhere in the statutes the loggia was designated as one of four places — along with the market field, the piazza, and the palace of the *podestà* — over which the government had special jurisdiction.[56]

The oratory of the *Compagnia di Piazza* is the only structure that we know of in fourteenth-century Scarperia whose site and architecture made it suitable as a public loggia. Whether it was used as such in addition to serving the confraternity is a question unanswered by the surviving documentation. The fusion of confraternal and government facilities would have been unusual but not unknown in Florentine territory. Indeed, Florence's largest fourteenth-century confraternity, the Company of the Virgin of Orsanmichele, had its seat in the city's grain market and warehouse. The association of a religious image with a place of political assembly posed no contradiction in the late Middle Ages. Churches were commonly the sites of government meetings,[57] while chambers within towns halls were often enriched with chapels and images of patron saints. The Sala del

Consiglio in Siena's Palazzo Pubblico contains perhaps the best-known example of a holy image in a political setting. Like the queen of the city that she was, the Virgin of Simone Martini's *Virgin in Majesty* dominates the council chamber from her position on its end wall and admonishes the town councillors to "search out justice, ye who rule the land." Siena's Palazzo Pubblico offers a further parallel to a politically engaged oratory in the Cappella di Piazza, which was begun in front of the town hall in 1352. A votive for the city's delivery from the plague of 1348, the Cappella provided an open-air altar facing Siena's Campo that could serve as the stage for public ceremonies in which the city's patron, the Virgin, was visibly present.

The association of the oratory of the *Compagnia di Piazza* at Scarperia with the public ceremonies of the town government is all the more plausible because of the special relationship that existed between the two institutions. While nominally a dependency of the Convent of San Barnaba, the Company was virtually unconstrained by the Augustinian friars. The two groups were mutually supportive, but there is no evidence of members of the order exercising authority over their lay brothers. Such religious autonomy was characteristic of most Florentine confraternities. The Scarperia Company's ties to the institutions of government, however, were more constraining and much less common. In the surviving documents of the fourteenth century the Company appears almost as an agency of the public authority. At mid-century the system for electing the Company's officers was fixed by the town council and registered in the official town records.[58] Control of the Company's estate was shared by the council and the Company's officers, and the administration of Company affairs was the equal responsibility of both bodies.[59] At the end of the fifteenth century the Company's officers were chosen in the palace of the Florentine official.[60] Behind this affiliation lay the Florentine government; it is hard to imagine that any of the activities of the Company were undertaken without the city's approval and support. The construction of a richly decorated oratory on a fine site in the center of Scarperia would seem to have demanded Florentine participation. Indeed, the oratory and the Madonna on its very public altar served Florentine interests more directly than did any other aspect of the Company's presence in the town.

The institution of the lay confraternity was largely an urban phenomenon. Its participatory and emotional form of devotion and its corporate and republican administrative structure were probably unknown to Scarperia's immigrants in the villages of their earlier lives.[61] The *Compagnia di Piazza* introduced all this—and something more—to the residents at

Scarperia. The Company was not generically urban, but very specifically Florentine. Its model was the Company of the Virgin of Orsanmichele, the largest and richest confraternity in the city and the only one to enroll members from the countryside.[62] Attention was paid to the Virgin of Orsanmichele not only by the people but by the Florentine government as well. The Madonna had a reputation for miraculous powers, established in 1292, and had won a great following. Her status in the city was given formal recognition in 1365, when the Florentine *Signoria* declared the Mother of God the special advocate of the republic. The *Signoria* proclaimed the Feast of the Assumption a state holiday and initiated a public celebration that required the rectors of the city's churches, the superiors of its convents, and all the members of the government to march in procession to Orsanmichele where the Virgin was venerated at the Company's altar.[63]

As a society of devotion, dedicated to the singing of lauds and services for the salvation of its members, Scarperia's *Compagnia di Piazza* was the same type of religious brotherhood as that of Orsanmichele. Two wills from Scarperia attest to the townsmen's devotion to the Company in Florence as early as 1341.[64] What defines the *Compagnia di Piazza's* specific connection to the Orsanmichele institution is the image of the Virgin on the altar of the oratory and loggia. Painted by Jacopo del Casentino and executed shortly before his death in 1349,[65] the picture in Scarperia is of an enthroned Madonna (Fig. 98). As befits the queen of such a modest province, the size of the image is not large — 1.45 by 0.85 meters — and the royal court is no more than two angels. The Madonna, however, has a noble lineage. The model for the painting is the magnificent image, painted by Bernardo Daddi, that by 1347 stood on the altar at Orsanmichele (Fig. 99).[66]

The similarity between these two images lies, in large part, in the way the Madonna addresses the worshipper. In both pictures one is led into the sacred environment through the steady gaze of the Virgin. In both, her eyes are fixed, looking directly forward, but the features of her face and the rest of the picture are in movement. The pose of the child, especially, is energized. He shifts in his mother's embrace as she supports him familiarly with one arm behind his torso and the other across his legs, grasping the back of his knee and thigh. He gazes, like the viewer, at her face, and she tilts his body outward to display him. In both images Christ holds a finch in his left hand and reaches toward his mother with his right.

Bernardo Daddi's painting was the third picture of the Madonna to be venerated at Orsanmichele.[67] Like the image that preceded it, Bernardo's picture copied the original, thereby claiming a connection to it. If the

98 Jacopo del Casentino, *Virgin and Child with Angels,* ca. 1349. Oratory of the *Compagnia di Piazza,* Scarperia (Photograph: Soprintendenza alle Gallerie, Florence).

99 Bernardo Daddi, *Virgin and Child with Angels*, 1347. Orsanmichele, Florence
(Photograph: Soprintendenza alle Gallerie, Florence).

enormous popularity of the Orsanmichele Company after the plague of 1348 is any measure, Bernardo's new copy was a success. The Company at Scarperia may have hoped, in the same way, to call on the power, or at least on the popularity, of the Orsanmichele Madonna by a similar act of reference. The devotees of the Virgin of the *Compagnia di Piazza* held that she came to them already endowed with miraculous powers. According to an eighteenth-century history she was found in a well on the site where Scarperia was to be established.[68]

Although they belong to the same closely defined tradition of images, the Virgins of Orsanmichele and Scarperia differ in a way that seems especially significant. At the center of both pictures is Christ's right arm, which mediates the relationship between mother and child. In the Orsanmichele altarpiece the child's gesture is a tender caress of the Virgin's cheek. The more generous proportions of the Scarperia picture would seem to have forced a makeshift posture. Instead of touching his mother's face, Christ's stiffly extended arm now reaches only as far as the Virgin's bodice. Christ clasps Mary's robe in his outstretched hand, holding its two sides together. The gesture is unnatural both anatomically and as the action of a child. It is not, however, the result of a lack of skill; the picture is otherwise too accomplished. The awkwardness has a deeper root. Both the Orsanmichele and Scarperia altarpieces make reference to the themes of the marriage of Christ and the Church and the identification of Mary with the Church.[69] These themes receive an extremely human interpretation at Orsanmichele, where the relationship portrayed is gentle and affectionate. The mother and child at Scarperia are joined by less personal bonds. The pose of the figures is more formal, the spatial structure of the picture is flatter, and the gesture of Christ, wrapping the Virgin in a starry mantle, has a quality of ritual that is absent in the work at Orsanmichele.[70]

The difference between the two images has much to do with the historical circumstances surrounding their execution. The plague of 1348 which separates the dates when they were painted may well play a role. The different character of the two confraternities is equally important. The devotion at Orsanmichele was spontaneous in origin, emotional in character, and enriched with a vivid history. The *Compagnia di Piazza* was a step removed from the original spiritual forces of the confraternal movement; it received its form from a well-established model and was set in motion by powers outside the brotherhood. The prominent role of the Orsanmichele company in Florentine society was a result of the Company's own success. Just the opposite must be said of the *Compagnia di Piazza*. It was a creature of Florence and an instrument of Florentine authority. Its success was the success of Florentine territorial policy.

The Virgin of the *Compagnia di Piazza* was a unique focus of public attention in Scarperia. Her position within the town could not have been more central and her architectural surroundings could not have been more flattering. When the cloth that draped her was pulled back, she could be seen from almost anywhere on the square. When she was covered, her tabernacle pronounced the importance of her place. Hers was, without competition, the most prominent altar in the town.

The Virgin's presence made a strong statement. To the contemporary visitor it spoke about the town's allegiance to Florence. The architecture of the oratory prepared the onlooker for the Virgin's message. In both its original form and after its enclosure in the 1480s, the building was easily identified by its style with the city on the Arno. The picture was even more specific, recalling the city's special protectress at Orsanmichele. Astride the road from Bologna, northern Italy, Germany, and eastern Europe, Scarperia was for a century the first safe town inside Florentine territory. In a settlement exactly a day's ride from the city, and the major stopping point along the best route through the Apennines, there was no more advantageous place to site such a monument. To the fourteenth- and fifteenth-century population of the town, the Madonna of the *Compagnia di Piazza* represented the urban life that they had adopted by moving to the new town, and the unity of their new community. She oversaw the most solemn events in the town, and protected it in the same way that the Virgin of Orsanmichele protected Florence.

The relationship between Florence and its new towns was not initially intended to be one of mutual benefit. The towns were established as bulwarks against the city's enemies, their residents a resource that the Florentines had won in battle or acquired by purchase and treaty. The rough country folk who populated the new towns were subjects of the Florentines, not their equals. The civilizing process initiated by the *Compagnia di Piazza* and other public institutions of the new towns took time, and it was not only the immigrants who had to change. The attitude of the Florentines was as much a barrier to cooperative relations as were the limitations of the townsmen. By the end of the fifteenth century, however, citizens of the city had revised their perception of the townsmen. A chapter in the history of Scarperia clearly illustrates the stages of their changing point of view.

In 1349 and 1350 Scarperia was the center of command and supply for the Florentine war against the Ubaldini.[71] As a result the town became a target of the family's Milanese allies when they entered the Mugello in the fall of 1351. The thirteen-thousand-man army of the Visconti paid siege to Scarperia for fifty-seven days, attacking it three times and turning the battle over this small position into the most important encounter of the war. For Matteo Villani, who reported the events of the siege of Scarperia in an unprecedented nine chapters of the second book of his chronicle,[72] it was at the siege of Scarperia that Florence demonstrated its ability to defend its new territorial state.

Villani's account is full of details of the battle: the overwhelming strength of the enemy, the violence of its attack, the sophistication of its military engineers. By contrast, Scarperia was "a weak town, small in size, and walled on only one side,"[73] and its defenders were few. But the Florentine captain was "loyal and brave," the two hundred horsemen "hand picked and of good stock," and the three hundred infantrymen "expert."[74] Surrounded by an enemy so numerous that it "covered the plain" the defenders refused to surrender; "they intended to die on the battlements rather than give one merlon to the enemy."[75] The battle was furious. Catapults, sappers, a continual renewal of the attack by fresh troops, all the resources of the huge army were brought to bear on the Florentine fortress. Finally, in desperation, the Milanese commanders called on their best German mercenaries and offered them the lordly prize of ten thousand florins to attack. "Moved by vainglory and avarice," the German captain accepted the challenge. But the exhausted defenders, "throwing off their fear and disdaining rest," calmly held their fire until the enemy was on the walls and then repelled this midnight attack, too.[76] The Milanese were humiliated. The magnificent army, "led by good captains and supported by all the Ghibellines of Italy," could not take the "vilissimo castello" of Scarperia.[77] The heroes of the defense were the captain of the Mugello, the Florentine patricians who led reinforcements into the besieged town, and the city's foot soldiers who bore the brunt of the fighting.

In Villani's version of this story the battle for Scarperia was a victory for Florence alone. Its brave citizens were the primary heroes. We are told that the foot soldiers were led by Florentine sergeants, not that they — like their Milanese counterparts — were foreigners who fought for pay. If the commander of the Florentine forces was also a foreigner, then it was to the city's credit to have attracted such a man. Conspicuously absent from Villani's account is any mention of the local community's effort. Neither the bravery of its residents in battle nor the losses they suffered from the enemy's bombardment were especially significant. Like his brother, Giovanni Villani, forty years before, Matteo Villani considered the new towns exclusively as instruments of Florentine policy. His account of Scarperia's successful resistance to the Visconti siege is meant to be read in connection with the doleful tale of the Florentine army's failure in the field; it proves the city's wisdom in investing in the new towns.[78]

Subsequent accounts of the events of 1351 depend largely on that of Matteo Villani, retaining his emphasis on the importance of the siege of Scarperia in the defense of Florentine territory. The evolution of the story is in the identity of its heroes. The histories of Florence written in the fifteenth and sixteenth centuries play down the role of the German commander of the Florentine forces, Jacopo di Fiore, while the achievement of a Florentine patrician from the "house of the Medici" is, understandably, emphasized. In addition, these histories recognize and even dramatize the contribution of the Scarperia residents. In the early fifteenth century Leonardo Bruni begins his reconstruction of events by introducing the "terrazini" into the story and reporting the full contents of the Florentine *Provvisione* of 20 October 1351, in which the terms of official gratitude were outlined, including a recognition of the townsmens' role.[79] Writing in the middle of the fifteenth century, Poggio Bracciolini, himself a native of a new town, Terranuova, reverses Villani's priorities and makes the residents of Scarperia the backbone of the defense. A speech that he composes and sets in the voice of the Milanese commander is addressed to them. Demanding their surrender, it describes the horrors that await them: "to be a prisoner together with your children," and "the shame that must befall women and wives." These are domestic threats, meaningful only to men with families. Their poignancy comes from the fact that the defenders risked these dangers to remain faithful to the city. Poggio's "oppidani" are accomplished soldiers. It is they who foiled the enemy's attempt to tunnel into the town.[80] The official history written by Scipione Ammirato at the end of the sixteenth century focuses on the Medici contribution. It takes pains to identify the Giovanni de' Medici involved in the battle and even composes an oration to the troops for him. In Ammirato's history, the residents of Scarperia are presented as a significant percentage of the defenders. Loyal, strong, and skillful in arms, they are described as putting up a vigorous fight.[81]

The difference between Villani's account of these events and Ammirato's is startling. A few pages of history witness the emergence of an attitude toward provincial populations that is the basis of the modern territorial state. Judging from Bruni's and Poggio's versions of the story, the changes were already in the making in the fifteenth century. Thanks to these historians, the community at Scarperia became a respected if not yet equal partner in a political enterprise that drew on the resources of a broad geographic base.

Scarperia, like San Giovanni and Firenzuola, represented Florence in a special way. The vicarate of the Mugello was officially settled at Scarperia in 1415, but from the middle of the fourteenth century the new town was, in practice, the seat of the vicarate. The vicar administered a territory that stretched across the Apennines, circling Florence from Vicchio and Borgo San Lorenzo in the Mugello to Campi and Carmignano in the lower Arno valley.[82] The regional mission of the office made large demands on the town. The residence of the vicar and the seat of his court housed a staff of twenty-one soldiers, notaries, and servants, who assisted the Florentine patrician in executing his military and judicial duties.[83] Meetings of the council representing the residents of the vicarate, and the activity of the court with its broad jurisdiction both put pressure on the town's inns, its markets, its streets and central square.

The building that was the focus of the vicar's presence in Scarperia is the tremendous castlelike structure at the center of the town (see Figs. 46, 47). Begun about 1355 and the residence of the Florentine garrison five years later, the building occupies the entire western half of the original square.[84] It stretches from the town wall to the main street, a distance of almost seventy meters. Its blank side walls, opened only with shooting embrasures, loom over the adjacent residential streets; its tower dominates the townscape. The facade that faces onto the square has a more civil appearance: three stories of windows and colorful coats of arms open the wall and give it plastic relief. But even this decoration reinforces the building's primary message: the arms represent the succession of vicars in Scarperia, and like those men, the Palazzo Vicarile served Florence directly.

While all of the buildings around the square accommodated institutions that, in one way or another, were at the service of the mother city, the Palazzo Vicarile was the only one actually occupied by men who were the paid employees of Florence. Built by a Florentine official, commanded by a Florentine castellan, and the seat of the Florentine vicar of the Mugello, the castle served first the city and then the town. As a fortress its ultimate purpose was to preserve Florence's occupation of the site; as a civic building it housed the Florentine administration of a large provincial territory. Its dominant physical presence was on the scale of the whole Mugello. To the residents of the town and the province, and to the travelers on the road from Bologna who passed below its eastern facade, the castle represented Florentine rule.

All the new towns represented Florence, but the vicarial capitals did so more assertively. The buildings of Scarperia's central square gave visual expression to all aspects of the new-town mission. The oratory of the *Compagnia di Piazza* reflected Florentine influence within the community; the Palazzo Vicarile symbolized the city's political power in the province. Surrounded by these monuments, the town center witnessed the most significant events in the life of the region: the swearing in of the vicar, the public reading of the statutes, the devotions to the Virgin, and the assembly of the vicar's council. The most spectacular event in the town's history was celebrated in 1452. In that year the Hapsburg prince, Frederick, archduke of Austria and king of the Germans, passed through Tuscany on his way to Rome to celebrate his marriage and to be crowned Roman Emperor by Nicholas V. Florence offered its most splendid hospitality. The *Signoria* sent three ambassadors to Ferrara to greet Frederick and to accompany him across the Apennines. On 29 January the royal party broke its journey at Scarperia. The following morning a mission of twenty Florentine patricians and one hundred richly dressed young gentlemen went out to the new town. The Florentine and the royal suites confronted each other with full ceremony. A formal welcome was offered by Giannozzo Manetti for the Florentines and the appropriate compliments graciously returned for the future emperor by Aeneas Silvius Piccolomini. After the official reception the royal entourage and its Florentine escort began their parade south. From Scarperia they rode for a day through Florentine territory, arriving at the city at ten in the evening.[85] The splendid celebration at the Porta di San Gallo was the climax of the city's welcome, which began when Frederick had physically entered the Florentine state two days earlier, at Firenzuola. tine state two days earlier, at Firenzuola.

One hundred and fifty-three years after the foundation of the first Florentine new towns, the political organization of the Tuscan countryside had been completely reformed. From the Apennine watershed to Arezzo and Poggibonsi, the land had become Florentine. The city's ceremonial welcome of Frederick reflects the important role of the new towns in that change.

CHAPTER 7

NEW TOWNS AND THE URBANISM OF THE FLORENTINE MERCHANT COMMUNE

MEDIEVAL TOWNS AND CITIES were often represented as the re-creation of other, more famous places. Even authors who wrote about a city of the stature of Florence did not hesitate to identify a model that flattered it. The historian Wolfgang Braunfels drew attention to the importance of the exemplum for city planning by citing Dante, who declared Florence the most beautiful and famous of the daughters of Rome, fashioned in her image, and Giovanni Villani, for whom Florence had been built "al modo di Roma."[1] Florence's Roman heritage enhanced the city's claims to virtue and status,[2] but her lineage was not only ideological. Dante and Villani spoke about a physical similarity as much as a political or cultural one. For Villani the dedication and location of Florence's churches defined the ties between the two cities: "Let us begin in the east, at the Porta S. Piero. From that gate there is a street that goes to S. Pier Maggiore, just as in Rome."[3] The likeness was not to be found in exact imitation; the qualities of the original that medieval planners considered significant could be captured in abstract physical schemes.[4]

The identity of new towns could also be enhanced by borrowing and the very names of the medieval European towns reveal the founders' attempts to do so. Sometimes these names expressed merely the hope of success. If Frankfort an der Oder, Strassburg im Neumark, and Neubrandenburg in the German East, Pampelonne and Beauvais in the French department of Tarn, or Barcelonne, Cologne, Pavie, and Fleurance in the department of Gers prospered like their namesakes, their founders would have been more than satisfied. Often there was no political connection between a medieval new town and its model; there seems never to have been a physical one. Here the Florentine towns were the exception. Their names expressed commitment as well as expectation and were intimately tied to the city's honor. They marked the Florentine occupation of the countryside. The plans of the new towns, too, were inspired by Florence. It was not, however, the construction of like-named churches, the basis of the Florence – Rome resemblance, that connected Florence and its off-spring. In fact, the topography of the city had little to do with the bond. The new towns did not emulate the mundane Florence of late-thirteenth-century reality. They invoked, instead, the ideal Florence of contemporary imagination.

When Florentine writers and painters of the fourteenth and fifteenth centuries described the form of their native city, they glossed over specific topographical details, giving a generalized account of regular and recognizable shapes. Inevitably this produced some distortions. Florentine history was too long and the city too thickly built up for the physical environment to conform to any pattern simple enough to be put into words or even, given the limited survey technology of the age, to be reproduced graphically. The city described by Giovanni Villani was structured by two main streets, one that ran east and west, between the Porta alla Croce and the Porta al Prato on the city's new circuit of walls, the other north and south, between the Porta di San Gallo and the Porta Romana. Their intersection, Villani wrote, was the center of the town, "the intersection of the arms of the cross and the center of the circle of the city." He further defined the spot as "about where today one finds the hall of the consuls of the wool guild," [5] the only building in the city to which he made specific reference. He did not mention it because it actually marked the intersection—indeed, he acknowledged that it was a bit displaced—but in his opinion it was the most important site in the city, the seat of the industry that employed, by his count, an astounding thirty thousand workers. In this ideal view, the functional core of the city and the formal hub of its plan had to coincide.

The coincidence of formal and functional centers was the theme of Leonardo Bruni's panegyric to the city of Florence, the *Laudatio Florentinae Urbis* of 1403 / 4.[6] Bruni organized the physical fabric of the entire Florentine territorial state as a series of concentric rings. The walls, the suburbs, the citizens' rural estates, and the dependent towns all revolved around what Bruni, as chancellor of the republic, considered to be the most significant feature of the city. Again, it is a building, the Palazzo della Signoria, that is the seat of government.

The same approach as Villani's and Bruni's is evident in a figural image

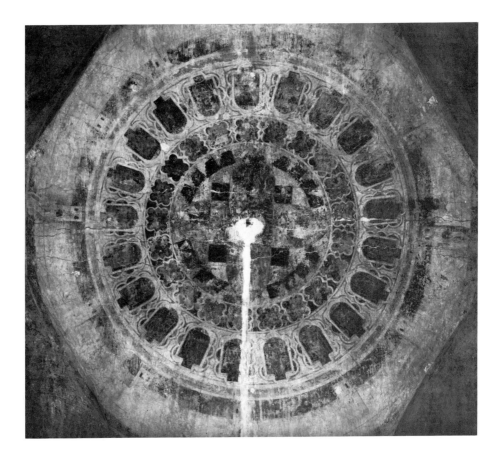

100 A symbolic image of the Florentine government, 1366. Palazzo dell'Arte dei Giudici e Notai, Florence (Photograph: Soprintendenza alle Gallerie, Florence).

of 1355 that decorates the vault of the audience chamber of the palace of the lawyers and notaries, the Arte dei Giudici e Notai, on the Via Pronconsolo.[7] The image uses heraldic symbols and elements of architecture to represent the political organization of Florence (Fig. 100). It is structured, like Bruni's Florence, as a series of concentric rings. Two outer circles of panels contain the coats of arms of the twenty-one guilds and the images of their patron saints. Inside the circle of saints are the arms of the sixteen *gonfalone,* the geographic divisions of the city, and the four quarters into which they were grouped. Each of these sets, professional and geographic, is directly related to the city's government. The guilds dominated the city's politics and membership in one of them was a prerequisite for participation in the government. The *gonfalone* and quarters were the administrative divisions of the community; the collection of taxes, the city's defense, and even the selection of the priors who formed the government were organized by quarter. The center of the fresco is occupied by a cross-shaped configuration of four emblematic shields. The *giglio*, or lily, of the Florentine commune and the eagle of the *parte Guelfa* fill two of them. The less-well-preserved emblems seem to contain the cross of the Florentine *popolo* and the vertically divided red and white fields that represent the combined Florentine and Fiesolan communities. The rings and shields represent the political institutions, alliances, and history that made up Florentine government in the mid-fourteenth century. Around the outside of the fresco, a final ring cements the relationship between this political abstraction and the real city. It is a naturalistic representation of the city walls, complete with eight towers, four gates, a moat, and bridges.

Villani, Bruni, and the designer of the Giudici e Notai fresco did not invent the patterns they used. Villani's metaphor of a cross of streets inscribed within a circle goes back to the earliest images of inhabited sites and rationalized space.[8] In the Middle Ages it had, in addition, the authority of religion. According to medieval city builders and their chroniclers, Christian communities derived protection from an arrangement of churches "in modum crucis."[9] Four religious foundations sufficed to mark the perpendicular axes that formed the cross. The cathedral, seat of the bishop who orchestrated the layout, occupied the point of the streets' intersection. The medieval use of this pattern was not only emblematic. The expression "crux viarum" describes the intersections of special importance within the city.[10] The concentric circles of Bruni's Florence and the vault fresco of the Giudici e Notai palace are also based on a venerable tradition, at least as old as Plato's description of Atlantis in his *Critias*, where a central acropolis is surrounded by five circles of land and water.[11] In the Middle Ages, the scheme was occasionally used to describe cities,[12] but it more frequently represented abstract concepts such as the organization of Aristotelian science or the structure of the Ptolemaic universe.[13] Dante used it to describe heaven, hell, and purgatory.

Because they were familiar schemata, concentric rings and the crossed circle were used to describe Florence. They reveal little about the city's actual topography, but a good deal about the fourteenth-century urban ideal. In both schemes the center dominates, marked geometrically either by an intersection of axes or by its unique position at the center of concentric circles. Architecture and planning celebrated this central spot. The chief building of the community — which changed according to the author's point of view — was sited at the geometrically defined middle point. In the scheme used by Bruni and the Giudici e Notai palace fresco the concentric rings separate the different parts of the composition in descending order of importance. Both this scheme and Villani's are complete, bound either by the ring of dependent towns or by the city wall. They are strongly centralized, hierarchically ordered, and closed. One could hardly devise a more apt description of a Florentine new-town plan.

The translation of these schemes into the language of orthogonal planning required only a few changes. What was lost, at least visually, was the circle. While the occasional medieval foundation acquired a curved (though never geometrically circular) line of defense, only the few new towns that had to come to terms with a hilltop site were organized in concentric rings. Within the context of straight streets and rectilinear lots and squares, the Florentine new-town plans reproduced ideal layouts almost literally. An intersection defined the center and a public square "nel mezzo della terra" (Document 19) accommodated not just one public building but all of them. The intersection of the main streets quartered the towns, and neighborhood centers created from the crossing of secondary streets expressed the identity of each quarter with the same clarity as did the groupings of banners in the Giudici e Notai palace fresco. Even the hierarchy of rings finds a place within the orthogonal system. The diminishing depth of lots and blocks on either side of the central axis accommodated a class structure with four full distinctions of grade. Finally, surrounding and enclosing this skillfully knit system of public streets and private property was the town wall. Isolated from adjacent buildings both inside and outside the town, complete in its circuit from the earliest days of the foundation, the wall perfectly expressed the idea behind all the descriptions of Florence: the city's unity and the special status of the urban community.

The period of new-town foundation was one of dramatic change in the political organization of Florence. In the early 1280s a merchant patriciate gained control of the government and ruled for most of the next one hundred and fifty years. During this time the political role of the traditional ruling class, the nobility with origins in the feudal countryside, was severely limited. Membership in a guild became a requirement for all elected officials. The new government wrote laws and established judicial authority that it attempted to enforce throughout the population. It declared resolutely independent nobles to be outlaws and established government control over previously autonomous social institutions. Where it could, it replaced private jurisdiction with the authority of the government. This was a long process and it was considerably slowed by Florentine respect for tradition and, especially, for the nobility. Its progress, however, was irreversible and by the fifteenth century the impulse to centralize and unify had significantly reshaped Florentine politics and society.

This political and social change had many implications for the city's physical character. While in idealized images Florence was unified and centralized, in the real city the government faced a complicated task. Its efforts, however, were heroic. Within a few decades of taking power the priors had begun work on a new cathedral, a monumental town hall, major churches like Santa Croce and the Badia, a new circuit of walls that increased the size of the city more than five fold, and many streets and squares in both the new and old parts of the town. Unique in the city's history, the scale of the new architecture established landmarks for the whole community. Even more revolutionary was the creation, by the Florentines, of one of the first modern urban environments. The physical city of the merchant commune was an open one. The uniformity of authority and jurisdiction that the government strove for translated directly into a concept of urban space, in which every part of town was to be equally accessible and all buildings, both private and public, would be visible to everyone.

Streets were the basic unit in the new urbanism of the Florentine merchant commune. Singly, sometimes in pairs, rarely in larger clusters, streets were the subject of a body of legislation that extended throughout the fourteenth and fifteenth centuries. Properly formed roadways were considered beautiful. They reflected honorably on the city, facilitated its work, and allowed it to prosper. A government committee in 1298 built streets "for the honor and beauty and fulfillment of the city."[14] A project to establish a thoroughfare along the river in 1287 was thought "useful and proper and beautiful."[15] Regularity was the primary requirement of a beautiful street. Straightness, a smooth, paved surface,[16] and a consistent slope[17] were essential as was a continuous wall of facades on either side of the roadway. Vacant lots were to be closed with garden walls, "for the greater beauty of the city,"[18] and firm regulations restricted the demolition of buildings.[19] The materials of facades were of public concern, too. Stone and brick were required to a height of as much as 9.3 meters.[20] The houses themselves were considered an ornament to the city.

The demands of regularity could bring the government into conflict with its citizens. One thorny issue was the projection of private construction over the building line. In the late Middle Ages there were many ways to steal public space. Ephemeral structures represented the most constant

101 Viterbo. Via Bellavista (Photograph: Fine Arts Library, Harvard University).

threat. The booths that vendors established at public market places, the counters that projected onto the street from the windows of shops, and the awnings that protected the counters from the sun all used public space and all had the terms of their use restricted by law. Because they could be removed so easily—indeed, structures like these were sometimes taken in nightly—the regulations concerning them were comparatively lenient. A rental fee for the occupation of public ground, a size limit, or an established schedule of times of use provided adequate control over these potential obstacles. Governments across central Italy proceeded more strictly against permanent structures, such as jetties (cantilevered upper stories), bridges between buildings, and external stairs, to defend the public domain.

The results varied considerably from site to site. The commune at Viterbo battled these obstructions as strenuously as any. Its mid-thirteenth-century statutes prohibited the construction of external stairs because they "prejudiced the appearance of the street."[21] Nevertheless, the stairs, jetties, and bridges survive (Fig. 101) and give the city a picturesque appearance that is now highly prized as an example of medieval urbanism. In Florence prohibitions against jetties first appeared in connection with projects to build major new streets like the Via Maggio project of 1295.[22] A general proscription of *sporti*, as the jetties were called in Florence, was written in 1299, but even that law applied only to new streets. Elsewhere, the government had to accept the jetties and contented itself with imposing a tax that, according to Giovanni Villani, brought in seven thousand florins a year.[23]

Of all the qualities of the Florentine aesthetic of streets, straightness was preeminent. Ambitious projects, like the Via Larga (now Via Cavour), which was built in the early fourteenth century to facilitate the transportation of grain to the market at Orsanmichele, ran from the gate in the old wall to one in the new circuit along a "straight line measured by a cord." It was built "to enhance the decorum of the city of Florence and to be useful and especially to increase the number of beautiful straight streets and entrance routes."[24] In the very center of the old city roadways could only approximate this ideal. The city's surveyors defined new thoroughfares there by the position of preexisting buildings. Doors, wall planes, and the corners of houses became markers as street builders sought piecemeal regularity.[25]

New construction was only part of the responsibility of the city's officers in charge of planning. More frequently they worked to improve existing facilities. The government sought to protect public streets against the encroachment of private construction and to foster an ordered spatial environment in the city. The earliest surviving regulation, dated to 1248 and preserved in the 1325 statutes of the city's *podestà*, required only that new construction conform to the building line of adjacent properties and present a straight facade to the street.[26] As the officials gained experience and authority they increased the degree of the city's intervention. In a *provvisione* of 1294 a whole area was described as "narrow and ill formed." The government decreed that the fronts of all the houses in the offending area be rebuilt; the street was "to be straightened and the deformity eliminated."[27] At the same time the government maintained existing streets more aggressively. Occasional attention — defined by the rhythm of private building initiative — gave way to regular inspection. A law written for the statutes of the *capitano del popolo* of 1322 – 25 provided for repair and paving of the streets under government supervision and

102 Florence. Borgo Ognissanti.

constant vigilance against private usurpation. At the beginning of the
six-month term of each new *capitano*, local officials in both the city's
parishes and the communities of the Florentine countryside reported ille-
gal occupation of the "viae publicae." The *capitano* had the authority to
order trespassers to dismantle offending construction within ten days.[28]

In the new towns it was never necessary to straighten streets. Main
street, residential streets, cross streets, alleys, and perimeter roads were all
as straight as the most successfully executed thoroughfares within the city.
Their width, too, satisfied Florentine standards. The main roadway at San
Giovanni (see Fig. 1) had the same width as the Via Maggio, the Via
Serragli, and the Borgo Ognissanti in Florence (Fig. 102), and as the other
important new streets laid out in the city in the late thirteenth century. Like
the best of the city's new thoroughfares, those in the founded towns were
graded during construction (Document 4), paved and cleaned to guarantee
drainage,[29] and defended by legislation against the encroachment of private stairs, bridges, and jetties (Document 15).

The straightness required of a street that a fourteenth-century Florentine would have considered beautiful implied an orthogonal relationship
between that street and adjacent ones. In the new towns this relationship

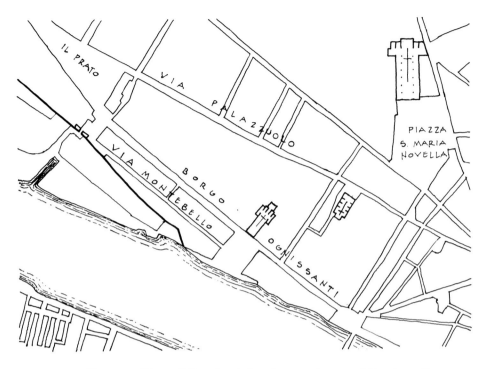

103 Florence. Plan of the street development around Ognissanti.

characterized the whole plan. In Florence it could be achieved only approximately, on a limited scale, and with many contradictions. Borgo
Ognissanti was one of the city's most successfully orthogonal developments (Fig. 103). The Borgo itself was laid out in 1278 by the government
and the Umiliate friars at Ognissanti, who owned the land. This straight
street, 20 *braccia* (11.7 meters) wide, replaced an old path by the river and
provided access to lots 50 *braccia* (29.2 meters) deep. On the land behind
the lots a spillway and mills exploited the water power of the river Arno. In
1291 a street 8 *braccia* (4.7 meters) wide and a second strip of houses 20
braccia (11.7 meters) deep were laid out between the Borgo and the spillway. Because all the lots on the Borgo Ognissanti had the same depth, the
subsequent development around the present-day Via Montebello was
exactly parallel with the first. An open space 100 *braccia* (58.4 meters) wide
in front of the church of Ognissanti, whose straight sides were perpendicular to the axes of the streets, gave the area a focus and balance.[30] The only
complex of street, square, and building lots in Florence that was more
rigorously composed was the rebuilt Ponte Vecchio of the 1340s. In this

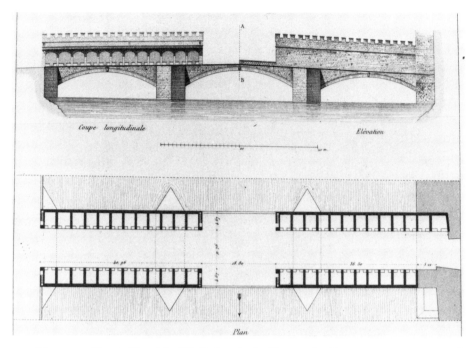

Coupe longitudinale   Elévation

Plan

104 Florence. Ponte Vecchio (G. Rohault de Fleury, *La Toscane au moyen age*, I, 1870).

completely controlled environment the 9.76-meter-wide and 101.48-meter-long roadbed was flanked by forty-eight shops and opened at its center to a piazza measuring 18.8 by 19.1 meters, overlooking the river (Fig. 104).

Despite the restricted size of the Ognissanti project, the composition took shape in stages. Its construction was guided by circumstances, and where these were unpropitious no cohesive development took place. The Via Palazzuolo, for instance, a straight street 16 *braccia* (9.4 meters) wide built by the Umiliati in 1279, bore no formal relation to Borgo Ognissanti not 50 meters away. Its course was determined by the location of the city's new Prato, the older Borgo San Paolo, and the limit of the convent's property.[31] Its connection to the river development was limited to the point at the Prato at which the two systems intersected.

The informal coordination of the two parts of the Umiliati project is typical of the plan of Florence. Everywhere around the periphery of the city, neighborhoods developed with straight streets and irregular relations. In some places, such as the area around the church of San Barnaba at the intersection of the Via Guelfa and the Via San Zanobi, approximate orthogonality approaches geometric precision. But the effort at regularity was never sustained over a wide area. The planners of Florence conceived grand schemes, like the construction of the streets along the Arno or the roads that circled the city walls, but there was too long a history of architecture, too discontinuous a process of development, and too varied a purpose among the developers to produce a master plan. It was only in the new towns that integrated street compositions were possible.

The straightening of Florentine streets and the removal of obstacles for the free passage of men and merchandise was not motivated by practical and aesthetic considerations alone. The creation of a domain of public space and the extension of the system of transit and communication to the entire area within the city walls had the same political motivation as the foundation of towns. City streets, too, could confront the nobility and reinforce the government's control of its territory. A street that the commune proposed in 1287 was not only "bright and open" but would allow "everyone to pass along it freely."[32] Obstacles to free passage were not necessarily innocent; sometimes they were conceived and built as barriers. At least one document explicitly addresses this aspect of restructuring the city. In 1301 the government built an approach to the town hall from the eastern countryside to facilitate the importation of grain and to provide for loyal *popolani* a route that would be safe from attack by "magnates" — as members of the great families were called — who opposed the guild-based regime.[33] The new street, called the Via San Procolo, fulfilled the same function as did the new roads in the countryside. Like the route to Bologna that passed through Scarperia and Firenzuola, the Via San Procolo liberated the city's traffic from the control of the nobility.

The renovated and newly built streets of Florence were public streets. As such, they were distinguished in law from other parts of the city.[34] Neighborhood streets, *viae vicinales*, sometimes defined as dead-end streets,[35] were controlled jointly by the owners of the property abutting them; private streets were themselves a possession, part of the holdings of an individual or family. Only public streets, limited in number in the early Middle Ages, were fully under the jurisdiction of the government. Florence's new street system aimed to unify a city that in the immediately preceding centuries resembled a feudal landscape more than what we would today call a city. In the precommunal city each quarter was dominated by a few families that had established fortified precincts functioning very much like the castles of the feudal nobility in the countryside. The

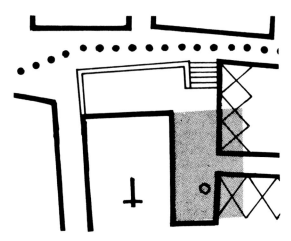

105 Genoa. The Doria family compound (L.G. Bianchi and E. Poleggi, *Una città portuale del medioevo, Genova nei secoli X – XVI*, 1980).

precincts flourished; the physical and political links between them were weak.

Record of the precincts of medieval Florence has been preserved primarily in the toponymy of the city. Names like the Piazza dei Figlioli della Tosa (which stood immediately north of the site of the Piazza della Repubblica) and the Corte dei Macci (next to Orsanmichele) record the appropriation of areas of the city by family groups (see Figs. 51, 52).[36] Thanks to the success of the commune in integrating these once purposely isolated places with the rest of the urban environment, the precincts themselves are largely unrecognizable. A similar situation exists in most Italian cities. In Genoa, however, where the nobility preserved its independence longer than elsewhere, good examples survive. The most complete example, but also the most uncharacteristically monumental, is the compound of the Doria family around the church of San Matteo (Figs. 105, 106).

The center of a family precinct was an open space, often very small, called a *curia*, meaning, in this case, court or meeting place. Around it, the patriarchs of the clan built their residences. At San Matteo, the buildings on the north and west sides of the space were opened at ground level by loggie, which served as the site of such family ceremonies as marriages and funerals and the signing of important documents.[37] The church of San Matteo dominates the Doria compound from its uphill position on the east side of the square.[38] Only remnants of the towers, which are probably the best-known features of the family compound, survive at San Matteo. They

106 Genoa. The *curia* of the Doria compound at San Matteo.

were once the focus of the precinct's defense. Almost none of the family compounds were isolated from the adjacent fabric of the city. A description of 1329 of the parish of San Matteo reveals just how extensive and how continuous the Doria compound was with the surrounding houses (Fig. 107).

Nonetheless, the boundary between one territory and the next, or between family ground and the "neutral" ground of unaffiliated burghers, was once more obvious and more easily defensible than would now appear possible. Gates closed what are now public streets, and towers defended the major entry points into the compound.[39] In times of hostilities between families the Doria called their country dependents into town and closed the gates of the compound, where wells and storehouses prepared the family against siege. Catapults and other weapons were mounted in the towers, and city streets below became the scene of battle. Chronicles of Genoa recount numerous, devastating civil wars within the city walls.

Noblemen lived together because it was the family that defined their social identity. Before any political body, a nobleman owed loyalty to an

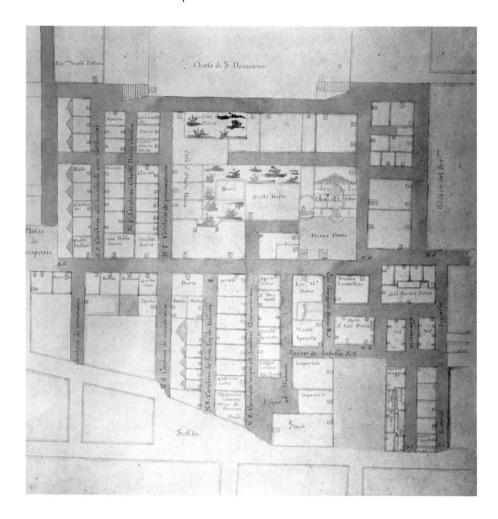

107 Genoa. The parish at San Matteo, from a description of 1329 (Collezione topografico del Comune di Genoa, 3464).

extended group of relatives.[40] He fought for them in feuds that defended family interests and honor and he submitted himself to the judgment of family courts. In principle, he shared ownership with his relatives in a family estate, and it is based on this relationship, which goes back to an original feudal investiture shared by the many descendants of an original vassal, that the members of these extended families are called *consorte*.

In 1281 and 1286 the Florentine government proceeded against the city's great families, whether they were legitimately noble or not, who behaved in the characteristically collegial and independent manner of the nobility, with legislation whose goal was "to control the unbridled presumption of the great and strong of the city and county of Florence."[41] The government demanded a bond of two thousand lire from each person it declared an outlaw. Ostensibly the new legislation asked only that the magnates respect the city's laws.[42] Specific provisions reveal the kind of behavior Florentines expected of the nobility. Magnates were ordered to obey the city's officials. They were warned against assisting outlaws or enemies of the state, against joining in conspiracies, and against participating in riots. Couched in the form of an apolitical appeal for peace, the bond laws, like the Ordinances of Justice of 1293 and 1295 which blocked magnates from participating in city government, had profound social and political significance.

The bond laws challenged the nobility's basic privileges by forcing it to conform to a civic standard defined by the merchant class. Legal jurisdiction, which derived from feudal investiture, was the nobles' most important forfeiture. The new laws demanded that magnates surrender their dependents to the communal courts if they were accused of crimes in town, and that they turn over criminals of any kind captured on their country estates. By establishing financial penalties for acts of violence, the laws frustrated traditional means of resolving differences among peers and thereby sought to curb the cycle of revenge that the noble code of honor generated. In attempting to control fortifications, the bond laws had a direct effect on the physical character of the city. The right to fortify was originally a privilege of the sovereign that was passed to tenants upon their investiture.[43] It came to town with the immigration of the nobility. In theory at least, this was the legal ground for the construction of the towers that were the main defense of the family compound. The challenge to private fortifications was another attack on the autonomy of the great families.

The Florentines had mixed feelings about the towers. They were proud of the presence of so many noble families within the city[44] and also of the towers that were the outward sign of this population.[45] They could not, however, tolerate the warlike behavior for which the towers were built. In the mid-thirteenth century, both Guelph and Ghibelline regimes dismantled the towers of their opponents and limited the heights of others.[46] From 1280 Florentine legislation against family towers was more restrained. The statutes of the 1320s tolerated construction of new towers, limiting only their height,[47] and confined their attack to towers in ruinous condition.[48] Magnates were prohibited from owning buildings of any kind in strategically important parts of the city, such as bridgeheads and the areas near the main squares,[49] but only a magnate who failed to post bond was threatened with the destruction of his tower.[50] At the same time, arming a tower with a catapult was punishable by the destruction of the tower, a thousand lire fine, and, for the craftsman who built the weapon, the loss of a limb.[51] The commune of the priors accepted the towers. Magnate and *popolano* alike were allowed to build them; no one, however, was permitted to use them for attack or defense. The form alone, with its connection to the city's proud and noble tradition, survived.

The Florentine merchant government dealt with family compounds in the same spirit in which it addressed the towers: it offered protection in exchange for the recognition of its authority. The simple geographic concentration of family members posed a limited threat to the government so long as the topographic units were not also military and political ones. The government allied itself with family interests by taking over duties of the traditional family council. Documents drawn up by twelfth- and thirteenth-century *consorterie* had tried to strengthen the hold of each group on the area around its center. In 1179 an association of families living around the Florentine *mercato vecchio* defined a zone in which it would attempt to establish ownership of all real estate. Any associate who entered into a contract for property in the area was obliged to share his interest with all the other members of the group.[52] The agreement of 1287 – 88 that served as the constitution of the Corbolani *consorteria* of Lucca made a similar provision. It asked any member who learned of the sale of a piece of property within the three "chapels," or neighborhoods, dominated by the *consorteria* to announce it to the council.[53] In the fourteenth century the same obligations were defined as communal law. In Florence, the statutes of the *podestà* required *consorti* to offer their relatives property that they wished to sell, and protected the family's right to repossess buildings and land.[54]

While the isolated family precinct was the characteristic environment of the old nobility through the thirteenth century, the new public streets of Florence became increasingly attractive sites for residential construction in the period that followed the institution of the priorate of the guilds in 1282. A landmark of this critical shift of architectural focus was a project to build a street through the heart of the oldest part of Florence (Fig. 108; see Figs. 49, 51). In January 1298 the *Signoria* received a petition from the residents in

108 Florence. Via Cimatori, looking toward Orsanmichele.

the area of Orsanmichele requesting that the priors and the committee in charge of defending and improving the commune's property create a new street in their neighborhood. According to the petition the street was to begin at the piazza of Orsanmichele, penetrate the densely constructed area to the east of the square, and reach to the "pallatium comunis et populi Florentine," i.e., the Bargello.[55] Jetties, bridges, and even strongly projecting roofs were prohibited, and a width of 10 *braccia* was proposed despite the crowded conditions.

The route of the new street led between the palaces of the Cerchi family and through the "plathea de Cerchiis," with its loggia. Thus, the street was not only designed to connect two public monuments, but also to open to public view the innermost core of the precinct of a powerful family. Significantly, the project was not opposed by the Cerchi. Indeed, it must have been their idea. The representatives of the Florentine Badia, who successfully opposed the part of the street that would have run through their property, said the project was initiated "at the time when the Cerchi and their allies ruled the city."[56]

The Cerchi were members of a "new" family whose power rested on their recent achievements in business and politics and whose rivals, led by the great nobleman Corso Donati, ridiculed them for their lack of aristocratic breeding.[57] Family solidarity must have meant something very different to the Cerchi from what it meant to the old nobility. Perhaps for this reason they seized on a new way to reinforce their visibility within the city. Rather than retreating to the internal court of the family compound, they exploited the public stage of the city's streets. By this choice the Cerchi, and the families who built the big new palaces that began to appear in Florence in the late thirteenth century, created a new building type. Large in size, permanent in construction, and oriented to the streets with elegant masonry facades, the palaces of the city's most prominent citizens soon took their place alongside churches and town halls as the great monuments of the urban environment.

In November 1294 the Florentine *Signoria* proposed a general reorganization of the laws of the state, in order to eliminate the overlapping and contradictory legislation that had accumulated in the statutes of the *podestà* and *capitano,* and in the ordinances that supplemented them.[58] The sponsors of the reorganization bill, the same political figures who wrote the antimagnate Ordinances of Justice, hoped to produce a legal code that was "clara et aperta," with laws recorded "secundum debitum ordinem." Nicola Ottokar, who quoted these phrases in an important article on the

Florentine urban aesthetic, pointed out that this was the same language the city's officers used to describe the projects to renew and expand the city's physical environment.[59] He argued that the two programs shared the same drive for order, regularity, and organization. What Ottokar did not emphasize was that, in late-thirteenth-century Florence, both schemes failed. The reorganization of the legal code faltered in the face of the suspicions of powerful citizens; the rebuilding of the city was hampered by the physical obstacles of Florence's past. Only in the new towns could these radical projects succeed.

The ability of the new towns to represent the urban ideal of the Florentine merchant commune is based on a decision that preceded any design. It is spelled out in the documents of foundation, which said that "no magnate may buy a house, field, or lot in these towns" (Documents 2, 3, 16). The message was the same in the Arno valley and in the Apennines: magnates could not acquire land or build fortifications within two miles of a new settlement. The immediate motivation for this policy was the adversarial position of the country nobility. They were the enemy against whom the towns were founded and their armed opposition to the new settlements continued throughout the fourteenth century. But it was not just the nobility in the countryside that was excluded from the new towns; the foundation charters were just as explicit about magnates from the city. These same charters welcomed the subjects of the noble families, promising immigrants freedom from feudal obligation (Document 3). Both tactics were successful and the towns developed without noblemen or serfs.

This uncompromising aspect of the new-town program had its effect upon the settlement plans. There was no place for the nobility within new-town walls. A hierarchy of lots accommodated the variety of rich and poor farmers, not the distinction between farmers and lords. The organization of property, with rows of lots facing onto public streets, well served the needs of rustics and artisans but not the extended family of the nobility. New-town plans eliminated the possibility of building a private precinct focused on an internal *curia* just as surely as the law prohibited the immigration of magnates.

The ordered disposition of elements that Giovanni Villani, Leonardo Bruni, and the guild of lawyers and notaries had to invent to give meaning to the plan of Florence was realized at the new-town sites. Their street systems fulfilled the fundamental political mission of the government of the priors, guaranteeing to all members of the community access to all areas of the town. The open plan and the enclosing walls represented the unity of the settlement. The geometric proportions of the blocks epito-

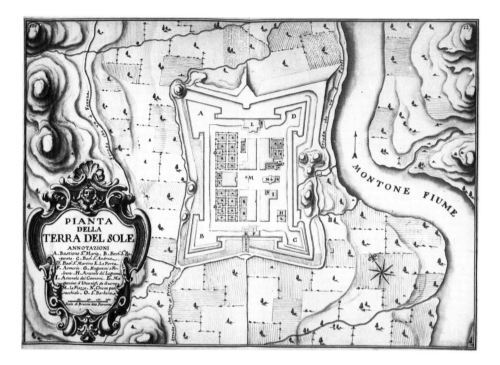

109 Terra del Sole, ca. 1743 (ASF, *Gabinetto* 695, fols. 126, 127).

mized the orderliness of the whole. The collection of public buildings around the open space at the center of the plan expressed the government's aspirations after a public authority that had jurisdiction over the entire urban population and a role in a broad spectrum of human activities. The product of a collaboration between office-holding Florentine citizens and design professionals from the city's sophisticated architectural establishment, the new towns embodied the most progressive ideas about urban form in an age of profound change in city life.

Urban design from the Renaissance to modern times has depended on the achievements of the late Middle Ages. The rich Renaissance tradition of public squares, and the emergence of the facade as a primary focus of architectural interest are basic themes of urbanism pioneered between the twelfth and fourteenth centuries. The Florentine new towns offered both an elegant summation of what had been accomplished to 1350 and a significant contribution of their own. Their value was not lost on succeeding generations. Piero della Zucca, after preparing a meticulous survey of San Giovanni in 1554 (see Fig. 5), complimented the "invenzione" of the

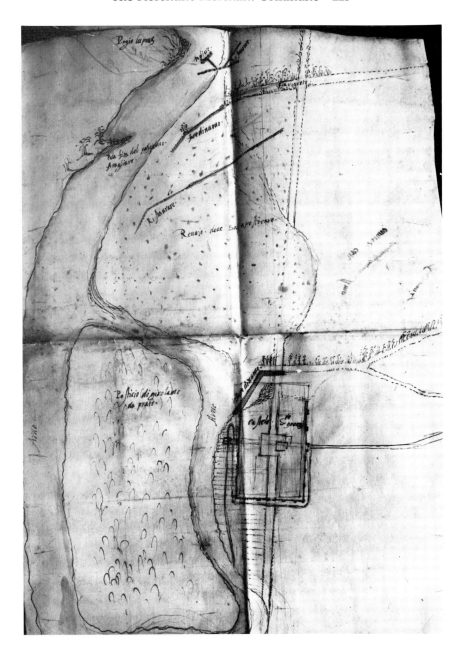

110 Bernardo Buontalenti, plan of San Giovanni (ASF, *Capitani di parte,* numeri
neri 722, fol. 181, 1 August 1568).

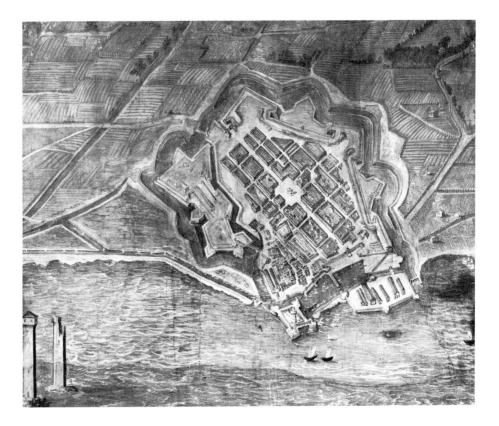

111 Bernardino Pocetti, plan of Livorno, 1609. Palazzo Pitti, Florence, Sala di Bona.

medieval design and wrote that the piazza, especially, was made with "grande arte" (Document 23). Vasari apparently agreed. He attributed the design of the towns to the leading architects of the day.[60] When, in the mid-sixteenth century, Florentines again began to design towns, they took as their models the plans of the fourteenth-century new towns.

Terra del Sole is a garrison town on the north slope of the Apennines (Fig. 109). It lies within ten kilometers of Forli in an area that was occupied by the Florentines in the first decade of the fifteenth century. A modest settlement overwhelmed by its fortifications, it is, nonetheless, a place with some urban pretensions. A handsome square lies at the heart of the plan, one side of it occupied by the palace of the Florentine official, the other by the church of a parish centered in the town. A single street accommodates all the residential structures and also serves as the spine of the composition. Terra del Sole is a fortress laid out as a town. The plan that it mimics is the one created for San Giovanni. Bernardo Buontalenti, who designed Terra del Sole in 1564 for Duke Cosimo I, was well aware of the relationship between his design and the medieval one. As advisor to the state on architectural and engineering matters he traveled in the countryside with some regularity. There is even a document to show how he interpreted San Giovanni. In 1568, in connection with a project to improve the bed of the Arno river, Buontalenti made a rough sketch of San Giovanni's plan (Fig. 110).[61] In the drawing the long piazza of the medieval town becomes almost square and the Palazzo Pretorio stands at the head of the open space rather than in its center. As a result San Giovanni looks very much like Terra del Sole. A piazza even more similar to that blocked out in Buontalenti's sketch appears in a project for the Medici port city of Livorno. The design for the city that Buontalenti submitted in 1576 contained no central square, but by 1610, when a fresco in the Pitti Palace recorded the scheme under construction, a piazza had become an important feature (Fig. 111).[62] It sits astride the main road, a monument at its center, the church and a government palace facing each other across the open space.

The designs of Terra del Sole and Livorno reinterpret the central space of the medieval new town in a uniquely Renaissance way. The balanced proportions of the square at Terra del Sole must be read as a criticism of the extended piazza of its model. The axial coordination of church and palace in the two Renaissance projects would have been impossible in the earlier age. At a more basic level, however, the debt of the sixteenth-century plans is inescapable. The symmetry, centrality, and unity that is the distinctive quality of these designs is the special legacy of the Florentine new towns.

NOTES

ABBREVIATIONS IN THE NOTES

ASF Archivio di Stato, Florence
Cap. Capitoli del Comuni di Firenze
Provv. Provvisioni
SS. Miss. Signori Missive, I Cancelleria
Stat. Com. Statuti di Comuni Soggetti
Uff. Cast. Ufficiali delle Castella
Uff. Cast., Rocche Ufficiali delle Castella e Rocche

GV *Cron.*
Giovanni Villani. *Cronica di Giovanni Villani a miglior lezione ridotta coll'aiuto
de'testi a penna con note filologiche di I. Moutier
e con appendici storico-geografiche comp. da Franc. Gherardi-
Dragomanni.* Florence, 1844 – 45

MV *Cron.*
Matteo Villani. *Cronica di Matteo Villani, a miglior lezione ridotta coll'aiuto
de'testi a penna con appendici storico-geografiche compilate da Franc. Gherardi-
Dragomanni.* Florence, 1846

All documents not quoted from secondary sources retain the original
orthography.

A NOTE ABOUT DATES

The Florentine calendar begins the new year on March 25. Thus, documents issued between 1 January and 24 March carry a date of one year earlier than they would in the modern calendar. To avoid confusion, the dates of both years are given (e.g., 1298 / 9). When the year of a document is referred to in the text I use the modern convention.

NOTES TO THE INTRODUCTION

1. The foundation document of 1299 may well represent only the *terminus ante quem* for a project already initiated. Giovanni Villani gave the date of the foundation as three years earlier, with this succinct description of the Florentines' motives:

   Nel detto anno [1296] essendo il comune e popolo de Firenze in assai buono e felice stato, con tutto che i grandi avessono incominciato a contradiare il popolo, come detto avemo, il popolo per meglio fortificarsi in contado, e scemare la forza de' nobili e de' potenti del contado, e spezialmente quella de' Pazzi di Valdarno e degli Ubertini ch'erano ghibellini, si ordinò che nel nostro Valdarno di sopra si facessono due grandi terre e castella; l'uno era tra Fegghine e Montevarchi, e puosesi nome castello Sangiovanni, l'altro in casa Uberti allo 'ncontro passato l'Arno, e puosongli nome Castelfranco, e francarono tutti gli abitanti de'detti castelli per dieci anni d'ogni fazione e spese di comune, onde molti fedeli de' Pazzi e Ubertini, e quegli da Ricasoli, e de' Conti, ed altri nobili, per esser franchi si feciono terrazzani de' detti castelli; per la qual cosa in poco tempo crebbono e multiplicaro assai, e fecionsi buone e grosse terre (GV *Cron.*, VIII, chap. 17).

   San Giovanni was already a town of some substance in 1312 when, according to Villani, it was conquered by the emperor, Henry VII (GV *Cron.*, IX, chap. 65). Castelfranco (called di Sopra to distinguish it from a town of the same name founded in the lower Valdarno, with the assistance, it seems, of the city of Lucca) appears in a document of 1320, in which members of the town's governing body describe the foundation of the town as a past event (ASF *Provv.*, 24, fols. 51r and v, 12 April 1320).
2. J. Plessner, *Una rivoluzione stradale del Dugento* (Copenhagen, 1938), pp. 52 – 53.
3. From an inscription, "MCCCXXXVII SI POSE Q(UE)STA," on the lintel of a door into the central church, we know that the building of Terranuova began immediately after the document of foundation. The town's population was

addressed by the Florentine *Signoria* in November 1338 (ASF *Provv.*, 29, fol. 76r). The incident that occasioned the communication from Florence, an attack by the town's residents on the village of Gangheretto, was reported by Giovanni Villani, who dated it to 1336 (GV *Cron.*, XI, chap. 53). At the same point in his text Villani gives an account of the founding of Terranuova. After discussing the rebellion of the towns of the area against the young Count Guido da Battifolle "per male reggimento che 'l giovane facea a'suoi fedeli d' opera di femmine," and their protection and then purchase by the Florentines, Villani writes, "E poi appresso, in calen di Settembre 1337, il comune di Firenze ordinò e fece cominciare in Valdarno in fra quelle terre nel piano di Giuffrena in luogo proprio del comune di Firenze una terra, e puosele nome castel santa Maria, faccendovi tornare dentro uomini di tutte le ville e terre d'intorno con certa franchigia e immunità, per torre in perpetuo ogni giuridizione e fedeltà a' detti conti."

4. The Florentines appointed an officer to oversee the project in 1306 (Document 4). Two acts of his immediate successor are preserved in documents of 1308 (Document 5). In November 1308 the Florentine government sent instructions to the "sindico, rectoribus, consilio, universitati, hominibus et personis Comunis castri Sancte Barnabe" (ASF *SS. Miss.*, 1, 1 November 1308; published in *Bollettino storico-letterario del Mugello* 1 [1893], p. 12). Villani gives this account of the foundation:

Nel detto anno del mese di Maggio (1306) i Fiorentini andarono ad oste sopra 'l castello di Montaccianico in Mugello, e puosonvi l'assedio; il quale castello era de'signori Ubaldini, ed era molto bello e ricco, e fortissimo di sito e di doppie mura, perocchè l'avea loro fatto edificare con grande spendio e diligenzia il cardinale Ottaviano loro consorto; nel quale castello s'erano ridotti gran parte degli Ubaldini, e quasi tutti i ribelli bianchi e ghibellini usciti di Firenze, e faceano guerra e soggiogavano tutto il Mugello infino all'Uccelatoio. E al detto castello stette l'oste infino all'Agosto, gittandovi dificii e faccendovi cave, ma tutto era invano, se non che gli Ubaldini tra loro vennero in discordia, e il lato di messer Ugolino da Senno il pattegiaro co' Fiorentini per mano di messer Geri Spini loro parente, e diedonlo per promessa di quindicimila fiorini d'oro onde di gran parte n'ebbono male pagamento. E quegli che v'erano dentro l'abbandaro e andarne sani e salvi, e 'l castello fu tutto abbattuto e disfatto per gli Fiorentini, che non vi rimase casa nè pietra sopra pietra. E feciono fare i Fiorentini giùso al piano di Mugello nel luogo detto la Scarperia, una terra per fare battifolle agli Ubaldini, e torre i loro fedeli, e feciongli franchi, acciocchè Montaccianico mai non si potesse riporre. E cominciossi la detta terra e edificare a dì 7 di Settembre gli anni di Cristo 1306, e puosonle nome santo Barnaba. E ciò fatto, del mese d'Ottobre vegnente i Fiorentini cavalcarono con loro oste oltre l'Alpe, e guastarono tutte le terre degli Ubaldini, perch' aveano fatta guerra e ritenuti i bianchi e' ghibellini (GV *Cron.*, VIII, chap. 86).

5. There is some confusion about this date. Villani gives 8 April 1332 as the foundation date of Firenzuola, referring to the ceremony of laying the first stone (GV *Cron.*, X, chap. 199). M. Richter ("Die 'Terra murata' im florentinischen Gebiet," *Mitteilungen des kunsthistorischen Institutes in Florenz*, 5, no. 6 [July 1940], pp. 351 – 386) includes documents from ASF *Cap.*, 32, fol. 271 (see Document 13), which describe the plan and call the town by name; she dates these 9 April 1330. Their correct date is two years later (9 April 1332), which tallies with Villani's report. E. Repetti (*Dizionario geografico, fisico, storico della Toscana*, supp. [Florence, 1845], s.v. "Firenzuola"), following G. Gaye (*Carteggio Inedito d'Artisti dei secoli XIV, XV, XVI*, I [Florence, 1839], p. 472), refers to contracts of 27 June and 28 November 1328 for construction at Firenzuola. These contracts are the same as documents in ASF *Cap.*, 35, fols. 221r and 225v, which are dated 17 June and 28 November 1338. S Cassini (*Dizionario biografico geografico storico del comune di Firenzuola* [Florence, 1914] I, pp. 149 – 150) refers to a document of 1315 concerning Firenzuola also published by Gaye, but I cannot find this in Gaye's work. Villani's account of the circumstances of the foundation is:

> Nel detto anno [1332] avendo i signori Ubaldini dissensione e guerra insieme, ciascuna parte a gara mandando al comune di Firenze di volere tornare all' ubbidienza e alla signoria del comune, traendogli di bando, per gli Fiorentini fu accettato; ma ricordandosi che per molte volte s'erano riconciliati per simile modo col comune di Firenze, e poi rubellatisi a loro posta e vantaggio, come si può trovare per addietro, si provvide per lo detto comune di fare una grossa e forte terra di là dal giogo dell'Alpe in sul fiume del Santerno, acciocchè i detti Ubaldini piu non si potessono rubellare, e' distrittuali contadini di Firenze d'oltre l'Alpe fossono liberi e franchi, ch'erano servi e fedeli de' detti Ubaldini; e chiamarono a far fare la detta terra sei grandi popolani di firenze con grande balìa intorno a ciò. Ed essendo i detti uficiali in sul palazzo del popolo co' signori priori insieme in grande contasto, come si dovesse nominare la detta terra, e chi dicea uno nome e chi un altro, noi autore di questa opera trovandomi tra loro, dissi: Io vi dirò uno nome molto bello e utile, e che si confà alla 'mpresa. Perocchè questa fia terra nuova e nel cuore dell'Alpe, e nella forza degli Ubaldini e presso alle confini di Bologna e di Romagna; e s'ella non ha uno nome che al comune di

Firenze ne caglia e abbiala cara, a' tempi avversi di guerra che possono avvenire, ella fia tolta e rubellata spesso; ma se le porrete il nome ch'io vi dirò, il comune ne sarà più geloso e più sollecito alla guardia: perch'io la nominerei, quando a voi piacesse, *Firenzuola.* A questo nome tutti in accordo sanza alcuno contasto furono contenti, e il confermarono, e per più aumentare e favorare il suo stato e potenza le diedono per insegna e gonfalone mezza l'arme del comune, e mezza quella del popolo di Firenze; e ordinarono che la maggiore chiesa di quella terra, conseguendo al nome, si chiamasse san Firenze; e feciono franco chi l'abitasse dieci anni, recando tutte le genti vicine e ville d'intorno ad abitarla, e traendogli d'ogni bando di comune; e ordinarvi mercato uno dì della semmana. E cominciossi a fondare al nome di Dio a dì 8 d'Aprile del detto anno quasi alle otto ore del dì, provvedutamente per istrolagi, essendo ascendente il segno del Leone, acciocche la sua edificazione fosse più ferma e forte, stabile e potente (GV *Cron.,* X, chap. 199).

6. GV *Cron.,* XI, chap. 139; MV *Cron.,* II, chap. 6.

7. The *Cronica d'incerto* (ed. D.M. Manni [Florence, 1733]), q.v. 1373, reports "Comincansi a rifare Firenzuola." Gaye (*Carteggio,* I, p. 524) includes a document from the *Provvisione* of 22 October 1371, which he presents as "Balia ad faciendum et reponendum terram et fortilitiam Firenzuole." In ASF *Cap.,* 3, fol. 236r, 21 February 1373, eight men are appointed to oversee the work; fol. 243r gives the committeemen for 1374, fol. 245r those for 1375. The walls and gates and even the interior of the town were significantly repaired in the period 1471 – 76. An account book of the officials in charge of the work is preserved in ASF *Uff. Cast.,* 13. A number of letters between these officials and the *Cinque Ufficiali sopra le Fortificazioni* are in ASF, *Lettere Varie,* 2. Between 1495 and 1499 the city had further work on the defenses of the town directed by their architect Antonio da Sangallo the elder (G. Severini, *Architettura militare di Giuliano da Sangallo* [Pisa, 1970], p. 34). Gaye (*Carteggio,* I, p. 587) reports on a payment of 8 May 1497 (ASF, *Stanziamenti,* 17) to Antonio as *capomaestro at,* among other things, Poggio Imperiale (the new-town project above Poggibonsi) and Firenzuola.

   The town described by the building officials in 1332 was to have been 633 *braccia* (370 meters) long, and 342 *braccia* (200 meters) wide (Document 13). The town inside its late-fifteenth- and sixteenth-century walls measures, today, ca. 200 by 180 meters.

8. The sixteenth-century historian Scipione Ammirato gives this account of the foundation: "In questo tempo [1350] gli ufiziali delle castella, per fare abitare Civitelle secca, concedettero a quelli che vi andassero a fare elezioni straordinarie, e fecero distibuir fra essi alcuna somma di danari.

Dettero anche ordine che in Valdambra nel luogo detto Selvapiana si fabbricasse una terra assai forte per quei tempi acciocchè quelli di Castiglione Alberti, della badia d'Agnano, della Pieve di Prisciano, di Capannole, di S. Lorenzo, di Monteluco, di Cacciano e di Cornia ve andassero ad abitare, parendo che con questo cambiamento si desse a'popoli maggior occasione d'esser fedeli alla Republica, e con lasciar i luoghi di nuovo acquistati disabitati e spesse volte rovinati, fosse tolta a'vecchi signori la speranza di aver più a riaverli" (*Istorie fiorentine* [Florence, 1847], II, pp. 477 – 478).

9. P. Pirillo, "Un caso di pianificazione territoriale nel contado di Firenze (seccolo XII e XIV)," *Studi e Ricerche* 1 (1981), pp. 179 – 200.

10. Richter, "Terra Murata," p. 379, Document 2.

11. ASF *SS. Miss.*, 1, 11 January 1308 / 9; published in *Giotto; bolletino storico-letterario del Mugello*, 1892, pp. 15 – 16.

12. For the events of 1324, see *Istoria fiorentina di Marchonne di Coppo Stefani*, VI, rubric 379; GV *Cron.*, IX, chap. 273. For those of 1364, see ASF *Provv.*, 54, fols. 110r and v, 11 February 1364 / 5. ASF *Uff. Cast.*, 6, records the progress of the work between 19 March 1364 / 5 and 18 December 1367.

13. ASF *Provv.*, 64, fols. 273r and v, 23 March 1376 / 7.

14. MV *Cron.*, VII, chap. 45: "E in questo medesimo tempo [1356] ne fecc porre il comune una [terra] di nuovo al Pontassieve di costa ove si dice Filicaia, la quale è più per ridotto d'una guerra, che per abitazione o per mercato che vi potesse allignare." Gaye, *Carteggio*, I, p. 527, from *Provvisione* 65, 11 December 1375: "Che si finisca la fabbrica castri S. Angeli pontem Sevis."

15. ASF *Uff. Cast., Rocche*, 44, fol. 44, 21 September 1382.

16. Gaye, *Carteggio*, I, p. 539, from *Provvisione* 90, 9 June 1394: "Fiat forum in castro Sancti Angeli de ponte Sevis. Essendo questo paese ben situato e desiderando la republica di vederlo piu forte, credeva di poter arrivare a tal scopo, e di radunarvi piu gente, dando il permesso di farvi un mercato."

17. MV *Cron.*, VII, p. 45; A. Bossini, *Storia di Figline* (Florence, 1970).

18. MV *Cron.*, V, chap. 73; ASF *Provv.*, 41, fols. 48r and v, 6 August 1354, initiates the project; fols. 95r and v, 25 October 1354, names the building committee; ASF *Provv.*, 45, fol. 165r, 14 April 1358, which deals with the survey and distribution of house lots, is the last notice of the project of which I have record. ASF *Uff. Cast.*, 11, preserves the resolutions of the building committee in charge of the project in July and August 1356.

19. Gaye, *Carteggio*, I, p. 527, from *Provvisione* 66, 10 June 1376, records the Florentine decision to enlarge and fortify the "burgo de Campi"; ibid., p. 533, from *Provvisione* 80, 23 April 1389, "Castrum Campi quasi comple-

tum''; ASF *Uff. Cast., Rocche*, 44, fols. 15r – 16v, 5 June 1382, describes the plan for the enlarged town.

1. In 1392 Scarperia had only a castellan and twenty-three soldiers in its keep (ASF, *Camera del Comune*, 70, fol. 51r) and in 1401 a castellan and four soldiers (ASF *Uff. Cast., Rocche*, 2, fol. 7v). In 1339 the captain of Firenzuola had one aide (ASF *Uff. Cast.*, unclassified [the cover of the volume has ''Castellani 1339 – 1341, armadio 9, palco 2, 36''], fol. 15v); the *podestà* of Castelfranco also had one aide (ibid., fol. 29r).

2. ASF *Uff. Cast., Rocche*, 1, fols. 54r and v, 13 January 1366/7:

> In prima provedemo alla tera della Scarperia cioè dalla parte di fuori si radesse e rimondasse tutto l'antifosso e che il fosso si radesse 4 braccia a piè dè brocchati.
>
> Anche provedemo alle bertesche choridoi, parapetti e ventuno stecchati e palcora delle tori e al ponte della porta bolognese che lla predette chose si riconcino e rinuovino pero che sono molto guaste a le spese del detto comune.
>
> Anche comandamo a'retori degl'infrascritti popoli cioè
>
> a duccio fecini rettore di Sa'Michele a lezano
>
> a michele tedaldini rettore di San Piero a Sieve
>
> a piero manni rettore di San Giusto a Fortuna
>
> a bancho celli rettore del Sa'Iacopo a Coldaia
>
> ad andrea pinuccini rettore de Sa'Lorenzo a Ghabiano per cio che no'gli trovami coscritti a veruna guardia
>
> Che cho'lor popoli siono a dare aiuto con opere e a contribuire la spese che concorerano al comune della Scarperia a fornire e fare le sopradetta chose, alla pena di lire cinquanto per ciaschuno de detti populi
>
> Anche a dì XIII di genaio facemo fare mostra generale degl' uomeni della detta terra della Scarperia e veduta la detta mostra chomandamo che infra XV dì ciascheduno uomo della detta terra dovesse essere armato di quattro pezi d'arme, cioè cervelliera, rotella over pavese [?], lancia, coltello overo spada; e acerti piu suficienti in numero di cinquanto sieno armati di coraza overo coretto oltre a sopra detti pezi darme nominati, alla pena di libre diece per ciascheduno pezi d'arme che non avessero. / / fol. 54v / / Anche veduta la camera dell'arme della detta tera. Comandamo a Francescho Gharducci e Tura Mattei, sindachi e rettori della detta tera, e a'loro consiglieri che di qui all'mese prosimo che viene debano aver meso nella detta chamera quattro bombarde

grosse fornite e quattro balestre grosse e due chasse di buoni verrettoni oltre al'fornimento chev'è

Anche veduta la chamera del chasero della detta tera comandamo a detti sindachi che nel detto termine d'u' mese abiano rinovato il grano e il saetamento che nella detta chamera trovamo.

Anche che in sulla tore della guardia del chastagno si rifacciano quattro merli che son' di[s]fatti e chaduti.

E i predetti chomandamenti di fare le sopredette chose infra il detto termine d'u' mese facemo a'detti Francescho e Tura e lor consiglieri alla pene di lire mille. Delle quali tutte chose apare carta per mano di Ser Stefano di Matteo da Prato notaio del detto comune della Scarperia.

3. MV *Cron.*, II, chap. 14.

4. ASF, *Signori Responsive, I Cancelleria*, 5, fol. 69r, 20 April 1359. In 1551, the earliest date for which there are records, Borgo San Lorenzo had a population of 1889 and Scarperia 978. (Repetti, *Dizionario*, I [1833], s.v. "Borgo San Lorenzo," V [1843], s.v. "Scarperia.")

5. GV *Cron.*, VII, chap. 140.

6. ASF *Uff. Cast., Rocche*, 1, fol. 24, 1350 – 1366.

7. MV *Cron.*, II, chaps. 9, 10.

8. In 1356, 234 men were enrolled as heads of families in the tax lists of Scarperia (ASF, *Estimo*, 282, fols. 165r – 168v). They were undoubtedly aided by younger members of the families and by men who came into the fortress town from the surrounding area.

9. Matteo Villani tells this famous story in extended form in MV *Cron.*, II, chaps. 12 – 23, 29 – 33. Documents concerning the siege are published in *Giotto; bolletino storico letterario artistico del Mugello*, 1 (1902), pp. 133 – 141.

10. GV *Cron.*, VIII, chap. 86; see Intro., note 4.

11. MV *Cron.*, I, chaps. 23, 25.

12. On 3 May 1350 Matteo di Borgo di Rinaldo and Cionetto Giovenchi dela Stario were appointed "in offitiales ad standum et morandum in terra Scharperia super camera armorum et arnensis ac victuale et bladi dicti comunis [Florence] et ipsi recipiendum dandum et exhibendum prout viderint expedire" (ASF, *Balia*, 6, fols. 67r and v).

13. On 21 April 1350 the city sent 23 *maestri* to the war zone to make "edifitia ad prohicienda lapides" (ASF, *Balia*, 6, fol. 64v). On 17 May the masters' contract was extended "perficiandum dicta Edifitia per dicto comune in terra Scharperia et in partibus Mucelli" (ibid., fols. 70v, 71r).

14. Ibid., fol. 77r, 30 June 1350, payment for the delivery of twenty-eight letters, six to Scarperia, ten to the army; ibid., fol. 113r, 22 September 1350,

payment for the delivery of thirty-eight letters, ten to Scarperia, two to the army.

15. ASF *Provv.*, 105, fols. 3r – 5v, 11 April 1415.

16. San Giovanni became the seat of the vicar of the upper Valdarno on 1 December 1408 (ASF *Provv.*, 97, fols. 140v – 141v). Firenzuola was the seat of the vicarate of the "Alpe" from at least 14 October 1392, when Francesco di Michele Ghuicciardini was named vicar of Firenzuola (ASF, *Camera del Comune*, 70, fol. 53r). The two remaining new towns, Castelfranco di Sopra and Terranuova, lay in the province administered from San Giovanni.

17. In the list of the members of the *Arte degli Albergatori* of 1393 eleven men from Scarperia appear (ASF, *Albergatori*, 5, fol. 33r). The list of 1409 contains the names of five men from Scarperia and nine from Firenzuola (ibid., fol. 50r).

18. The route of the old road to Bologna is documented in a section of the statutes of the Florentine *capitano del popolo* of 1322, which was written before 1285: "strata per quam itur ad Sanctum Petrum de Sieve versus Bononiam et versus Gallianum et Sancte Aghatum et incipit a porta seu Burgho Sancti Laurentii" (R. Caggese, ed., *Statuti della repubblica fiorentina* [Florence, 1901], I, p. 174), and in ASF *Provv.*, 6, fol. 145, 3 December 1296: "Per stratam per quam a civitate Florentie itur Bononiam . . . duo idonei pontes de lapidibus et calcina fieri et construi debeant inter terram Cornaclarii et terram Valliam in strata publica . . . unum videlicet super flumen Risani et alterum super flumen Santerni." The road between Sant'Agatha and Cornacchiaia ran directly below the walls of the Ubaldini seat at Monteaccianico; see D. Sterpos, *Communicazioni stradali attraverso i tempi: Bologna – Firenze* (Rome, 1961), chap. 3, note 50.

19. The war against the Ubaldini in 1306 is described in GV *Cron.*, VIII, chap. 86 (see Intro., n. 4); see Document 3. For the attacks on Firenzuola in 1342 and 1351, see GV *Cron.*, XI, chap. 139; MV *Cron.*, II, chap. 6. For the Ubaldini war of 1348, see notes 11 – 14. For the siege of 1351, see note 9.

20. While Villani merely chronicles the destruction of Monteaccianico, another writer of the period notes that the purpose of the action was "c'ognuomo andasse sichuro da Firenze a Bologna" (see P. Santini, *Quesiti e ricerche di storiografia fiorentina* [Florence, 1903], pp. 128 – 129).

21. In letters of 13 February 1309 the Florentine *Signoria* advised the Ubaldini and the government of Bologna "quod strata qua itur Florentia Bononiam currat per partes et terram sancti Barnabe que dicitur Scarperia." ASF *SS. Miss.*, 1, fols. 99r – 100r.

22. F. Sartini, ed., *Statuti dell'arte degli albergatori della città di Firenze (1324 –*

1342) (Florence, 1955), pp. 156 – 157.

23. Marco di Coppo Stefani, *Cronica*, rubric 548.

24. These points are mentioned in the travel itineraries of Rinaldo degli Albizzi (*Commissioni di Rinaldo degli Albizzi per il comune di Firenze, 1399 – 1433* [Florence, 1867], 3 vols).

25. GV *Cron.*, VIII, chap. 86; see Intro., note 4.

26. GV *Cron.*, XI, chap. 53; see Intro., note 3.

27. GV *Cron.*, VIII, chap. 17; see Intro., note 1.

28. GV *Cron.*, X, chap. 199; see Intro., note 5.

29. ASF *Provv.*, 41, fol. 113v, 17 December 1354:

> Coram vobis, magnificis et potentibus viris, dominis prioribus artium et Vexillifero Iustitie populi et Comunis Florentie, reverenter exponitur pro parte hominum et universitatis et Comunis castri S. Barnabe, cui dicitur Scarperia de Mucello, subditorum fidelium et devotorum vestrorum, quod homines dicti castri pro maiori parte sunt progeniti et descendentes de hominibus et personis qui olim sub tirannide Ubaldinorum apud montem Accianichum et alibi tenebantur occupati. Et quod post de tirannide predicta per populum et Comune Florentie potenti manu fuerunt liberati et adunati ad habitandum in dicto castro S. Barnabe, hedificato et posito per populum et Comune predictum, ubi permanserunt et permanere intendunt sub dominatione, obedientia et fidelitate populi et Comunis predicta et Partis Guelfe.

30. P. Farulli, *Annali overo notizie istoriche dell' antica nobile e valorosa città di Arezzo in Toscana* (Foligno, 1717), I, p. 228: "Questa Badia (Agnano) fu padrona di tutto il territorio fino al Castello di Cappanole, di Castiglione Alberti, di Montelucci, di Cacciano, di Cornia, della Pieve a Presciano, chè poi tutti questi castelli divenne padrona, siccome di 24 comuni; ciò si prova dall' archivio di Santa Maria in Grado, dalla Cronica manoscritta di Don Tommaso Mini Nobile Fiorentino."

31. Johanne Benedicto Mittarelli and Anselmo Costadoni, *Annales camaldenses Sancti Benedicti* (Venice, 1761), V, pp. 555 – 558, document 320, 28 October 1340.

32. Farulli, *Annali*, I, pp. 227 – 228, also refers to the original donation dated AD 900.

33. Repetti, *Dizionario*, IV (1841), s.v."San Pancrazio."

34. P. Farulli, *Cronologia delle famiglie umbre e toscane*, I, pp. 239 – 240.

35. Castiglione Alberti and Cornia were listed as belonging to the Ubertini in the charters of Corrado II and Philip of Hohenstaufen. In 1221 the Conti Guidi promised not to disturb the Ubertini in these two towns (Farulli, *Annali*, I, pp. 239 – 240). Castiglione Alberti came into the hands of the abbey only in 1326, and then by the very questionable means of a donation

from Guido Tarlati, the head of the rival feudal clan of the Aretine *contado*, while he was bishop of Arezzo (ibid., pp. 229 – 230). It is not known when Cornia came into the abbey's possession, but it seems clear that the change of ownership was contested by the Ubertini. In the document of the clan's final surrender to Florence, written thirty-five years after the town was ceded to the city by the abbey of Agnano, Cornia was listed as having been under the rule of Farinato degli Ubertini (U. Pasqui, *Documenti per la storia della città di Arezzo* [Florence, 1937], III, pp. 247 – 258, document 85, 26 June 1385). In a similar manner, in the 1353 treaty to end the FlorentineVisconti war Casciano was recognized as belonging to Buoso degli Ubertini as bishop of Arezzo (Pasqui, *Documenti*, III, pp. 116 – 123, document 818, 31 March 1353).

36. Pasqui, *Documenti*, III, pp. 21 – 22, document 783, 28 May 1337. Pier Saccone and Tarlato Tarlati sold to the commune of Florence, "quinque partes et dimidiam alterius partis de otto partibus: videlicet castri et Comunis Bucini, castri et Comunis Galatronis, castri et Comunis Turris, castri et comunis Sancte Reparate ed ville de Renola et curias et territoria et districtus dictorum castrorum et Comunium ac ville predicte et cuiuslibet ipsorum."

37. P. Guidi, *Tuscia, I, Le decime degli anni 1274 – 1280* (Vatican, 1932), pp. 90 – 91; M. Giusti and P. Guidi, *Tuscia, II, Le decime degli anni 1295 – 1304* (Vatican, 1942), p. 109.

NOTES TO CHAPTER 2

1. Archivio di Stato, Siena, *Capitoli*, 3, 1. The Talamone plan is not an architect's drawing, but a notarial document that records the names of the men to whom the lots in the town have been assigned. A similar drawing, also from the fourteenth century, survives for the founded town of Ston in Yugoslavia (*Arhitektura*, 31 [1977], pp. 160 – 161). Technical plans of this kind are known to have existed for larger cities as well. Lapo di Castiglion-chio reported the existence of such a plan of Florence in a letter of 1377 (G. Bofitto and A. Mori, *Firenze nelle vedute e piante* [Florence, 1926], p. xix). It included the measurement of the city wall, the streets and squares, the houses and the gardens. The Sienese statutes of 1262 speak of a plan of the city prepared in 1218, which the government intended to update (L. Zdekauer, *Il costituto del comune di Siena dell'anno 1262* [Milan, 1897], section 3, rubrics 13, 56). The plan of Venice prepared in the early twelfth century by the Milanese surveyor Hellia Magadizzo survives in three later copies, including one from the fourteenth century. It presents a more

accurate representation of Venice than does the iconographical image of Rome in the *Chronologia Magna*. Still, its account is only an approximation, without a geometrical foundation and dependent, probably, on repeated corrections for its points of agreement with the reality of the city's physical shape. In the representation of the Grand Canal it is easy to see that the plan uses conventional forms—an even width and unbroken curves—to represent, rather than reproduce, the idiosyncratic course of this urbanized channel in the lagoon (J. Schulz, "Jacopo de' Barbari's View of Venice: Map Making, City Views, and Moralized Geography Before the Year 1500," *Art Bulletin* 60 [September, 1978], pp. 425 – 474, esp. p. 432, n. 20, p. 445, n. 60, fig. 9; W. Braunfels, *Mittelalterliche Stadtbaukunst in der Toskana* [Berlin, 1953], pp. 77 – 78).

2. The Florentine *braccio* equals 0.584 meters; see D.F. Zervas, "The Florentine Braccio da Panna," *Architectura* 9 (1979), pp. 6 – 10.

3. In a letter of 22 April 1350 the Florentine *Signoria* ordered the residents of the town to complete the defenses (ASF *SS. Miss.*, 10, fols. 37r and v). In a *Provvisione* of 1 June 1364 the attention of the *Signoria* turned to the gates and towers: "Comune et popolus Terrenuove debeant portas et turres dicti castri . . . perfici facere usque ad altitudinem quindecim bracchiorum super muros dicti castri" (Gaye, *Carteggio*, I, p. 514). The construction of the reinforcing towers was usually a secondary stage in the raising of a defense. The orders concerning them must indicate that the wall was already completed. On 27 October 1367 the *Signoria* approved the disbursement of Florentine funds for the completion of the defenses of Terranuova. The document notes that eight towers were already built and that there were sixteen still to go (Gaye, *Carteggio*, I, p. 519).

4. Richter, "Terra murata," pp. 382 – 384, document 5f, reproduces a contract of 24 May 1335 given out by the Florentine officials to two Florentine masons for the construction of the Porta Fiorentina. Another mason, Ceffus Lippi Manni, from the parish of San Tomaso in Florence, was paid for the construction of three gates with twenty-five *braccia* of wall on either side by Nepum Cecchi, the treasurer of the Florentine officials (ASF *Cap.*, 35, fol. 222r, 27 June 1338; fol. 225r, 28 November 1338), while three men, "omnibus habitatoribus dicte terre de Florenzuola," were paid by Clarus Nuti Mercoiani de Florenzuola, the treasurer of the town, for the construction of walls and towers (ASF *Cap.*, 35, fol. 224r, 4 September 1338; see also Richter, "Terra murata," document 5h). The records of both treasurers' payments are in the documents of the Florentine building committee. MV *Cron.*, II, chap. 6, at 1351, has: "I Ubaldini . . . corsono a Firenzuola, chè si redificava pe' fiorentini, ma non ancora cinta di mura,

nè di fossi, nè di steccati, ma incominciata, e dentro v'erano capanne per alberghi, e lieve guardia per tener sicuro il cammino, sicchè senza contrasto la presono e arsono." For the work of 1371, see Intro., note 7.

5. Gaye, *Carteggio*, p. 518, from *Provvisioni*, 57, 19 August 1367: "pro parte comunis et hominum de Scarperia comitatus flor. reverenter exponitur — quod, quum ipse homines a modico tempore citra multas expensas fecerint in conservatione fortilitie dicti castri, nichilominus inverunt et inveniunt steccatum dicti castri marcidium et distructum, quod impossibile esset eis illud absque dominationis vestrae subsidio reficere, et quod in ipsa expensa steccati, licet fuerit et sit utilis ad opportunitatem subito imminentem, nichilominius quia hius modo lignamina modico tempore durant, utilis esset, dum possible suppetit et tempus patitur, fortificare cum muris." Despite the *Signoria*'s positive response to this petition, it was necessary to repeat it in 1370 with the remark "quod multi credunt esse melius dictam terram paulatim murare" (Gaye, *Carteggio*, I, p. 523, from a *Provvisione* of 7 June 1370).

6. For the walls, ASF *Cap.*, 35, fol. 242, 28 February 1336 / 7; Richter, "Terra murata," document 5h. The walls were to rise ten *braccia* above the escarpement at their base and have machicolations of two *braccia* plus the height of the merlons, which I estimate at another two *braccia*. The escarpment should have been the same height, six *braccia,* as the one on the adjacent gates. The contract for one of the gates is recorded in ASF, *Cap.*, 35, fol. 232v, 24 May 1335 and is reproduced in Richter, "Terra murata," document 5f. For the gate, ASF *Cap.*, 35, fol. 227r, 28 February 1336; Richter, "Terra murata," document 5h.

7. The defenses of the new towns should be compared for scale with the walls of Florence which were 20 *braccia* (11.68 meters) high and 3.5 *braccia* (2.05 meters) thick, with reinforcing towers ranging from 40 to 60 *braccia* (23.36 to 35.04 meters) in height and gates of over 60 *braccia*. See D. Friedman, "The Porta a Faenza and the Last Circle of the Walls of Florence," in *Essays Presented to Myron P. Gilmore*, ed. S. Bertelli and G. Ramakus (Florence, 1978), II, pp. 179 – 192.

8. Richter, "Terra Murata," document 5h.

9. ASF *Stat. Com.*, 831, Statutes of the League of Scarperia, 1427, fol. 40r. No one was permitted to butcher an animal anywhere in the town between the months of April and November "except on the street that is next to the town wall."

10. "Terra di San Giovanni Valdarno[.] La via dentro alle mure large BXX[.] Le mura grosse B 1 ½[.] El fosso et la via intorna al fosso B XXXVII[.] Et [p]iù dove gli è fondamento."

11. D. Ballestracci and G. Piccinni, *Siena nel trecento,* (Florence, 1977), p. 82.

12. Braunfels, *Stadtbaukunst,* pp. 63 – 64, n. 151, citing a law of 1323.

13. For Scarperia's keep, see chap. 5, note 76; Repetti (*Dizionario,* II [1835], s.v. "Firenzuola"), without citing his source, says that Firenzuola received its *cassero* at this date. The paramilitary building that now stands on the west side of the town's piazza has been much rebuilt, but seems first to have been worked on by Antonio di Sangallo the elder between 1495 and 1499; G. Severini, *Architettura militari di Giuliano di Sangallo* (Pisa, 1970), p. 28, n. 27, p. 34, n. 39.

14. For the decoration of gates, see Braunfels, *Stadtbaukunst,* pp. 82 – 85; for San Giovanni, see E. Baldi, *L'Oratorio della Madonna delle Grazie in San Giovanni Val d'Arno* (Florence, 1914), pp. 15 – 20. The 1484 *Capitoli* of the company note that each of the town's four gates was decorated with an image of the Virgin; Baldi, *L'Oratorio,* p. 75.

15. Richter, "Terra Murata," documents 5f, m.

16. The contracts given out by the building committee for the Florentine wall were based on a regular sequence of towers (Friedman, "Porta a Faenza," pp. 179, 187, n. 5). Giovanni Villani, who served on the committee, criticized the walls at the place where, from necessity, they departed from this sequence (GV *Cron.,* IX, chap. 256).

17. ASF *Stat. Com.,* 831, Statutes of the League of Scarperia, 1427, fol. 37v:
Perche a niuno e lecito con dampno altrui farsi richo, ma solamente star contento a quello gli tocha in parte, statuto e ordinato é che niuno alberghatore o vinactiere o altro artefice di qualunche conditione si sia, maschio o femmina o altri mercatanti invitare o invitare fare ad albergho o bere o mangiare a comperare o vendere né uscire fuori del soglare dell' uscio della casa loro, per alcuno invitare o delle decte loro case chiamare forte, o pane, vino, orciuoli, o fieno, o niuna merchatantia o niuna altra cosa mostrare, se non quando coloro che passano et che vogliono alberghare o mercatanti fussino contro o per me' la casa dell albergatore o del vinatieri o i merchatanti, et dal mezo del righaguolo della strada.
If a passerby was interested in buying, the merchant or hotel keeper was permitted to:
invitare pianamente et per modo convenevole, et uscir fuori de casa sua per due braccia et non piu per invitare in modo predicto verso di cotale che invitare volesse. Al quale alberghatore sia lecito, o vinactiere, o merchatante nel decto caso invitare pianamente et per modo convenevole et uscir fuori di casa sua per due braccia et non piu per invitare al modo predicto, socto pena et a pena di soldi dieci per ciascheduno che

contrafacesse et per ciaschuna volta. Et che niuno albergatore del chastello predicto, di qualunque condictione si sia, per niuno tempo, et maximamente al tempo della quaresima quando i romei vanno al perdono, et quando tornano, ardischa overo presumma in niuno modo publicamente o occultamente andare usare el chastello della Scarperia o mandare alcuno huomo, overo persona, interpetro, o non interpetro a invitare o vero per invitare alcuno, a pena di soldi venti per ciascheduno et quante volte.

Et che niuno alberghatore overo vinactiere o altra persona venda o apparechi agl'albergatori che passano ardischa o presumma i'niuno modo cuocere, o cuocere fare, alcuna cosa, o aparechiare o apparechiato tenere nella strada maestra del decto chastello se non solamente nella casa della sua habitatione alla pena di soldi venti per ciascheduno et ciascheduna volta, et che niuna persona ardischi overo presummi vendere o vendere fare per alcuno tempo alcune carni di pecora di troia o mocticine cocte o crude senon solamente in piaza al canto del cassero o nel mercatale del chastello nel dì d'mercato, si veramente quelle non vendano presso a' becchai delle decte legha o oltre a di loro a 40 braccia (ibid., fol. 38r).

18. Homeowners at Scarperia were ordered to pave the section of the channel lying behind their houses to assure the free passage of water through and out of the town; ASF *Stat. Com.*, 831, Statutes of the League of Scarperia, 1423, fols. 32r and v (for the text of this document, see chap. 7, note 29).

19. ASF *Cap.*, 4, fols. 46 – 50 (also fols. 98v, 105v), in which seven documents were recorded by Francesco Masi, Florentine notary, April 3 – 10, 1350.

20. The street grid of the Giglio Fiorentino scheme provided for a maximum of 356 lots. There would have been 3 less, given that the *cassero* had to be accommodated, and another 1 less, at least, for both of the *palazzo* of the Florentine official and the church (see note 22). Another 16 lots would have been eliminated to make room for the streets by the walls at the short ends of the town, and another 12 if the lots of eight *braccia* on the main cross street were combined with the lots of ten *braccia* next to them to make large lots at these favored locations. The *palazzo* of the Florentine official might have been enlarged by another lot and the church by as many as 3. This gives a minimum of 320 lots.

21. The Giglio Fiorentino building program required that all houses on the streets leading from the town's gates be built to a height of at least ten *braccia* with facades "de lapidibus seu lateribus" (Document 19). The plan of San Giovanni of 1559 (Fig. 5), as well as the evidence of the remains at all the new-town sites, shows that the floor space on these lots was also

extended by the construction of an extra story.

22. At San Giovanni the church of San Lorenzo (Fig. 4), which lies on the south side of the town's central square and which appeared in the tithe rolls of 1274 / 5 and 1302 / 3 as S. Laurentii de Plano Alberti (Guidi, *Decima 1274 – 1280*, no. 865; Giusti and Guidi, *Decima 1295 – 1304*, no. 1187), seems to have been rebuilt on its present site in 1306 (F. Gherardi Dragomanni, *Memorie della terra di San Giovanni* [Florence, 1834], p. 27). The church of San Giovanni (Figs. 8, 9) stands opposite the Palazzo del Podestà on the north side of the square and seems to have been founded in 1312. Only in 1672 did it receive the status of parish church, making it the administrative superior of all the other churches in town (Dragomanni, *Memorie*, pp. 27, 138 – 140). Castelfranco has no church in its central square today, but according to the town's *statuti* of 1394, a church dedicated to San Piero was located there (G. Camerani Marri, ed., *Statuti di Castelfranco di Sopra*, 1394 [Florence, 1963], p. 44). The view of the town preserved in the archives of the Capitani di Parte shows the church in the northwest corner of the square (ASF, *Piante dei Capitani di Parte*, Piante dei popoli e steade, 121 / I, fol. 253v) (Fig. 12). It flanks the main street and faces the square. The site is presently occupied by a residential building. The parish church of the town, dedicated to San Tommaso, is now located two blocks from the square, on the main cross street. The church at Scarperia (Figs. 25, 90, 91) is located on the north side of the square. It was begun at the time of the foundation of the town, but was not made the head of an independent parish until 1364 (Document 9). The main church of Firenzuola, Santi Giovanni e Fiorenzo, was placed on the north side of the central square, facing onto the main road (the same position as the church at Scarperia). It may have been built within a few years of the town's foundation. A document of 24 May 1334 mentions diverting for the construction of the church all the income then being used to build the then almost complete *palazzo* of the Florentine official (Document 14). The main church of Terranuova, also on the central square, was placed there only in the fifteenth century (see page 169). At Giglio Fiorentino the parish church of San Piero was to have been transferred to the new town from the village of Pieve a Prisciano at the time of the new town's foundation. The church would have been placed in the central square, opposite the palace of the Florentine official (Document 19).

23. ASF *Stat. Com.*, 831, Statutes of the League of Scarperia, 1427, fol. 56v. Marri, ed., *Statuti di Castelfranco*, pp. 36 – 37.

24. ASF *Stat. Com.*, 317, Statutes of Firenzuola, 1418, fol. 22v.

25. Ibid., fols. 17r and v.
26. ASF *SS. Miss.*, 2, 22 July 1311.
27. Archivio Comunale di Castelfranco di Sopra, *Statuti del Comune di Castelfranco*, 21 March 1408 / 9, fol. 25r.
28. Ibid., fol. 26r; at Scarperia the market was regulated by three "castaldoni" elected by the league who were specifically empowered to check the quality of the grain sold at the market and to see that all measures were honest and sealed with the mark of Florence (ASF *Stat. Com.*, 831, Statutes of the League of Scarperia, 1423, fols. 11r – 13v).
29. Archivio Comunale di Castelfranco di Sopra, *Statuti del Comune di Castelfranco*, 21 March 1408 / 9, fols. 24v – 25r.
30. ASF *Stat. Com.*, 831, Statutes of the League of Scarperia, 1423, fol. 38r: "et che niuna persona ardischi overo presumi vendere o vendere fare per alcuno tempo alcune carni di pecore, di buia, o mocticine cocte o crude senon solamente in piazza al canto del cassero o nel mercatale del chastello nel dì del mercato."
31. Archivio Comunale di Castelfranco di Sopra, *Statuti del Comune di Castelfranco*, 21 March 1408 / 9, fol. 24v: "Che in sulla piazza di Castelfranco si facci ogni mercoledi mercato." The market loggia of the town, located on the square, is noted in the original edition of the statutes from 1394; Marri, ed., *Statuti di Castelfranco*, rubric 17.
32. ASF *Stat. Com.*, 317, Statutes of Firenzuola, 1418, fol. 30r, rubric 55: "Del mercato da non farsi nel castello di Firenzuola statuarono et ordinarono che il mercato predicto si faccia et fare si debbi continuamente fuori del castello di Firenzuola sul merchatale acciò deputato e in niuno modo fare si possa nè debba dentro nil dicto castello."
   In the fifteenth century the local commune was very careful about the organization of the booths on the *mercatale* and the rental of space there; ASF *Stat. Com.*, 831, Statutes of the League of Scarperia, 1423, fol. 48v: "Acciò che per niuna lungheza di tempo possa a ssè il terreno della decta lega et maximamente quello del merchatale apropriarsi, statuto et ordinato e . . . fra uno mese dal dì della publicagione del presente statuto sieno tenuti et debbino [the town officials] constringnere et gravare et constringnere et gravare fare tucte et ciaschune bocteghe, cioè coloro che ànno bocteghe o alcuno edificio nel decto mercatale della lega et coloro che da quinci inanzi la veranno a riconoscere quello terreno sopralquale averà edificato o edificato avesse per publica carta le quali carte che delle predecte cose si faranno registrare et scriversi debbano in su libri et registri della decta lega." Individuals were not permitted to erect booths on the *mercatale* "senon verso i fossi et verso la strada overo gli orti," that is,

except around the perimeter of the market field, so that the space at the center remained open (ASF *Stat. Com.*, 831, Statutes of the League of Scarperia, 1423, fol. 49r).

33. ASF *SS. Miss.*, 6, 8 June 1341; published in *Bollettino storico-letterario del Mugello*, 1 (1893), pp. 79 – 80: "Quoniam hiis, per que Sanctorum solepnia possint aliqualiter impediri, est summo studio resistendum, scientes quod in terra vestra festivitas Beati Barnabe apostoli, patroni vestri, est tam per fratres Agustinos quam per vestrarum ecclesiarum rectores honorifice in proximo celebranda, volumus et mandamus quatenus scandalis, que occasione quacumque in ipsa solepnitate verisimiliter possint occurrere, debeatis utiliter obviare, et prope loca ecclesiarum, in quibus in terra vestra ipsa sunt solepnia celebranda, removeri faciatis tabernas et lusores et reliqua, que ipsi solepnitati possint impedimenta prestare, nec patiamini quod in platea comuni vestri fiat aliqua copertura, huiusmodi mandata nostra effectualiter impleturi."

34. Today the side of the piazza north of the east – west road is between 15.88 and 17.6 meters deep (the building facades bordering the piazza are not exactly parallel) while the side to the south is 28 meters deep. If the two sides were once equal, which would be in keeping with the symmetry that characterizes all other aspects of the plans, it is more probable that the larger measurement is original. In any urban situation, but especially in the new towns, it is much easier to usurp public space than to enlarge it. Thus, the piazza would have had proportions of approximately 2 : 3.

NOTES TO CHAPTER 3

1. G. Maetzke, *Florentia* (Rome, 1941); C. Hardie, "The Origin and Plan of Roman Florentia," *Journal of Roman Studies* 55 (1965), pp. 122 – 140.
2. S. Lang, "Sull'origine della disposizione a scacchiera nelle città medioevali in Inghilterra, Francia e Germania," *Palladio*, n.s. 5 (July – December 1955), pp. 97 – 108.
3. E. Duprè Theseider, "Frederico II, ideatore di castelli e città," *Archivio Storico Pugliese* 26 (1973), p. 38, n. 33. For the ancient ritual, see J. Rykwert, *The Idea of a Town* (Princeton, 1976), pp. 65 – 68.
4. GV *Cron.*, I, chap. 38.
5. Ibid., chap. 36.
6. GV *Cron.*, III, chap. 2.
7. M. Biddle and D. Hill, "Late Saxon Planned Towns," *The Antiquaries Journal* 51 (1971), pp. 70 – 85; M. Biddle, "The Evolution of Towns: Planned Towns before 1066," *C.B.A. Research Report* 14, ed. M.W. Barley (London, 1975), pp. 19 – 32.

8. For a summary of the north German evidence, see M.W. Barley, *European Towns: Their Archeology and Early History* (London, 1977), pp. 127 – 157, 243 – 259; for the early French settlements, see P. Laveden and J. Hugueney, *L'Urbanisme au Moyen Age* (Geneva, 1974), pp. 61 – 67, figs. 177 (Nogaro), 184 (Saint-Nicolas-de-la-Grave).

9. P. Dinelli, *Camaiore, dalle origini ai giorni nostri* (Camaiore, 1971), I, pp. 178, 187.

10. F. Buselli, *Pietrasanta e le sue rocche* (Florence, 1970), p. 70; Dinelli, *Camaiore,* I, pp. 180 – 189.

11. In the thirteenth century the politics of Lucca and Florence were so closely intertwined that the two cities hired the same men to serve as public officials. Guiscardo da Pietrasanta, a Milanese nobleman of Guelph loyalties, served as foreign official, or *podestà,* in Florence in 1254. In the following year, and for unprecedented further terms in 1256 and 1257, he held the same office in Lucca (D. Scalabrella, *Vita Eroica del Milanese Guiscardo da Pietrasanta fondatore del "cuore della Versilia"* [Pietrasanta, 1964], p. 6; Dinelli, *Camaiore,* I, p. 179, n. 1). During his Lucchese service, Guiscardo led the city's armies against its feudal enemies in Versiglia. To secure the armies' conquests, he founded Camaiore and Pietrasanta. The chronicler Ptolemy of Lucca tells us that it was from Guiscardo that the eponymous town of Pietrasanta received its name (Ptolomei Lucensis, "Annales," *Documenti di storia Italiana* [Florence, 1876] VI, p. 78).

  Guiscardo's service to the Florentines was even more illustrious. The year of his tenure as *podestà* was "l'anno vittorioso" (G.V. *Chron.,* VI, chap. 58) of the Florentine Primo Popolo. The city's armies defeated the Sienese, winning Poggibonsi, Montalcino, and Volterra, entering the latter city and establishing a Guelph government there. They so intimidated Pisa, Florence's other Ghibelline enemy in Tuscany, that the city won trading concessions at Pisa's port and received (and gave to Lucca) the fortress of Ripafratta on the Serchio. Giovanni Villani reports these events in four chapters of his chronicle, repeating three times "essendo podestà di Firenze il detto messer Guiscardo da Pietrasanta di Milano" (GV *Cron.,* VI, chaps. 55 – 58).

  Lucchese Pietrasanta is one of two Tuscan new towns that bear this name. Florentine Pietrasanta, founded in 1285 (see Intro., note 9), failed, and its plan was destroyed. Whether that plan reproduced the design of its Lucchese predecessor could now only be uncovered by excavation. While the first Florentine new town might have been the intermediary between the Lucchese plan and San Giovanni, the idea to found towns in the Arno valley was under discussion in the Florentine councils during the whole period of the work at Florentine Pietrasanta (Document 1). For six months of that time, in 1288, Guiscardo's son Pagano was the Florentine *capitano del popolo* (Scalabrella, *Vita Eroica*, p. 19). Pagano died in 1300. His grave in San Ambrogio in Milan bears a tombstone that recalls his service to the Florentines.

12. C. Meckseper, "Rottweil: Untersuchung zur Stadtbaugeschichte im Hochmittelalter," 2 vols. (Ph.D. diss., University of Stuttgart, 1969), I, pp. 260 – 278. For the older interpretation, see E. Hamm, *Die Städtegründungen der Herzöge von Zähringen in Sudwestdeutschland* (Freiburg im Breisgau, 1932).

13. E. Leiwehr and O. Grimm, *Marktplätze in Sudostbayern* (Passau, 1976); see also L. Rothenfelder, "Die Wittelsbacher als Städtegründer in Bayern," *Verhandlungen des historischen Vereines für Niederbayern*, 47 (1911), pp. 1 – 106.

Straubing, the largest and most prosperous of the Wittelsbach new towns, founded in 1281 in an area dominated by the bishop of Regensburg, has a market street 38 meters wide and 600 meters long crossed at the approximate center of the plan by a street running between the town's north and south gates. In the middle of the market, astride the intersection, is a tower with a vaulted north – south passage at its base, built by the town in 1316. The tower is clearly visible in the wooden model of the town dated 1568, made by the local woodworker, Jacob Sandtner (Alexander Freiherr von Reitzenstein, *Die alte bairische Stadt* [Munich, 1967]; Freiherr von Reitzenstein discusses Sandtner's models of the towns of Munich, Landshut, Ingolstadt, Straubing, and Burghausen); see also K. Bosl, ed., *Straubing, das neue und das alte Geschichte einer Stadt im altbayerischen Kernland* (Straubing, 1968); J. Laschinger, "Die Stadtkorporationen in den Landstanden am Beispiel der Stadt Straubing," *Jahresbericht des historischen Vereins für Straubing und Umgebung* 83 (1981), pp. 27 – 42.

14. A. Klaar, "Strassenplatz und Rechteckplatz," *Unsere Heimat* (Monatsblatt der Vereins für Landeskunde und Heimatschutz von Niederösterreich und Wien), n.s. 6 (1933), pp. 7 – 19; idem, "Der gotische Städtebau in Österrich," in *Die bildende Kunst in Österreich, gotische Zeit*, ed. K. Ginhart (Raden in Wien, 1938), pp. 13 – 25; idem, "Die Siedlungsformen der Österreichischen Donaustadt," in *Die Städte Mitteleuropas im 12. and 13. Jahrhundert* (Beiträge zur Geschichte der Städte Mitteleuropas), ed. W. Rausch (Linz, 1963), I, pp. 95 – 96.

15. For plans of the Austrian towns discussed here, see *Atlas der historischen Schutzzonen in Österreich I: Städte und Märkte* (Graz, 1970); H. Koepf, *Stadtbaukunst in Österreich*, (Salzburg, 1972).

16. K. Dinklage, "Völkermarkt zwischen Abt und Herzog; ein Beitrag zur Gründungsgeschichte mittelalterliche Städte," *Mitteilungen des Institut für Österreichische Geschichtsforschung* 67 (1959), pp. 278 – 305.

17. G. Clonfero, *Venzone, guida storico-artistico*, 3d. ed. (Udine, 1975); idem, *La cerchia murata di Venzone* (Udine, 1976); L. Ciceri, ed., *Venzon*, 48th Congress of the Società Filologica Friulana (Udine, 1971); U. Michele, "Venzone," in *Storia dell'arte italiana*, pt. 3 (Inchieste su Centri Minori), ed. E. Guidoni (Turin, 1980) I, pp. 37 – 68.

18. To the west, where the Tagliamento ran by the town, the medieval street ended at the Augustinian church of San Giovanni.

19. All of the buildings of Venzone, including many handsome residential constructions of the fourteenth and fifteenth centuries, were heavily damaged in the earthquake of 1976.

   Versions of the intersection plan appear in northern Germany, too. While significantly different from their counterparts founded in the lands under Hohenstaufen influence in the south, the north German towns are the only other examples in Europe of the plan type under discussion here. Brunswick Altstadt, founded in the first decades of the twelfth century, is the earliest example of this type (E. Keyser, *Städtegründungen und Städtebau in Nordwestdeutschland im Mittelalter* [Remagen, 1958], pp. 191 – 204). The intersection plan is repeated in the later additions to Braunschweig itself and in the late-twelfth- and early-thirteenth-century foundations of the Ludowingian landgraves in neighboring Thuringia (W. Hesse, *Hessische Städtegründungen der Landgrafen von Thüringen*, Beiträge zur Hessische Geschichte [Marburg and Witzenhausen, 1966] IV). Examples elsewhere, like Itzehoe in Holstein, founded by the Schauenberg count Adolf IV in 1227 (Keyser, *Städtegründungen*, p. 150), and Freienstein in Pomerania carry this plan type well into the thirteenth century.

20. Clonfero, *Venzone*, p. 7.

21. For a discussion of the participation of masons from the cathedral workshop in the town building activity of Italian cities, see below, pp. 163 – 165.

22. C. Baracchini and A. Caleca, *Il duomo di Lucca* (Lucca, 1973), pp. 19, 21.

23. Ibid., p. 25.

24. Ibid., p. 24; Pietro Guidi, "Di alcuni maestri Lombardi a Lucca nel secolo XIII,"*Archivio Storico Italiano*, 7th ser., 12, no. 2 (1930), pp. 209 – 231. Guidi reproduces documents of 11 August 1242, 22 August 1242, 29 September 1248, 16 April 1250, 11 January 1251, 11 September 1251, and 16 June 1257 in all of which Lombardo is referred to as "operarius ecclesie Sancti Martini" or the like.

25. Baracchini and Caleca, *Duomo*, p. 22.

26. M.L. Cristiani Testi, *San Miniato al Tedesco* (Florence, 1967), p. 59.

27. G. Agnello, "Il castello svevo di Prato," *Rivista dell'istituto nazionale d'architettura e storia dell'arte*, n.s. 3 (1954), pp. 147 – 227; F. Guerrieri, ed.,

Il castello dell'imperatore a Prato (Prato, 1975).

28. G. Tommasi, *Sommario della storia di Lucca dall'anno MIV all'anno MDCC compilato in documenti contemporanei* (Florence, 1847), p. 79; A. Mancini, *Storia di Lucca* (Florence, 1950), p. 93.

    If it was through the empire that the intersection plan was transmitted to Tuscany, the foundations with which Frederick was himself involved in Sicily and the kingdom of Naples seem not to have played a role. Designed to fulfill very different requirements, the form of these towns bears no similarity to either the Tuscan or the German plans; see I. Nigrelli, "La 'fondazione' federicana di Gela ed Augusta," *Siculorum Gymnasium* 6 (1953), pp. 166 – 184; P.F. Palumbo, "La fondazione di Manfredonia," in *Contributi alla storia dell'età di Manfredi* (Biblioteca Storica, IV) (Rome, 1959), pp. 71 – 107; E. Duprè Theseider, "Federico II, ideatore di castelli e città," *Archivio Storico Pugliese* 26 (1973), pp. 25 – 40; A.M. Guidoni, "Architettura paesaggio e territorio dell'Italia meridionale nella cultura federicana," *Federico II e l'arte del duecento italiano*, Atti della III settimana di studi di storia dell' arte medievale dell'università di Roma, ed. A.M. Romanini (Galatina, 1980), I, pp. 75 – 98.

29. A.M. Romanini, "La Rielaborazione Trecentesca di Pavia Romana," in *Atti del Convegno di Studio sul centro storico di Pavia*, 4 – 5 July 1964 (1968), p. 127.

30. L. Simeoni, "Il comune," in V. Cavallari, P. Gazzola, A. Scolari, eds., *Verona e il suo territorio* (Verona, 1964), II, pp. 304, n. 4; 309.

31. My thanks to Professor Kurt Forster for pointing to the importance of the Piazza Erbe in this context.

32. The commune of Novara received the land and the residents of Borgo San Leonardo, later called Borgomanero, from the counts of Biandrate by virtue of a treaty signed in 1202. The document included a provision for payment to the counts for the land within the walls of the town "secundum quod valebat ante constructionem illius loci," suggesting that construction may have preceded the treaty (V. De Vit, *Memorie storiche di Borgomanero e del suo mandamento* [Milan, 1959], pp. 214 – 215). In 1259 the church of San Lorenzo was located outside the walls of Borgomanero. This does not preclude, however, the possibility that the walled Borgo San Lorenzo of 1202 and modern Borgomanero occupy the same site, since the separation of church and settlement was not unusual in medieval new towns. Florentine Scarperia, for example, was located two kilometers from the parish church at Fagna. The church on the central square at Borgomanero, San Bartolomeo, was first mentioned in 1225 in a document in which the town was still called Borgo San Leonardo (ibid., p. 92).

33. Borgomanero's position as the site of the first closed-corner square of

Western urban design has been challenged by H. Lillius, *Der Pekkatori in Raahe: Studien über einem eckverschlossenem Platz und seine Gebäudetypen* (Helsinki, 1967). Lillius tries to show that this piazza form was an invention of the Renaissance. He believes that the square at Borgomanero was rebuilt in its present state at the time of the reconstruction of the church of San Bartolomeo. He points out that none of the buildings on the square can be dated by architectural style to the Middle Ages. While this is true, such a problem is not unusual in medieval new towns, especially successful ones. Montauban, the first foundation of the counts of Toulouse established in 1144, has no building, except for the parish church, that appears to be medieval; the structures that surround the famous market place belong to the eighteenth century. In the southern quarter of the square at Borgomanero there is a set of colonnaded arcades that, while still not medieval, would appear to date to the beginning of the sixteenth century. If so, they establish the present form of the square as existing before the rebuilding of San Bartolomeo. The necessity for a Renaissance date for the Borgomanero square is contradicted, too, by the evidence of the squares at Villarreal and Castelfranco, both of which are bordered by buildings that are clearly medieval. If the Borgomanero square is not obliged by its formal character to be Renaissance and cannot be given a late date by documentary evidence, it should probably be dated with the rest of the plan.

34. Before the planning of Castelfranco di Sopra, but after the foundation of Borgomanero, the central square of the city of Parma, a city that inhabited the plan of a Roman colony, was regularized into a form very similar to the squares in the new towns. In 1221 the half of the present-day Piazza Grande that lies south of the Via Emilia, the site of the ancient forum, was cleared and paved in connection with the construction of a second town hall on the east side of the square. At the end of the thirteenth century the northern half of the piazza was given formal order with the construction of large-scale masonry palaces (E. Guidoni, "L'urbanistica dei comuni italiani in età Federicana," in *La città dal medioevo al rinascimento* [Bari, 1981], p. 82; also published in *Atti della III settimana di studi di storia dell'arte medievale dell'università di Roma, 15 – 20 Maggio 1978; Federico II e l'arte del duecento italiano* [1980], pp. 99 – 120; M.C. Cervi, "Evoluzione topografica della Piazza Grande di Parma dall'epoca romana alla fine del secolo XIII," *Archivio Storico per le Provincie Parmensi*, 4th ser., 14 [1962], pp. 31 – 52; J. Schulz, "The Comunal Buildings in Parma," *Mitteilungen des Kunsthistorischen Institutes in Florenz* 26, no. 3 [1982], pp. 277 – 324).

35. The foundation charter of Villarreal is published in P. Ramon de Maria,

El "Ripartiment" de Burriana y Villarreal (Valencia, 1935), pp. 118 – 121. On 22 February 1273, however, the king had already awarded the chaplaincy of the church of Villarreal to a relative of his secretary (R.J. Burns, *The Crusader Kingdom of Valencia; Reconstruction on a Thirteenth Century Frontier* [Cambridge, Mass., 1967], I, p. 70, II, p. 403, n. 120). On 18 April 1275, the king endowed a hospice at Villa regalis (Burns, *Crusader Kingdom*, I, p. 243, II, p. 489, n. 46). By 1400 Villarreal had 598 inhabitants and was a center of the Valencian textile trade (R.J. Burns, *Islam under the Crusaders; Colonial Survival in the Thirteenth Century Kingdom of Valencia* [Princeton, 1973], pp. 75, 93); see also J.M.ª Doñate Sebastia, *La Torre Mocha* (Villarreal, 1977), for an essay on the oldest surviving element of the town wall.

36. The distortion of strict orthogonality may be the result, as it appears to be at the Lucchese town of Camaiore, of the oblique relationship between the course of the main road and the descent of the slope on which the town was placed. The cross streets are oriented with the fall line to facilitate the flow of water through the town.

37. One fourth of the square's perimeter was destroyed in this century, when an entire block at the center of the town was cleared to provide a site for the seat of the provincial administration.

38. "Nos vingué un mestre d'Albenguena qui havia nom Nicoloso, qui feu lo trabuquet nostre de Mallorca, y nos digué: Micer, no us cal estar aqui si vos nos voleu per pendre aquest lloch, que vos lo podeu haver si vos voleu a quinze jorns. Nos demanaremli en qual manera. Ell digué: Doneume fusta, que molta n'hi ha aqui de lledoner y d'uns arbres y d'altres, y fervos tinch un castell de fusta d'ací a vuyt jorns, y fer l'hem allà, aixi com vos sabeu que ferem a Mallorca anar los trabuquets. Nos diguerem que veritat deya, més que'n voliem haver consell ab los Richs homens." James I, king of Aragon, *Cronica o Comentaris del Gloriosissim y invictissim Rey en Jaume I*, ed. A. Aguilo (Barcelona, 1905), pp. 177.

39. If Nicolosa designed the plan of Villarreal, he did not take his inspiration from the new-town foundations in the region of Albenga. The town of Villanuova di Albenga, in the valley of the Arroscia and Lerrone rivers, founded in 1250 and the most prominent of the city's creations, is laid out on an entirely different system. Its plan is organized around a wide central street that serves as a market. This thoroughfare runs between the two gates of the town and has some arcaded porticos. The residential streets are laid at right angles to the market street and intersect it at intervals of seventeen meters (J. Costa Restagno, "La Fondazione di Villanuova di Albenga," *Rivista Inguana e Intemelia*, n.s. 13 [July – December 1958], pp.

135 – 146; M. Celeste Paoli, "Il Restauro delle Mura di Villanuova di Albenga," *Rivista Inguana e Intemelia*, n.s. 13 [July – December 1958], pp. 167 – 169, with plan). The plan follows the type established in Germany by the Zähringer foundations, such as Neuenburg on the Rhine of 1171 – 1181, and in Italy by the plan of Gattinara, a town founded by the commune of Vercelli in 1242, located fourteen kilometers southwest of Borgomanero.

40. According to J. Puig y Cadafalch ("Les Influences Lombardes en Catalogne," *Congrès Archéologique de France* [1960], p. 699), Nicolosa's services to the king were a late event in a long history of Lombard sculptural and architectural activity in Catalonia. Puig y Cadafalch argues for the influence of Lombard masons on the formation of the first Romanesque style in the tenth and eleventh centuries, and cites a document of 1175 in which the master of the cathedral at Urgel says that he will keep five "Lombards" including himself at work on the project for the year: "Ita quod singulis anni habeam et teneam at servitium beatae Mariae me quinto de lombardius id est IIII lombardes et me"; J. Harvey, *The Medieval Architect* (New York, 1972), p. 245, also publishes the document.

41. For a history of Cittaducale, written in 1592 with the use of documents in the town and in Naples, see Sebastiano Marchesi, *Compendio storico di Cittaducale (dall'origine al 1592)* (Rieti, 1875); for the foundation document, dated 15 September 1308, see ibid., pp. 216 – 218; for the modern literature, see F.P. Fiore, "Fondazione e forma di Cittaducale," *Atti del XIX congresso di storia dell'architettura, L'Aquila, 15 – 21 Settembre 1975*, 2 (1980), pp. 475 – 488.

42. Repetti, *Dizionario*, I, (1833), s.v. "Castelfranco di Sotto."

43. GV *Cron.*, IX, chap. 61.

44. The open space that is the heart of the French designs is missing from the plan of Castelfranco di Sotto. A slight widening of the principal northeast – southwest street between the blocks just east of the central intersection passes for the town's main square. It is as inadequate to the requirements of Italian design as it is to the paradigm of the double intersection plan. The original situation may, however, have been different. The late date of the foundation of the church of Saint Peter offers the possibility that the block that the church occupies, adjacent to the present makeshift square, might have been dedicated to public use during the few decades that it was open. Reconstructed like this, the original plan of Castelfranco bears an even closer resemblance to the plan of Sainte-Foy.

The double intersection plan is perhaps the most international of all medieval new-town designs. It appears not only in the southwest of

France, but also in the German east. Two towns in Mecklenburg, for example
—Malchin, founded between 1236 and 1350 by Nikolaus of Werle, and
Neubrandenburg, founded in 1248 by the margrave of Pomerania—have
plans containing square and rectangular blocks that are generated by the
streets bordering the market square. In the course of the thirteenth and
fourteenth centuries German and Polish nobles, Bohemian kings, and the
knights of the Teutonic Order founded additional towns in the East
following this plan (H. Keller, *Die Ostdeutsche Kolonialstadt des 13. Jahrhunderts und ihre südlandischen Vorbilder*, Sitzungsberichte der Wissen-
schaftlichen Gesellschaft an der Johann Wolfgang Goethe-Universität,
Frankfurt-am-Main, vol. 16, no. 3 [Wiesbaden, 1979], with biblio.). Keller
finds Austrian and northern Italian sources for the characteristic "checker-
board" plan of east German colonial towns. The "double intersection"
plan is a subset of this larger category and does not appear in Austria or
northern Italy.

  C. Higounet ("Cisterciens et Bastides," *Le Moyen Age* 56, nos. 1 – 2
[1950], pp. 69 – 84), has shown that abbeys belonging to the Cistercian
order were involved, as partners with the French kings and the lesser nobility, in the foundation of towns laid out on the double intersection plan
in the southwest of France. E. Guidoni ("Cistercensi e città nuove," in *La
Città*, pp. 103 – 122) extended Higounet's arguments to claim that the
Cistercians were responsible for carrying the plan around Europe; he even
attributed its invention to them. The effort to understand the diffusion of
the double intersection plan as a historical event, rather than simply to
acknowledge the typological similarity between widely separated examples, is important, but as Guidoni himself says, the evidence is still incomplete.

  The earliest towns based on the double intersection idea seem to have
been founded in the area east of the Elbe. The first of them consists of
little more than house lots laid out around the square in imitation, according to the traditional interpretation of these plans, of the market at Lübeck
(refounded in 1158). The example cited by Guidoni—Trzebnica in Silesia,
founded in 1203—is only roughly orthogonal. This town does have the
advantage of some immediate connection with the Cistercians, who,
according to the information published by Guidoni, established a church
there at the time of foundation (Guidoni, "Cistercensi," p. 110). In the area
of the southwest of France studied by Higounet, the Cistercians were
associated with twenty-eight foundations. The first of them was Carbonne
on the river Garonne, founded by Alphonse de Poitiers in partnership
with the abbey of Bonnefont in 1256 (Higounet, "Cisterciens," p. 72). It has

only two streets (P. Lavedan and J. Hugueney, *L'Urbanisme au Moyen Age* [Geneva, 1974], fig. 236), which are parallel to each other and border an open space that lies between them at the middle of the town. This is not a double intersection plan. The earliest town of the double intersection type (albeit in incomplete form) that is connected through documents with the Cistercians is Castillones (Lavedan and Hugueney, *Moyen Age*, fig. 250). It was created in 1260 by Alphonse's seneschal for the Agenais on land belonging to the abbey of Cadouin (Higounet, "Cisterciens," p. 72). Since 1255 the Alphonsine administration on its own had been founding double intersection towns like Sainte-Foy that were both completely developed and rigorously surveyed. While it is possible that some influence from the east German towns may have crystallized the double intersection idea for the French royal planners, a very plausible development of the scheme can be constructed from the late foundations of Alphonse's predecessor, Raymond VIII, count of Toulouse (for instance, Lisle d'Albi, founded 1248; see Lavedan and Hugueney, *Moyen Age*, fig. 349) through to the early efforts of Alphonse's own administration (such as Villefranche de Rouergue, founded 1252; see Lavedan and Hugueney, *Moyen Age*, fig. 277). These early plans, like the mature ones that followed them, are focused on the market square. What they lack is a formal system — the double intersection — by which the square generates the plan of the whole town. Characteristic of the greater informality of these early plans is the absence of a consistent arrangement of lots and blocks.

Although it is unlikely that the Cistercians developed the double intersection plan, they may still have had a role in transmitting it across Europe, and their connection with Castelfranco, however tenuous, is worth noting. The Cistercian abbey in the lower Arno valley is the *badia* at Settimo. It was originally Benedictine, then Vallombrosan, and was transferred to the Cistercians in 1238. The Benedictine abbey was founded, along with a sister settlement at Fuccechio, by Lotario di Cadolo in the tenth century. Fuccechio, a powerful site with imperial patronage, dominated the intersection of the Via Romea, the major north – south road through medieval Tuscany, and the road along the Arno. Castelfranco is located less than seven kilometers from Fuccechio (G. Calzolai, *La storia della badia di Settimo* [Florence, 1958]).

45. Their ownership of the castle is first documented in 1217. In 1254 members of the family sold their shares of the castle, the new and the old *mercatale*, and the piazza in front of the presbytery of San Lorenzo (the church on the main square of the present town) to the city of Florence (Ripetti, *Dizionario*, III [1839], s.v. "Montevarchi").

46. G.V. *Cron.*, V, chap. 38; Count Guido Novello was King Manfred's vicar in Tuscany and one of the leaders of the victorious Ghibelline army at Monteaperti in 1260.

47. See note 19.

48. E. Keyser and H. Stoob, eds., *Deutsches Städtebuch* (Stuttgart, 1939 – 1974), III, *Nordwest-Deutschland*, pt. 2, *Westfalen*, ed. E. Keyser (1954), pp. 164 – 172, esp. para. 4a.

NOTES TO CHAPTER 4

1. L.B. Alberti, *L'Architettura* (Milan, 1966), I, p. 65.

2. Ibid., p. 21.

3. Ibid., II, p. 535.

4. Francesco di Giorgio Martini, *Trattati di architettura, ingegneria, e arte militare,* ed. C. Maltese (Milan, 1967), I, p. 4, plate 1. "Parmi di formare la città, rocca e castello a guisa del corpo umano, e che el capo colle appricate membra abbi conferente corrispondenzia, e che el capo la rocca sia, le braccia le sue aggiunte e ricinte mura, le quale circulando partitamente leghi el resto di tutto el corpo, amprissima città."

5. *Filarete's Treatise on Architecture,* trans., with intro. and notes, J.R. Spencer (New Haven, 1969), II, figs. 11v, 13v, 43r; 13r: "Eo to detto come io voglio . . . hedificare questa citta e prima fare il mio disegnio il quale stara in questa forma e proportione. La prima forma sara due quadri adosso luno allaltro non iscontrando gli angholi insieme ma luno angolo verra equalmente distante intradue angholi delluno e dellaltro quadro la proportione anghulare sara didistanza traluno anghulo all altro dieci stadii."

6. R. Mainstone, "Structural Theory and Design Before 1742," *The Architectural Review* 143, no. 854 (1968), pp. 303 – 310.

7. O. Kletzl, *Planfragmente aus der Dombauhütte von Prag* (Stuttgart, 1939); H. Koepf, *Die gotischen Planrisse der Wiener Sammlungen* (Vienna, 1969); F. Bucher, "Design in Gothic Architecture," *Journal of the Society of Architectural Historians* 37 (1968), pp. 49 – 71; idem, "Medieval Architectural Design Methods, 800 – 1560," *Gesta* 11, no. 2 (1973), pp. 37 – 51.

8. Translation from L.R. Shelby, "The Geometrical Knowledge of Medieval Master Masons," *Speculum* 47 (July 1972), p. 395; H.R. Hahnloser, *Villard de Honnecourt: kritische Gesamtausgabe des Bauhuttenbuches ms. fr. 19093 der Pariser Nationalbibliothek* (Vienna, 1935), pp. 11 – 17, pl. 2: "en cest livre puet o[n] trover grant consel de le grant force de maconerie [et] des engiens de carpenterie, [et] si troveres le force de le portraiture, les trais, ensi come li ars de iometrie le [com]ma[n]d[e] [et] ensiagne."

9.   Shelby, "Master Masons," p. 395; see also idem, "The Practical Geometry of the Medieval Mason," *Studies in Medieval Culture* 5 (1975), pp. 133 – 144.

10. P. Frankl, "The Secret of the Medieval Masons," *Art Bulletin* 27 (March 1945), pp. 46 – 64 (including E. Panofsky, "An Explanation of Stornoloco's Formula"); L.R. Shelby, *Gothic Design Techniques: The Fifteenth-Century Design Booklets of Mathes Roriczer and Hanns Schmuttermayer* (Carbondale, Ill., 1977).

11. Hahnloser, *Villard*, pp. 111 – 112, pl. 39.

12. Ibid.; Frankl, "Secret," pp. 57 – 60.

13. *Annali della fabbrica del Duomo di Milano dall'origine fino al presente*, I (Milan, 1877), pp. xvi – xvii; also published in H. Siebenhüner, *Deutsche Künstler am Mailander Dom* (Munich, 1944), p. 69. The document is a letter of 20 December 1401 to Gian Galeazzo Visconti. Its author is a partisan of the northern masters but otherwise unidentified.

14. J.S. Ackerman, "'Ars Sine Scientia Nihil Est,' Gothic Theory of Architecture at the Cathedral of Milan," *Art Bulletin* 31 (March 1949), pp. 84 – 111.

15. Ibid., p. 100, appendix 3, p. 109.

16. Close tolerances between geometrically generated proportions and constructed ones are essential for most analyses of design, but even when they are absent, geometry may still have played a role. Many designs begin with an abstract, geometric ordering system and evolve toward "compromised" solutions that accommodate more successfully the myriad requirements of a real-world object. Unfortunately, once modifications wipe out all trace of the geometric aspect of a design, it is lost to anyone who must depend entirely on the finished product for information. For this reason contemporary drawings are so valuable. They may record the evolution of a design or simply document its ideal form. The design history of the Sansedoni palace in Siena provides an example. The ideal form of the palace is represented in a drawing that is part of the contract of 1340 between the family and the builders. The project represented in the drawing has dimensions generated by an equilateral triangle and by a square whose sides equal the width of the facade, along with other measurements that conform to a modular system (F.K. Toker, "Gothic Architecture by Remote Control: An Illustrated Building Contract of 1340," *Art Bulletin* 67 [March 1985], pp. 67 – 95). The palace that was built represents a significant modification of that design and a departure from its geometry. The changes allow the floor levels of the new construction, for instance, to conform to the levels of the residential complex to which it was added. This practical requirement might well have been anticipated, but the drawing chooses to ignore it and presents a geometrically coherent

design instead. The changes that adapted the addition to the older structures took place only in the execution stage and, according to the contract, were the responsibility of the patron (ibid., p. 90, sections 28, 30, 31, 33 of the contract).

17. But see note 63.

18. The distance between the axis of the main street and the far edge of the first block (containing the first and second rows of lots) measures, at different places, 47.98, 48.45, 48.78, and 48.15 meters. Between the axis and the outer side of the second block, the distance measures 83.13, 83.7, 83.8, and 85.56 meters.

   The plan of Castelfranco (Fig. 11) shares the gradual and progressive diminution of the depth of its building lots that suggests the geometric base of its sister foundation, San Giovanni. The modern dimensions of the plan do not, however, reveal the geometry clearly. No combination of angles and diameters defines the significant intervals of the plan with any great accuracy or consistency. The system based on the sine values of thirty- and sixty-degree angles that was used at San Giovanni, however, fits a little better than the other alternatives. If the far side of the first block, a distance of 36.5 meters from the axis of the main street, is assumed to have been generated by a thirty-degree angle, a hypotenuse of 73 meters can be calculated. With an angle of sixty degrees, a triangle with a hypotenuse of 73 meters would have one side of 63.2 meters. The far side of the second block (comprising the third and fourth rows of lots) of the Castelfranco plan is 64.8 meters from the axis of the main street, a deviation of 2.5 percent.

   The presence at Castelfranco of a third block, comprising the fifth and sixth rows of lots, and a fourth block, comprising the seventh and eighth rows, is an exception to an otherwise consistent rule of Florentine planning according to which new towns were limited to four rows of lots on either side of the central axis. The third and fourth blocks at Castelfranco do not seem to participate in the geometry of the town plan. Their depth is determined much more pragmatically. Each block is composed of two rows of lots of equal depth—17 *braccia* in the third block, 16 in the fourth—plus the width of the intervening sewer. Without the outer blocks, the Castelfranco design would appear even more like San Giovanni than it does now; indeed its overall proportions, approximately $2\frac{3}{4}:1$, would be the same as those of San Giovanni.

19. The dimensions of this block have been obscured by the closing of the street next to the town wall and by the expansion of the houses into this space. An examination of the fabric of buildings in the outermost blocks shows that the original structures were about 9.3 meters deep. The nine-

teenth-century tax map reveals other structures on these blocks of about the same size.

20. *Ptolemy's Almagest,* trans. G.J. Toomer (London, 1984), p. 47; O. Pederson, *A Survey of the Almagest* (Odense, 1974).

21. G.J. Toomer, "A Survey of the Toledan Tables," *Osiris* 15 (1969), pp. 5 – 174. While the Arabic original of the tables is lost, the Latin translation by Gherard of Cremona survives in over one hundred manuscript copies. M. Curtze, "Urkunden zur Geschichte der Trigonometrie im christlichen Mittelalter," *Bibliotheca Mathematica,* 3d ser. 1 (1900), pp. 337 – 347.

22. Don Manuel Rico y Sinobas, ed., *Libros del saber de astronomía del Rey Alfonso X de Castilla,* III (Madrid, 1864), pp. 149 – 237.

23. For the text of the two-page work, "Figura inveniendi sinus kardagarum," see M. Curtze, "Urkunden," pp. 413 – 416; on John of Murs, John of Saxony, and John of Lignères, see *Dictionary of Scientific Biography* (New York, 1973), VII, entries by E. Poulle; for the history of trigonometry in the Middle Ages, see also A. von Braunmühl, *Vorlesungen über Geschichte der Trigonometrie* (Leipzig, 1900); J. Tropfke, *Geschichte der Elementar-Mathematik* (Berlin and Leipzig, 1923), V, chaps. 1, 2. A fourteenth-century treatise on the sine by Richard of Wallingford (ca. 1292 – 1336) is published in translation in E. Grant, ed., *A Source Book in Medieval Science* (Cambridge, Mass., 1974), pp. 188 – 198.

24. P. Knecht, ed., *I libri astronomici di Alfonso X in una versione fiorentina del trecento* (Zaragoza, 1965), esp. pp. xii – xiii. The manuscript, which is illustrated, is held in the Vatican Library (Cod. Vat. Lat. 8174). F. Saxl, *Verzeichnis astrologischer und mythologischer illustrierter Handschriften der lateinischen Mittelalters in römischen Bibliotheken* (Heidelberg, 1915), pp. 95 – 100, pl. IX, fig. 19.

25. M. Clagett, *Archimedes in the Middle Ages* (Philadelphia, 1978), III, pt. 1, pp. 11 – 18; the second of the eleven chapters is titled "de inventione cordarum quorumlibet arcuum circuli"; see also Braunmühl, *Vorlesungen,* pp. 92 – 118.

26. Shelby, "Master Masons," pp. 395 – 421 (biblio., p. 399, n. 12); Stephen K. Victor, *Practical Geometry in the High Middle Ages: "Artis Cuiuslibet Consummatio" and the "Pratike de Geometrie"* (Philadelphia, 1979), with extensive bibliography; F. Britt, *A Critical Edition of "Tractatus Quadrantis"* (Ann Arbor, Mich., 1972).

27. Curtze, "Urkunden," pp. 329 – 334.

28. B. Boncompagni, *Scritti di Leonardo Pisano matematico del secolo decimoterzo,* II (Rome, 1962) (La Pratica Geometriae di Leonardo Pisano secondo la lezione del codice urbinate n. 292 della Bibliotheca Vaticana).

29. Ibid., p. 1.

30. A fifteenth-century example was published as Leonardo Fibonacci, *La pratica di geometria, volgarizzata da Cristofano di Gherardo di Dino cittadino pisano dal codice 2186 della Biblioteca Riccardiana di Firenze*, ed. G. Arrighi (Pisa, 1966).

31. "Quem Tholomeus posuit in almagesto." Boncompagni, *Scritti*, II, p. 94.

32. Ibid., p. 95.

33. Full-scale construction presents many practical problems. It would have required a rope or chain of more than eighty meters for the radius of the circle. We can only speculate about the degree of accuracy of a construction that had to contend with the elasticity of fiber chords or the weight of metal chains, as well as the rough ground of the new town site on which they would have to be manipulated. I know of no medieval examples of geometric construction on this scale. For a possible, but not demonstrably medieval, solution to these problems, see note 62; on medieval survey practice, see E.G.R. Taylor, "The Surveyor," *The Economic History Review* 17, no. 2 (1947), pp. 121 – 133; D.J. Price, "Medieval Land Surveying and Topographical Maps," *The Geographical Journal* 121 (March, 1955), pp. 1 – 10; O.A.W. Dilke, *The Roman Land Surveyors, An Introduction to the "Agrimensores"* (Newton Abbot, 1971). For a discussion of survey instruments — mostly for measurement in the vertical plane — described in the medieval literature, see M. Curtze, "Uber die im Mittelalter zur Feldmessung benutzten Instrumente," *Bibliotheca Mathematica*, n.s. 10, no. 3 (1896), pp. 65 – 72; E.R. Kiely, "Surveying Instruments, Their History and Classroom Use," *Yearbook of the National Council of Teachers of Mathematics* 19 (1947), pp. 64 – 83.

Throughout the Middle Ages the surveyors' tools were the simple instruments they had inherited from the *agri mensores* of antiquity: the line, the rod, the groma (made from a pair of rods set at right angles), and the plumb bob. There is a single recorded instance of an angle-measuring instrument used in geographic survey — that is, survey in the horizontal plane — before the Renaissance, and it refers to measurements that were taken underground. The statutes of the mining guild of the commune of Massa Marittima, dated 1294, call for the recording of compass bearings in the registration of claims in the iron and silver fields within the commune's territory. The boundaries "debeant calamitari et cum calamita singnari postquam posita et facta erunt; et scribatur in instrumento sententie ad quem ventum partita respiciunt, et ut si dicta partita mutarentur possint refici et reformari in pristinum statum" ("Ordinamenta super arte fossarum rameriae et argenteriae civitatis Massae," *Archivio Storico Italiano*, Appendices, VIII [1850] p. 648, no. 27). Above ground the surveyor measured only distances and right angles. Oblique boundaries were recorded by reference to natural landmarks, such as trees, and markers placed on the ground. Maps like the one found in the Kirkstead Abbey Psalter of about 1300 (based on a survey of circa 1150) at Beaumont College, Old Windsor, have a very approximate relation to reality, despite the relative accuracy of distance measurements, because the angles between boundary lines were so distorted (Price, "Surveying," pp. 3 – 4, figs. la, lb). For an excellent review of medieval surveying technique as it bears on the construction of city plans, see J. Schulz, "Jacopo de' Barbari's View of Venice: Map Making, City Views, and Moralized Geography before the Year 1500," *Art Bulletin* 60 (September 1978), pp. 425 – 474, esp. pp. 430 – 436.

A practical surveyor, Bertrand Boysett (1372 – 1414) from Arles, writing on the problem of dividing a circular field into equal parts, resorted to a pragmatic, nongeometric approximation (P. Pausier, "Le Traité de l'arpentage de Bertrand Boysett," *Annals d'Avignon et du Comtat Venaissin* 12 [1926], p. 34). A rather unusual "round field" of medieval origin survives some distance to the west of Arles in the department of Hérault, near Narbonne. It is actually a set of fields covering a surface of 500 hectares (about 200 acres) that were reclaimed by a drainage project undertaken by three noblemen from the area around the castle of Montady and by a public notary (possibly acting for an association of future freeholders). The four men were given a charter by the archbishop of Narbonne on 13 February 1247. As the area appears today, the borders of the fields are radially oriented drainage ditches that carry water along straight lines toward a circular canal surrounding an "island" at the center of the whole area. The water collected from these ditches is channeled into a wider ditch pitched toward a point on the perimeter of the reclamation area, where a tunnel had been dug through one of the surrounding hills. The tunnel, 1,364 meters long and with an attached aqueduct, carries the water of the reclaimed land to the Etang de Poilhes, 6,218 meters away. The parts of the "field," now administered by a cooperative of the land owners, are equal neither in length (because the area is not truly round) nor in the number of degrees that each subsumes, but the radial character of the boundaries and drainage ditches is consistently maintained (L'Abbé Ginieis, "Sur L'Etang de Montady," *Bulletin de la Société Archéologique de Beziers* [1858], pp. 3 – 17; illustrated in George Gerster, *Grand Design* [New York and London, 1976], pp. 166 – 167, fig. 116).

In the Renaissance, angle-measuring techniques became the foundation of a new, mathematically based form of city plan. Leonardo da Vinci's plan of Imola of about 1502 is the earliest surviving monument of the new mapping technology, but the methods and instruments on which that achievement depend were set out by Leon Battista Alberti in the first half of the fifteenth century. In the *Descriptio Urbis Romae,* written between 1432 and the early 1450s (L. Vagnetti, "La 'Descriptio Urbis Romae,' uno scritto poco noto di Leon Battista Alberti," *Quaderni,* University of Genoa, Faculty of Architecture, 1 [1968], pp. 25 – 78), and the *Ludi matematici* dedicated in 1450 (L.B. Alberti, "ludi rerum mathematicarum," in *Opere volgari,* ed. C. Grayson [Bari, 1973], III, pp. 131 – 173), Alberti presented a system in which the measurements of angles and of distance were coordinated to produce a geometrically accurate image of the city of Rome. Alberti used an instrument that he called a "horizon," a disc whose circumference was divided into 40 degrees, each with four internal divisions called minutes, that was equipped with a "radius," or sighting rule, that pivoted around its center. Alberti placed his horizontally oriented instrument on the Campidoglio and rotated the radius to point to the city's most prominent monuments. In each case he recorded at what degree and minute the radius intersected the circumference of the horizon. To that information he added a measurement of the distance of the monument from the sighting point, which he obtained by pacing or by triangulation. By reproducing these two coordinates — orientation and distance (at a reduced scale) — on a piece of paper, again with the aid of the horizon, he was able to rationalize the map-making process (Joan Gadol, *Leon Battista Alberti: Universal Man of the Early Renaissance* [Chicago and London, 1969], pp. 70 – 74; J.H. Pinto, "Origins and Developments of the Ichnographic City Plan," *Journal of the Society of Architectural Historians* 25 [March 1976], pp. 35 – 50).

34. Boncompagni, *Scritti,* II, p. 95.

35. D.F. Zervas, "The *Trattato dell'Abbaco* and Andrea Pisano's Design for the Florentine Baptistry Door," *Renaissance Quarterly* 28 (Winter 1975), pp. 483 – 503, 485, nn. 6, 7. Zervas lists the treatises of arithmetic and of the *abbaco* in Florentine libraries, including an Italian language *Aritmetica e geometria di Leonardo Fibonacci* from ca. 1290 in the Biblioteca Riccardiana (Codex 2404).

36. Ackerman, "Ars," p. 90, nn. 22, 23.

37. Frankl, "Secret"; Shelby, "Gothic Design."

38. E. Guidoni, the first to perceive the proportional base of the new-town plans, claimed that the elevations of contemporary Tuscan palaces had story levels fixed by the same system that structured the new-town plans (E. Guidoni, *Arte e urbanistica in Toscana, 1100 – 1350* [Rome, 1970], pp.

215 – 217, fig. 113). He provided only drawings to support his conclusions.

39. F. Boucher, "Medieval Design Methods, 800 – 1560," *Gesta* 11, no. 2 (1972), p. 43, fig. 15. The sides of the square blocks are 55.4 meters long (with variations of 20 centimeters). Using Boucher's system the side of the first rectangular block should be 78.3 meters long ($55.4^2 + 55.4^2 = 78.3^2$). The actual measurement is around 82.4 meters. A similar calculation for the third row of blocks generates a dimension of 99.3 meters ($82.4^2 + 55.4^2 = 99.3^2$). The actual dimensions of the long sides of the outer blocks are 109.2 and 112 meters.

The interaxial dimensions are clearly more relevant, but even they will not produce a third term that has a significant relationship to the measurements of the plan. The third term would be the diagonal of a rectangle with sides of 90.4 and 64 meters: 110.8 meters. The distances between the first and the second secondary axes are approximately 116.6 and 119.4 meters, depending on where in the town one measures. The difference between the blocks on the two sides of the town not only shows a failure to agree with the ideal dimensions, but also suggests that any geometric base for the length of these blocks was overridden by other considerations.

The primacy of survey lines at Grenade agrees with the geometry of the Florentine towns. It is also the approach documented in the 1391 report of the mathematician Gabriele Stornaloco on the proportional scheme for Milan cathedral: "I have taken all the widths according to the measurement from center to center; therefore I have not bothered to enter into the drawing of the thickness of the piers because it is sufficiently clear to the master architects how much they occupy within the bodies (*scil.*, central nave and aisles) of the church" ("Omnes lactitudines acepi mensuratione centri ad centrum icdeo non curavi in designamento ponere spissitudinem colonarum quia satis est manifestum Magistris Inzigneriis quantum occupant in corporibus ecclesie"; Frankl, "Secret," p. 55).

F. Buselli (*Pietrasanta e le sue rocche* [Florence, 1970], pp. 40 – 66, fig. after p. 64) has proposed a geometric interpretation of the plan of the Lucchese foundation of Pietrasanta (1255) which includes a number of systems, some geometric, some modular. According to Buselli the length of the town corresponds both to four times the distance across it and three times the golden section of twice its width. The dimension that he defines as the width of the town differs for the two calculations. Only for the second of them does it include the roads inside the walls. The dimension he assigns to the length of the town also varies. He finds justification for this in the absence of any fixed points for the west end of the town, which was destroyed in a fire of 1343 and rebuilt with the renewal of the city's fortifications in the 1480s. I feel that the absence of a secure terminus for this important dimension makes any geometrical proposal extremely hypothetical.

40. R. Salomon, *Opicinus de Canestris: Weltbild und Bekenntnisse eines Klerikers des 14. Jahrhunderts* (London, 1936), I, p. 60, nn. 2, 3; Opicinus himself, anything but a seafaring man, used the Portolan's distinctive system of charting for his own fantastic images and maps.

41. The English monk Alexander Neckam, in his *De Utensilibus* of about 1180, described among a ship's stores "a needle placed upon to a dart [*jaculo suppositum*], and it is turned and whirled round until the point of the needle looks northeast of north. And so the sailors know which way to steer when the Cynosura is hidden by clouds" (E.G.R. Taylor, *The Haven Finding Art* [London, 1956], p. 95). In 1268 Pietro di Maricourt, writing in the camp of Charles I at Lucera in Apulia, described a compass much like the modern instrument. It was composed of a box, covered with glass, that contained a magnetized needle rotating over a regularly divided wind rose (T. Bertelli, "Sopra Pietro Peregrino di Maricourt e la sua epistola de magnete," *Bulletino di bibliografia e di storia della scienze matematiche e fisiche pubblicato da B. Boncompagni,* [Rome, 1868], pp. 1 – 32, 65 – 99 [pp. 70 – 89 contain Pietro's text], 101 – 139, 319, 420). By the end of the century a modest ship, like the one described in a document of 1294, carried two *calamita* (compasses) and three mappamundi (portolan charts), one with an accompanying text or Portolan (Taylor, *Haven*, p. 115).

42. The Carta Pisana is preserved in the Bibliothèque Nationale, Paris (Galerie des Cartes, no. 214). This parchment, measuring 104 by 50 centimeters, is thought to have been prepared around 1275, following a prototype of 1250 – 1260 (B. Motzo, *Il compasso da navigare* [Cagliari, 1947], p. xlvii). Motzo discusses the attribution of the sea chart to Catalans, Genoese, and Pisan navigators and comes down in favor of the Pisans (ibid., pp. l – liv). He notes the special marks surrounding the port of Pisa on the chart, the Tuscan character of the language, and the absence of information about the Black Sea, an area of special interest to the Genoese but untraveled by the Pisans. He also cites the Pisan provenance of the chart.

43. The atlas, in the Nationalbibliothek, Vienna, no. 594, measures 19 by 18.5 centimeters and has ten sheets. It is signed on the last sheet "Petrus Vesconte d'ianua fecit istas fabulas anno domini MCCCXVIII"; K. Kretschmer, *Die italienischen Portolane des Mittelalters* (Berlin, 1909), p. 112.

44. The most consistent tradition of the Portolan chart is the division of the compass rose into 8 winds (Motzo, *Compasso*, pp. lxxxv – xcii). In the course of the thirteenth and fourteenth centuries the original units were

increased by subdivision to a maximum of 128. At that point the smallest unit subsumed an arc of $2\frac{13}{16}$ degrees. The half-wind, which is the base unit for the compass pattern on the charts, had an arc of $22\frac{1}{2}$ degrees, and the wind itself, an arc of 45 degrees.

45. An introductory bibliography on the astrolabe and related instruments would include: M. Destombes, "La Diffusion des instruments scientifiques du haut moyen age au XVe siècle," *Cahiers d'Histoire Mondiale* 10, no. 1 (1966), pp. 31 – 51; R.T. Gunther, *The Astrolabes of the World,* 2 vols. (London, 1932); W. Hartner, "The Principle and Use of the Astrolabe," in W. Hartner, *Oriens-Occidens* (Hildesheim, 1967), pp. 287 – 318; Keily, "Surveying Instruments"; F. Maddison, *Medieval Scientific Instruments and the Development of Navigational Instruments in the XV and XVI Centuries* (Coimbra, 1969); L.A. Mayer, *Islamic Astrolabists and Their Works* (Geneva, 1956); H. Michel, *Traité de l'astrolabe* (Paris, 1947); J.D. North, "The Astrolabe," *Scientific American* 230 (January 1974), pp. 96 – 106; E. Poulle, "L'Astronomie du moyen age et ses instruments," *Annali dell'Istituto e Museo di Storia della Scienza di Firenze* 6, no. 2 (1981), pp. 3 – 16; D.J. Price, "Precision Instruments to 1500," in *A History of Technology,* ed. C. Singer et. al. (Oxford, 1957), III, pp. 582 – 619.

46. A treatise, *De Astrolabia,* known in an eleventh-century manuscript, is sometimes attributed to Gerbert of Aurillac, later Pope Sylvester II (999 – 1003) and another, *De Mensura Astrolabii,* has been ascribed to Hermannus of Reichenau (1013 – 1054) since the thirteenth century. On the quadrant, see P. Schmalzl, *Zur Geschichte des Quadranten bei den Arabern* (Munich, 1929); G. Boffito and G. Melzi d'Eril, *Il quadrante d'Israel* (Florence, 1929); R.T. Gunther, *Early Science in Oxford* (Oxford, 1923), II, pp. 154 – 181 on quadrants in general, pp. 164 – 169 on Profacius's quadrant, with modern and medieval illustrations, pp. 161 – 163 on the quadrant of Robert Anglicus (called here John of Montpellier); P. Tannery, "Le Traité du quadrant de maître Robert Angles," *Notices et Extraits* 35, no. 2 (1897), pp. 561 – 640; G. Sarton, *Introduction to the History of Science,* II, pt. 2 (Baltimore, 1931), pp. 850 – 853, 993 – 994.

47. The exception is the translation in 1263 of al-Zarquali's treatise on the *saphaea.* Jacob ibn Tibbon ed., J.M. Millas-Vallicrosa trans., *Tractat de l'assafea d'Arzaquiel* (Barcelona, 1933); E. Poulle, "Un Instrument astronomique dans l'occident latin: La 'saphea,'" in *A Giuseppe Ermini* (Spoleto, 1970), pp. 491 – 510.

48. D.J. Price, "An International Checklist of Astrolabes," *Archives Internationale d'Histoire des Sciences* 8 (1955), pp. 243 – 263, 363 – 381.

49. T.O. Wedel, *The Medieval Attitude toward Astrology* (1920; reprint ed.,

Hamden, Conn., 1968), pp. 67 – 69. The clergyman Michael Scot (fl. first third of the thirteenth century) wrote a lengthy introduction to astrology, the *Liber Introductorius,* and was employed for much of his life as court astrologer to Frederick II (L. Thorndike, *A History of Magic and Experimental Science,* I [New York, 1923], pp. 307 – 337.)

50. *Purgatorio,* canto 16, LL. 64 – 81. V. Laraia, *Enciclopedia Dantesca,* I (Rome, 1970), s.v. "Astrologia."

51. G. Boffito, "Perchè fu condannato al fuoco l'astrologo Cecco d'Ascoli?," *Studi e Documenti di Storia e Diritto* 20 (1899), pp. 357 – 382; Wedel, *Medieval Attitude,* pp. 75 – 77; Thorndike, *Magic,* p. 94; J. Seznec, *The Survival of the Pagan Gods* (New York, 1961), pp. 42 – 83; GV *Cron.,* X, chap. 40.

52. GV *Cron.,* XI, chap. 2.

53. Ibid., X, chap. 198; further discussion of astrology in GV *Cron.,* XI, chaps. 1, 20, 33, 67, 99, 113; XII, chap. 41.

54. From *De eodem et diverso,* written ca. 1109, quoted in Wedel, *Medieval Attitude,* pp. 49 – 50.

55. R. Varese, *Trecento Ferrarese* (Milan, 1976), pl. xxi a; L. Coletti, "Un Affresco, due miniature, tre probleme," *L'Arte,* n.s. 5 (March 1934), pp. 101 – 122.

56. Brunetto Latini, *Li Livres dou Tresor,* ed. F.J. Carmody (Berkeley, 1948), p. 34.

57. M. Fiorini, *Sfere terrestre e celesti di autore italiano oppure fatte o conservate in Italia* (Rome, 1899). In the rhomboid-shaped reliefs of the campanile's second row of panels, there is a second astronomical figure, a seated woman who focuses her attention on a celestial globe that she holds in her left hand. For more astrologers / astronomers, see: J. Diamond Udovitch, "Three Astronomers in a Thirteenth-Century Psalter," *Marsyas* 17 (1974 – 75), pp. 79 – 83; J.E. Murdoch, *Album of Science: Antiquity and the Middle Ages* (New York, 1984).

58. On Petrarch see Wedel, *Medieval Attitude,* pp. 82 – 85. The suggestion that the purpose of the astrolabe was often only to identify the Doctor of Astrology was made to me by Professor George Saliba of Columbia University.

59. D. de Solla Price, "Philosophical Mechanism and Mechanical Philosophy: Some Notes toward a Philosophy of Scientific Instruments," *Annali dell'Istituto e Museo di Storia della Scienza di Firenze* 5, no. 1 (1980), pp. 77 – 85; D. de Solla Price, "Instruments of Reason," *The Sciences* 21 (October 1981), pp. 15 – 17.

60. L.A. Mayer, *Islamic Astrolabists and Their Works* (Geneva, 1956), p. 59, pl. iva; *Catalogo degli Strumenti,* ex. cat., Museo di Storia della Scienza (Florence, 1954), pp. 61 – 62, no. 1105; Gunther, *Astrolabes,* pp. 122, 263.

61. Guidoni, *Arte e urbanistica,* pp. 229 – 234, figs. 116 – 118.

62. Whether the polygons would have been drawn on a tracing floor or a

piece of parchment and the proportions that were extracted from the construction transferred, by multiplication, to the scale of the town, or whether a full-sized construction would have been prepared at the new-town site, is not a question addressed by Guidoni. Professor Noel Swerdlow, historian of astronomy at the University of Chicago, who helped me to understand both the astronomy and geometry of this problem, offered a very attractive alternative to full-scale construction. The builders of the new towns needed only to survey a circle of, say, ten feet in diameter with its center at the future intersection of the main streets. They would then have divided the circumference of the circle into 6 sections by using the radius as a chord, and into 12 sections by bisecting those chords. Once the ten-foot circle had been subdivided into 15-degree units, a rope or chain the length of the radius of the full circle could have been stretched from a stake that marked the center of the construction, over a stake that marked a 15-degree division. Sighting along the two stakes (which were five feet apart and therefore gave a very accurate measure), whoever was setting out the plan would make a visual check that the cord was straight and taut. The far end of the cord would mark the position of the 15-degree point on the circumference of the full circle. Moving the cord to the next 15-degree interval on the ten-foot circle, the next position on the large one could be similarly set. When all the intervals were marked, the sine lines could be constructed by connecting the appropriate points. A survey of this kind would have been very accurate; however, I favor the survey that used right angles and mathematically derived values, given what we know of the practice of medieval surveyors and what we do not know about medieval architectural geometry, namely that masons ever constructed sine values.

63. Of all the medieval architectural geometries, the only one to have a relationship to the proportions of the Florentine new-town plans is the "Archimedes" spiral drawn by Master 2 in the *Sketchbook* of Villard de Honnecourt (Hahnloser, *Villard,* p. 40, fig. 8) and surviving in a series of figures engraved on the lower bed of a discarded capital from one of the piers of the south transept porch of Chartres cathedral (R. Branner, "Villard de Honnecourt, Archimedes, and Chartres," *Journal of the Society of Architectural Historians* 19 [October 1960], pp. 91 – 96; see also Cox to Branner and Branner's reply, *Journal of the Society of Architectural Historians* 20, [October 1961], pp. 143 – 146). According to the *Sketchbook,* the spiral was used to determine the incalculable third side of triangles that fixed the lower angles of the keystones of pointed arches. Values generated by the spiral are measured on lines perpendicular to its axis. These lines originate at the two centers used to construct the spiral's many turns. One perpen-

dicular line produces values of $\sqrt{3}$, $\sqrt{15}$, etc., with the radius of the first turn taken as the base unit. The other perpendicular, the one used in the *Sketchbook,* generates values of $2\sqrt{2}$, $2\sqrt{6}$, etc. It is this one that bears on the new-town plans.

The concordance of the values of the spiral with the proportions of the plans can be ascertained by establishing the relationship between the two terms $2\sqrt{2} \approx 2.828 : 2\sqrt{6} \approx 4.898 = 1 : 1.7319$. This is the relationship between the sine of a 30-degree angle (.5) and the sine of a 60-degree angle (.8660). Thus, everywhere that equivalents of the sines of 30- and 60-degree angles appear in a design, so the values of the spiral do too. At San Giovanni and Castelfranco, where only two dimensions conform to a consistent system and can be explained as 30- and 60-degree sines, the spiral could be the source of the ratio. It should be noted, however, that this application is very different from the one documented in the *Sketchbook.*

If the proportions of the San Giovanni and Castelfranco plans were derived from the spiral, the real dimensions were almost certainly established through a transfer of scale. The spiral 180 meters in diameter required for a direct construction is almost unimaginable. Spirals of 0.67 meter like the ones at Chartres might provide the proportions, but multiplication would be required to ascertain the dimensions.

The overwhelming disadvantage of the spiral is that it generates only the 30- and 60-degree sine values. Its other terms have no relation to the other proportions of the more comprehensive system at Terranuova. For those proportions Fibonacci's table of arcs and chords, or some equivalent, was essential. One might imagine that the spiral was responsible for San Giovanni and Castelfranco, the earliest of the plans, and that the chord table entered the picture only with the later project for Terranuova. Such an argument has the advantage of making some connection, however problematic, with the architectural tradition of geometry; its weakness is the difficulty of describing the shift between systems. The ability to shift presupposes an understanding of the relatedness of the proportional systems of the spiral and the chord table, and this is impossible to demonstrate. There are no contemporary equations of the two systems and the geometric forms are so dissimilar as completely to discourage recognition. I am skeptical about the likelihood that the Florentine planners ever applied the "Archimedes" spiral to their proportional problem.

64. The drawing in the Uffizi (UA 4124r) attributed to Fra Giocondo, which was once associated with the project of Alfonso II to renew the plan of ancient Naples (Per Gustaf Hamberg, "Vitruvius, Fra Giocondo and the City Plan of Naples," *Acta Archeologica* 36 [1965], pp. 105 – 125, figs. 4, 6), seems,

as Professor Giorgio Ciucci suggested in conversation, to represent the
geometry of a spiral staircase. The geometry, however, is sine geometry,
and the format of the drawing, which collapses the geometries of plan and
section into one, is characteristic of images from both medieval architectural practice and medieval astronomy.

65. The graphic interpretation of the wind rose by Palladio (M. Vitruvii
Pollionis, *De architectura libri decem, cum commentarii Danieli Barbari*
[Venice, 1567], p. 34) follows Fra Giocondo in coordinating the rose with a
representation of a town plan and allowing the octagon of the rose to
define the limits of the central portion of the street system. Unlike Fra
Giocondo, Palladio and Barbaro give their city a perimeter that is also octagonal and has sides that are parallel to the sides of the rose. The orthogonal street grid matches up only awkwardly with both the shape of the
town and the gates in the defenses. Fra Giocondo as well as Palladio and
Barbaro provide wind roses independent of a street plan. The two texts
include roses divided into 22.5-degree arcs, as Vitruvius describes, and
15-degree arcs as one finds in the astronomical tradition.

66. L.B. Alberti, *L'Architettura* (Milan, 1966), II, pp. 819 – 821.

67. H. Saalman, "Santa Maria del Fiore: 1294 – 1418," *Art Bulletin* 46 (December
1964), pp. 471 – 500, esp. pp. 483 – 487, 491 – 494.

NOTES TO CHAPTER 5

1. "Notum sit omnibus tam futuris quam presentibus, qualiter ego Cunradus
   in loco mei proprii iuris scilicet Friburg forum constitui anno ab Incarnatione Domini MCXX. Mercatoribus itaque personatis circumquaque
   convocatis quadam coniuratione id forum decrevi incipere et excolere.
   Unde unicuique mercatori haream in constituto foro [ad] domos in proprium ius edificandas distribui atque de unaquaque harea solidum publice
   monete mihi et posteris meis pro censu annuatim in festo beati Martini
   persolvendo disposui. Singule vero haree domorum in longitudine centum
   pedes habebunt, in latitudine quinquaginta"; F. Keutgen, *Urkunden zur
   städtischen Verfassungsgeschichte* (1901; reprint ed., Aalen, 1965), p. 117, no. 133.

2. *Calendar of the Patent Rolls* (I, Edw. 1, 1281 – 1292), Public Record Office
   (London, 1893), pp. 81 – 82, 13 October 1283. Le Waleys, a wine merchant,
   had been mayor of Bordeaux and London and, between 1284 and 1294,
   held the tax farm on six of the King's new towns in Gascony. M. Beresford,
   New Towns of the Middle Ages (London, 1967), pp. 6, 9.

3. M. l'Abbé Brueils, "Montreal," *Bulletin de la Société Archéologique du Gers*

11 (1910), p. 47; P. Lavedan and J. Hugueney, *L'Urbanisme au Moyen Age* (Geneva, 1974), p. 73.

4. H. Reincke, "Uber Städtegrundung: Betrachtungen und Phantasien" (1957), *Die Stadt des Mittelalters*, ed. C. Haase (Darmstadt, 1969), I, pp. 331 – 363, esp. pp. 343, 356 – 367.

5. E. Lavisse, *La Marche de Brandenbourg* (Paris, 1875), p. 206.

6. Reincke, "Städtegrundung," pp. 336 – 337, 344 – 345.

7. G. Camarani Marri, *Statuti dei Comuni di Castelfranco di Sopra (1394) e Castiglione degli Ubertini (1397)* (Florence, 1963), pp. 167 – 168. The document is held in ASF *Notarile antecosimiano*, F66, fol. 177v, 21 April 1300.

8. GV *Cron.*, X, chap. 198, describes the committee this way: "Chiamarono a far fare la detta terra sei grandi popolani di Firenze con grande balia intorno a ciò."

9. The first committee was appointed for a six-month term on 13 February 1331 / 2 (ASF *Provv.*, 211, fols. 101r and v). As part of the terms of their office, the priors and *gonfaloniere* "providerunt quod suprascripti sex sapientes viri habent et habere intelligantur per totum tempus dictorum eorum offitio omnem et totalem baliam . . . quam habent et habuerunt predicti domini priores et vexillifer iustitie." Among their powers was the authority to determine the "magnitudines et modo et forma" of the settlement.

10. In its own documents as well as those of the city government, this committee was not always referred to by the name of the town it was established to found, but also by the title *Offitiales communis florentine super facto alpium* (ASF *Cap.*, 32, fol. 273r, 12 March 1331 / 2) and ultimately as the *offitiales alpium* (ASF *Cap.*, 35, fol. 229r, 24 September 1338). In fact, the committee was concerned with the administration of many aspects of the city's northern frontier territory, including political matters that had only indirect bearing on the building of the new town. As an example, on 12 March 1331 / 2 the committee's representatives received from the Ubaldini, the city's baronial rivals in the Apennines, possession on behalf of Florence of a number of towns and castles. According to the agreement with the Ubaldini, these places were to be kept by the city for a period of five years. On the same day the committee placed them in the care of other noble families (ASF *Cap.*, 32, fol. 273r).

11. ASF *Provv.*, 211, fols. 102v – 107r.

12. Gaye, *Carteggio*, I, p. 487, from ASF *Provv.*, 29; 21 November 1337; ASF *Cap.*, 35, fol. 221r, 3 June 1338.

13. Gaye, *Carteggio*, I, p. 448, from ASF *Provv.*, 30, 21 May 1339.

14. ASF *Provv.*, 41, fols. 95r and v.

15. Ibid., 40, fol. 73r, 15 October 1353.

16. Ibid., 44, fol. 9v, 21 November 1356.

17. Ibid., 54, fols. 110r and v.

18. The project to enlarge and fortify the town of Campi, which lies to the west of Florence, had been under an independent committee in 1376 (Gaye, *Carteggio*, I, p. 527; ASF *Provv.*, 66, 10 June 1376. The record of payments made by the committee in 1378 – 79 are preserved in ASF *Uff. Cast.*, 10). The records of 1382 indicate that responsibility for the project had passed to the *Ufficiali delle Castella* (ASF *Uff. Cast., Rocche*, unnumbered [volume is marked Arm. 9, palco 4, numero 44], fol. 16r, 5 June 1382): "Advertentes et considerantes castrum et terra de Campi noviter constructum et edificatum et circumdatum muris et foveis per Comune Florentie et expensis dicti Comunis, et hodie dictum opus commissum est dicto offitio et offitialibus castrorum." Entries in the same volume show the following town projects also to have come under the control of the *Castella*: Pontassieve, fols. 21v – 22v, 27 June 1382, fols. 44r and v, 21 September 1382; San Casciano, fol. 46r, payments of 27 September 1382; Firenzuola, and Scarperia, fol. 26r.

19. The earliest step toward the formation of an office charged with the administration of the fortifications of the Florentine state is contained in a *Provvisione* of 26 January 1345 / 6 (ASF *Provv.*, 36, fols. 87v, 88r), in which the *Signoria* and the captains of each guild appointed a committee made up of the priors and the *gonfaloniere*, the twelve good men, and up to six men from each of the quarters of the city. This rather unwieldy body was given a stricter form on 14 July 1349 (ASF *Provv.*, 36, fol. 133r), when the representation from each quarter was set at two and the government's participation was limited to the priors and *gonfaloniere*. The body was given a six-month term and responsibility for the fortification of the state, but it still did not have an official name. The title appears only in the document that announced the next set of officers (they were named "ad offitium supradictum quod vulgariter appellatur et appellari debet offitium castrorum") on 25 January 1349 / 50 (ASF *Provv.*, 37, fols. 82r and v). This is the document in which the intention to found Giglio Fiorentino was first enunciated.

20. In the early fifteenth century the office of the *Castella* was merged with other government agencies. In 1408 we have the records of the sixteen officers "offitialium chastrorum et fortilitiarum et habundantia grani et bladi et alia vittualia e molendinum dicti comuni florentie" (ASF, *Uff. Cast.*, 14, 1408). In 1419, the authority of the *Castella* was transferred to a committee called the *Sei di Arezzo* (G. Prunai, "Firenze [secolo XII – 1808],"

Acta Italica, Piani particolari di pubblicazione 6 [1967], p. 68).

21. ASF *Uff. Cast., Rocche,* 1, fols. 5r and v, 26 June 1350, at Uzzano.

22. ASF *Uff. Cast.,* 15, fol. 1r, 1352, for the town of Barga.

23. ASF *Uff. Cast.,* unnumbered (volume is marked 303, arm 9, palco 4, no. 48.), 1360, concerning the Val di Nebule.

24. ASF *Uff. Cast.,* 1, fols. 54r and v, 13 January 1366 / 7. Francescho di Buto and Chantino di Agnoli are the authors of this notebook "chessi faccia nelle terre e rocche le quali son poste nel quartiere di Santa Maria Novella requitando il comandamento ella comesione de nostri signori." Their report concerns the town of Scarperia. See chap. 1, note 2.

25. ASF *Uff. Cast.,* 1, 13 May 1350, fol. 4.

26. The committee for 18 February 1364 / 5 to 17 August 1365 (ASF *Uff. Cast.,* 6, fol. 1r) was composed of Johannes Cambii, a member of the Lana guild (Johannes cambii de Medicis was listed, in 1372, among the men eligible to serve on the merchants' tribunal from the Lana guild [ASF, *Mercanzia,* 187]); Filippo Lorini Bonaiute, who appears on the merchant tribunal list of 1385 from the Calimala (ASF, *Mercanzia,* 209); Nofrio Johanis domine Lapi Arnolfi, a member of the Cambio (ASF, *Mercanzia,* 209); and Bartolomeo Mancini Sostegni.

27. ASF *Uff. Cast.,* 6, fol. 1r (for the term 18 February 1364 / 5 – 17 August 1365) and fol. 17r (for the term 18 February 1365 / 7 – 17 August 1366).

28. M. Mansfield, *A Family of Decent Folk, 1200 – 1741; A Study in the Centuries Growth of the Lanfredini* (Florence, 1922), pp. 9, 28 – 45.

29. ASF *Cap.,* 35, fol. 225, 10 November 1338.

30. ASF *SS. Miss.,* 10, fol. 94v, 17 June 1351.

31. ASF *SS. Miss.,* 11, fol. 1v, 6 July 1353.

32. Beresford, *New Towns,* pp. 3 – 13.

33. Lavedan, *Moyen Age,* p. 73.

34. Reincke, "Städtegrundung," pp. 348 – 351, 361 – 363.

35. GV *Cron.,* IX, chap. 273.

36. ASF *Provv.,* 54, fols. 110r and v, 11 February 1364 / 5, for the governmental legislation; ASF, *Notarile antecosimiano,* N66 (Paulo Nemmi), fols. 159r and v, 5 April 1365, for the document in which the terms of the project, including financial obligations, are made known to the representatives of the league of Vicchio; ASF *Uff. Cast.,* 6, containing the records of the building committee for the period between 18 February 1364 / 5 and the end of July 1367.

37. Repetti, *Dizionario,* IV (1841), s.v. "Vicchio."

38. "Guilglielmus olim Ugolini de Stracciabendis populo s[anct]i Pan[cratii] de

Florentie, Iure proprio et in perpetuum dedit, vendidit, tradidit et concessit Stefano Berti de Romanescha et Latino Nemmi de Sancto Stefano in Botena de Mucello comitatus Florentie presentibus recipientibus et stipulantibus pro liga universitatis lige Vicchii de Mucello comitatus Florentie, et eorum sucessoribus vel quibus concesserit ipsa liga septem bracchia terrenim platee sive castri Vichii praedicti siti in populo plebatus Sancti Casciani de Badule comitatus Florentie, loco dicto la piaza di Vicchio, summendo et incipiendo a domo et muro domus dicte lige Vichii, mensurando versus stratam et palatium quod est in ipsa terra sive castro et a[m]pletudinis tantum quantum est dicta domus sita in terra Vichii praedicti latere superiori, cui rei vendite a primo dicta domus lige, a ii, iii, iiii platea terre Vichii." Guglielmus received four hundred florins for his property (ASF, *Notarile antecosimiano*, N66 [Paulo Nemmi], fols. 131r – 132v.

39. ASF *Uff. Cast.*, 6, fol. 1v, 19 March 1364 / 5, fol. 37r, 26 June 1367.

40. Ibid., fol. 37v, 26 June 1367. "Domino Nichole Lapi advocato dicte offitio et consultori qui consulerit eis et eorum in offitio precedessoris" was paid two florins.

41. Ibid., fol. 34v, 24 January 1366 / 7. ASF *Cap.*, 35, fol. 221r, 3 June 1338. The six members of the Firenzuola committee selected Nepum Cecchi, the committeeman from the Ultrarno section, as "camerarius apud quem perveniat et pervenire debeat pecuniam percipienda et exigenda ex quibuscumque gabella, redditibus et proventibus deputatis vel deputandis ad constructionem et perfectionem portarum terre et murorum" of Firenzuola.

42. The notary at Vicchio for the January 1366 / 7 – July 1367 term was Paulo Nemmi from Santo Stefano de Botena in the Mugello (ASF *Uff. Cast.*, 6, fol. 33r). Nine of his cartulary books are preserved in the Florentine archives (ASF, *Notarile antecosimiano*, N65 – 68, 1345 – 89).

43. ASF *Uff. Cast.*, 6, fol. 1r, 18 February 1364 / 5.

44. Two years after Bacino's original appointment, the committeemen for the 1366 / 7 term reaffirmed his authority (ibid., fol. 34v, 24 January 1366 / 7).

45. ASF *Uff. Cast.*, 3, fol. 19v, 4 May 1345, fol. 34r, 20 May 1345.

46. ASF *Uff. Cast.*, 6, fol. 21v – 22r. Bacino was reimbursed for money that he spent to entertain the committeemen during their visit on 7, 8, and 9 May 1366.

47. Ibid., fol. 37v, June 1367.

48. Ibid., fol. 38r, 26 June 1367.

49. Ibid., fols. 3r – 5v, 14 April 1365:

   locatio edifitii murorum: Item postea, dittis anno et inditione, et die quartadecima aprilis. Actum Florentie, in palatio populi florentini in quo domini priores moram trahunt, presentibus testibus Bacino Cambiuzii

populi S. Michelis Bertelde de Florentia et Iohanne Salvi Vespuccii
populi S. Petri Bonconsigli et Francisco Batini dicti populi S. Michelis ad
hec habitis et rogatis.

Prenominati Iohannes Cambii, Nofrius Iohannis et Filippus Lorini
officiales predicti, Simul existentes pro eorum offitio exercendo, absente
tamen dito Bartolomeo eorum colega, volentes diligenter providere circa
constructione, edificatione et fortificatione terre Vichii, vigore eorum
offitii et autoritate et potestate eis concessa per Comune Florentie, omni
modo, via et iure, quo et quibus magis et melius potuerunt, locaverunt
et concesserunt ad faciendum construendum, edificandum et murandum
Piero et Leonardo, fratribus et filiis olim Masi Leonis, populi S. Marie
Novelle de Florentia, omnes et singulos muros, ianuas et tures circhi
terre Vichii de Mucello, comitatus Florentie, noviter construendos et edificandos infrascriptis modis, ordinibus et cautelis, per eosdem condutores construendos et edificandos et fiendos, et ultra et plus et minus ad
declarationem offitialium pro tempore existentium, videlicet:

Ianue dicte terre et quelibet ipsarum sint et esse debeant isto modo,
videlicet: funditus cave sub terra prout videbitur dictis offitialibus et
eorum successoribus et eorum capud magistro, grosse in cosciis ianue
sub terra usque in altitudinem brachiorum trium usque ad primam
sigham brachiorum septem, et longitudinis brachiorum sedecim, et facia
anterior grossa brachia quatuor in fundamentis usque ad dictam secam.
Et super dicta seca moveatur barbacane in altezza brachiorum septem
barbacanis, et super dicto barbacane moveatur dirittus ianue predicte. Et
sic respondeant sighe trium faciarum, et ibi moveant solgliam cum
pilastrellis in altitudine ut et prout et quomodo et quanto videbitur capud
magistro dicti operis pro tempore existenti, voluta et fatta et serata
diligenter tamen prima volta arcorum ianue sive ianuarum, et ragualg-
liatis usque ad altitudinem quatuordecim sive sedecim brachiorum primi
archiis.

Turres autem dite terre sint et esse debeant fundate sub terra prout
videbitur ditis offitialibus et eorum sucessoribus, et grosse brachia
quatuor vel circa, videlicet, coscie, et in facia anteriori brachiorum trium
usque ad primam segham, et super dicta sigha moveatur barbacane
usque ad altitudinem brachiorum septem, reducendo murum grossum
ad brachia duo a barbacane supra, et sic sit usque ad par et equalem
murum, sive ad altitudinem merlorum. Et dicte tures sint omnes aperte a
parte anteriori cum balestreriis, tot et tales, quot et quales, que et prout
videbitur capud magistro; reducendo muros turium extra muros circhi

terre in quatuor facis, cum tribus cantis et prout videbitur capud magistro pro tempore existenti.

Alii autem muri dicte terre Vichii Vichii [sic] sint fundati et cavi sub terram prout et quantum videbitur capud magistro, grossi in fundamentis brachiis duobus usque ad primam risegham, et risegentur dicti muri in tribus partitis et seghis ex parte exteriori, et reducantur et sint equali terra grossi brachio uno et medio, sive super ditis reseghis sit talis murus in altitudine a terra supra, brachia quatuordecim usque in sedecim sodum, ad voluptatem et deliberationem uficialium pro tempore existentium, videlicet a quatuordecim usque ad sedecim brachia. Et infra quam mensuram sint et esse debeant bechadelli et volteciuole et coridori sportati brachio uno et quarto uno, prout videbitur capud magistro, ragualgliate et lastricate volticiole et l'andito dele mura e dele torri, et ibi moveantur petorali et merli in altitudine brachia quatuor in totum sive circa, cum balestariis, tot et tales, quot et quales, et prout et eo modo quo et quibus expediunt et expedient, ad deliberationem capud magistri.

Et teneantur et debeant dicti magistri condutores rimbocchare muros quoslibet ex parte interiori et exteriori, ad puntam cazuole, et debeant acapezare lapides; et intelligatur vanus pro pleno a peduccio cuiuslibet archi supra, tam ianuarum quam cuiuslibet alterius archi, et debea[n]t murare quodlibet contium quod sibi daretur penes muros et becchadellos.

Et debeant habere dicti magistri conductores a Comuni Florentie et offitialibus predictis, pro predictis laboreriis sic fiendis, calcinam vivam, lapides, renam, lengniamina, ferros et piobbum, mattones sive lateres et concia, penes muros, videlicet illa et illos qui et que remaneant seu remanere debent in dictis muris, et fundamenta cavata expensis locatoris et dicti offiti. Et teneantur et debeant dicti magistri conductores murare, construere, edificare et facere tales muros, ianuas et tures et cetera edifitia et quodlibet eorum bene et diligenter, ad arbitrium capud magistri et ad arbitrium et declarationem cuiuslibet boni et legalis magistri eligendi per dictos offitiales vel eorum in offitio sucessores, pro solidis tribus florenorum parvorum quolibet brachio quadro, reducendo quemlibet murum ad brachium quadrum. Et intelligatur dittos merlos vanum pro pleno. Qui pretius solvendus sit et solvi debeat eis per camerarium dicti offitii.

Que omnia promiserunt et solempniter convenerunt preditti conduttores dictis offitialibus locatoribus, recipientibus et stipulandibus pro Comuni Florentie et dicto offitio et eorum in dicto offitio successoribus, facere, construere edificare et murare bene et diligenter et sine fraude, ad arbitrium et declarationem boni viri et boni magistri et dicti capud magistri eligendi ut supra dicitur, temporibus, modis, conditionibus et formis et cautelis dicendis et declarandis per dittos offitialis vel in dicto offitio sucessores, pena librarum mille et plus et minus ad arbitrium et volu[m]ptatem dictorum offitialium et eorum in dicto offitio sucessorum. Obligantes. . . . Renuntiantes. . . .

Insuper predicti Pierus et Leonardus conductores et quilibet eorum in solidum obligando, promiserunt et solempniter convenerunt dictis offitialibus recipientibus et stipulantibus ut supra, dare et prestare sex bonos et idoneos fideiussores ad predicta, artifices seu mercatores, hinc ad per totam diem sabati proxime futuri, per totam diem, pena florenorum quingentorum auri et qualibet alia pena per ditos offitiales declaranda. Et quod etiam licitum sit et liceat dictis offitialibus, si non prestabunt fideiussores predictos, dicta laboreria alteri locare, non obstantibus predictis, et dicti conductores nichilominus teneantur ad penam et dampna et interesse. Obligantes. . . . Renuntiantes. . . .

50. "Coppum olim Lapi Aglionis de Florentie virum utique providum et expertum super videndo providendo et sollicitando laborerium magistros et conductores dictorum murorum" was selected by the committee on 16 June 1338 (ASF *Cap.*, 35, fol. 221r). On 22 June, Nepum Cecchi, the committee's treasurer (himself a committeeman), Coppo, and a scribe were commissioned to go to Firenzuola for ten days "ad videndum providendum et corrigendum et ordinandum faciendum et fieri faciendum quecumque utilia et necessaria viderint expedire et fieri et ordinare debere nec non etiam cum ambaxiata et commissione eis facta pro constructione et hedificatione dicte terre" (ibid., fol. 221v).

51. A. Gherardi, ed., *Le consulte della repubblica fiorentina* (Florence, 1896), III, p. 321, 11 September 1292. Of an even earlier date and equally laconically described are two technical assistants at the foundation of the Bolognese town of Castelfranco on the Via Emilia. In 1228 the Bolognese official in charge of this project was directed to lay out a palisade as it had been indicated "ab ingignerio" (Archivio di Stato, Bologna, *Comune, Registro Grosso*, fol. 500v). When the town was enlarged with a ring of garden plots in 1231, the records included: "De omnibus supradictis facta ratione per Iulianum Erri mensuratorem Communis ad hoc specialiter missum a Potestate Bononie" (G. Ghirardacci, *Della Historia di Bologna* [Bologna, 1596], I, p. 151); Francesca Bocchi, "Centri minori e fonti catastali; strutture sociale e spazio urbano nel territorio bolognese attraverso il catasto Boncompagni (1787): un metodo di analisi," *Storia della Città* 2 (1979), pp. 8 – 9).

52. On 31 January 1357 / 8, Francesco received twenty-one florins for three months' work (ASF *Uff. Cast.*, 5, fol. 9r).

53. Taddeo received twelve florins for two months' work on 14 February 1357 / 8 (ibid., fol. 9v).

54. H. Saalman, *Filippo Brunelleschi, the Cupola of Santa Maria del Fiore* (London, 1980), p. 177; A. Grote, *Das Dombauamt in Florenz, 1285 – 1370, Studien zur Geschichte der Opera di Santa Reparata* (Munich, 1959), pp. 62, 69.

55. ASF *Uff. Cast.*, 11, fols. 2r and v, 11 July 1356. Three days after Giovanni's appointment the committee's documents record this payment: "Johanni Lapi Ghini capomagistro pro suo salario triginta dierum quibus tum stetit et tum stare debet apud Sanctum Cassiani ad ordinandum et pro curandum dictum laborerum ad rationem soldi viginti pro quolibet die, lire 30 fp" (ibid., fols. 4r and v).

56. Ibid., fols. 5r and v, 19 July 1356.

57. Grote, *Dombauamt*, p. 73; C. Guasti, *Santa Maria del Fiore* (Florence, 1887), p. 84.

58. Guasti, *Santa Maria*, pp. 140 – 220; H. Saalman, "Santa Maria del Fiore: 1294 – 1418," *Art Bulletin* 46 (1964), pp. 471 – 500.

59. Two officers appointed by the councillors of the Mercanzia "sopra la nuova constructione overo edificatione del nuovo palagio il quale sifa nuovamente per labitatione dell ufficiale della mercantantia et per la sua famiglia" pay "A Giovanni di Lapo Ghini maestro il quale tolse affare il detto lavorio con certi patti intra lui e dicti soprastante et uffitiali del detto lavorio fiorini trecento cinquanta doro" (ASF, *Mercanzia*, 172, fols. 80v – 81r, 17 December 1359, published in G. Milanese, *Nuovi documenti per la storia dell'arte Toscana* [Florence, 1885], document 72, p. 56). On 4 September 1360 Giovanni was paid another sixty florins "per parte del pagamento per lo lavorio chesso fece e tolse a fare in nella casa nova della detta universita" (ASF, *Mercanzia*, 173, 4 September 1360).

60. The building committee went to Pontassieve on 28 June 1358 "et secunt duxerant Jacobum Conti et Tomassum Davizzi mensuratores et Johanem Gherardini et Bencium Cionis magistros et ser Taddeum Lapi notarium ad providendum laborerium, constructionem dicte terre et ad faciendum mensurari muros dicte terre propter errorem commiserunt pro prima mensura" (ASF *Uff. Cast.*, 5, fol. 11v). The second trip, which Benci alone made with three of the officials, a notary, six horses, and five *famulos*, "ad providendum Laborerio constructionem et operi dicti castri," took place on 2 through 6 December 1358 (ibid., 5, fol. 29v).

61. Benci received two florins for his three days of service in June (ASF *Uff. Cast.*, 5, fol. 25v, 21 July 1358).

62. Saalman, *Cupola*, p. 183; Guasti, *Santa Maria*, pp. 260, 262, 267.

63. C. Frey, *Die Loggia dei Lanzi zu Florenz* (Berlin, 1885), p. 272. On 23 October 1383 Lorenzo di Filippo was paid thirteen florins for two months' work as *capomaestro* of the loggia (Guasti, *Santa Maria*, p. 271). On 19 August of the same year he was made *capomaestro* of the cathedral as well (Saalman, *Cupola*, pp. 182 – 183).

64. ASF *Uff. Cast., Rocche*, 44, fol. 46r, 27 September 1382.

65. ASF *Uff. Cast.*, 5, fol. 45v, 27 September 1382. Gattoli also received a per diem of one lire when he traveled for the *Castella*.

66. ASF *Uff. Cast., Rocche*, unnumbered (jacket is marked no. 2, 45), fol. 60r, 10 February 1401 / 2.

67. Ibid., fols. 24v – 25r, 11 February 1401 / 2.

68. Ibid., fol. 61v. Francesco appeared for the *Castella* at Panzano in the hills south of Florence.

69. W. Paatz, "Zur Baugeschichte des Palazzo del Podestà (Bargello) in Florenz," *Mitteilungen des kunsthistorischen Institutes in Florenz* 3, no. 6 (January 1931), pp. 311 – 312, 320, documents 51, 59, 60, 62 – 65.

70. W. Paatz and E. Paatz, *Die Kirchen von Florenz*, I (Frankfurt, 1940), pp. 411, 418, n. 5.

71. M. Trachtenberg, *The Campanile of Florence Cathedral* (New York, 1971), pp. 186 – 189, document 12.

72. Saalman, *Cupola*, pp. 45 – 54.

73. ASF *Uff. Cast., Rocche*, 1, fol. 5r, 26 June 1350.

74. ASF, *Consulte e Pratiche*, 1, fol. 38r, 3 August 1353: "Neri Fioravantis per offitio Castrorum consuluit ut supra Mattheus."

75. The *Provvisione* empowering the *Ufficiali delle Castella* to look into the foundation of a new town in the Val d'Ambra is dated 25 January 1349 / 50 (Document 18). The rough copy of the Giglio Fiorentino project in the records of the *Ufficiali delle Castella* (ASF *Uff. Cast., Rocche*, 1, fols. 15v – 18r) is dated 19 May (1350) (Document 19). The official act for the foundation of Giglio Fiorentino is dated 2 June 1350 (Document 20).

   The first signature of ASF *Uff. Cast., Rocche*, 1, consisting of fols. 1 – 8, bears the dates 29 June 1350 through 4 July 1350. The second signature, consisting of fols. 9 and 10, bears the dates 1 and 4 July and contains Neri's name. The third signature, fols. 11 – 18, begins with 13 May. The signature is not dated to a year, but because of its relation to the Giglio Fiorentino project it must belong to the year 1350. It contains a paragraph advising the construction of "una terra grossa a pie di castello S. Niccolo allato alla pieve a vado in luogo chessi chiama donichata" (fol. 11v), recommendations for the reinforcement of the keeps at Borro and Laterina in the Val d'Ambra (fols. 14 – 15), and the description of Giglio Fiorentino (fols. 15v – 18r). The fourth signature, fols. 19 – 36, contains no dates and is written in a new, fourteenth-century hand. It deals with the defenses of towns in the upper Arno valley and the Val d'Ambra. The fifth signature, fols. 37 – 52, also undated, contains similar material. In the sixth and final signature, fols. 53 – 71, a report on the defenses of Scarperia (fols. 54r and v) contains the date 13 January 1366 / 7.

76. The building that occupies the western half of the piazza at Scarperia serves today as the town hall (see Figs. 46, 47). It is a long (sixty-nine meters), thin (twenty-two meters), castellated structure that consists of a main nucleus of rooms on the piazza connected by twelve-meter-high walls to a gate complex on the edge of the town. The building was constructed in at least three stages. The first, which enclosed all the space presently occupied by the building, created a structure whose primary purpose was military. In the other two stages, this structure was adapted for use as the residence of the Florentine vicar of the Mugello.

The building is first mentioned in 1355, when it was under construction or at least in the planning stages. At that date the vicar of the Mugello wrote from Scarperia to the *Signoria* in Florence: "Richordovi dell'opera del chassero chessevoi sapeste quello che porta voi lo studiareste a vostro podere" (ASF, *Signori Responsive, I Cancelleria,* 4, fol. 137r, 16 July 1355). By 1360 the project was largely complete. A petition of 22 June from the town's residents to the *Signoria* about the ringing of the town bells contains the information that the old tower was no longer accessible because of the new construction and that a castellan and soldiers appointed by the Florentines were already in residence in the building:

Vobis dominis prioribus artium et vexillifero iustitie popoli et Comunis civitatis Florentie, reverenter exponitur pro parte hominum et personarum Comunis castri Sancti Bernabe de Scarperia, et pro salute, commodo et honore dicti Comunis Florentie et castri predicte de Scarperie quod tempore fundationis et ordinationis casseri dicti castri cum hoc esset quod turris magna dicti castri, in qua est eorum campana, recludi et micti opportebat in dicto cassero, fuit permissum hominibus dicti castri quod per famulos et familiares castellanorum qui pro tempore essent deputati ad custodiam dicti casseri, pulsaretur et pulsari deberet campana dicti Comunis et castri Scarperie que est in et super dicta turri casseri, ad consilium dicti comunis Scarperia et ad vocandum custodias nocturnas et ad omnia et singula alia necessaria dicto Comuni et castro Scarperie et ad custodiam dicti Comunis et castri et hominum et personarum ipsius (ASF, *Provvisione, Protocolli,* 8, fol. 44r, 22 June 1360).

The officially approved version of the petition appears in ASF, *Provv.*, 47, fol. 205v.

77. In 1375 a restructuring of the committee charged with the construction of the Loggia della Signoria led to the administration of the project by the cathedral *opera*. The rebuilding of the city's prison, the Stinche, in 1397 – 98 was supervised by the *opera*. In the early fifteenth century the *opera* oversaw construction at the Palazzo della Signoria and at the city's castles in the countryside (Saalman, *Cupola*, pp. 182 – 185).

78. Saalman, *Cupola*, pp. 173 – 176; Grote, *Dombauamt*, pp. 68 – 69, 99 – 100.

79. ASF *Provv.*, 10, fol. 235, 1 April 1300; Braunfels, *Stadtbaukunst*, p. 260, document 24. The translation by the seventeenth-century historian Ferdinando del Migliore of what appears to be a piece of thirteenth-century legislation, now lost, asserts that Arnolfo was "capomaestro del nostro comune" when he was called to design the new cathedral; Ferdinando del Migliore, *Firenze città Nobilissima Illustrata* (1684; reprint ed., Bologna, 1976), p. 6.

80. ASF *Provv.*, 26, fol. 84, 12 April 1334; Braunfels, *Stadtbaukunst*, p. 262, document 27; Trachtenberg, *Campanile*, p. 182, document 1.

81. Braunfels, *Stadtbaukunst*, pp. 236 – 237.

82. Ibid., pp. 237 – 238.

83. Ibid., p. 263, document 28.

84. G. Milanesi, *Documenti per la storia dell'arte Senese* (Siena, 1854), I, p. 231: "Item magistro Lando aurifici pro salario quia steti ad faciendum rationem murorum Paganici, libri viiii, soldi v."

85. Braunfels, *Stadtbaukunst*, pp. 261 – 262, documents 25, 26.

86. Vasari writes: "Volendo, in questo mentre, i Fiorentini murare in Valdarno di sopra il castello di San Giovanni, e Castel Franco, per commodo della città e delle vettovaglie, mediante i mercati; ne fece Arnolfo il disegno, l'anno 1295, e soddisfece di maniera così in questa, come aveva fatto nell'altre cose, che fu fatto cittadino fiorentino" (Vasari, *Le Vite*, ed. G. Milanesi [Florence, 1906], I, p. 286). Two details of this passage are of particular interest. The first is the date — four years earlier than the document for the foundation of the town. The difference does not discredit Vasari, since the Valdarno projects had been under consideration since 1285. In fact, Giovanni Villani had given a similar date, 1296. The one year difference indicates that Vasari did not get his information from the fourteenth-century chronicler. The language of the passage points to another potential source. The phrase "for the convenience of the city and for the supply of victuals to their markets" is the language of the Florentine chancery. In a slightly modified form these words appeared in the records

of the debates of 1285 about the foundation of the town of Pietrasanta (now Casaglia): "quod de reffectione dicte terre obveniant honor commodum et utilitas Comuni Florentie, et maxime pro copia grani et bladi habenda de partibus Romandole" (Document 1). Vasari discussed an award of citizenship given to Arnolfo for his plans of the new towns. It is possible that his language, as well as his date for the new-town plans, comes from a government document that has not survived.

Vasari offered another attribution of a new-town design and again the artist was a man who held the office of *capomaestro* at the cathedral. According to Vasari, Andrea Pisano prepared the plans for the "castle at Scarperia . . . because Arnolfo was dead and Giotto absent" (Vasari, *Vite*, I, p. 486). Clearly something is wrong. The documents for Scarperia are unequivocal in giving the design of the town to the Florentine soldier and judge Matteus, who administered the project. They also certify the date of the foundation, 1306, which is almost twenty-five years before we have any evidence of Andrea's presence in Florence. Vasari may have been entirely wrong in attributing to Andrea any activity as a planner of new towns, or he may have been mistaken about the project in which Andrea participated. Andrea held the position of *capomaestro* at the cathedral in about 1340. He is recorded then as "maior magistro dicte opere," the successor to Giotto, who died in 1337 (ASF *Cap.*, 17, fol. 77; Trachtenberg, *Campanile*, p. 184, document 5). This was, of course, the period in which the city found Terranuova.

NOTES TO CHAPTER 6

1. GV *Cron.*, XI, chap. 53, quoted in Intro., note 3.
2. C. Bec, "Le Paysan dans la nouvelle toscane (1350 – 1430)," in *Civiltà ed economia agricola in Toscana nei seccoli XIII – XV: problemi della vita delle campagne nel tardo medioevo*, Ottavo convegno internazionale del centro italiano di studi di storia e d'arte, 21 – 24 April 1977 (Pistoia, 1981), pp. 29 – 52; O. Merlini, *Saggio di ricerche sulla satira contro il villano* (Turin, 1894).
3. E. Conti, *La formazione della struttura agraria moderna nel contado fiorentino* (Rome, 1965), I, pp. 394, 411.
4. G. Fasoli, "Ricerche sui borghi franchi dell'alta Italia," *Rivista di Storia del Diritto Italiano* 15, 2 (May – August 1942), pp. 174 – 175.
5. Ibid., p. 177.
6. G. Spagnesi and P. Properzi, *L'Aquila: problemi di forma e storia della città* (Bari, 1972); G. Budelli et al., "L'Aquila: nota sul rapporto tra castelli e

'locali' nella formazione di una capitale territoriale," in *Città, contado e feudi nell' urbanistica medievale,* ed. E. Guidoni (Rome, 1974), pp. 181 – 195; G. Gizzi, "La città dell' Aquila: fondazione e preesistenze," *Storia della Città* 28 (1983), pp. 11 – 42.

7. These are the churches of San Bartholomeo al Pozzo in the south quarter, San Nicolo in Ganghereto in the east quarter, and Santa Maria in Pernina in the north quarter. All three of them appear in the episcopal tax records of the late thirteenth and early fourteenth centuries when they were located in the original villages. M. Giusti and P. Guidi, Tuscia, II, *Le decime degli anni 1295 – 1304* (Vatican, 1942), pp. 128 – 129, no. 2319 for S. Bartolomeo de Puteo, no. 2308 for S. Nicolao de Gangareto, no. 2303 for S. Maria de Pernina.

8. The 1306 letter of instructions to the Florentine official in charge of the construction of Scarperia lists Sant' Agatha, Santa Maria di Fagna, San Giovanni Maggiore, and San Michele di Ferrone among the villages that were obliged to help in the work (Document 4). As listed in the tax records of 1356, from which the population data are also taken, the quarters of Scarperia were Sant' Agatha with 32 families recorded, Santa Maria with 45, San Giovanni with 53, and San Michele with 104 (ASF, *Estimo,* 282, fols. 165r – 168v).

9. Padre D. Bacci, *Terranuova Bracciolini nella sua storia* (Florence, 1956), pp. 197 – 198, refers to a bull of Eugenio IV, which was read publicly in San Biagio on 17 June 1443, making the church in the piazza the new "chiesa madre" and also "chiesa plebana" with jurisdiction over all the other churches in the town. The new church was built on the site of two oratories, one dedicated to the SS. Crocefisso and the other to Santa Maria. For the name of Terranuova in the fourteenth century, see Intro., note 3.

10. In a letter of 18 March 1407 / 8 to the *podestà* of Scarperia the *Signoria* wrote: Dilectissimo nostro. Acciò che gli huomini di codesta Comunità vivano in concordia, et che pel tempo che viene si ripari agli inconvenienti et danni che hanno sostenuti per lo essere divisa cotesta terra della Scarperia ai quattro Quartieri et per noi et per loro di nostro consentimento, si è deliberato che codesta terra ritorni a unita et a uno corpo, et che si levi via la detta divisione. Pertanto vogliamo et comandiamo che tu ordini e facci che questa divisione si levi, avendo in ciò buona diligenzia che si facci reposatamente et concordia. Et perchè faccendo questo è bisogno similmente da te forma et modo che gli ufici di cotesta Comunità ritornino a essere in altra forma che di dividergli in quattro parti della terra, ma che sieno distribuiti e ordinati sanza questa divisione, et che

tutti gli uffici della Lega et Comune della Scarperia si riformino in modo che sia pace et riposo di tutti gli huomini della Lega et Comune. Però vogliamo et comettiamo che,

fatto che fia la detta reduzione delle quattro parti della terra a una, che tu facci d'avere e di ragunare insieme gli uomini della Lega et del Comune, et quegli che si conviene secondo gli ordini di cotesta Lega et Comune, et vincendosi per le due parti delle tre, vogliamo et comettiamo che si facci la detta reformagione per modo che stia bene. Et perchè non vi si faccia ingiustizia né inconveniente, agiugniamo alla parte detta di sopra del riducere la terra a uno corpo, che quando si riduce, che questa ordinazione duri in perpetuo, et acciò che per niuno s'ardisca di cercare o fare in contrario, vogliamo che tra gli huomini della detta terra si metta una pena nella quale caggia chi cercasse o facesse in contrario et paghisi a quegli che observassono.

Confidianci nella tua prudenza, e per tanto fa' di avere in questi fatti tale diligenzia, che quanto comandiamo abbi effecto et tu possa quindi essere comendato.

ASF SS. Miss., 27, reproduced in *Giotto; Bollettino Storico, Letterario, Artistico del Mugello* 1 (1902), pp. 30 – 31.

11. On the political and social geography of Florence, see R. Weissmann, *Ritual Brotherhood in Renaissance Florence* (New York, 1982), chap. 1, biblio; on the settlement of immigrants in the city, see C. Greppi and M. Massa, "Città e territorio nella repubblica fiorentina," in *Un'altra Firenze, l'epoca di Cosimo il Vecchio: riscontri tra culture e società nella storia fiorentina* (Florence, 1971).

12. See note 10.

13. The dramatic difference between the settlement schemes for Terranuova and Giglio Fiorentino may have as much to do with the circumstances of the foundations as with a sudden shift in Florentine policy. Terranuova was founded, at least according to the public documentation, in response to a petition of free villages who turned to the city for assistance. Giglio, on the other hand, was to have been constructed from villages that were the feudal possession of the abbey of Agnano. It was the abbey not the villagers who approached the city, and this may have cast the Florentine government in the role of seigneur rather than liberator.

14. The legislation begins, "Cum libertas . . . non ex aliene, sed ex proprio dependet arbitrio." P. Vaccari, *Le affrancazioni collettive dei servi della gleba,* Instituto per gli Studi di Politica Internazionale (Milan, 1939), p. 59. L.A. Kotel'nikova, *Mondo contadino e città in Italia dall'XI al XIV secolo*

(Bologna, 1975). For an analysis of the limits of the opportunity offered serfs by the city of Florence, see B. Stahl, *Adel und Volk im florentiner Dugento* (Cologne, 1965), pp. 40 – 45.

15. ASF, *Provv.*, 29, fol. 76r; GV *Cron.*, XI, chap. 53. Richter, "Terra Murata," p. 359, n. 38.

16. MV *Cron.*, II, p. 55.

17. For the structure of government in the new towns, see the following sets of statutes from the late fourteenth and early fifteenth centuries: ASF *Stat. Com.*, 173, Statutes of Castelfranco di Sopra, 1393; ibid., 175, Statutes of Castelfranco di Sotto, 1425; ibid., 317, Statutes of Firenzuola, 1418; ibid., 779, Statutes and Amendments of San Giovanni, 1382 – 1586; ibid., 830, Statutes and Amendments of the vicarate of Scarperia, 1415 – 1643; ibid., 831, Statutes of the League of Scarperia, 1423, Amendments to 1569; ibid., 877, Statutes and Amendments of Terranuova, 1462 – 1600.

18. On Cardinal Ottaviano, see *Fonti per la storia d'Italia*, Istituto Storico Italiano, VIII (Rome, 1890), *Registro del Cardinale Ottaviano degli Ubaldini*, G. Levi, ed.; idem, "Il Cardinale Ottaviano degli Ubaldini secondo il suo carteggio ed altri documenti," *Archivio della Reale Società Romana di Storia Patria*, 9, nos. 3 – 4 (1891); A. Hauss, *Cardinal Ottavian Ubaldini: ein Staatsmann des 13 Jahrhunderts*, Heidelberger Abhandlungen zur mittleren und neuren Geschichte (Heidelberg, 1913), XXXV; L. Magna, "Gli Ubaldini del Mugello: una signoria feudale nel contado fiorentino," *Atti del II Convegno del Comitato di Studi nella Storia dei ceti dirigenti in Toscana*, 14 – 15 December 1979 (Pisa, 1982), pp. 13 – 65.

   A plaque dated 1592, placed on the facade of the Fagna church by the parish priest, commemorates the Ubaldini tomb removed in 1570 by Pius V: "Cum oli[m] Octaviani Ub / aldinii Cardi[nalis] ossa ex h[oc] / loco ubi marmoreo sepul[crum] / asservaba[n]t. In Ecclesiam / essent illata Iulius Deius / plebanus ut rei memo / riam vivam retinere / hunc lapidem posuit / A.D. MDLXXXXII."

19. At San Giovanni the town government established a relationship with the new parish that repeated the relationship between the feudal lords and the old parishes. Archivio Comunale di San Giovanni, 265, *Comunità di San Giovanni, Partiti*, 1513 – 1532, fol. 24r, 29 October 1514. The priest and rector of San Lorenzo at Castel San Giovanni: "per observatione della antiqua consuetudine solito farsi di sei mesi in sei mesi in dicto soprascripto di, ricognobbe da sua populani alhora existenti consiglieri della Credentia retenere la dicta chiesa et quelli affirmo essere veri et legiptimi signori et patroni di quella con le usate cerimonie et prandio"; *ibid.*, fol. 78r, 25

October 1517: "piovano della pieve di Castel San Giovanni per observantia della antiqua consuetudine quo questo sopradicta dì nella dicta chiesa ricognobbe dal consiglio della Credentia per dicto comune stipulante et recevendo la dicta pieve di San Giovanni et per dicto comune tenerla et possiderla ex quelli, disse et affermo essere veri et legiptime patroni di quella dandoli in segno di vero patronato le chiavi in mano con le altre bone et solite cerimonie."

20. The convent, dedicated to San Barnaba, was founded by a Frate Napoleone Galuzzi from Bologna on the authority of a bull of John XXII dated 8 June 1324. The pope gave the Augustinians permission to found two houses in the territory between Bologna and Tuscany for the benefit of the local residents but also in order to provide hospices for members of the order when they traveled across the mountains; L. Torelli, *Secoli Agostiniani* (Bologna, 1678), V, pp. 402 – 403. Frate Napoleone placed the convents at Loiano, on the Bolognese side of the watershed, and at Scarperia.

21. In 1326 the prior of Fagna, feeling his rights in the new town threatened by the Augustinian foundation, petitioned the pope to have the friars removed. The pope responded in a letter of 15 October 1326 instructing the *guardiano* of the convent of Santa Croce in Florence to investigate the claims of the two sides; Archivio Segreto Vaticano, *Registri Vaticani* 113, fols. 300r and v.

22. Since the bull of 1324 had specifically instructed Frate Napoleone not to place the convents where they would cause a conflict with the parochial clergy, it is likely that the *guardiano* found against the friars. A bull of 1331 ordered the Tuscan inquisitor to remove the Augustinians from Scarperia. The bull is cited as "Registri Vaticani titolo 3, ep. 1767," and its content described in T. Herrera, *Alphabetum Augustiniani* (1644), II, p. 415, and in S. Bellandi, "L'antico convento degli Agostiniani in Scarperia," in *Scarperia Illustrata* (Borgo San Lorenzo, 1906), p. 9. Nonetheless, I have not been able to trace a copy of it either in the Archivio Segreto or the Augustinian archives in the Vatican City. An important detail of the decision suggests that the Curia may not really have been in favor of getting rid of the friars. Rather than simply ordering them to be sent away to look for a new site, or even having his lieutenants select alternative ground, the pope ruled that the friars were to be settled in the buildings of the parish chapter at Fagna. If the prior did not want the friars at Scarperia, it is doubtful that he would have been pleased to give them his own church.

23. ASF, *Conventi Soppresse*, 252, 29, fols. 17r and v, 16 December 1439: the syndics of the vicarate of the Mugello for the peace and repose of all the persons of the vicarate, "mossi con tucti i vicari di dicto Vicariato per lo

magnifico Comune di Firenze mandati et che verrano al reggimento et governo di dicto vicariato sieno tenuti et cum salvo che ogni di loro e di ciaschuno di loro [con] reverentia debbino socto vinculo di juramento Iurare et promectere come si costuma solempnemente di fare et exercitare el lor ufficio predicto dinanzi fanno la loro residentia li frati predicti."

24. ASF, *Conventi Soppresse*, 252, 21, fols. 5r and 6v, will of Guido Ser Imolese, 25 June 1341; Guido wished to be buried at San Barnaba and left the revenue from a piece of land for construction at the church. ASF, *Archivio Diplomatico, Compagnia di Santa Maria di Piazza di Scarperia*, 14 February 1380, will of Antonio di Berto Passerini of Scarperia; Antonio gave 25 lire for building at San Barnaba.

25. ASF, *Provv.*, 47, fols. 200v – 201r, 22 June 1360. The priors and *gonfaloniere* "possint providere et ordinare quid et quantum et quemadmodum per ipsum comune Florentie expendi debeat in reparationem ecclesie sancti Barnabe de Scarperia comitatus Florentie et pro conservatione indempnitatis dicte ecclesie a dampno quod passa fuit propter destructionem et occupationem muri et terreni dicte ecclesie facto pro fortificatione castri de Scarperia predicta." The sum decided on, 100 florins, was 150 florins less than the residents of Scarperia had requested.

26. In villages in which it was the largest building and perhaps the only one of masonry construction, the church could be the center of defense, the last retreat of embattled residents. In the village of Agnano, which was supposed to send its inhabitants to settle Giglio Fiorentino, the east end of the abbey church forms part of the outer perimeter of the site's defenses; at Viterbo the church of Santa Rosa had its apse built into the city wall; and in the thirteenth-century expansion area of Massa Marittima the church shares its bell tower with the city's defenses.

27. ASF, *Compagnie Soppresse*, M. XCII, *Santa Maria di Piazza di Scarperia*, 10, fol. 58v.

28. ASF, *Conventi Soppresse*, 252, 29, fol. 2r, undated in a late-sixteenth-early-seventeenth-century hand: "Questa Compagnia della Beata Vergine di Piazza di Scarperia fu istituta l'anno 1327 [27 July written above], sotto il nome della Natività della Madonna da fra Ventura fiorentino Augustino nel convento di Santa Barnaba in Scarperia nella loro chiesa, et feci i primi quattro Capitani elettori—Vanno da Montepoli, Maestro Guiduccio Bili, Vanni di Ser Davanzato, Vanetto Puccini . . . quali originali capitani soli governavano la Compagnia con un Camerlingho che fu Vanni di Ser Davanzatto. . . . Il primo Cancelliere o scrivano fu fra Giovanni Arighetti fiorentino. La Compagnia si cominciò il dì di S. Jacopo l'anno come è detto

1327. Le sudette cose si veggono al suddetto libro molto vecchio al quale mancano molte carte."

29. ASF, *Compagnie Soppresse*, M. XCII, *Santa Maria di Piazza di Scarperia*, 10, fol. 35r: "Memoria come la compagnia fu aprovata l'anno 1364 da monsigneur Arcivescovo di Firenze." These lines were also written in the sixteenth or seventeenth century.

30. The members "pray to God to have mercy on [the dead man's] soul and, if for any demerit, he has been condemned to punishment in purgatory, let it please You, in Your charity, to forgive him and to lead him to glory of the eternal life to which, [we pray] let it please your Majesty to lead us all, Amen" (ibid., fols. 17r – 18r).

31. ASF, *Capitoli, Compagnie Soppresse*, 54, 1 November 1567, fols. 10r and v.

32. ASF, *Archivio Diplomatico, Compagnia di Santa Maria di Piazza di Scarperia*, July 1348.

33. ASF, *Capitoli, Compagnie Soppresse*, 54, fol. 11v. This book of documents and ASF, *Compagnie Soppresse*, M. XCII, *Santa Maria di Piazza di Scarperia*, 10, and ASF, *Conventi Soppresse*, 252, 29, are the sources of information in this paragraph not otherwise credited.

34. ASF, *Archivio Diplomatico, Compagnia di Santa Maria di Piazza di Scarperia*, 25 October 1354:

In Christi nomine amen. Anno ab eius incarnatione millesimo trecentesimo quinquagesimo quarto, indictione octava, die vigesimaquinta mensis Octubris. Convocatis et cohadunatis probis viris Nuto Manecti, Francischo Andreini et Mattheo Corsini de castro S. Barnabe cui dicitur Scharparia, comitatus Florentie, sindici Comunis et Universitatis dicti castri, ut de ipsorum sindicatu constare dixerunt in publico instrumento scripto manu publici notarii, absente tamen Francischo Gharducii eorum collegha in dicto offitio sindicatus; et ser Filippo ser Ugholini, Ghino Albizzini, Tura Mei et Ianne Nuti dicti loci, capitanei sotietatis beate et gloriose Marie Virginis de dicto Castro, ut de ipsorum electione, offitio et balia contineri dixerunt in publico instrumento scripto manu publici notarii, in platea dicti castri Sancti Barnabe de mandato sapientis et discreti viri ser Scharfangni ser Dini de Prato, notarii et offitialis dicti Comunis dicti castri ad numptii requisitionem, ut moris est. In qua quidem adunatione interfuerunt omnes sindici et capitanei suprascripte, predicti quidem sindici et capitanei dicentes et asserentes ad se ipsos sindicos et capitaneos spectare et pertinere de iure gubernationem et administrationem dicte sotietatis et bonorum et rerum dicte sotietatis, nec non hospitalis dicti Comunis et dicte sotietatis hedificati prope dictum castrum sub vocabulo S. Iacobi, et bonorum et rerum dicti hospitalis.

35. ASF, *Archivio Diplomatico, Compagnia di Santa Maria di Piazza di Scarperia,* 13 March 1320 / 21. In this document the priest at Fagna received the contribution for the hospice.

36. It was not only the poor that the Company touched with its funds. Awards for dowries were structured to give greatest assistance to those families who already had resources of their own. One of the dowry funds, which offered one award of fifty lire and two of twenty-five, gave the larger sum to candidates who, within limits, already had most (ASF, *Capitoli, Compagnie Soppresse,* 54, fols. 20r and v). To be eligible for the fifty-lire award, a girl had to have a dowry of her own of less than seven hundred lire. Girls with dowries of less than three hundred lire were eligible for the twenty-five-lire awards.

37. The town's first schoolmaster, brother Andrea da Sesto Fiorentino, whose name appears in records of 1486, was paid a salary and given the use of a garden plot, vineyards, and pasturage from an endowment established by the Company (ASF, *Conventi Soppresse,* 252, 29, fol. 57v: "Frate Andrea di Sesto fiorentino fu il primo maestro di scuola di Scarperia: con Salario di soldi 30 l'anno del 1486 ed più certi campi vigna e prati con obbligho ancora oltre allo scuola di tenere canto all oratorio"). By 1506 one-third of the teacher's salary was paid by the local government (ibid., fol. 59v). The schoolmaster at this time, brother Piero di Jacopo di Donato, received a salary of one hundred *soldi.* In the 1520s the commune's contribution ceased and students paid tuition fees, but the Company continued to pay its two-thirds share (ibid., fol. 62v) and to maintain the building in which classes were held. The Company's seventeenth-century books of *ricordi* note two improvements to the schoolhouse. One is the painting of an image of the Virgin "sopra alla porta della scuola" in 1517 (ASF, *Compagnie Soppresse,* M. XCII, 10, fol. 35v); another, dated 1509, concerns a "muricuola luogo la scuola el Oratoria" (ASF, *Conventi Soppresse,* 252, 29, fol. 60r). If the school and oratory did, in fact, share a wall, the school was located in the building on Via San Martino that today houses the stairs that give access to the rooms in the upper story of the oratory structure.

38. The Company supported building and maintenance at both San Barnaba and Santi Iacopo e Filippo (ASF, *Compagnie Soppresse,* M. XCII, 1, fascicle A, unpaginated, and 10, fols. 48 – 64; *Conventi Soppresse,* 252, 29, fols. 55v – 56v) and donated properties to help establish a living for the town's priest. "El podere che laciò Vanni del Gudeo da Firenze posto a S. Giorgio alla Rena, luogho detto al Poggio, fu conceduto alla chiesa dei Santi

Iacopo e Filippo per sussidio del parrochiano, a libro vecchio a carta 7, roghato per Bernardo Baldi, 1348"; this refers to the act of donation of the farm to the Company. "E di più si concesse a detta parochia e per lei a ser Piero di Franco Romoli alora parochiano, 2 pezi di terra lavoratia, luogho detto S.M. et G. alla Rena, la quale aveva comprata la Compagnia. E li concesse con obligho che in perpetuo si facesse dire ogni maria et messe in detta chiesa al'altare della Nunziata per l'anima di Madalena di Antonio di Michele di Tura che laciò fiorini 50, a libro rosso vecchio a c. 4 e 6." This entry is next to another dated to the year 1474 (ASF, *Compagnie Soppresse*, M. XCII, *Santa Maria di Piazza di Scarperia*, 10, fol. 58r).

39. ASF, *Estimo*, 282, fols. 165r – 168v.

40. ASF, *Archivio Diplomatico, Compagnia di Santa Maria di Piazza di Scarperia*, 10 February 1352 /3. In this document twenty-four men, all of whom were named, and the four officers of the company, declaring themselves to be at least two-thirds of the membership, in congregation "sub logie et tabernachulo prefate sotietate," gave two of the officers authority to represent them in court.

41. ASF,*Estimo*, 282, fols. 165r – 168v. The quarter of Sant'Agatha, which had a population of 32 families, was home to 5 brothers; the quarter of Santa Maria, with a population of 45 families, was home to 4; the quarter of San Giovanni, with a population of 53 families, was home to 9; San Michele, with a population of 104 families, was home to 10. The statutes of the Company, though written only in the sixteenth century, expressly forbade more than one member of a family at a time from participating in its ruling council (ASF, *Capitoli, Compagnie Soppresse*, 54, fol. 2r).

42. R.F.E. Weissman, *Ritual Brotherhood in Renaissance Florence* (New York, 1982).

43. Ibid., p. 91, citing ASF, *Cap.*, 439, *Capitoli della Compagnia della Disciplina in Santa Maria del Carmine*, 1431, prologue.

44. Ibid., citing L. de Prete, ed., *Capitoli della Compagnia della Madonna d'Orsanmichele dei secoli XIII e XIV* (Lucca, 1859), statutes of 1294, chap. 5, p. 4.

45. Ibid., p. 89, citing Biblioteca Nazionale, Florence, *Banco Rari*, 336, *Statuti della Compagnia di San Gilio*, 1278.

46. Two documents give names of councillors who served the town in the mid-fourteenth century. One is the note prefacing the *Estimo* of 1364 (ASF, *Estimo*, 214, fol. 218r); the other is the *Ufficiali delle Castella* report of 1366, which charges two town officials with repairing the defenses (see chap. I, note 2). One of these officials was a syndic of the Company in 1354 (see note 34); one of the town councillors in 1364 was named on the list of Company members of 1353 (see note 40).

47. The western wall of the oratory, the wall facing Via San Martino, preserves the walled-up remains of two upper story windows and the bases of four sandstone brackets, now broken off flush with the wall (Fig. 95). The brackets, which suggest a cantilevered upper story, contradict the windows and may be a later addition. The windows, however, must predate the oratory because their sills lie at a level that is lower than the height reached by the vaults of the oratory.

48. See note 40.

49. ASF, *Compagnie Soppresse*, M. XCII, *Santa Maria di Piazza di Scarperia*, 10, fol. 35r: "Del'anno medesimo [1484] si fece alzare el tetto dell oratorio perchè era basso insino alla volta a dette libro 181." This text comes from a collection of notices about the Company prepared in the eighteenth century.

50. H. Saalman, *The Bigallo, The Oratory and the Residence of the Compagnia del Bigallo e della Misericordia in Florence* (New York, 1969).

51. Examples can be found in the Chiostro Grande at Santa Maria Novella, which was built between 1303 and 1340 (Paatz and Paatz, *Kirchen*, III [1952], pp. 698 – 699), and at San Domenico al Maglio, founded in 1297 (ibid., II [1941], pp. 2, 7, n. 7).

    The loggia's vaults are covered with fresco decoration and though in very bad shape (the whitewash that covered them was cleaned off with rasps in the 1953 – 57 restoration), they too seem datable to the middle of the fourteenth century.

52. The canopy is faced with three gables; the two lateral ones are opened in trefoil arches while the wider one on the front is five lobed. Flanking the gables on the forward corners are pinnacles of an almost ungothic solidity that matches the weight of the columns on which they stand. Parallels for all of these forms can be found in tombs in the transept of the church of Santa Croce in Florence. The heavy twisted columns and five-lobed arch appear on the Baroncelli tomb inscribed with the date 1327 in the right transept; the arch and the distinctive single-leaf crockets that stud the gables are also to be found on the Bardi tombs of the 1340s in the left transept (Paatz and Paatz, *Kirchen*, I [1940], pp. 556, 647, n. 282 for the Baroncelli tomb, 576, 667, n. 409 for the Bardi tomb). The capitals, too, have Florentine counterparts from the mid-fourteenth century. The same serrated-edge leaves rolled at both top and sides appear in the capitals from the late 1330s in the four corners of the ground-floor chamber of the campanile of Florence cathedral (Trachtenberg, *Campanile*, figs. 39 – 42).

53. G. Leinz, "Die Loggia Rucellai, ein Beitrag zur Typologie der Familienloggia" (Ph.D. diss., University of Bonn, 1977); K. Frey, *Die Loggia dei Lanzi zu Florenz* (Berlin, 1885); J. Paul, "Die mittelalterlichen Komunalpaläste in Italien" (Ph.D. diss., University of Freiburg im Breisgau, 1963).

54. Camerani Marri, ed., *Statuti di Castelfranco;* rubric 17 is entitled "De la electione d'uno notaio che legga gli statuti a la loggia"; rubric 2 is concerned with controlling gambling in the town and its territory: "E che niuna persona possa ne debbia nel detto castello o sua corte giucare a tavole in alchuno luogo furche alla casa del comune o alla loggia ch'e in sulla piazza."

55. ASF *Stat. Com.,* 831, fol. 41r: "Chiaschuno huomo habitante nel chastello della Scarperia sia tenuto et debba andare al corpo di qualunque morisse nel detto castello et il corpo morto acompagnare infino alla chiesa dove si soppellisse. . . . Et poi seppellito il corpo i suoi parenti acompagnare insino ala casa donde el corpo morto e uscito et a quindi con quegli huomini et persone alla loggia della decta legha tornare. Et ivi tucti coloro che saranno stati acompagnare el morto per lo modo decto di sopra rassengare. Et i colpevoli et tucti color che non seranno stati al corpo morto come decto e sieno condempnati nella decta pena."

56. Ibid., fol. 55v.

57. J.G. Davies, *The Secular Use of Church Buildings* (London, 1968), pp. 57 – 60; Frey, *Loggia,* pp. 78 – 79.

58. ASF, *Archivio Diplomatico, Compagnia di Santa Maria di Piazza di Scarperia,* 1 October 1354: "In Dei nomine amen. Anno ab eius Incarnatione millesimo trecentesimo quinquagesimo quarto, indictione octava, die prima mensis Octobris. Actum in castro S. Bernabe cui dicitur Scarperia de Mucello, presentibus testibus Bartolo Gerii et Iohanne Guiducci, ambobus dicti castri, ad hec vocatis et rogatis. Ser Filippus quondam ser Ugolini, notarius, Tura Mey, Chinus Albizzini et Giannes Nuti, omnes de Scarperia, Capitanei et gubernatores Sotietatis seu fraternitatis S. Maria de Scarperia (ut de ipsorum electione constare dixerunt in actis dicti Comunis, scriptis manu ser Nicchole ser Archolani notarii), vice et nomine dicte sotietatis, omni via iure modo et causa, quo et quibus magis et melius potuerunt, nomine quo supra fecerunt constituerunt et solepniter ordinaverunt pro dicta sotietate ac eius vice et nomine, sindicos procuratores actores factores negotiorum gestores et certos numptios speciales, Iohannem Andreini et Nuccium vocatum Palafuta Bindi de Scarperia."

59. See note 34.

60. ASF, *Conventi Soppresse,* 252, 29, fol. 58r: "Si dice del Imborsare Capitani a Palazzo del Sig. Vicario," between entries dated 1499 and 1500.

61. C.M. de la Roncière, "La Place des confréries dan l'encadrement religieux du contado Florentin: l'example de la Val d'Elsa," *Mélanges de l'École Française de Rome: Moyen Age – Temps Modernes* 85 (1973), 1, pp. 31 – 77; 2, pp. 633 – 671. De la Roncière calculated that seventy-six percent of the confraternities in the area of the countryside that he examined were sited

in towns of "micro-urbain" character. Of the four confraternities in the eastern Mugello before 1330, none was connected to the parishes from which the residents of Scarperia were drawn. Indeed, according to de la Roncière, it was the rare confraternity that was allied with the nobility. See also G. Meerseman and G.P. Pacini, *Ordo fraternitatis: confraternite e pietà dei laici nel medioevo*, 3 vols. (Rome, 1977), (*Italia Sacra* 24 – 26).

62. G. Richa, *Notizie istoriche delle chiese fiorentine*, I (Florence, 1754), pp. 8 – 9. Richa has his information from a set of the company's statutes no longer extant, written in 1291.

63. L. Passerini, *Storia degli stabilimenti di beneficienza e d'istruzione elementare gratuita della città di Firenze* (Florence, 1853), p. 435.

64. ASF, *Conventi Soppresse*, 252, 29, fols. 5r – 6v, 25 June 1341; ASF, *Archivio Diplomatico, Società di Santa Maria di Piazza di Scarperia*, 19 July 1348.

65. The picture has been attributed to Jacopo by R. Offner (R. Offner, "Jacopo del Casentino, integrazione della sua opera," *Bollettino d'Arte* 3 [1923 – 24], p. 264; idem, *Studies in Florentine Painting* [New York, 1927], pp. 30 – 31; idem, *A Critical and Historical Corpus of Florentine Painting*, section 3, II, pt. 2 [New York, 1930], p. 146, pl. LX). Offner's attribution has been supported in the subsequent literature (B.C. Kreplin in *Allgemeines Lexikon der Bildenden Künstler von der Antike bis zur Gegenwart*, eds. U. Thieme and F. Becker, XXIII [Leipzig, 1928], ed. H. Vollmer, s.v. "Jacopo Landino"; B. Berenson, *Italian Pictures of the Renaissance* [1932, reprint ed., London, 1963], p. 102).

The date of the Scarperia panel can be fairly closely pinned down. It cannot have been executed before 1347, for reasons discussed late in this chapter, and it must have been finished by Jacopo's death which occurred, according to the most accepted evidence, before 8 August 1349, when Jacopo's two sons were assigned to the care of guardians (H. Horne, "A Commentary Upon Vasari's Life of Jacopo del Casentino," *Rivista d'Arte* 6 [1909], p. 99. Horne also notes that Jacopo's name appears in the statutes of the guild of Saint Luke in a list made after 1350 in this form: "Jacopo di Casentino dipint MCCCIL"). Vasari, on the other hand, says in the 1568 edition of the *Lives* that Jacopo died at the age of eighty (Vasari-Milanesi, *Vite*, I, p. 675) and was buried in the Camaldolese church of San Agnolo outside of Pratovecchio. The *Annales Camaldensis* gives the date of Jacopo's death as 1358 (J.B. Mittarelli and A. Costadoni, *Annales Camaldenses Ordinis Sancti Benedicti* [Venice, 1761], VI, p. 52).

66. The date and attribution of the Orsanmichele altarpiece depend, aside from the style of the panel, on the records of two payments to Bernardo by the Company of Orsanmichele of 1 March and 16 June 1347 "per parte

dell dipintura dela tavola di nostra donna" (R. Offner, *The Works of Bernardo Daddi* [New York, 1930], pp. 2 – 3). The work must have been largely completed by 18 August 1348, the date of Bernardo's death.

67. The first picture, which began to work miracles in July 1292, was apparently destroyed by fire in 1304 (GV *Cron.*, VIII, chap. 71). It was replaced with another picture when the grain loggia was rebuilt in 1304 – 8 (Frey, *Loggia*, pp. 59 – 60) and this image was replaced by Bernardo's altarpiece in 1347. We have no secure idea of what the first image looked like, although an early-fourteenth-century fresco in the Santa Croce museum has been connected with it (B. Cole, "On an Early Florentine Fresco," *Gazette des Beaux Arts* [July – August 1972], pp. 91 – 96). There are, however, at least two representations of the second image, and even a candidate for identification as the actual painting! (W. Cohn, "La seconda imagine della loggia di Orsanmichele," *Bollettino d'Arte* [July – December 1957], pp. 335 – 338). The representations occur in manuscript illuminations, one in the Biadaiuolo Codex of 1335 – 40 in the Biblioteca Laurenziana (ms. Tempi 3, fol. 79), another in a register of the *capitani* of Orsanmichele, 1340 – 47, in the State Archives of Florence. The picture suggested as the image itself is now in the Oratory of Santa Maria Maddalena in the town of Pian di Mugnone just north of Florence.

Werner Cohn thought the second image to have been a copy of the destroyed miracle-working Madonna of the thirteenth century. The Santa Croce museum fresco also supports that idea. All the pictures related to the second image show full-length enthroned Madonnas surrounded by varying numbers of angels. The child is in every case posed in a seated posture on his mother's knee holding a goldfinch (except in the Pian di Mugnone panel). The Santa Croce fresco, probably a pale reflection of the Orsanmichele image but of some importance because it could have been one of the sources used for reconstructing the appearance of the lost altarpiece in 1308, has all these features. One particular detail of the fresco, the angels' delicate touching of the Virgin's throne, is repeated in both the State Archives and Pian di Mugnone versions of the second image.

The Daddi altarpiece continues this tradition, although naturally with some changes. Ideas of what was essential in a copy may well have changed in the forty years between the painting of the second and third images and certainly alterations were necessary to update the image for contemporary taste and adapt it to the artist's personal style. Yet there is a clear intention to reproduce the older image and even, it seems, an attempt to revive features of the first image that had been neglected in the 1308 copy.

The 1347 image maintains all the features, except the posture of the Christ Child, that tied the second Maddona at Orsanmichele to the first, famous altarpiece. In addition, the kneeling angels holding censers and oil lamps occur, in some formulation, in all the second-image copies, and most specifically in the Archivio di Stato illumination. This version also has the hand of the Madonna tucked between the child's arm and torso.

It is in the structure of the throne that Bernardo Daddi's picture may go back to the first image. At least it shows connections, in ways not taken up in the versions of the 1308 image, to the Santa Croce fresco. The second-image copies all have bare-backed thrones which, in both manuscript illumination versions, are inset with a blind trefoil arcade. The back of the throne of Bernardo's picture is covered with an embroidered cloth supported at the peak and the bases of the gable and at three other points on each side. A jewel-bordered roll of cloth follows this contour while the back drape, embroidered in a separate pattern, falls flat behind this support. The throne of the Santa Croce fresco is decorated in exactly this way. The scrolls that make up this throne's arms are also more like Bernardo's throne than anything connected to the second image.

68. G.M. Brocchi, *Descrizione della provincia del Mugello* (Florence, 1748), p. 120; Brocchi relates the story that before the foundation of Scarperia, houses stood on the site along with "quel pozzo, che è in mezzo di Piazza, in cui dicono che fosse trovato quell Immagine miracolosa della Santissima Vergine, che si venera nella Compagnia detta di Piazza."

69. M. Aronberg Lavin, "The Joy of the Bridegroom's Friend: Smiling Faces in Fra Filippo, Raphael, and Leonardo," in *Art the Ape of Nature, Studies in Honor of H.W. Janson* (New York, 1981), pp. 193 – 210; G. Schiller, *Ikonographie der Christlichen Kunst*, (New York and Kassel, 1966 – 80), IV, pt. 1 (1976), s.v. "Mater Ecclesia," and "Sponsa-Sponsus"; pt. 2 (1980), s.v. "Maria-Ekklesia"; E. Kitzinger, "A Virgin's Face: Antiquarianism in Twelfth-Century Art," *Art Bulletin* 62 (March 1980), pp. 6 – 19. My thanks to Professors Marilyn and Irving Lavin for suggestions about the iconography of the two Madonnas.

70. In her categorization of Tuscan Madonnas, Dorothy C. Shorr (*The Christ Child in Devotional Images in Italy during the XIV Century* [New York, 1954]) put the Orsanmichele and Scarperia altarpieces into different groups, based on the gesture that the Christ Child makes with his right hand. Because Shorr sought a system with the broadest possible application, she limited the number of qualities used to characterize the groups. For this reason she excluded the more complex combinations of gesture and form that define the very localized sort of relationship discussed here.

71. See chap. 1, notes 9 – 14.

72. MV *Cron.*, II, chaps. 14, 15, 21, 23, 29 – 33.
73. MV *Cron.*, II, chap. 15.
74. Ibid., chap. 14.
75. Ibid., chap. 15.
76. Ibid., chap. 32.
77. Ibid., chap. 33.
78. The government itself, in the spirit of the agreements that it had made with the settlers at the time of their immigration (Document 7), showed more concern for the townsmen. In its *Provvisione* written four days after the siege of Scarperia had been lifted, the much relieved *Signoria* awarded honors to the Florentines who had led the defense. The government fulfilled its promise to Jacopo de Fiore, the foreign captain of the Mugello, to provide extra pay to the mercenary soldiers; and granted a ten-year tax exemption to the residents of Scarperia "who suffered great damage to their persons and their possessions" and who "were energetic in their defense of the town" (ASF, *Provv.*, 40, fols. 35 – 36.). Additional documents relating to the siege of Scarperia can be found in *Giotto; bollettino storico lettarario artistico del Mugello* 1 (1902), pp. 133 – 141. For a decade after the events of 1351 the city's *Provvisioni* are peppered with extensions of the tax relief and reparations awarded to the residents.
79. Leonardo Bruni, *Istoria Fiorentina* (Florence, 1864), pp. 383, 394 for the "terrazzani," 391 – 392 for his version of the exploits of Giovanni de' Medici. For the *Provvisione* of 20 October 1351, see note 78.
80. Jo. Baptista Recenato, ed., *Poggii Historia Florentina* (Venice, 1715), pp. 15 – 16: "Auleguis ad Scarpariam castrametatus, cum pollicitationibus ad deditionem oppidanos cohortatus parum profecisset, minas addidit, praemonens, ne calamitates, quae expugnatis imminent, experiri vellent: 'considerare' admonet bonorum direptionem, suam liberorumque captivatatem: mulierum, ac uxorum ignominiam: verbera, bulner, caedem, quae omnia victos fortuna subire cogat. Satius esse slava patria gaudere, quam ea amisa extorres, atque inopes miseram vitam ducere: illis eas haud esse vires, ut tanto exercitui resisti queat; conducere suis rebus, ut potius pacato, quam infesto hoste uti malint, neve experiri cupiant, quid libido, atque ira militaris possit."
81. F. Ranalli, ed., *Istorie Fiorentine di Scipione Ammirato con l'agguinte di Scipione Ammirato il Giovane*, II (Florence, 1847), p. 505. "Il presidio era d'uomini valorosi, e i medesimi terrazzani, per non conoscer altri signori che i Fiorentini, i quali erano stati edificatori di quel luogo quarantiacinque anni addietro, e per naturo del loro mestiere, che trattano il ferro, eran forti, e fedeli; onde la resistenza era gagliarda."
82. In the fourteenth century the office of vicar was a peripatetic one. The

incumbent moved through his territory maintaining the peace and protecting Florentine interests. In the Mugello, however, Scarperia seems always to have had a special importance in vicarial affairs. In 1352 the vicar's treasury was fixed there (ASF, *Provv.*, 39, fol. 145v, 30 May 1352; for the collection of fines "fiat pro vicarius totus mucelli camerlingho deputat, seu deputando in terra Scarperia") and in 1353 a notary was provided for the vicar's use by the town's residents. The salary of the vicar was determined at 377 lire per month, from which he had to pay his staff. The vicar was given use of the notary "cum offitio contentum in statutum terre di Scarperia" (ASF, *Provv.*, 40, fol. 93r, 16 April 1353).

When the vicarate was reorganized in 1415, Scarperia became its permanent seat (ASF *Provv.*, 105, fols. 3r – 5v, 11 April 1415). The new vicarate of the Mugello included the *podesterie* of Mangone, Vicchio, San Piero a Sieve, Borgo San Lorenzo, Belforte, Scarperia, Calenzano, Campi, Signa, Sesto, Brozzi, and Carmignano. In the statutes of 1415 the powers of the vicars were described along with those of the *podestà* and *capitani* of the Florentine state (*Statuta Populi et Comunis Florentiae*, 1415, [Freiburg, 1783], III, pp. 621 – 634, 4th Book, rubric 59: "De iurisdictione, authoritate, et balia potestatem, et Vicariorum, comitatus, et districtus Florentine").

The vicar was a military officer who maintained the defenses of his territory. He also kept civil order within that area. As a judicial official he had the power to hear civil and criminal cases and to impose sentences according to a schedule fixed by the central government. His decisions were open to appeal to a Florentine judge. The vicar was responsible for the protection of the property of Florentine citizens in his territory and was also the intermediary for the collection of taxes and for communication between the city and its provincial subjects. Vicars had precedence of honor over *podestà*s, but their jurisdictions were not intended to overlap or to be in a hierarchical relation to each other. The statutes of 1415 established the term of office of vicars and *podestà*s at six months. At the end of this term each vicar was reviewed by an official of the *podestà* of Florence and three residents of the vicarate (ASF *Stat. Com.*, 830, fols. 94v, 95r). To assure his honorable behavior each vicar deposited ten thousand lire in security with the city before entering the office. In 1424 the vicarate of the Mugello absorbed the office of the *podestà* of Scarperia (ASF, *Tratte*, 67, fol. 100: "Die 16 Novembre [14]24 pro habentes baliam sommiss[ione] in vicaritus et non extrahitur potestas").

83. ASF, *Tratte*, 67, fols. 21r – 22r 1418 – 24: "Vicarius Mucelli cum uno milite socio, uno notario, quatuoro domicellis, quindecim famulis, quinque equis per eum retinere. Et cum salario libras duarum milium fp, solvendo hoc vs libre CXXV per potestarium Scarperia."

The 1418 allotment represents a reduction of two domestic servants, eight attendants, and two horses from the household that the vicar maintained before he was settled at Scarperia. At that time, too, the vicar's salary was guaranteed by Florence but paid by the residents of the vicarate (ASF, *Tratte*, 66, fol. 37r).

84. See chap. 5, note 76.

85. The reception of Frederick III is first recorded in a letter written by Niccolo Strozzi less than a week after the emperor's arrival. He reports on the city's sending three ambassadors to Ferrara and continues: "sabato sera stete [the Emperor and his train] alla Scarperia, e di quivi s'ordinarono per ambasciadori ala Scarperia 20 nostri citadini di principali, accompagniati da circa a 100 giovani vestiti ricamente, a bene a cavallo, chè domenica mattina si andarono alla Scarperia e visitorollo colle debite cierimonie, e di poi il dì ne vennono in Firenze, che come è detto di sopra, giunse alla porta con grand trionfo a ore 22" (ASF, *Carte Strozziane*, 178, letter 50, 5 February 1451 / 2; published in *Bollettino storico – lettararia del Mugello* 1 [1893], p. 29).

Vespasiano da Bisticci, writing in the 1480s in his life of Giannozzo Manetti, gives further, and partly contradictory information: "Ispedita la sua [Manetti's] commessione a Roma, tornò a Firenze; e fu tratto di collegio, ed in questo tempo passò l'imperadore in Italia, e fu fatto messer Gianozzo uno de' quindici ambasciadori chè gli andorono incontro con degnissima compagnia, con commessione che, dove lo trovassino, messer Gianozzo gli parlasse in nome della Signoria, e ricevesselo. Andando inverso il Mugello, lo trovorono a Vaglia, accompagnato da messer Carlo Pandolfini e messer Otto Nicolini. Ismontò l'imperadore con tutti i signori ch'erano con lui, e con messer Enea, che fece fare cardinale, e di poi fu papa Pio. Messer Giannozzo ismontò, lui e tutti gli ambasciadori smontorono. Fece messer Giannozzo una degna orazione accomodata secondo il tempo e il luogo; di poi messer Enea rispuose in nome dell'imperadore molto accomodate parole, e rimontorono a cavallo, e vennono alla via di Firenze, dove fu molto onorato. Tutti i cittadini di qualche condizione gli andorono incontro a cavallo, oltre a' quindici ambasciadori, e dua n'erano collo imperadore" (Vespasiano da Bisticci, *Vite di uomini illustri del secolo XV*, ed. P. d'Ancona and E. Aeschlimann [Milan, 1951], p. 280).

The disagreement about the location of the encounter between the emperor and the Florentines is compounded by the account of the event in Scipione Ammirato's sixteenth-century *Istorie Fiorentine:* "A 29 venne [the emperor] a Scarperia, ove trovò una gran parte della nobiltà fiorentina con ordine e apparecchio maraviglioso. I quali a casa Cosimo e Bernardetto de' Medici se e la sua corte riceverono. Il dì seguente gli uscirono incontro infino all'Uccellatoio l'arcivescovo Antonino co' suoi canonici, e ventidue cittadini cavalieri con più di sessanta giovani nòbili tutti pomposamente vestiti e bene a cavallo: co' quali a S. Gallo essendo ancor molto del giorno ne venne" (Ranalli, *Scipione Ammirato*, IV [1849], p. 121).

Ammirato's identification of three separate receptions makes it possible to accommodate both Niccolo Strozzi's and Vespasiano da Bisticci's accounts, yet there is much that is suspicious about Ammirato's version of the story. The reception and hospitality by the Medici, presumably at their estates of Trebbio and Caffaggiolo, like Ammirato's reconstruction of the family's part in the siege of 1351, suits the circumstance of the sixteenth century very well, but it does not appear in the fifteenth-century sources. Ammirato's three receptions also have a kind of symmetry that makes them suspect. The emperor is met by the city's three "estates," the nobility, the lord, and the citizens and clergy. The fifteenth-century accounts mention only the citizens. Ammirato does, however, give a prominent role to Scarperia and perhaps in this we can believe him. He did not get his information from Niccolo Strozzi's letter, yet what he did learn conforms to the account which is, after all, the closest in time to the events themselves.

NOTES TO CHAPTER 7

1. Braunfels, *Mittelalterliche Stadtbaukunst in der Toskana* (Berlin, 1953), pp. 131 – 134.
2. N. Rubinstein, "The Beginnings of Political Thought in Florence," *The Journal of the Warburg and Courtauld Institutes* 5 (1942), pp. 198 – 227.
3. GV *Cron.*, III, chap. 2.
4. R. Krautheimer, "Introduction to an 'Iconography of Medieval Architecture,'" *Studies in Early Christian, Medieval, and Renaissance Art* (New York, 1969), pp. 115 – 150.
5. GV *Cron.*, XI, chaps. 91 – 94.
6. H. Baron, *Crisis of the Early Italian Renaissance* (Princeton, 1955), I, pp. 168 – 171, 178 – 189; for dating of the essay, II, pp. 517 – 518, n. 16. Bruni's essay is also published, in translation, in B.G. Kohl and R.G. Witt, eds., *The Earthly Republic: Italian Humanists on Government and Society* (Philadelphia, 1978), pp. 121 – 174.
7. The fresco is too poorly preserved for the style of painting to indicate any precise date. There are some documents, however, that illuminate the question. A payment of ten florins, made on 15 July 1366 for the decoration of the Palazzo dell'Arte dei Giudici e Notai and particularly for frescoes in the "volta magna," could well refer to the Florence image (S. Calleri, *L'arte*

dei giudici e notai di Firenze [Milan, 1966], p. 131; document from ASF, *Arti, Giudici e Notai,* 28). The 1427 *catasto* tells us that only the ground floor of the palazzo was vaulted (Calleri, *L'arte,* pp. 132, 135). These vaults seem to have existed from 1349, when Neri Fioravanti was paid for the construction of vaults in the guild hall (ibid., p. 128). By comparison with the vaults in the Palazzo della Mercanzia on the Piazza della Signoria, which were executed shortly after the fall of 1359 by Giovanni di Lapo Ghini (ASF, *Mercanzia,* 172, fols. 72r and v, 27 September; fols. 81r and v, 17 December), and especially with the prismatic corbels of those vaults, which are exactly repeated in the Palazzo dell'Arte dei Giudici e Notai, the present vaults would seem to date to 1349. The frescoes were certainly done by 1406 when Ambrogio dei Baldesi was paid for the decoration on the walls of the hall (W. Cohn, "Franco Sacchetti und das Ikonographische Program der Gewölbemalereien von Orsanmichele," *Mitteilungen des kunsthistorischen Institutes in Florenz* 8, 2 (September 1958), pp. 75 – 76). Although these latter frescoes, too, have all but disappeared, we can be sure that those on the ceiling were not painted with them. Fragments of the decorative border of the two sections—fictive Cosmati work in the ceiling and acanthus scrolls on the walls—sit uncomfortably together and certainly do not belong to the same project. The ceiling frescoes belong to an earlier project, very probably to be connected with the document of 1366. Professor Miklos Boskovitz kindly brought the Giudici e Notai fresco to my attention.

8. A relief carving from Nimrud dating to the tenth century B.C. and representing a fortified camp testifies to the antiquity of the cross and circle image. The diagrams, or *templum,* of the sky and the earth from the Roman tradition of the *agri mensores* may have transferred this emblem to medieval Europe (J. Rykwert, *The Idea of a Town* [Princeton, 1976], figs. 6, 26, 168).

9. E. Herzog, *Die Ottonische Stadt* (Berlin, 1964), p. 251.

10. E. Guidoni, "La croce di strade; funzione sacrale ed economica di un modello urbano," *Lotus International* 24 (1979), pp. 115 – 119.

11. P. Leveque and P. Vidal-Naquet, *Clisthène l'Athéneien, Annales Littéraires de L'Université de Besançon,* 65 (Paris, 1964), pp. 123 – 146.

12. Milan's topography lends itself to this form of characterization. The early-fourteenth-century drawing of the city of Galvano Fiamma, however, depends more on the conventions of geometry than on an accurate record of the shape of the city. J.K. Hyde, "Medieval Descriptions of Cities," *Bulletin of the John Rylands Library* 48 (1966), pp. 308 – 340.

13. The Florence "figure" is surely related to the abstract schemata used to demonstrate the laws of Aristotelian science in European illuminated manuscripts from the sixth century on (see H. Bober, "An Illustrated

Medieval Schoolbook of Bede's 'De Natura Rerum,' " *Journal of the Walters Art Gallery* 19 [1956 – 57], pp. 65 – 97; idem, "In Principio, Creation Before Time" in *De Artibus Opuscula XL, Essays in Honor of Erwin Panofsky* [New York, 1961], pp. 13 – 28). It is particularly close to representations of the universe like the one of 1389 – 91 in the Campo Santo in Pisa, in which the earth is shown in the center of a series of concentric rings representing the elements, the planets, the stars, and the nine grades of angels (M. Bacci et al., *Camposanto monumentale di Pisa* [Pisa, 1960], pp. 99 illus. 103).

14. G. Pampaloni, *Firenze al tempo di Dante: documenti sull'urbanistica fiorentina* (Rome, 1973), p. 115, document 66, from ASF, *Archivio Diplomatico*, Badia di Firenze, 7 January 1298.

15. Ibid., p. 106, document 61, from ASF, *Archivio Diplomatico, Santa Croce*, 11 May 1287.

16. According to GV *Cron.*, VI, chap. 26, the paving of Florentine streets in 1237 made the city "più netta e più bella e più sana."

17. Pampaloni, *Firenze*, pp. 132 – 133, document 72, from ASF, *Archivio Diplomatico, Comenda Covi*, 29 August 1314.

18. R. Caggese, ed., *Statuti della repubblica fiorentina*, II, *Statuto del podestà, anno 1325* (Florence, 1921), bk. 4, rubric 65, p. 353.

19. G. Salvemini, *Magnati e popolani in Firenze del 1280 al 1295* (Florence, 1899), p. 137, n. 1; Braunfels, *Stadtbaukunst*, p. 109. The city's policy is reflected in the statutes of Castelfranco di Sopra of 1394, which established a penalty against anyone who demolished a house in the town that was not in ruinous condition (Camerani Marri, ed., *Statuti di Castelfranco*, bk. 2, rubric 84, p. 117).

20. Braunfels, *Stadtbaukunst*, p. 253, document 7, from ASF *Provv.*, 52, 27 February 1363. In Siena houses of packed earth (pisé) were required to have facades of brick; L. Zdekauer, ed., *Il costitutio del comune di Siena dell'anno 1262* (Milan, 1897), distinctio V, rubric 409; A. Lisini, ed., *Il costituto del comune di Siena volgarizzato nel MCCCIX – MCCCX* (Siena, 1903), I, distinctio II, rubric 409, pp. 406 – 407: "se infra la città di Siena et li borghi avenisse chè si facesse alcuna casa di terra murata ad arche, che le more et le facce denanzi si murino et si facciano et sieno di mattoni, acciò che cotali case rendano bellezza a la città." G. Chierici, "La casa senese al tempo di Dante," *Bollettino senese di storia patria* 28 (1921), p. 348; D. Ballestracci and G. Piccinni, *Siena nel trecento, assetto urbano e strutture edilizie*, (Florence, 1977), pp. 79 – 80. The description of the Giglio Fiorentino project required that houses on the main street of the town have masonry facades at least ten *braccia* high (Document 19).

21. Braunfels, *Stadtbaukunst*, p. 111, n. 401; V. Feridici, ed., "Statuti di Viterbo"

in *Statuti della provincia romana, fonti per la storia d'Italia*, VIII (Rome, 1930), distinctio III, rubric 39: "Quo nullus edificat caligam in strada. Item, statuimus quod nullus faciat vel hedificat caligam aliquam de novo seu murum in strata vel via publica, cuius occasione via, vel eius status vel aspectus vie ledetur vel choarceatur."

22. P. Moschella, "Le case a 'sporti' in Firenze," *Palladio* 6, nos. 5 – 6 (1942), pp. 167 – 173.

23. Gaye, *Carteggio*, I, p. 443, document of 24 March 1299. GV, *Cron.*, XI, chap. 32.

24. Pampaloni, *Firenze*, p. 144, document 76; R. Caggese, ed., *Statuti della repubblica fiorentina*, I, *Statuto del capitano del popolo degli anni 1322 – 1325* (Florence, 1910), bk. 4, rubric 8, pp. 175 – 181.

25. For the description of the projected course of the street between Orsan-michele and the Bargello, see Pampaloni, *Firenze*, pp. 114 – 118, document 66, from ASF, *Archivio Diplomatico*, Badia di Firenze, 7 January 1298.

26. Braunfels, *Stadtbaukunst*, p. 110, n. 393; Caggese, ed., *Statuto del podestà*, bk. 2, rubric 22, pp. 101 – 102.

27. Pampaloni, *Firenze*, pp. 111 – 112, document 64, from ASF, *Provv.*, 4, fol. 126, 6 December 1294.

28. Caggese, ed., *Statuto del capitano*, bk. 4 rubric 8, p. 178.

29. ASF *Stat. Com.*, 831, Statutes of the League of Scarperia, 1423, fols. 32r – 33r: Acciò che'l chastello della Scharperia necto si conservi, et perche tra vicini niuna lite si possa genare [*sic*, generare], statuto et ordinato é che ciascheduno che [h]a nel chastello della Scharperia casa propria o daltrui condocto sia tenuto et debba da uno mese dal dì della publicagione del presente statuto lastricare et lastricare fare dinanzi alla sua casa dove lastricato non fusse, o se vi fusse et fusse in parte guasto, raconciare alle sue spese. Ancora sia tenuto ciascheduno lastricare tralle case del decto chastello ciascheduno, cioè, presso alla sua casa propria o condocta fra'ldecto archipenzolata per si facto modo che ciascheduno riceva acon-ciamente l'acqua del suo vicino che gli è di sopra et per si facto modo che l'acqua che corre delle case aconciamente senza alcuna ingiuria et schoncio altrui scolare possa et correre fralle decte case da una via a un altra del decto chastello et i decti lastricati continuamente mantenere a tucte sue spese.

Sia tenuto ancora ciaschuno che [h]a casa propria o condocta nella quale guardaroba o acquaio non fusse, fare et far fare la guardaroba et ac-quaio predicto o qualchesia di quelli che non vi fusse fra'l termine predicto socterra coperto et di sopra lastricato si et per si facto modo che scorrere possa et che puzo non gicti et che a niuno de' vicini niuno rincrescimento generare possa socto la pena di soldi quaranta per ciascheduno che per le predecte cosa o alcuna di quelle fra il decto termine ad exicutione non ara mandato o contro alle dete cose facesse. Et acciò che l'acqua che corre tralle case // c. 32v // che sono l'una alato all'altra del decto chastello a niuno vicino dia puzo, niuna persona ardischa o presumma nel chiasso sopra ove fusse lastricato tralle case, che l'una allato all'altra, porre niuno legniame o cosa puzolente o alcuna altra cosa per lo corso della decta acqua si che la decta acqua o corsa di quella simpedischa o impedire o nuocere possa o che la decta acqua a vicini puzolente o fracida vengha et loro non offenda socto la decta pena. El podestà et ufficiale della decta lega siano tenuti et debbino per obligagione di giuramento di tucte le predecte cose cerchare ciascheduno mese una volta et color che contro fanno o faranno punire et condemp-nare nelle decte pene. Et niente di meno ciascheduno possa delle predicte cose et ciaschuna di quelle dinuntiare et accusare. Et abbi la quarta parte della condempnagione el podestà et ufficiale soldi due per lira di quelle condapnagioni che per le predecte cose fara et rischotera che schorrono et si sparghono tralle decte case quando fanno capo alla via o vie del chastello raghunare si debbino et condurre alla strada publica o a quella via per la qualle piu agevolmente schorrere et andare possino, non mectendo quelle per la casa o tralle case che fassino dall' altre parte della via. Et l'altre acque che piovano et caggiono delle case della decta terra nella strada publica et vie del decto chastello dal muro della porta bolognese insino al muro della porto [sic] fiorentina per la directa via precedano et eschano del castello donde usate sono d'uscire. Salvo che l'acqua la quale discende et spargesi per la via diricto del quartiere di Santo Michele tralle case che anticamente furono di Dino di Leone et di Partino Ughectini con quella che discende delle case del decto Ughectino anticamente insieme sono, escha et uscire debba per la fogna della porta di Sanct Agata per si facto modo che non guasti, consumi, o disfacci il lastricato // c. 33 r // della decta porta et che quello che e guasto rachonciare si debba per spatio d'uno mese per la decta legha.

30. Pampaloni, *Firenze*, pp. 100 – 102, document 58, from ASF, *Cap.*, 29 fol. 356; F. Sznura, *L'espansione urbana di Firenze nel dugento* (Florence, 1975), pp. 79 – 84.

31. Sznura, *L'espansione*, p. 79.

32. Pampaloni, *Firenze*, pp. 106 – 107, document 61, from ASF, *Diplomatico*, Santa Croce, 11 May 1287.

33. Ibid., pp. 125 – 130, document 70, from ASF, *Diplomatico*, coperte libri, 28

April 1301; M. Barbi, "L'ufficio di Dante per i lavori di via S. Procolo," *Studi Danteschi* 3 (1921), pp. 89 – 128. For the term "magnate," see note 42.

34. Braunfels, *Stadtbaukunst*, p. 90.

35. *Lo statuto del 1342 del comune di Perugia*, in *Corpus Statutorum Italicorum*, IX (Rome, 1916), bk. 4, rubric 19, p. 288.

36. F.J. Carmody, "Florence: Project for a Map, 1250 – 1296," *Speculum* 19 (1944), pp. 39 – 49, with biblio.

37. F.W. Kent, "The Rucellai Family and Its Loggia," *Journal of the Warburg and Courtauld Institutes* 35 (1972), pp. 397 – 401; Leinz, "*Loggia Rucellai*."

38. F. Niccolai, "I consorzi nobiliari ed il comune nell'alta e media Italia," *Rivista di Storia del Diritto Italiano* 13 (May – August, 1940), p. 313.

39. L. Grossi Bianchi and E. Poleggi, *Una città portuale del medioevo, Genova nei secoli X-XVI* (Genoa, 1980), pp. 109 – 116, and 211 – 223, figs. 190, 193 – 196.

40. J. Heers, *Family Clans in the Middle Ages* (1974; reprint ed., Amsterdam and New York, 1977), p. 39.

41. "Ut infrenata [sic] precipue Magnatum et Potentum de civitate et comitatu Florentie audax presumptio refrenetur"; Salvemini, *Magnati e popolani*, p. 364.

42. The definition of the term "magnate" for Florentine and other Italian communes is a vexed question (G. Pampaloni, "I magnati a Firenze alla fine del dugento," *Archivio Storico Italiano* 19, no. 4 [1971], pp. 387 – 423; G. Fasoli, "Ricerche sulla legislazione antimagnatizia nei comuni dell'alta e media Italia," *Rivista di Storia del Diritto Italiano* 12 [January – April, 1939], pp. 86 – 133; idem, 2 [May – August 1939], pp. 241 – 309). While only a small percentage of the families required to post bond in Florence in 1281 and 1286 were demonstrably members of the old feudal nobility, all are described as "nobiles" in the documents. For some, popular reputation was the only authority for their rank; others had received the official distinction of knighthood (Salvemini, *Magnati e popolani*, p. 144). The significant issue for the Florentine lawmakers was that all magnates behaved in a way that the commune considered violent, proud, and lawless and that this way of life was associated with the nobility. The commune treated the magnates as members of extended families, requiring distant relatives to take legal responsibility for one another. In the other towns of Italy, magnates were described as *casatici, de maioribus, de hospicio,* and *de parentelis,* all terms referring to the importance of family ties (Fasoli, "Legislazione antimagnitizia," p. 291).

43. Niccolai, "Consorzi Nobiliari," p. 306; G. Mengozzi, *La città italiana nell'alto Medioevo* (1931; reprint ed., Florence, 1971), p. 374.

44. GV *Cron.*, IV, chaps 9 – 14.

45. L. Meus, ed., *Epistola o sia ragionamento di Messer Lapo da Castiglionchio* (Bologna, 1753), p. 72: "La città dentro era unita di cittadini, et era molto forte di mura, e di fossi pieni d'acqua, e di grosse torri: e dentro alla detta piccola città ebbe in poco tempo appresso di cento cinquanta torri di Cittadini d'altezza di CXX braccia l'una, senza le torri delle mura della detta città: e per l'altezza delle molte torri che erano allora in Firenze, si dice ch'ella si dimostrava di fuori di lungi, e d'appresso la più bella, e rigogliosa terra del suo piccolo sito che si trovasse"; quoted in P. Santini, "Società delle torri in Firenze," *Archivio Storico Italiano*, IV (1887), p. 25.

46. GV *Cron.*, VI, chap. 39. A Florentine tower pact of 1209 refers to a limit on the height of towers in effect at that time (Niccolai, "Consorzi Nobiliari," p. 46, document 20). The legislation, however, does not survive.

47. Caggese, ed., *Statuto del podestà*, bk. 4, rubric 41, p. 333.

48. Ibid., bk. 2, rubric 30, p. 109.

49. *Statuto del capitano*, bk. 3, rubric 81, p. 290 – 291.

50. Salvemini, *Magnati e popolani*, pp. 137, 364.

51. *Statuto del podestà*, bk. 3, rubric 53, p. 218; Niccolai, "Consorzi Nobiliari," p. 332 for related legislation in other towns.

52. Niccolai, "Consorzi Nobiliari," pp. 463 – 464, document 17.

53. Ibid., p. 459, document 15.

54. *Statuto del podestà*, bk. 2, rubric 68, pp. 138 – 139. For similar laws in other Italian cities, see Niccolai, "Consorzi Nobiliari," pp. 123 – 124.

55. Pampaloni, *Firenze*, pp. 114 – 118, document 66, from ASF, *Archivio Diplomatico*, Badia di Firenze, 7 January and 24 January 1298; M. Barbi, "L'ufficio di Dante per i lavori di Via S. Procolo," *Studi Danteschi* 3 (1921), pp. 117 – 124, document 3, from ASF, *Archivio Diplomatico*, Badia Fiorentina, August 1301. The two documents give slightly different forms of the description of the physical situation. The later document no longer speaks of a street that will go all the way to the Bargello. For an analysis of the Cerchi palaces and new documents from the later fourteenth century, see B. Preyer, "Two Cerchi Palaces in Florence," *Renaissance Studies in Honor of Craig Hugh Smyth*, ed. A. Morrogh et al. (Florence, 1985), II, pp. 613 – 630.

56. Barbi, "Via S. Procolo," 127 – 128, document 7, from ASF, *Archivio Diplomatico*, Badia Fiorentina, 26 May 1310.

57. Giovanni Villani (GV *Cron.*, VIII, chap. 39) describes the Cerchi: "di grande affare, e possenti, e di grandi parentadi, e ricchissimi mercatanti, che la loro compagnia era delle maggiore del mondo; uomini erano morbidi e innocenti, salvatichi e ingrati, siccome genti venuti di piccolo tempo in grande stato e podere." The Donati, on the other hand, "erano gentili uomini e guerrieri." Dino Compagni described the Cerchi as

"uomini di basso stato, ma buoni mercatanti e gran ricchi, e vestiano bene, e teneano molti famigli e cavagli, e aveano bella apparenza" (I. del Lungo, ed., *Dino Compagni e la sua Cronica* [Florence, 1879], II, bk. 1, chap. 20, p. 83).

58. N. Ottokar, *Il comune di Firenze al fine del dugento* (Turin, 1962), p. 211, n. 3.

59. N. Ottokar, "Criteri d'ordine, di regolarità, e d'organizzazione nell'urbanistica ed in genere nella vita fiorentina dei secoli XIII – XIV," in *Studi comunali e fiorentini* (Florence, 1948), pp. 143 – 149.

60. See chap. 5, note 86.

61. Buontalenti and others reported on the condition of the Arno riverbed on 1 August 1568 (ASF, *Capitani di Parte,* numeri neri 722, fols. 181r and v): "So that your excellency may see the whole situation at once we include the drawing made by master Bernardo. The yellow signifies the work that is needed." The report proposed the removal of a waterbreak "made by Pasqualino" and the reinforcement of others toward the road and below the "fiumicello Fracheratto." All of this is visible in the drawing, as is the levy that the group suggested as protection for the town proper. Professor Caroline Elam kindly brought this drawing to my attention.

62. G. Nudi, *Storia urbanistica di Livorno* (Venice, 1959), pp. 105 – 116.

LIST OF DOCUMENTS

Document 1 ASF, *Consulte e Pratiche*. In Alessandro Gherardi. *Le consulte della repubblica fiorentina dall'anno MCCLXXX al MCCXCVIII*. 2 vols. Florence, 1896 – 98. The first discussions of the foundation of towns in the Florentine councils.

Document 2 ASF *Provv.*, 9, fols. 136r – 137r, 26 January 1298 / 9. Legislation for the foundation of towns in the upper Arno valley.

Document 3 ASF *Provv.*, 12, fols. 206r and v, 207v, 29 April 1306. Legislation for the foundation of two towns in the Apennines.

Document 4 ASF, *Diplomatico Generale*, 18 July 1306. Patent of authority to the official in charge of the foundation of Scarperia.

Document 5 ASF, *Archivio Diplomatico*, Compagnia di Santa Maria di Scarperia, 17 January 1307 / 8, 30 January 1307 / 8. The Florentine official in Scarperia re-assigns a house lot.

Document 6 ASF, *Archivio Diplomatico*, Monastero di Luco, 21 April 1308. The town council of Scarperia assigns a garden plot outside the north gate to one of the settlers.

Document 7 ASF, *Archivio Diplomatico*, Monastero di Luco, 25 April 1308. Florentine officials assign a house lot in Scarperia to a settler.

Document 8 ASF, *Archivio Diplomatico*, Compagnia di Santa Maria di Scarperia,

21 October 1368. Will of Bartolo di Piero, carpenter, in which he describes his house in Scarperia.

Document 9 ASF *Notarile Antecosimiano*, L35 (Lando Fortini), fols. 69v – 71v, 19 September 1364. The grant of parish rights inside the walls of Scarperia to the church of SS. Jacopo e Filippo by the vicar of the bishop of Florence.

Document 10 ASF *Notarile Antecosimiana*, L292 (Lorenzo di Ser Tano di Luziano), fol. 31v, 18 April 1375. The enlargement of the privileges of the church of SS. Jacopo e Filippo in Scarperia.

Document 11 Archivo generale degli Agostiniani, Rome, Li:4, *Relazione della Provincia Pisana*, fol. 246r, 4 April 1650. Report on the Convent of San Barnaba in Scarperia.

Document 12 ASF *Cap.*, 32, fols. 70r and v, 11 October 1329. Legislation for the foundation of a town on the Consuma pass between Pontassieve on the Arno and the Casentino.

Document 13 ASF *Cap.*, 32, fols. 271r and v, 9 April 1332. Legislation for the foundation of Firenzuola.

Document 14 ASF *Cap.*, 35, fols. 231v, 232r and v, 24 May [1334]. The Florentine officials at Firenzuola order settlers to build on their lots; they also make arrangements for the construction of public buildings.

Document 15 ASF *Cap.*, 35, fols. 223r and v, 25 August [1338]. The Florentine officials at Firenzuola prohibit bridges across the main street of the town.

Document 16 ASF *Provv.*, 28, fols. 152r and v, 2 April 1337. Legislation for the foundation of Terranuova.

Document 17 ASF *Cap.*, 4, fols. 36v – 39v, 16 January 1349 / 50. The Abbey of Agnano surrenders its possessions in the Val d'Ambra to Florence.

Document 18 ASF *Provv.*, 37, fols. 82r and v, 25 January 1349 / 50. The *Ufficiali delle Castella* are instructed to search for a site in the Val d'Ambra for the foundation of a town.

Document 19 ASF *Uff. Cast., Rocche,* 1, fols. 15v – 18r, 19 May [1350]. Description of the Giglio Fiorentino project by the *Ufficiali delle Castella* and translation of the document.

Document 20 ASF *Cap.,* 4, fols. 63r – 66r, 2 June 1350. Legislation for the foundation of Giglio Fiorentino.

Document 21 ASF *SS. Miss.,* 13, fol. 40r, 2 April 1365. Florence gives the Abbey of Agnano permission to build fortifications.

Document 22 ASF, *Piante dei Capitani di parte,* cartone XVIII, no. 28. Sixteenth century. Captions of the plan of San Giovanni Valdarno. (See Fig. 4.)

Document 23 ASF, *Cinque conservatori del Contado,* 258, fol. 602 bis. Report on the flood damage to San Giovanni made 10 March 1553 by Maestro Piero della Zucca. Captions. (See Fig. 5.)

Document 24 ASF, *Conventi soppresse,* 136, 143 / I no. 23. Captions of the plan of Scarperia from the convent of the Padre di San Firenze, after 1776. (See Fig. 22.)

The documents have been reproduced with the original orthography. My thanks to Professor Gino Corti for reviewing my transcriptions.

DOCUMENTS

Document 1 ASF, *Consulte e Pratiche.* In Alessandro Gherardi. *Le consulte della repubblica fiorentina dall'anno MCCLXXX al MCCXCVIII.* 2 vols. Florence, 1896 – 98. The first discussions of the foundation of towns in the Florentine councils.

ABOUT THE TOWN OF PIETRASANTA

[26 February 1284 / 5; Gherardi, I, p. 170] Item, quod officiales eligantur, et eis detur pro Comuni peccunia opportuna, pro complemento castri Pietresancte, ita quod ad honorem et utilitatem Comunis compleatur ipsum castrum.

[15 May 1285; Gherardi, I, p. 217] Item, si videtur dicto Consilio utile fore pro Comuni Florentie teneri Consilium super expensis faciendis ad presens pro Comuni usque in quantitatem librarum V [hundred] in fundando et faciendo muris Pietre Sancte; et hoc cum dicatur quod de reffectione dicte terre obveniant honor commodum et utilitas Comuni Florentie, et maxime pro copia grani et bladi habenda de partibus Romandiole.

[3 August 1285; Gherardi, I, p. 272] Item, si videtur dicto Consilio utile fore pro Comuni Florentie teneri Consilium super expensa V [hundred] librarum in refectione Pietre Sancte, scilicet in murando ipsum castrum, et in faciendo palatium Comunis ibidem. Dominus Oddo Altoviti consuluit secundum propositiones predictas.

[23 September 1293; Gherardi, II, p. 321] Primo videlicet, quod solvatur et solvi possit, de pecunia et avere Comunis Florentie et per Camerarios ipsius Comunis presentes vel futuros, ser Tinaccio magistro et mensuratori et Banducio Rustichi, superstitibus operis castri de Pietrasanta, pro complendis muris dicti castri, libras CL florenorum parvorum: quam pecunie quantitatem, ad ipsos perveniendam dicta occasione, dicti Superstites convertere et expendere possint eisque liceat absque eorum preiudicio in dicto opere et eius occasione, secundum quod eisdem videbitur fore utilius pro Comuni.

Item, quod habentes casolaria in dicto castro, qui nondum edificaverunt ibi domus, compellantur per dominum Capitaneum et Defensorem hedificare et construere domos super eorum casolaribus in dicto castro; secundum quod facere promisserunt et tenentur.

[29 September 1293; Gherardi, II, p. 369] Item, quod habentes casolaria in castro Pietresancte, qui nondum hedificaverunt domos super eorum casolariis, secundum quod facere promiserunt, compelantur per dominum Capitaneum.

ABOUT THE ARNO VALLEY TOWNS

[13 August 1285; Gherardi, I, pp. 276 – 277] In Consilio speciali domini Defensoris et Capitanei et Capitudinum xii maiorum Artium et aliorum Sapientum ad hoc vocatorum, in presentia Priorum, proposuit dominus Capitaneus de facto Vallis Arni et Casuberti, de exbannitis qui conversantur ibidem. Narratis hiis que dicta sunt Prioribus, de una terra vel duabus faciendis, in plano, in quibus morentur, pro obviando malitiis exbannitorum: item auditis hiis que dicta sunt in presenti Consilio per dominum Bonacursum Lisei, de processu facto contra d. Bonacursum predictum, scilicet de excomunicatione, narrata causa quare hoc factum est.

Manectus Tinioci consuluit, quod Potestas, Capitaneus et Priores, cum illo Consilio quod habere voluerint, habeant bayliam providendi et ordinandi de duabus terris faciendis et fieri faciendis, et de cogendo homines contrate, quos voluerint, venire ad habitandum et habitare; et omnia possint providere et facere in dictis terris faciendis, et de loco, secundum quod viderint convenire.

Manellus de Manellis consuluit, quod negocium Vallis Arni differatur ad presens, sed ex militibus stipendiariis mittantur Fighinum. In aliis acquievit dicto predicti Sapientis.

Dominus Symon de Salto consuluit, quod aliqua novitas non fiat de aliqua terra facienda in Casuberti, sed Capitaneus provideat de procedendo contra exbannitos et condempnatos.

Rubeus Fornarii consuluit, quod procedatur ad duas terras faciendas et fieri faciendas in partibus Casuberti, in plano, sine magna fortilicia, in quibus homines contrate debeant habitare.

Dominus Iacobus de Certaldo . . . De facto autem terre seu terrarum fiendarum in Casuberti, consuluit quod predicta reducantur ad multa et diversa Consilia, magnatum per se, et artificum per se, et magnatum et artificum insimul; ita quod predicta non recipiant initium in presenti Consilio. Et si contingerit fieri, fiant terre in tali plano quod not sit in magna fortilicia.

Factis partitis per dominum Defensorem et Capitaneum, placuit secundum dictum domini Iacobi predicti super facto Vallis Arni.

[25 August 1285; Gherardi, I, pp. 281 – 282] Dominus Gherardus de Vicedominis . . . consuluit, quod provideatur et ordinetur de una terra facienda in Casuberti, in qua morentur homines contrate societatis. Item, quod procedatur ad exactionem librarum detemptarum, secundum provisionem Priorum, que locum habeant tantum in civitate Florentie. De viis et pontibus faciendis, procedatur secundum petitiones; et fiant expensis plebatuum contrate, et qui soliti sunt facere et aptare stratas predictas. Et illis per quorum terras mitteretur via predicta satisfiat iuxta extimationem.

Dominis Adimari de Adimaris consuluit . . . quod terra non fiat in Valle Arni: tamen quelibet Comunitas teneatur securare stratam.

Dominus Aldobrandinus Melliorelli . . . consuluit quod una vel plures terre fiant in Casuberti; dummodo tales ponantur qui debeant ponere ad habitandum homines cuiusque conditionis, et dummodo aliquis ex magnatibus non possit ibidem habitare, vel domum vel casolare habere. Et ad hoc ponantur boni homines, ita quod non inspicerent aliquam specialitatem. Et non sint murate.

Item, de terris Casuberti, placuit duabus partibus quod procedatur ad unam vel . duas terras faciendas in plano, non muratas et non in magna fortilicia. Item, quod in ipsis vel ipsa terra nullus ex magnatibus civitatis vel comitatus possit habitare vel domum vel casolare habere; et ad predicta facienda eligantur boni homines et legales qui provideant et faciant ita quod contrate homines ponantur in dictis terris, non inspiciendo ad aliquam specialitatem.

[28 August 1285; Gherardi, I, pp. 284 – 285] Item, super facto terre fiende in Valle Arni, pro resistendo maliciis exbannitorum.

Dominus Albiczus Corbinelli . . . consuluit, quod non procedatur ad terram vel terras faciendas in partibus Vallis Arni modo aliquo, nec ad proposita super hoc.

Iohannes del Brodaio . . . consuluit, quod terre fiant in plano, ut dictum est, in partibus Vallis Arni, in tali loco quod se revidere possint cum Fighino et Montevarchi; ad hoc ut alique expense ibidem non fiant pro Comuni, nisi forte in foveis cavandis.

Franciscus Torselli consuluit . . . quod supersedeatur de dicta terra facienda in Valle Arni.

Manectus Tinioci consuluit . . . super facto Vallis Arni, quod ubi videbitur Potestati, Capitaneo et Prioribus, cum illis quos secum habuerint, fiant terre secundum quod eisdem videbitur; que non sint in magna fortilicia: dummodo aliquis ex magnatibus vel potentibus non possit ibidem habitare vel domum vel casolare habere.

Dominus Loctus de Alleis consuluit . . . quod in Potestate, Capitaneo et

Prioribus remaneat de habendo Consilium super facto terrarum Vallis Arni, vel de non faciendo eas, secundum quod eisdem videbitur.

Item, quod provideatur per Potestatem, Capitaneum et Priores, et alios Sapientes quos et quot habere voluerint, super facto dictarum terrarum fiendarum an non; et super hoc premeditate provideatur, et secundum quod eisdem videbitur, de ipsis faciendis an non.

[31 August 1285; Gherardi, I, pp. 289 – 290] In Consilio quam plurium Sapientum militum congregato coram Potestate, Capitaneo et Prioribus, occasione providendi super facto Casuberti, scilicet de terris faciendis an non, vel de providendo super predictis: naratis hiis que facta sunt super hoc.

Presentibus testibus domino Alberto milite Capitanei et ser Lapo Cienghetti.

Dominus Talanus de la Tosa consuluit, quod due terre fiant in partibus Vallis Arni et Casuberti, secundum quod videbitur officialibus ad hoc ponendis per Potestatem, Capitaneum et Priores, et secundum quod per alia Consilia firmatum fuit.

Dominus Gualteroctus de Bardis consuluit, quod nichil fiat de predictis terris, sed per Potestatem, Capitaneum et Priores inveniatur via secundum quod viderint convenire ad hoc ut strata sit secura.

Placuit duabus partibus quod terre non fiant in Casuberti. [The vote was six for, twelve against.]

Document 2 ASF *Provv.*, 9, fols. 136r – 137r, 26 January 1298 / 9. Legislation for the foundation of towns in the upper Arno valley.

[In left margin: Tres terre fiant in partibus Vallis Arni superioris, due in planitie de Casuberti, alia iuxta burgum Casalberti.]

Pro honore et iurisdictione Comunis Florentie amplianda et melius conservanda per dominos priores artium et vexilliferum iustitie populi Florentie prehabita in hiis diligenti examinatione et quam [plurium] sapientum virorum consilio nec non inter eos secundum formam statutorum secreto et solempni scruptinio ad pissides et palloctas celebrato et facto, eorum offitii auctoritate et vigore provisum deliberatum et firmatum fuit quod pro iamdicto Comuni Florentie et ad ipsius Comunis laudabile incrementum // fol. 136v // tres terre seu comunitates de novo construantur hedifficentur et fiant et popullentur in partibus vallis Arni, videlicet due ex eis in planitie et partibus de Casuberti, tertia vero in burgo seu juxta burgum Plani Alberti, in illis locis et in ea latitudine et longitudine et eo modo et forma quibus placuerit et videbitur et prout et secundum quod placuerit et videbitur dominis prioribus artium et vexillifero iustitie populi florentini, tam presentibus quam futuris. Que quidem terre proprio nomine nominentur, ac etiam muris et foveis et aliis fortilitiis, hediffitiis, domibus et aliis opportunis munitionibus hedifficentur construantur et fiant et prout et secundum quod de ipsorum dominorum priorum et vexilliferi provisione et voluntate processerit et mandato. Ipsarum vero terrarum et cuiuslibet earum habitatores et perpetui terrazzani sint illi quos et quot ipsi domini priores et vexillifer voluerint et de quibus et in quantitate et numero quibus duxerint providendum. Qui etiam habitatores et terrazzani per quoscumque rectores seu offitiales dicti Comunis ad hoc deputandos, realiter et personaliter, sicut expediens fuerit, ad ipsas terras ut predicitur construendas hedifficandas et faciendas et fieri et construi, hedifficari et murari et aliis fortilitiis murari faciendas, nec non ad domos et habitationes eorum ibidem construendas et hedifficandas prout et sicut pro ipsarum terrarum et cuiuslibet earum hedifficatione, constructione et popullatione expedire videbitur effectualiter compellantur. Illi igitur qui, ut iam dictum est, fuerint habitatores et terrazzani alicuius ipsarum terrarum, ab omnibus et singulis libris et prestantiis decetero pro Comune Florentie imponendis et quomodocumque et quacumque de causa exigendis, sint et esse debeant liberi et immunes pro illud tempus quod ipsi iamdicti domini priores et vexillifer duxerint providendi, dummodo tempus et terminus ipsius immunitatis et provisionis super ea fiende decem annorum tempus et spatium non excedat. Et interim, ipsa provisione et immunitate durante, ipsi iamdicti terrazzani et habitatores aliquo modo iure vel causa non teneantur nec per aliquem rectorem vel officialem dicti Comunis Florentii presentium vel futurorum vel per aliqua aliam personam cogantur vel quomodolibet astringantur ad ipsarum librarum seu prestantiarum solutionem seu mutuationem faciendam. Illi namque quorum sunt vel erunt terrena seu hediffitis sita in locis in quibus provisum et deliberatum fuerit ipsas terras, ut dictum est, construi hedifficari et fieri debere sicut expediens fuerit, cogantur et cogi possint et debeant ad ipsa terrena et hediffitia concedenda et vendenda pro ipsarum terrarum constructione et hedifficatione, ut predicitur, facienda, pro illo pretio seu pretiis quo vel quibus ipsi domini priores et vexillifer vel illi quos ad hoc eligerint et deputaverint duxerint providendi. Superstites vero offitiales quos et quot ipsi domini priores et vexillifer, tam presentes quam futuri, voluerint per eos eligantur et deputentur et eligi et deputari possint et debeant quando et quotiens et pro illo tempore et cum illo salario ac etiam licentia bailia et offitio, quibus et prout et sicut eisdem prioribus et vexillifer placuerit et videbitur convenire ad predicta omnia et singula et pro preditis omnibus et singulis faciendis et fieri faciendis et executioni mandandis pro Comuni iamdicto. Et insuper quod ipsi iamdicti domini priores et vexillifer, tam presentes quam futuri, possint eisque liceat, in predictis omnibus et singulis et circa ea, providere ordinare firmare et facere et fieri facere omnia et singola que eisdem videbitur expedire seu utilia fore in predictis et pro predictis omnibus

// fol. 137r // et quolibet predictorum faciendis observandis et fieri faciendis et ut predicitur executioni mandandis. Ac etiam in hiis, de hiis et super hiis omnibus et singulis ipsi domini priores et vexillifer, tam presentes qua futuri, possint eisque liceat in alios quos et quot voluerint commissionem facere et offitium, licentiam et bailiam aliis concedere et committere et exibere quando et quotiens et prout et sicut de eorum processerit voluntate. Dum tamen omnia et singula suprascripta fiant et fieri debeant sumptibus et expensis hominum et personarum, qui et que in ipsis terris vel aliqua earum, ut supra dicitur, venerint ad habitandum et ipsarum terrarum seu alicuius earum fuerint seu esse debebunt terrazzani et habitatores. Que idem expense et quantitates pecuniarum predictorum occasionibus neccessarie, eisdem imponantur et inter eos sortiantur et dividantur et ab eisdem totaliter exigantur per offitiales ad predicta, ut supra dicitur, eligendos et deputandos prout et secundum quod de ipsorum offitialium voluntate processerit et mandato. Providentes insuper et firmantes quod nullus de magnatibus civitatis vel comitatus Florentie possit seu audeat vel presummat in ipsis terris vel aliqua earum, aliquo modo, iure vel causa, per se vel alium, emere seu alio quocumque titulo, iure vel causa seu modo, acquirere vel habere seu ad pensionem conducere vel tenere aliquam domum, terrenum seu casolare, ac etiam decetero, extra aliquam ipsarum terrarum infra seu prope duo miliaria aliquam fortilitiam seu domum construere, hedifficare et facere seu hedifficari et fieri facere aliquo modo, iure vel causa, non obstantibus aliquibus statutis, ordinamentis seu consiliorum reformationibus, tam editis quam edendis, in predictis vel aliquo predictorum quomodolibet contradicentibus vel repugnantibus.

Document 3 ASF *Provv.*, 12, fols. 206r and v, 207v, 29 April 1306. Legislation for the foundation of two towns in the Apennines.

[In margin: Super quampluribus ordinamentis, pro duabus terris in Muccello et ultra alpes faciendis et pro obsidione Castri Montis Accianichi et pro favore citatorum tertia propositio.]

In nomine domini amen. Ad reprimendum effrenandum superbiam Ubaldinorum et aliorum de Mucello et de ultra alpes, qui Comuni et populo Florentie rebellaverunt castrum Montis Accianichi et alias fortilitias et guerram faciunt et non hactenus fecerunt dicto Comuni et populo Florentie, non habentes Deum pre oculis et non reminiscendo quod nati sunt Comuni et populo predicto, et que hactenus Comune Florentie misericorditer remisit eisdem et eorum antecessoribus, ut eorum vires radicitus enerventur provida deliberatione provisum et ordinatum est quod pro Comuni Florentie fiant due terre, una videlicet in Mucello, alia vero ultra alpes, ubi et sicut videbitur offitialibus ad predicta ponendis per dominos priores artium et vexilliferum iustitie presentes vel futuros. Item quod in dictis terris cogantur redire et domos facere et habitare homines et persone locorum qui ipsis offitialibus videbuntur. Item quod omnes et singuli facientes domum et habitantes in dictis terris vel aliqua earum, sint liberi et immunes ab omnibus libris et factionibus realibus Comunis Florenties per decem annos, ita quod per offitiales Comunis Florentie presentes vel futuros nullatenus inquientententur dictis occasionibus realiter vel personaliter. Item quod omnes et singuli qui in dictis terris vel aliqua earum domum fecerint et habitaverint cum eorum familiis per decennium saltem per duas partes cuiuslibet anni ipsius decennii, sint et intelligantur cum effectu esse ipsi et eorum descententes liberi et franchi ab omni vinculo et iugo servitutis et fidelitatis et omagii et recommendationis et anghariis et per anghariis et cuiuslibet annue prestationis et ab omni alio vinculo cuiuscumque condictionis exsistat. Hoc tamen locum non habeat in illis que stabunt in castro Montis Accianichi per tres dies postquam positus fuerit campus circha dictum castrum, nec in eorum ascendentibus et descendentibus. Item quod in dictis terris // fol. 206v // vel aliqua earum vel prope dictas terras vel earum aliquam, per unum miliare nullus de magnatibus et nullus de domo de Salto, plebatus sancti Johannis Maioris, et nullus de domo de Burgensibus sive de Ripaiuolis, et nullus de domo de Cingnano de Mucello possit vel audeat, per se vel alium, nec sit ei licitum habere vel tenere domum aliquam propriam vel conductam vel gratis concessam, vel aliquod immobile emere habere vel adquirire iure legati sive institutionis vel quocunque alio titulo vel etiam pro debitis vel occasione debitorum contractorum hactenus vel que in futurum contraherentur per aliquem, qui in aliqua dictarum terrarum hedifficaverit vel hedifficari fecerit vel ibi steterit. Item quod nullus de magnatibus et nullus de dictis tribus domibus de Mucello superius nominatis, possit vel ei liceat prope aliquam dictarum terrarum per unum miliare, hedifficare vel facere hedifficari aliquod hediffitium, et si habet vel haberet aliquod hediffitium infra duo miliaria, illud debeat omnino vendere infra duos menses a die inceptionis hedifficationis terre, vere et non fititie alicui popolari vel universitati ipsius terre, cui proximius esset hediffitium, pro eo pretio quod deliberatum esset per ipsos offitiales, sub pena librarum quingentarum florenorum parvorum. Et si non vendiderit infra dictum tempus, tale hediffitium funditus destruatur incontinenti. Et quod potestas et capitaneus qui pro tempore fuerint, teneantur predicta executioni mandare infra decem dies postquam aliquis eorum exinde fuerint requisitus, sub pena librarum ducentarum. Et intelligatur talis vendictio fictitie fatta esse si probetur per publicum famam saltem per quattuor testes.

Item quod terrenum quod ponetur in dictis terris et in fossis et infra fossos dictarum terrarum ematur de pecunia Comunis Florentie et pro eo pretio et pretiis que videbuntur offitialibus antedictis.

Item quod in dictis terris fiant vie et platee et ecclesie prout ipsis offitialibus videbitur. Item quod possint domini priores artium et vexillifer iustitie presentes et futuri eligere offitiales superstites ad predicta et infrascripta facienda et procuranda, quos et quot et quotiens et eos removere et alios substituere et cum eo salario et prout eisdem videbitur convenire. Item quod possint facere ipsi offitiales construi in qualibet dictarum terrarum, portas et pontes circa castrum et super foveas, prout eis videbitur. Item quod possint et debeant habere dicti offitiales salarium et tenere de militibus et equitatoribus Comunis Florentie ad custodiam ipsorum et contratarum, si expedierit, in ea quantitate prout et sicut videbitur dominis prioribus artium et vexillifero iustitie pro tempore existentibus. Item quod possint habere ipsi offitiales a Comunibus a quibus voluerint et videbitur dominis prioribus artium et vexillifero iustitie, pedites de contrata, cum armis, quos et quot voluerint ad custodiam dictorum locorum. Dumtamen nullam pecuniam extorqueant vel recipiant ab aliqua comunitate vel singulari persona. Item quod nullus de magnatibus vel de dictis tribus domibus de Mucello possit esse offitialis vel in offitialem eligi ad predicta vel aliquod predictorum, et si eligeretur talis electio sit inanis, et si tale offitium accepteraverit puniatur per dominum potestatem in libris quinquaginta florenorum parvorum et ab ipso offitio infra tres dies removeatur.

[The *provvisione* continues with remarks concerning the siege, not yet begun, of the Ubaldini castle of Monte Accianico.] Item provisum et ordinatum est quod nullus audeat vel presummat esse et stare in castro Montis Accianicchi maxime postquam insignia Comunis Florentie felicis exercitus florentini fuerint et iverint terram Burgi Sancti Laurentii per tres dies sub pena eris et persone et ipsius patris avi et filiorum omnium descendentium. [The *potesta* and the *capitano* shall be the judges of guilt in this matter and everyone they condemn shall be considered a rebel against Florence. Anyone who stays at Monte Accianico beyond the three day terminus and is later brought to the Florentine camp] suspendatur per gulam prope Monte Accianichum [and anyone who makes a treaty with the Ubaldini will be punished] sub pena averis et persone. [The *potestà* and *capitano* are to be in charge of questioning such people and are to get at the truth] cum tormentis et qualibet alia via. [Reconciliation with the Ubaldini was anathema; the mere suggestion of it was punishable by decapitation. Enemy "soldiers" were treated as prizes; the city put up a bounty for them: fifty lire alive, twenty-five dead.]

// fol. 207v // Item pro bono publico et defensione populi et Comunis Florentie et singulorum civium et districtualium ipsius. Et ut singoli tam metu penarum quam premiorum et protectionis exortatione invitentur ad defensionem eiusdem ut sic nostra res publica circuncincta muro inexpugnabili defensorum, facilius resistatur insurgentibus ex adverso, et eorum superbia deprimatur, provisum ordinatum et stabilitum fuit quod domini priores artium et vexillifer (iustitie) populi et Comunis Florentie presentes et futuri possint eisque liceat facere ac condere provvisiones et ordinamenta, que et quot, quando quoniam et qualiter et quotiens voluerint eis placuerit contra rebelles et inimicos Comunis Florentie et tenentes et eos qui hactenus castra in rebellione Comunis prefati vel in eis stantes vel reparantes et qui hactenus steterunt et reparaverunt et contra turbantes et subvertere nitentes statum pacificum et tranquillum civitatis eiusdem.

Item quod ipsi possint eisque liceat providere stantiare et firmare super terris reponendis, faciendis et construendis de novo et reponi et construi faciendis in quocumque loco comitatus et districtus Florentie quecumque voluerint eisque placuerit, pro defensione et conservatione pacifici et tranquilli status civitatis Florentie et jurisdictionis et territorii eiusdem, et circa ea et eorum occasione et in favorem redeuntium ad habitandum et hedifficandum in eis. Et quidquid fecerint in predictis et circa predicta et eorum occasione et pro eorum executione, sint et intelligantur facta pro honore et utilitate Comunis et populi Florentie.

Document 4 ASF, *Diplomatico Generale*, 18 July 1306. Patent of authority to the official in charge of the foundation of Scarperia.

. . . prefati domini priores Artium et Vexillifer vigore eorum offitii et ex balia, licentia et auctoritate, potestate eis adtributis, datis et concessis per solempnia et opportuna consilia populi et Comunis Florentie, prout de ipsis publice scriptum est per ser Bonsignorem Guezzi, notarium reformationum dictorum consiliorum . . . providerunt . . . quod comunantia sive universitas, que de nove construi debet . . . in partibus Mucelli per dominum Matteum Judicem Magistri de Egimo [?] offitiale et capitaneum ad hoc pro Comuni Florentie spetialiter deputatum, sint et fiat in loco dicto La Scarperia, et quod in ipsa comunantia mictantur infrascripta pleberia sive comunia vel populi, et quod ipsa comunantia sive terra sit amplitudinis et longitudinis prout idem dominus Matheus providerit et ordinaverit, et vocetur ab inde in antea castrum Sancti Bernabe ad sui laudem et reverentiam. Et quot sit licitum dicto domino Matteo fieri facere in dicta terra putea, fontes, vias, stratas, et dirizzare et splanare quocumque et qualitercumque agnoverit et deliberaverit fore decens et ad sui liberam voluntatem, et predicta fieri et ad secutioni mandari debeant ad voluntatem et mandatum dicti domini Mattei per hominibus vicariatus Mucelli et appenditiis ipsius et per alios homines vicariatuum et popolorum qui sint de Mucello sicut ydem dominus Matteus agnoverit et viderit expedire, cui predicti domini priores et Vexillifer in predictis et circa predicta vices eorum totaliter commiserunt.
Comunia sunt haec:
Comune de Sancto Johanne Maiori cum popolo Sancte Maria de Castello
Comune et popolus Sancti Michelis de Figliano
Comune de Luco

Comune et populus Sancti Stefani de Grezzano
Comune de Prata et Covignani cum popolo de Miralbello
Comune et populus Sancti Johanis de Senne
Comune et populus Sancti Bartoli de Petrone
Comune de Trisanti cum populo de Fagna
Comune de Castagniuolo
Comune et populus Sancte Crucis de Ubaldinis
Populus Sancti Clementis de Signano
Populus Sancti Simonis dela Roccha
Populus Sancti Michelis de Ferrone
Populus Sancti Donati de Monte cercho [?]
Populus Sancti Martini de Lacho
Populus Sancti Andree de Cirliano
Comune de Manfriano
Comune de Monte Accianico
Comune et populus Sancte Agathe
Populus Sancti Gavini in Connochio
Comune et populus de Villa Nova
Populus Sancti Laurentii de Montepoli
Populus Sancti Benedicti de Mezalla
Populus Sancte Maria de Mercoiano
Populus Sancti Michelis de Lomena
Comune de Guinizzingho

Document 5 ASF, *Archivio Diplomatico*, Compagnia di Santa Maria di Scarperia, 17 January 1307 / 8, 30 January 1307 / 8. The Florentine official in Scarperia reassigns a house lot.

Certum est quod Bernardus de Bordonibus, honorabilis et generalis capitaneus castri S. Barnabe de Mucello pro Comuni Florentie deputatus, ex vigore sui offitii privavit Turam quondam Viviani de S. Cruce, ut paret in actis curie dicti Capitanei per sententiam per eum latam, de quodam casolari posito in dicto castro, in via S. Barnabe, et est longitudinis decem et octo brachiorum et amplitudinis duodecim brachiorum, tenor cuius talis est. Tura Viviani de S. Cruce, contra quem procedimus per inquisitionem nostri offitii in eo et super eo quod preceptum fuit eidem per nuntium nostrum, de nostro mandato, quod certo termino iam ellapso deberet coram nobis personaliter comparere ad tractandum et ordinandum et conferrendum nobiscum de refectione et constructione eius domus super casolari vel terreno eidem dato et assignato in dicta terra S. Barnabe. Qui vel aliquis pro eo [non] convenit et non comparuit, et dictum preceptum sprevit, ut in actis nostre curie plenius continetur. Et ideo ipsum, habito pro confesso propter suam contumaciam et inobedientiam, a dicto eius casolari et terreno ei dato et assignato in dicta terra, et omni sui iure et causa et iurisdictione et parte vel sorte, quod et quam habet vel ad eum spectat quocunque titulo vel modo vel iure in dicto casolari vel terreno, et omnibus hedifficiis vel lignis super dicto casolari vel terreno positis, privamus et cassamus, et ipsum in solidis viginti florenorum parvorum, dandis et solvendis camerario dicte terre, recipienti vice et nomine dicti Comunis, in hiis scriptis sententialiter condemnamus. Salvo quod si ipse comparuerit coram nobis ad obediendum et fatiendum predicta, et domum fatiendum et complendum super dicto casolari hinc ad quinque dies proxime venturos, non teneatur ad predictam condempnationem. Item salvo et reservato quod dictus dominus Capitaneus possit facere quidquid sibi placuerit. Lata, publicata et pronuntiata fuit dicta condempnatio et sententia condempnationis per dictum Bernardum capitaneum et offitialem eo pro tribunali sedentem in domo ubi habitat dictum Capitaneum, presentibus testibus ser Ugolino de Grezzano, notario, Iohanne de Villa et Landuccio Bonaiuti nuntium, in millesimo trecentesimo Septimo, indictione sexta, die XVII mensis Ianuarii.

Quare hodie, sub eodem millesimo et indictione, et die penultima dicti mensis Ianuarii, dictus Bernardus de Bordonibus, Capitaneus generalis dicti castri ad dandum et concedendum casolaria hominibus et personis venientibus ad standum et habitandum in dicto castro, prout in statuiis et ordinamentis dominorum priorum artium et Vexilliferi iustitie civitatis Florentie plenius continetur, iure proprio et in perpetuum dedit, tradidit et concessit Cionino quondam Iannis de Grecci de Manfriano, recipienti pro se et suis heredibus aut cui ius suum im posterum concedere voluerit, unum casolare positum in dicto castro, in via S. Barnabe, cui a primo dicta via a II Vannetti Ciaballie, a III Benini magisti Iacobi, a IIII terrenum Comunis. Qui Cioninus promisit mihi notario, stipulanti et recipienti vice et nomine dicti domini Capitanei pro Comuni Florentie dictum casolare incasare et in ipso domum construere et coperiere de tegulis, et dictum casolare et domum retinere pro Comuni et populo Florentie et dominis prioribus et Vexillifero iustitie prefatis et ad eorum et cuiuslibet eorum mandatum, obedientiam et voluntatem . Et promisit etiam dictum casolare et domum non vendere et non alienare nec concedere alicui persone nobili seu magnati seu de progenie magnatum, nec alicui persone ecclesiastice seu alicui ecclesie, sub pena et ad penam librarum centum florenorum parvorum semper Comuni Florentie applicanda si contra fecerit in aliquo predictorum. Et promisit etiam dictum casolare incasare et habitare cum sua fami[li]a, et domum construere et perficere hinc ad Kallendas Marti proxime Venturi, sub pena et ad penam librarum decem florenorum parvorum sollempni stipulatione promissa si contra fecerit in aliquo predictorum. Et prefatus dominus Capitaneus, nomine dicti Comunis Florentie, promisit dicto Cionino, recipienti et stipulanti nomine quo supra, ipsum casolare et domum contra omnes personas defendere et guarantire, sub obligatione bonorum dicti Comunis Florentie et sub pena dupli extimationis dicte domus et casolaris, que pro tempore plus valuerit. Pro quibus omnibus et singulis firmiter observandis, precibus et mandato dicti Cionini, Gherarduccius frater suus, filius quondam dicti Iannis, in omnibus et singulis supradictis extitit in solidum fideussor, Et renuntiavit beneficio de fideussoribus, et se ut principalis in omnibus et singulis in solidum obligavit. Qui Cioninus sponte et suo plano animo iuravit corporaliter ad Sancta Dei Evangelia manualiter tacta scriptura, se esse de eo velle quod nunc est populus florentinus, et semper dilligere bonum et tranquillum statum Comunis et populi Florentie et hominum et universitatis castri predicti.

Actum in dicto castro S. Barnabe, presentibus testibus ser Francisco notario quondam Guidonis de Sala, Naddo quondam Iohannis de Querceto, et Nuto quondam Bencivieni de Lavorniano.

Ego Franciscus olim Iohannis de Mutina, notarius et nunc [scriba] predicti domini Capitanei, predictis omnibus interfui et rogatus scripsi et publicavi.

Document 6 ASF, *Archivio Diplomatico*, Monastero di Luco, 21 April 1308. The town council of Scarperia assigns a garden plot outside the north gate to one of the settlers.

In Dei nomine amen. Anno ab incarnatione eiusdem millesimo trecenteximo octavo, die vigesimo primo mensis Aprelis, indictione sexta. Requisitis consiliariis comunis castri S. Barnabe de Mucello per nuntium spetialem dicti Comunis et in cassero dicti castri more solito congregati, quorum nomina inferius denotantur, videlicet Naddus de Querceto, Naddus Botii, Puccius de Filetto, ser Marsilius Gucci, Lippus Sostengi, ser Ceccus Cursi, Vanturius Guiducii, Cordinus Benincase et Cenne Aldebrandini, qui sunt due partes et ultra consiliarum dicti Comunis, plena concordia et utriusque consensu, nemine discordante, ex vigore bailie concesse consiliariis dicti Comunis et duabus partibus eorundem a Comuni et populo florentino (ut constat et plenius continetur in statutis provisione Comunis et populis florentini factis sub annis Domini millesimo trecentesimo septimo, transcriptis et exemplatis per ordinem ex constituto Comunis et populi florentini et domini Capitanei populi suprascripti per ser Iohannem notarium, filium quondam ser Lapi Bonamichi notarii), omni mode et iure quibus melius et validius potuerunt, iure proprio et in perpetuum dederunt, tradiderunt et concesserunt pro orto faciendo Iohanni quondam Becciardi de Rocca, terragini dicti castri, pro se et suis heredibus recipienti, unum stariorum terre ad rectam mensuram corde Comunis Florentie, posite extra portam Bononiensem, de retro ortis qui sunt iuxta stratam publicam, mensuratum per Bacuccium de Rabatta mensuratorem, cui a primo via que est infra ortos antiquos et posteriores, a II Buti quondam Spillecti de Lago, a III via Vecchia, a IIII Baldi Berriandi de Rocca. Ad habendum, tenendum, possidendum et quicquid sibi et suis heredibus deinceps placuerit perpetuo faciendum, cum omnibus et singulis que infra predictos continentur confines vel alios si qui forent accessibus et egressibus suis usque in viam publicam, et cum omnibus et singulis que habent super se vel infra seu intra se in integrum, omnique iure et actione, usu seu requisitione sibi ex ea vel pro ea re aut ipsi rei modo aliquo pertinente. Pro pretio dando et solvendo vero domino talis terreni a festo S. Michelis de mense Septembris proxime venturi ad unum annum proximum, videlicet librarum trium florenorum parvorum. Quam dationem et concessionem et omnia e singula in hoc contracta contenta predicti consiliarii modo et iure quo supra approbaverunt et ratificaverunt.

Actum in dicto cassero, presentibus Gherarduccio quondam Drudi, populi S. Martini de Bubiano, Guiduccio Casini de Tasso Vallis Arni, ser Bianco quondam domini Thomasii de Magreto, districtus Mutine, et Iacobo quondam Terii Zati de S. Petro ad Sevem, tesibus ad hec vocatis et rogatis.

Ego Franciscus quondam Guidonis, notarius de Sala, imperiali auctoritate iudex ordinarius et notariis, hiis omnibus interfui et rogatus scripsi et publicavi.

Document 7 ASF, *Archivio Diplomatico*, Monastero di Luco, 25 April 1308. Florentine officials assign a house lot in Scarperia to a settler.

In Dei nomine amen. Anno ab incarnatione eiusdem millesimo trecentesimo octavo, die vigesimo quinto mensis aprelis, indictione sexta. Probus vir Barberius quondam Sinibaldi de Aretio, vicarius generalis nobilis et potentis viri Bernardi de Bordonibus, honorabilis Capitanei castri S. Barnabe de Mucello (ut constat de vicariatu predicto publico instrumento facto manu ser Francisci quondam Iohannis de Mutina, notarii dicti domini Capitanei), ex vigore dicti instrumenti vicariatus, vice et nomine dicti domini Capitanei, omni modo e iure quibus melius potuit, iure proprio [et] in perpetuum dedit, tradidit et concessit, vice et nomine Comunis Florentie, Mannellino quondam Mannuccii de Preta, pro se et suis heredibus et cui vel quibus ius suum in posterum concedere voluerit stipulanti et recipienti, unum casolare positum in dicto castro, in via S. Laurentii, cui a I dicta via, a II terrenum Comunis S. Barnabe, quod fuit olim Fasiani Privetti per Capitaneum dicti Castri, a III Tignosi de Ruosine, a IIII domine Rose de Senne, et est longitudinis sedecim brachiorum et amplitudinis duodecim brachiorum. Que

Mannellinus promisit stipulatione sollempni dicto domino vicario recipienti vice et nomine Comunis Florentie et pro ipsum Comune, ipsum casolare incasare et cooperire de tegulis et domum complere et in ea [redire] cum sua familia in dicta domo hinc ad calendas septembris proxime venturi, et ipsum casolare et domum non vendere nec alienare neque concedere alicui magnati seu alicui de progenie magnatum, nec alicui ecclesie seu alicui ecclesiastice persone, sed ipsum casolare et domum retinere pro Comune et populo florentino et dominis prioribus et vexillifero iustitie civitatis Florentie presentibus et futuris, et ad eorum et cuiscunque eorum voluntatem, obendientiam et mandatum, sub pena librarum ducentarum bonorum denariorum florenorum parvorum sollempni stipulatione promissa, semper Comuni Florentie applicanda si contra fecerit in aliquo predictorum. Pro quibus omnibus et singulis observandis et firmis tenendis, precibus et mandatu dicti Mannellini, Forese quondam ser Lapi, notarius de Preta, in omnibus et singulis suprascriptis extitit fideiussor et renuntiavit beneficio de fideiussoribus et se, ut principalis, in solidum obligavit. Et prefatus dominus vicarius, nomine quo supra, promisit dicto Mannellino stipulanti et recipienti ut supra, ipsum casolare et domum contra omnes personas defendere et auctorizare et disstrigare, sub pena dupli extimationis dicti casolaris et domus, que pro tempore plus valuerit, stipulatione sollempni promissa, et obligare bona dicta Comunis Florentie pro omnibus servandis, ut dictum est.

Qui Mannellinus sponte et suo plano animo iuravit, corporaliter ad Sancta Dei Evangelia manu autem tactis scripturis, se esse de eo velle quod nunc est populus florentinus, et semper diligere bonum et pacificum et tranquillum statum Comunis et populi florentini et dicti castri et hominum et universitatis castri predicti.

Et ego Francisus quondam Guidonis notarius de Sala, imperiali auctoritate iudex ordinarius et notarius, hiis omnibus interfui et de mandato dicti domini vicarii scripsi et publicavi.

Document 8 ASF, *Archivio Diplomatico,* Compagnia di Santa Maria di Scarperia, 21 October 1368. Will of Bartolo di Piero, carpenter, in which he describes his house in Scarperia.

In Dei nomine amen. Anno Domini ab incarnatione eiusdem millesimo trecentesimo sexagesimo ottavo, indictione septima, die vigesima prima mensi ottobris. Bartolus olim Pieri, faber de Scaperia comitatus Florentie, sanus per gratiam Yesu Christi mente sensu et intellectu licet corporis egritudine languens, suarum rerum et bonorum omnium dispositionem per presentem nu[n]cupativum [?] testamentum sine scriptis in hunc modum facere ordinavit et procuravit.

Imprimis quidem divotissime recommendavit animam suam Domino Yesu Christo creatori nostro et eius Matri Virginis Marie et omnibus sanctis curie celestis, et eis redidit animam suam quandocunque eum de hoc seculo migrari contingerit.

Item elegit sui corporis sepulturam in ecclesia fratrum Heremitarum ordinis S. Agosti[n]i loci S. Bernabe de Scarperia, et ibi iussit et voluit sepelliri.

Item reliquid et dari voluit per infrascriptos suos heredes dicte ecclesie S. Bernabe, pro anima sua salute, libras vigintiquinque florenorum parvorum.

Item pro anima sua salute et omnium de domo sua, reliquid domine Iohanne, uxori quondam Bertini Petruccini de Manfriano et filie quondam Iunte de Scarperia, unam madiam et unum paiuolum et unum paiuoluzum et unam sicula cum fune et unam capsam cum uno seramine et unum mantellum cilestrum menatum et unam quarnachiam cilestram menatam ad usum dorsi dicti testatoris et unum boticellum trium vegetarum.

Item reliquid eidem domine Iohanne moram et habitationem unius anni unius sue medietatis domus site in castro Scarperie, in quarterio S. Iohannis dicti castri, cuis medietatis talis dixit esse confines: a primo strata publica, a secundo heredum Ricucci Luccii, a tertio heredum Spigliati Bertini, et a quarto Iacopi Turini; et ab inde supra libere remanere voluit infrascripto heredi suo.

Item voluit disposuit et mandavit ac commisit et licentiam omnimodam dedit atque concessit dicte domine Iohanne quod ipsa det et distribuat et dare et distribuere possit, pro anima sua salute, omnia sua superlectilia et frumentum piis et miserabilibus personis, videlicet illis personis quibus magis utilius videbitur, pro anima sua et parentum suorum salute, sine ulla ratione redenda.

Item reliquid eidem domine medietatem porcis sui.

Item dixit et confessus fuit dictus testator quod ipse vendiderat Iacopo olim Turini de Scarperia medietatem domus sue versus domum dicti Iacopi pro pretio florenorum quadraginta auri, et quod de dictis quadraginta florenis auri iam habuerat ab eo et sibi dederat florenos viginti otto auri et libram unam et soldos decem florenorum parvorum. Quapropter volendo observare dictam venditionem, voluit et disposuit, imposuit, commisit et mandavit infrascripto heredi suo quod eidem Iacopo vendant et vendere teneantur et debeant dictam medietatem versus domum dicti Iacopi, dicto Iacopo statim cum dictus Iacopus dederit infrascripto heredi suo residuum dictorum quadraginta florenorum auri, cum promissione de legiptima rei evictione et defensione. Et eum inducant in tenutam et corporalem possessionem dicte medietatis domus, et de dicta venditione faciant et fieri faciant publicum instrumentum venditionis manu publici notarii conficiendum, cum pactis obligationibus stipulationibus promissionibus chautelis obligationibus, penis et pene adiectionibus, renuptiationibus et omnibus aliis sole[m]nitatibus usitatis et opportunis in talibus contractibus vallatis et vallandis.

Item reliquid eidem Iacopo unam capsam co[per]tatam cum duobus coperchis et unum boticellum capacitatis quatuor salmarum vini.

Item dixiti quod murus qui est inter eius domus et domum heredum quondam Ricuccii Luccii est pro medietate fundatus super suum terrenum, et alia medietas super terrenum dicti quondam Ricuccii, et quod est medius suus prout tenet tectus domus sue et quod ab inde supra est totus heredum dicti quondam Ricuccii.

Item dixit quod murus in quo et super quo sunt lignamina lodie sue, ex parte posteriori est filiorum Spigliati quondam Bertini et quod in eo nullum ius habuit nec habet, et ideo voluit et mandavit quod ad omnem requisitionem heredes dicti quondam Spigliati eleventur et extollantur de dicto muro dicta lignamina.

Item reliquid pro salute anime sue et suorum remissione pechatorum et aliorum de domo sua, hospitale S. Iacopi de prope Scarperia, medietatem unius sui orti versus terram heredum quondam Iacopi Baldi, positi in populo S. Michaelis de Feroni, cui toti orti a primo, secundo et tertio vie, et a quarto heredes dicti quondam Iacopi Baldi. Cum hac conditione quod non possit nec debeat vendi, alienari, permutari nec alicui ullo modo sive iure obligari nisi quando Capitanei et gubernatores sotietatis Virginis Marie de Scaperia sive hospitalarius dicti hospitalis fieri faceret apud dictum hospitale unum puteum et non aliter, et si contra feceret tunc in eo casu dictam medietatem orti reliquid infrascripte societati Virginis Marie de Scarperia.

Item reliquid hospitali S. Marie del Merchatale de propre Scarperia unum lectum cum trispidibus et assis, sacone, cultrice et duobus pimacis et duobus paris lintiaminum et uno copertorio pro hospitando pauperes pio amore Dei.

In omnibus autem aliis suis bonis mobilibus et immobilibus, iuribus et actionibus presentibus et futuris, sibi heredem universalem [in]stituit et esse voluit sotietatem sive fraternitatem Virginis Marie de Platea de Scarperia. Cassans et inritans omne aliud testamentum et omnem aliam ultimam voluntatem hinc retro per eum factam manu cuiuscunque notarii, non obstantibus aliquibus verbis derogatoriis in eo appositis. Et hanc suam asseruit esse velle ultimam voluntatem, quam valere voluit iure testamenti, et quod si iure testamenti non valeret, valere voluit iure codicillorum vel alterius cuiscunque ultime volunatis melius valere potest et tenere.

Actum in castro S. Bernabe de Scarperia de Mucello, comitatus Florentie, in domo habitationis dicti testatoris, sita in dicto castro, presentibus testibus Cionino olim Brungniuoli, Bragio olim Iacopi, Nicholaio olim Compangni, et Piero olim Boschuccii, omnibus de Scarperia, et Andrea olim Puccini et Iohanne filio dicti Andree, populi plebis S. Petri ad Sevem, et Poglino olim Chiaruccii Comunis Scarperie, et Betto olim Sostengni, populis S. Gavini ad Cornochium, ad hec vocatis et a dicto testatore rogatis.

Ego Phylippus olim ser Ugolini Benedicti de Scarperia, imperiali auctoritate iudex ordinarius publicusque notarius, predicta omnia et singula coram me acta rogatus hic public scripsi et publicavi, ideoque me subscripsi.

Document 9 ASF, *Notarile Antecosimiano*, L35 (Lando Fortini), fols. 69v – 71v, 19 September 1364. The grant of parish rights inside the walls of Scarperia to the church of SS. Jacopo e Filippo by the vicar of the bishop of Florence.

[In margin: Comunis de la Scarparia pro ecclesia Sanctorum Jacobi et Filippi dicti loci.]

In Christi nomine amen. Pateat omnibus evidenter quod constituti personaliter coram infrascripto domino Simone de Paganis vicario infrascripto, Andreas quodam Lapi, Comunis de la Scarperia de Mucello, Florentine diocesis, sindicus et procurator universitatis et personarum castri predicti de la Scarperia, sindicario et procuratorio nomine dicte universitatis et personarum eiusdem, ac etiam venerabilis vir dominus Ventura, plebanus plebis Sancte Agathe de Mucello dicte diocesis, sindicus et procurator et sindicario et procuratorio nomine domini Benedicti plebani canonicorum et capituli plebis Sancte Marie de Fagna de Mucello dicte diocesis cum consensu etiam et volunta[te] et in presentia domino Rodulfi Bartoli Simonis, prioris Sancti Petri Scheradii, et Arduini, rectoris ecclesie Sancti Johannis Evangeliste florentini, canonicorum dicte plebis de Fagna, ibidem presentium et expresse dicto domino Venture, sindico et procuratore predicto, consentientium et eidem consensum et volutatem prestantium in omnibus et singulis infrascriptis, de quorum Andree et domini Venture sindicatus et procuratio constant publicis instrumentis exinde confectis per Ser Mattheum Lippi de Scarperia notarium publicum, dicto domino Simoni vicario predicto exibuerunt et tradiderunt atque fecerunt supplicationem, significationem et petitionem infrascripte continentie et tenoris, videlicet.

Significat dominationi vestre universitas castri Scarperia de Mucello, florentine diocesis, quod in dicto castro est quedam ecclesia sive oratorium sub vocabulo beatorum Jacobi et Filippi cum quadam domuncula per se, cui domuncule a primo latere via, a secundo et tertio dicte universitatis, et a quarto Laurentii Cacini. Que ecclesia sive oratorium fundata et hedificata est super fundo et solo dicte universitas ad hoc per ipsam universitatem dudum concesso et deputato // fol. 70r // Quod quidem oratorium sive ecclesia est subiecta et pertinens ad plebem Sancte Marie de Fagna dicte diocesis et in ipsius parrocchia seu plebatu constituta, ac per priorem et canonicos dicte plebis solita gubernari et offitiari nec alium habet proprium rectorem nec etiam dotem vel redditus ad substentationem ipsius, propter que et quia dictum castrum de Scarperia est magne custodie propter guerras et suspitiones partium vicinarum nitentium actenus invadere dictum castrum, ipsa plebes in eadem ecclesia seu oratorio ad celebrandum cotidie misarum solempnia et divina offitia et personis dicte universitatis exibendum ecclesiastica ut expedit sacramenta, non retinet continuum ut expedit sacerdotem, nec commoditatem habent die et nocte libere accedendi ad illam homines de dicta universitate, propter que universitas et persone de dicta universitate et castro Scarperie receperunt actenus et cotidie recipiunt in predictis offitiis et sacramentis multipliciter detrimentum. Et quia etiam dicta ecclesia minatur ruinam ita et talis, quod nisi de presenti eidem de opportuno remedio provideatur, de facili destruetur, quod redundaret in maximum dampnum, dedecus et obrobrium universitatis predicte. Propter que dicta universitas et homines dicte universitatis ad eorum consolutionem quietem et animarum salutem deliberaverunt, in quantum de vestra voluntate et ordinatione procedat, dictam ecclesiam seu oratorium de eorum bonis reficere et sufficienter dotare, ita quod ibi sit et morari possit honorifice perpetuus rector, qui tempore presentationis ipsius sit sacerdos, cum ministro per ipsam universitatem, tamquam patronam ipsius ecclesie et oratorii, presentando priori pro se et canonicis et capitulo dicte plebis qui nunc sunt et pro tempore fuerint, et per priorem ipsius plebis et capitulum de Fagna, suo nomine et vice et nomine dicti capituli dicte plebis instituendum ad presentationem huiusmodi. Cui priori et capitulo et plebi ipsa ecclesia et rector subsit quoad institutionem predictam dumtaxat, et quoad alios honores per alias ecclesias dicti plebatus debitos dicte plebi. Reservato etiam dicte plebi omni jure decime et quartisesii, quam decimam et quartisium dominus Benedictus prior dicte plebis vel alius prior ipsius plebis vel capitulum vel alius pro ipsa plebe recolligisset sive recepisset hactenus in dicto castro Scarperie. Quam decimam et quartisium in antea prior et canonici dicti plebis qui sunt et pro tempore fuerint, vel alius pro eis et plebe predicta, recolligere possint eodem modo et forma quibus hactenus consueti sunt, non obstantibus aliquibus supradictis vel infrascriptis. Et reservato batisimo hominum et personarum cuiuslibet condictionis dicti castri. Et etiam quarta funeralium eorum qua sepellirentur apud ecclesiam fratrum Heremitarum dicti castri et // fol. 70v // omni alio jure et actione dicte plebi competenti contra fratres, capitulum et conventum fratrum Heremitarum ipsius castri. Sitque deinceps dicta ecclesia parrocchialis et curata, et habeat pro sua parrocchia totum dictum castrum de Scarperia infra fossos seu muros aut stecchatos dicti castri, et personas degentes in illo et ipsarum personarum curam et regimen pleno jure. Et quod decedentium corpora eorundem non electa alibi sepultura per ipsos ante decessum, apud dictum ecclesiam possint et debeant sepelliri. Ita tamen quod rector qui pro tempore fuerit in dicta ecclesia Sanctorum Jacobi et Filippi teneatur et debeat dare priori et capitulo dicte plebis medietatem cere et omnium dopleriorum sive

torchiorum venientium cum funeribus, que sepellientur in dicta ecclesia rema-
nentium sacerdoti eiusdem ecclesie. Et insuper ut dicta plebes conservetur in-
dempnis, volunt et intendunt ipsa universitas dare et donare eidem plebi et in
ausilium reparationis et reattationis dicte plebis et reluendi certa bona dicte plebis
pignori obligata, florenos quadragintaquinque auri boni et puri et recti ponderis et
conii florentini, qui perveniant ad manus alicuius de antiquioribus dicte plebis,
convertendos in causam praedictam, vel alicuius mercatoris de dicto castro vel
aliunde, de quo concordaverint predicti prior et canonici ut dictum est. Et insuper,
in signum honoris et reverentie, teneatur et debeat rector qui pro tempore fuerit in
dicta ecclesia sanctorum Jacobi et Filippi, in festo principali dicte plebis de Fagna,
silicet in festo Assumptionis beate Marie Virginis gloriose de mense Agusti, offer-
ere sive offerri facere cuilibet canonicorum dicte plebis qui nunc sunt et eorum
successoribus sive alteri pro eis recipienti nomine census, dummodo non sint ultra
sex canonici, unum cereum ponderis unius libre. Et priori qui nunc est vel pro
tempore fuerit, teneatur et debeat ipse rector offerre sive offerri facere in ipsa die
qui cantabitur missa, duos cereos accensos ponderis in totum librarum sex. Et si
non esset prior illa die nichilominus teneatur offerre sive offerri facere ipsi plebi
super altari dicte plebis vel procuratori suo, secundum quod superius continetur.
Et insuper quod in festo principali dicte ecclesie, videlicet in festo beatorum Jacobi
et Filippi, prior et capituli dicte plebis de Fagna qui nunc sunt et pro tempore
fuerint, debeant esse et libere possint ibi presse // fol. 71r // in offitio ordinando
et prandio et cena et aliis and honorandum dictum festum spectantibus, a vespero
vigilie usque ad vesperum festivitatis tamquam maiores ipsi festo Sanctorum
Jacobi et Filippi, et de ipso festo disponere sicut maiores prefati festi, non obstante
contradictione rectoris, ut dictum est. Et quod prior et capitulum dicte plebis,
advertentes predicta veritate fulciri et cupientes quantum in eis est, ut dictis
hominibus et universitati circa predicta sicut eis videtur jure consonum satisfiat, et
quod hec cedunt in utilitatem et commodum et profectum plebis praedicte, super
hiis invicem habuerunt colloquium et tractatum pluries iteratum, et matura deliberatione habita super predictis inter se ad invicem, solempniter deliberaverunt
predicta fieri et executioni mandari in quantum ad hoc accedat dominationis
vestre legiptima auctoritas et consensus. Quare cum ad vos et vestrum offitium
spectat providere utilitatibus ecclesiarum pariter et subditorum, et ex predictis
cultus divini numpminis amplietur, dictaque universitas et personae ipsius divin-
orum recipiant incrementum et dicta plebes inlesa conservetur et augeatur, eidem
dominationi supplicant reverenter quatenus ipsam ecclesiam seu oratorium cum
dicta domuncula, que domuncula consuevit esse pro habitatione presbiteri qui ibi
degebat pro divinis ofitiis celebrandis a dicta plebe, ex predictis causis utilibus et
neccesariis eximatis et parrocchialem et principalem ecclesiam constituatis in
castro et loco predicto propter utilitates, neccesitates et commoda suprascripta

consequenda, et vitanda incommoda de quibus supra fit mentio et que in evidenti apparent. Ipsique ecclesie dictum castrum, territorium et parrocchiam et personas ipsius assignetis et concedatis sub modis et formis prefatis perpetuo predictis omnibus permansuris. Et eisdem priori et capitulo sic, ut predicitur, eandem ecclesiam et domunculam concedendi et super predictis cum dicta universitate et sindico conveniendi iuxta formam petitionis predicte et tratatuum per eos in vicem propterea habitorum, licentiam concedatis interponentes predictis et contractibus propterea celebrandis vestram et episcopalis curie florentine auctoritatem nichilominus et decretum, cum omnibus non obstantibus clausulis opportunis et in talibus consuetis, prout etiam manifeste apparet posse fieri de jure, iuxta sanctorum patrum decreta.

Document 10 ASF, *Notarile Antecosimiana*, L292 (Lorenzo di Ser Tano di Luziano), fol. 31v, 18 April 1375. The enlargement of the privileges of the church of SS. Jacopo e Filippo in Scarperia.

[In margin: Comunis et ecclesie de Scarparie. Concessio baptismatis.]

In Christi nomine amen. Anno ab Incarnatione ipsius millesimo trecentesimo septuagesimo quinto, indictione tertiadecima, die decima octava mensis aprilis. Actum in monasterio et loco monasterii et ecclesie Sancte Marie de Sancto Seppulcro prope Florentiam, presentibus testibus venerabili viro domino Nicholao priore ecclesie Sancti Andree de Maiano, Spoletane diocesis, infrascripti domini Episcopi vicario generali, et presbitero Francischo rectore ecclesie Sancti Miniatis de Quintole, Florentine diocesis, et aliis pluribus etc.

Appareat omnibus manifeste quod Reverendus in Christo pater et dominus, dominus Agnelus, Dei et apostolice Sedis gratia Episcopus florentinus, ciertis justis et rationabilibus causis motus et maxime infrascriptis, ad infrascriptam, utilem et necessariam ac rationabilem gratiam grandi etiam meditatione ac consilio prehabitis, descendit modo infrascripto et per infrascripta verba, videlicet. Angelus, Dei et apostolice Sedis gratia Episcopus florentinus, ad ecternam rei memoriam, devotis subditis fidelibus nostris, nostrique episcopatus florentini hominibus et personis castri et fortilitie Sancti Bernabe, quod Scarperia vulgariter nupcupatur, plebatus Fagne florentien nostre diocesis, atque tibi presbitero Benedicto, rectori ecclesie Sanctorum Filippi et Iacopi de dicto loco, tuisque subcessoribus in perpetuum, pius pater et pastor, moleste gerens animarum inconmoda subditorum, eo diligentius ipsarum necessitatibus atque cotidie imminentibus periculis providet opportune, quo graviora conspicit pericula imminere et percipit scandala suboriri, ut quantum fieri potest pericula evitentur et scandalis salubriter obvietur. Sane cum cordis diligentia, non sine mentis amaritudine percipientes, oretenus a Iohanne, presentialiter generali vicario nostro, quam enormia et ineffabilia reperit apud plebem Sancte Marie de Fagna, dum visitaret ipsam, cum inibi visu vidit et a multis percepit quod nec per priorem dicte plebis nec per alium sacerdotem ministrabantur ecclesiastica sacramenta et maxime baptismum, januam aliorum. Et quod plures infantes utriusque sexus delati ad illam de castro predicto et de superioribus partibus, maxime versus Alpes per quattuor milliaria distantes a dicta plebe, per totam diem tenebantur ante quam sacerdos aliquis qui baptizzaret eosdem reperiri posset. Ea propter diligentius adtendentes quanta possunt propter hec hominibus et personis in dicta terra et territorio ipsius degentibus, et aliis prelibatis circa sacri fontem baptismatis animarum et corporum pericula imminere et scandal resultare, cum ipsa terra sive castrum et oppidum sint magna custodia indigen[te]s, nocturnis precipue temporibus, et quandoque diurnis, et cuius porte clause sepe per totam diem minime aperiuntur, qua de causa tunc temporis ad dictam plebem de Fagna, que situata est extra ipsam terram per miliare, pro sacro fonte baptismatis nullus accedere potest nocturno tempore vel diurno, et guerrarum precipue ac etiam tenpestatum inundationis temporibus. Cuius rei occasione multotiens parvulorum aliqui per mulierculas, aliqui vero in ecclesia fratrum heremitarum in dicto castro ne sine baptismo decederent baptizzati fuerunt. Et aliqui etiam sine baptismo perierunt et alii nonnulli propter periculum quod imminebat animarum et corporum scandalizzati fuerunt. Hiis vero providere utiliter cupientes, pietate paterna et inmitantes ea que alias dicte ecclesie Sanctorum Filippi et Iacopi circa animarum curam et funera defuntorum et alia ad conmoditatem fidelium dicti loci concessa per predecessores nostros et largita fuerunt, dignis et devotis etiam hominum et personarum dicti loci meritis inclinati, tibi presbitero Benedicto, nunc dicte ecclesie Sanctorum Filippi et Iacopi rectori, ac tuis subcessoribus canonice intrantibus ipsique ecclesie in perpetuum, non obstantibus constitutionibus quibuscumque, qua fungimur auctoritate concedimus ut omnes de dicto castro et terra de Scarparia et habitantes in dicto castro et in territorio Scarperie supra versus Alpes, videlicet quanto trahitur totum dictum castrum Scarparie ab intra et ab extra supra versus Alpes, et non ab inde infra versus plebem prefatam Sancte Marie de Fagne, de plebatu de Fagna solumodo, libere licite et impune valeas baptizzare, tibique et tuis subcessoribus antedictis atque eidem ecclesie presentium auctoritate concedimus, ut fontes sacri baptismatis habeas in ecclesia antedicta eosque de cetero in ea possis erigere, et pro ipsis benedicendis secundum ordinem consuetum tempore ab ecclesia constituto et pro pueris baptizzandis petere liceat et habere valeas crisma et oleum cathecuminorum in die cene Domini, sicut et alie ecclesie baptismales a nobis et subcessoribus nostris, ac etiam oleum infirmorum santum pro infirmis ungendis habent, et hactenus consueverunt habere dicta die. Et uti liceat eisdem fontibus pro hominibus et personis castri et territorij ipsius versus Alpes predictas die noctuque prout fuerit opportunum, absque aliqua requisitione plebani sive prioris et capituli dicte plebis de Fagna, et ipsorum contradictione aliquatenus non obstante. In quorum omnium testimonium et certitudinem pleniorem tibi, ut predicitur, presens privilegium duximus concedendum huius scripti tenore nostrique sigilli appensione munitum. Nulli ergo omnino hominum liceat hanc nostre concessionis et gratie paginam perturbare, seu eidem ausu temerario contrahire. Si quis autem contrarium adtentare presumpserit, indignationem omnipotentis Dei et beatorum Apostolorum eius Petri et Pauli ac nostram se noverit incursurum. Cuntis vero predicta servantibus sit pax et securitas et spem habeant retributionis ecterne.

Document 11   Archivio generale degli Agostiniani, Rome, Li:4, *Relazione della Provincia Pisana*, fol. 246r, 4 April 1650. Report on the Convent of San Barnaba in Scarperia.

Il monasterio di S. Bernaba dell' Ordine degli Eremitani di S. Agostino situato nel castello di Scarperia, Diocese Fiorentina, fondato et erecto l'anno 1325 con consenso della Republica di Firenze e della Comunita di Scarperia, fu dato il Placet assegnando essa la grandezza della chiesa, Cemeterio, Orto, e Convento, E Fra Gregorio di Barolomeo di Firenze prese il possesso. Item la Chiesa sotto il titolo di S. Bernaba Apostolo.

Item il claustro quadro, nel claustro da basso vi è una Compagnia, o confraternita della Santissima Nunziata, delle tre stanze che servono per Camere e Celle, dall'altra parte della porta principale la Muraglia della Chiesa, in un andito La Cantina divisa in tre parti, reffectorio, Cucina, et di tucto cinto di Muro, Granaio, Dormitorio da una parte del quale stanno tre Camere, un andito con altre 4 camere. Dal Dormitorio s'entra su le loggie di sopra e vi e un stanzone che serve per granaio, due Camera a man sinistra e due a man destra, e due altre Camere con studiolo, et un'altra Camera.

This document names the first fathers of the convent. Five of them, including the father superior, were from Scarperia, one, the treasurer, was from Pistoia, one was from Prato.

Document 12 ASF, *Cap.*, 32, fols. 70r and v, 11 October 1329. Legislation for the foundation of a town on the Consuma pass between Pontassieve on the Arno and the Casentino.

Ordini della terra da Montalpruno

Vobis dominis prioribus Artium et Vexillifero Iustitie civitatis Florentie, reverenter exponitur quod a civitate Florentie usque in Castentinum nulla terra est, propter quod comitatus Florentie, maxime tempore guerre, est in magno periculo et potest per hostes Comunis Florentie faciliter, absque aliqua contrarietate, discurri, et sepissime contingit robarias et capturas personarum in eorum comintatu fieri, et per stratam non itur secure. Et quod a domibus positis super dicta strata, loco dicto Borselli, usque ad finem dicti comitatus versus Casentinum, est distantia per quattor miliaria et ultra, inter quam distantiam est terrenum adeo bonum et fertile quod vix simile reperiretur in toto comitatu et districtu Florentia. Et quia fortilitia non est aliqua, remanet quasi totum dictum terrenum incultum, et si construeretur aliqua terra intra dictum locum, maxime prope dictos confines, homines de contratis redirent ad habitandum in ea, et totum dictum terrenum laboraretur et acquireret Comune Florentie terrenum per spatium quatuor miliarum, quod quasi dici potest Comune Florentie non habere vel possidere ullatenus, et Casentinenses et alii circunstantes et Romandioli confluerent cum frumento, blado, forratico et bestiis tam domesticis quam silvestribus et aliis victualibus, et haberetur maior solito eorum copia in civitate Florentie, ac Aretini et Comites Guidones, ghibellini et rebelles Comunis Florentie, guerram facere non possent contra Comune predictum de partibus Casentini vel aliis circunstantiis. Quare vestre providentie supplicatur quod vobis placeat, una cum offitio XII bonorum virorum, deliberare et per Consilia populi et Comunis Florentie stantiari et firmari facere quod de novo ordinetur et construatur una terra prope extremitates dicti comitatus, intra locum predictum, super strata predicta, in loco qui dicitur in Plano dell'Asentio, prope Montem al Prunum, qui est aptior et habilior quam aliquis alius intra dictum locum, tam ratione planitiei quam copie fontium qui sunt ibi vel in circumstantiis dicti loci super ipsa strata, et quia Casentinenses et alii circumstantes facilius et citius ad ipsum locum fluerent quam ad alim ubi construeretur terra predicta. Que terra ponatur et fiat in dicto loco, in Plano dell'Asentio vel circumstantiis eius, super dicta strata, secundum deliberationem que fuerit facta per officiales ad id deputatos per dominos priores Artium et Vexilliferum Iustitie presentes vel futuros. Que terra construatur et fiat hoc modo, videlicet. Scilicet quod plebatus Pomini, plebatus Glaceti, plebatus Castillionis, plebatus S. Cervasii de Pelago et plebatus Pitiane, et homines ipsorum plebatuum et cuiuslibet eorum, faciant et facere teneantur et cogantur fossas et steccata circa locum ubi dicta terra esse debuerit vel ordinatum fuerit eam esse, et bertescas circa ipsa steccata. Et pro predictis steccatis et berteschis faciendis, possint accipere de lignaminibus que sunt ibi prope, quorum abundantia non est ibi parva. Et sit dicta terra in longitudine saltem sexcentorum bracchiorum, et amplitudine trecentorum bracchiorum. Et Comune Florentie ibi construat duas portas, unam versus Casentinum et aliam versus civitatem Florentie, de quo loco per ignem et fumum poterit responderis signis ignis et fumi que fierent super turrim palatii populi, more dominorum priorum et Vexilliferi Iustitie. In quibus et pro quibus portis et constructione eorum, de pecunia Comunis Florentie percepta seu percipienda ex defunctibus stipendiariis Comunis Florentine et castellanis et custodibus terrarum et castrorum ipsius Comunis, expendantur et convertantur usque in quantitatem quingentarum librarum florenorum parvorum, que dentur et solvantur per camerarios Camere Comunis Florentie illi persone et personis, de qua et quibus deliberatum fuerit per dominos priores et Vexilliferum Iustitie presentes vel futuros.

Item quod quelibet persona de dictis plebatis vel aliunde, guelfa tamen, que not sit civis Florentie vel nobilis comitatus Florentie, que infra duos menses proxime construet vel construi faciet in dicta terra domus in qua habitet et stet continue cum sua familia, sit immunis per septem annos incipiendos ab ea die in antea, qua talis persona edificaverit vel edificari fecerit dictam in dicta terra et in ea redierit ad habitandum cum sua familia, ab omnibus libris, presantantiis, // fol. 70v // impositis et gabellis, factionibus et quibuscumque aliis oneribus et servitiis Comunis Florentie, personalibus et realibus, que infra dictum tempus imponerentur, indicerentur vel fierent per Comune prefatum seu solvi deberent ipsi Comuni, salvo quod a gabella contractuum et instrumentorum, et [a] gabella portarum civitatis Florentie. Et quod extimum et libra, seu summa ipsius extimi et libre illius, videlicet que construxerit vel construi fecerit in dicta terra domum et in ea habitaverit cum sua familia, detrahatur et detrahi et cassari possit et debeat de extimo seu libra populi in quo fuerit allibrata, per notarium Camere ad cancellationum, condemnationum et bamnorum offitium deputatum. Et quod contra dictam immunitatem nihil fieri vel deliberari possit vel debeat per Comune Florentie vel Consilia ipsius Comunis et populi, vel offitiales eiusdem, vel aliquid aliud per quod veniri possit in dimunitionem immunitatis predicte, et si contra fieret non valeat nec teneat nec ab aliquo debeat observari vel executioni mandari.

Item quod unaqueque persona que voluerit construere seu construi facere domum in dicta terra, possit habere de terreno quod situm fuerit intra fossas et steccata dicte terre pro ipsa domo edificanda, dando ei cuius fuerit terrenum, ad rationem duorum denariorum, eius videlicet quod ad presens valet unus denarius, et etiam possit haberede lignaminibus que sunt in circumstantiis dicte terre, necessariis constructioni dicte terre, pro simili pretio statuendo ut dictum est. Item quod in dicta terra vel extra ipsam terram iuxta eandem terram, possit et debeat fieri mercatum saltem semel singulis septimanis, ea videlicet die que placuerit hominibus dicte terre, in quo vendatur frumentum, bladum, formaticum, bestie et alia victualia et mercantie, sine solutione gabelle Comuni Florentie facienda pro ipso mercato vel rebus que adducerentur vel venderentur in ipso mercato.

Document 13   ASF *Cap.*, 32, fols. 271r and v, 9 April 1332. Legislation for the foundation of Firenzuola.

[In margin: Consitutio terre nove de Fiorenzola]

In Dei nomine amen. Anno Domini millesimo trecentesimo trigesimo secundo, indictione XV, die nono mensis Aprilis. Predicti Pierus, Philippus, Cennes, Benincasa, Giovencus et Bernardus offitiales (=superfacto alpium), facta discussione in dictis partibus ultra alpes in pluribus et pluribus locis et diversis diebus, et cum sindicis, rectoribus et aliis hominibus et personis contratarum Santerni, Rivocornacchiarii, Bordignani, Rapezi et aliarum contratarum, et cum ipsis hominibus ratiocinio et etiam una cum Finuccino de Aretio et Lotto de Montecchio, conistabilibus, stipendiariis Comunis Florentie, et habita plena et matura deliberatione inter se ipsos, et nullo discordante, et vigore eorum balie et auctoritatis eisdem a Comuni Florentie concesse, deliberaverunt, stantiaverunt, providerunt quod quedam terra nove ponatur et construatur et poni et construi debeat et edificetur pro iamdicto Comuni Florentie et ad ipsum Comune et populum Florentie expectantem. Et ad honorem, pacificum et bonum statum Comunis et populi Florentie et Partis Guelfe et sancte matris Ecclesie, in loco qui dicitur Piano dell'Arca. Que terra nominetur, vocetur et appelletur pro dicto Comuni Florentie et ad ipsum Comune pertinentem, terra sive castrum de Fiorenzuola, et que terra sit et esse debeat longitudinis bracchiorum VI[hundred]XXXIII, et amplitudinis bracchiorum III[hundred]XLII, et plus et minus ad voluntatem dictorum officialium. Et in qua et per quam terram Fiorenzuole sit et esse debeat una via que vadat versus Florentiam et recte versus Bononiam. Et in capite ipsius vie versus Florentiam, sit et esse debeat una ianua, que ianua appelletur et nominetur ianua Florentina et in capite ipsius vie recte fiat una alia ianua versus Bononiam que ianua appelletur et vocetur ianua S. Iohannis, et que via sit mastra et vocetur via Florentina. Et etiam in ipsa terra, ex alia parte, mittatur et esse debeat alia via mastra, que vadat recte versus Santernum, et in capite ipsius vie, ex parte Santerni, ponatur et constuatur una ianua, que ianua vocetur ianua S. Petri. Et in alio capite versus Rivocornacchiaium, alia ianua que vocetur ianua S. Maria, et etiam ipsa via voceture via S. Maria, et etiam ipsa via voceture via S. Maria. Et ambe vie, ut dictum est, sint mastre et maternales. Et ad ispam terram et castrum debeant pertinere infrascripta

Comunia et populi, et esse unum Comune per se tantum, et ad unum extimum et libram et distributionem extimi, et voceture Comune Fiorenzuole. Nomina quorum Comunium sunt hec, videlicet.

Comune et populus S. Petri de Santerno
Comune et populus S. Nicholai de Casanuova
Populus S. Maria de Rifredo
Populus S. Iohannis de Rivocornacchiaio
Populus S. Martini de Castro et S. Iacobi
Populus S. Bartholomei de Vallibus
Populus S. Marie de Frena
Populus S. Nicolay de Pogialto

Omnes predicti populi et Comunia et homines et persones eorumdem debeant repondere ad ipsum Comune de Firenzuola et ad unum extimum et libram extimi tantum, et respondere Comuni Florentie ut // fol. 271v // alii comitatini ipsius civitatis Florentie. Et quod Comune dicatur, vocetur et nominetur Comuni et Castrum de Firenzuola comitatus Florentie et ad ipsum Comune expectante. Et quod dictum Comune terre nove de Fiorenziola habeat et habere et tenere debeat arma cum campo albo, intus cum medietate crucis et medio lilio simul coloris rubei per longitudinem et in longitudinem clipei sive scudi, ad honorem et statum Comunis et populi Florentie et Partis Guelfe.

Document 14 ASF *Cap.*, 35, fols. 231v, 232r and v, 24 May (1334). The Florentine officials at Firenzuola order settlers to build on their lots; they also make arrangements for the construction of public buildings.

[In margin: Quod habentes casolaria cogantur ad perficiendum.]

Die xxiiii Maii

Predicti offitiales [=ad hedificandum casolaria in terra de Fiorenzuola], absente Coppo Borghesis eorum collega, vigore ipsorum offitii et balie eis concesse per dominos priores Artium et Vexilliferum Iustitie Comunis et populi Florentie et offitiales duodecim bonorum virorum, et omni modo via et iure quibus melius potuerunt, stantiaverunt ordinaverunt et firmaverunt quod omnes et singuli homine infrascripti quibus data fuerunt casolaria per Comune Florentie seu per ipsius offitiales in terra de Fiorenzuola, cogantur cives et aliis omnes hinc ad quindecim dies ad incipiendum hedificationem et constructionem domorum super infrascriptis casolaribus, et hinc ad medium mensem Augusti ad complendum et completas ostendendum ipsas domos: Stantiantes ordinantes et firmantes quod ab inde in antea, si quis ipsa casolaria non compleverit et domos non fecerit cum effectu super ipsis casolaribus, eisdem tollantur et dentur aliis, videlicet cui et quibus deliberatum fuerit per dictos offitiales vel eorum successores.

// fol. 232r // Item stantiaverunt ordinaverunt et firmaverunt quod palatium Comunis et populi florentini, quod nunc per ipsum Comune Florentie in dicta terra de Fiorenzuola construitur et fit, habeat et habere debeat viam ex parte posteriori et versus Bernardum Ardinghelli, que sit amplitudinis [quactuor] bracchiorum. Et quod dictus ordo ponatur in statuto comunis de Fiorenzuola.

// fol. 232v [In margin: // Quod completo palatio pecunia deponatur pro ecclesia.]

Item stantiaverunt ordinaverunt et firmaverunt via et modo predictis, quod completo palatio Comunis et populi incepto per ipsum Comune et populum florentinum in terra Fiorenzuole, pecunia que post modum recepta fuerit et exacta occasione passetti, starii et stadere, mictatur et deponature pro constuctione et perfectione ecclesie Sancti [blank] de Fiorenzuola usque ad integram perfectionem ipsius ecclesie.

Document 15 ASF *Cap.*, 35, fols. 223r and v, 25 August (1338). The Florentine officials at Firenzuola prohibit bridges across the main street of the town.

[In margin: Statutum pontium]

Die xxv mensis Augusti (1338)

Supradicti offitiales (= super constructione et perfectione et bono statu terre de Florenzuola), exceptis dictis Iohanne et Philippozio eorum collegis, simul congregati in palatio priorum pro dicto eorum offitio exercendo, unananimi concordia et volunte, pro bono et pulcro statu dicte terre de Florenzuola et ut omnis scandali materia pretollatur, vigore eorum offitii et autoritatis et balie, et omni modo quo melius potuerunt, providerunt, stantiaverunt et ordinaverunt quod de cetero in dicta terra de Florenzuola, in aliqua parte vie que recta linea vadit et trahit a ianua Florentina ad ianuam Bononiensem, vel in via que vadit et trahit recta linea a ianua Imolensi usque Santernum ad ianuam Cornaclariam, nulla persona cuiuscumque condictionis existat, audeat vel presummat hedificare, construere vel facere, per se vel alium, aliquem pontem ligneum sive lapideum aut laterum vel de aliqua re, sub // f. 223v // pena librarum centum florenorum parvorum pro qualibet persona contrafaciente et vice qualibet auferenda per capitaneum et rectorem dicte terre qui pro tempore fuerit de facto, et nichilominus removere teneatur et debeat etiam de fatto pontem predictum. Quod si capitaneus vel rector, qui pro tempore fuerit, non fecerit, perdat de suo salario libras centum florenorum parvorem. Quas libras centum Camerarius Comunis Florenzuole que pro tempore fuerit, sibi retinere debeat de facto, et nichilominus sequens capitaneus vel rector predicta, modo et sub pena predictis, facere protinus teneatur.

Document 16 ASF *Provv.*, 28, fols. 152r and v, 2 April 1337. Legislation for the foundation of Terranuova.

Item infrascripta provisio, ut supra dictum est et infra dicetur, super infrascriptis edita et facta, cuius quidem provisionis tenor talis est. Audita et diligenter intellecta et examinata quadam expositione dominis prioribus Artium et Vexillifero Iustitie populi et Comunis Florentie supradictis, pro parte hominum et personarum infracriptarum terrarum, castrorum, comunium et populorum et locorum, videlicet:

Comunis de Ganghereta ⎤
Comunis de Terrano ⎥
Comunis de Pozzo ⎥ plebatus Gropine

Comunis delle Cavi ⎥
Comunis de Pernina ⎦

. . . . .

Comunis de Pietravelse
Comunis de Moncione
Comunis de Barbischio
Comunis de Veschia et Ville Bone
populi S. Nicholai de Forlle et
populi S. Donato de Menzano
porrecta et facta, inter cetera continente quod nuper cum magno gaudio sperantes eorum libertatem recuperare, redierunt ad solitam obedientiam Comunis et populi civitatis Florentie, velut filius ad ubera pie matris, et hoc ut de cetero possint, ut desiderant, ipsi et eorum descendentes in libertate vivere nec non parere et respondere Comuni Florentie in factionibus et aliis honoribus realibus et personalibus ipsius Comunis ut alii comitatini et districtuales civitatis eiusdem, et ut de cetero tenus non opprimantur et occupentur per tirannos vel alios iniustos dominos, sed ab eis et ab eorum iniustitia valeant se tueri. Et quod ea commode perfici per eosdem non possunt absque Comunis Florentie auxilio, domini priores Artium et Vexillifer Iustitie supradicti volentes eisdem Comunibus et populis de opportuno et salubri subsidio providere, habita prius super hiis cum offitio duodecim bonorum virorum diligenti deliberatione et demum inter ipsos dominos

priores et Vexilliferum Iustitie et dictum offitium duodecim bonorum virorum secundum formam statutarum, premisso facto et obtento partite et secreto scruptinio ad fabas nigras et albas, eorum offitii auctoritate et vigore, et omni modo et iure quibus melius potuerunt, providerunt ordinaverunt et stantiaverunt quod ipsi domini priores Artium et Vexillifer Iustitie, una cum affitio duodecim bonorum virorum, possint eisque liceat eligere et deputare aliquos bonos viros populares, cives florentinos, quos et quot voluerint et pro eo tempore et termino quo voluerint, non tamen maiori unius anni, in offitiales et pro offitialibus pro Comuni Florentie ad faciendum construi et de novo fieri unam vel duas terram et terras in partibus Vallis Arni a Castro S. Ciconie citra, in eo loco et locis dictarum partium, et in ea longitudine, amplitudine ac latitudine, et cum hiis portis, turribus, viis, fossis et muris quibus et prout et sicut expedire seu convenire videbitur et voluerint ipsi offitiales eligendi ut dictum est, et maior pars eorum, predicta possint eisque liceat ordinare et deliberare de hominibus et personis que redire voluerint vel debuerint ad domos hedificandum et habitandum in ipsis terris. Ac etiam possint eisque liceat dare et concedere pro Comuni Florentie hiis qui hedificaverint domum et ad habitandum cum eorum famuliis redierint in ipsis terris vel altera eorum, immunitatem et privillegium de libris et a libris et factionibus, honeribus realibus et fructibus bonorum rebellium, exbannitorum et condempnatorum et cessantium, a libris et factionibus ipsius Comunis et gabella ipsius, et a solutione ipsarum, salvo quod a gabella portarum civitatis Florentie et a gabella contractuum et instrumentorum et a gabella vini quod venditur ad minutum in civitate, comitatu et districtu Florentie pro tempore et termino quo convenire congnoverint, non tamen maiori decem annorum, salvo quod non possint aliquam concedere inmunitatem alicui civi florentino vel nobili comitatus Florentie. Et quod extimus et libra sive summa extimi et libra illius scilicet persone que construxerit seu hedificaverit aut construi vel hedifacari fecerit // fol. 152v // in tali terra domum et in ea habitaverit cum sua familia, detrahatur et detrahi et cassari possit et debeat de extimo seu summa libre et extimi populi in quo fuerit alibratus, per notarium offitialium predictorum. Et quod contra dictam inmunitatem nichil fieri vel provideri vel deliberari possit vel debeat per Consilia ipsius populi et Comunis seu offitiales eiusdem populi vel Comunis, vel aliquid aliud per quod venire posset in diminutionem vel derogationem inmunitatis iamdicte. Et si contra fieret, non valeat nec teneat, neque ab aliquo debeat observari vel executioni mandari. Et quod nullus de magnatibus civitatis, comitatus vel districtus Florentie seu aliunde, moretur vel habitet in ipsis terris vel aliqua earum vel eorum territorio, seu in eis vel eorum territorio emat seu acquirat per se vel alium, aliquam domum vel terrenum seu possessionem; et si quas possessiones haberet huiusmodi magnas in tali terra seu eius territorio, teneatur et cogature eas vendere pro iusto pretio Comuni vel hominibus ipsius terre. Et quod nulla persona vendat vel alienet aut aliquo titulo vel modo transferat aliquam domum, terram vel possessionem, que posita sit vel fuerit in ipsis terris vel aliqua earum vel alicuius earum territorio vel districtu alicui vel aliquem magnatem civitatis vel comitatus seu districtus Florentie vel aliunde, vel in aliquem alium pro ipso magnate vel ad preces seu in obsequium ipsius magnatis.

Document 17 ASF *Cap.*, 4, fols. 36v – 39v, 16 January 1349 / 1350. The Abbey of Agnano surrenders its possessions in the Val d'Ambra to Florence.

Cum dominus Basilius abbas monasterii Sancte Maria de Agnano, ordinis sancti Benedicti, Aretine diocesis, filius quondam Junte de Uglignano, Comunis Santi Geminiani, asserat dictum monasterium et ipsius monasterii possessiones et bona et fideles descriptos, iam sunt multa tempora invasa, usurpata et detenta fuisse a certis magnatibus et potentibus et maxime inimicis et rebellibus populi et Comunis Florentie dicte contrate de Ugnana propter que maxime ipse abbas non potuit vel potest pacifice habere, tenere seu possidere dictam abbatiam, possessiones et bona ipsius abatie eiusque fideles. Et considerans auxilio, bracchio et potentia Comunis Florentie ipsiusque Comunis Florentie gubernatione, regimine et potestate, ipsam abbatiam eiusque possessiones et bona libere habere, tenere et possidere, et ex eis fructus et redditus percipere et habere. . . . [the monastery, with its persons and possessions, submits itself to Florence with the following conditions:]

Imprimis quod dictus dominus abbas tradat dicto Comuni Florentie seu sindico dicti Comunis vel alio pro dicto Comuni Florentie recipienti, fortilitias dicte Abbatie in custodiam et accomandigiam, et ipsum Comune Florentie seu dictum sindicum vel alium pro dicto Comuni recipientem, inducat et immictat in tenutam et possessionem fortilitiarum ipsius abbatie ad custodiendum, protegendum et impediendum ne ab aliquo occupentur seu adprendantur.

Item quod pro dicta custodia, tuitione et defensione fienda, dictum Comune Florentie possit et ei liceat mictere et ponere in dictis fortilitiis abbatie predicte, unum offitialem cum quatuor famulis, quos dictus dominus abbas, capitulum et conventum et homines infrascripti promictere teneantur esse et stare in fortilitiis supradictis et ipsos manutenere et defendere iuxta posse in possessione et tenuta predicta. Quibus offitiali et famulis satisfiat de ipsorum salario et mercede expensis dictorum fidelium et hominum castri de Cappannole et castri Castilionis Albertorum et plebis de Presciano et castri de MonteLuccii et castri de Cacciano et castri de Cornie. Quod salarium seu expense ordinarie taxari et inter predictos homines dictarum terrarum, locorum et castrorum distribui et per ipsos solvi eo

modo et forma, tempore, temporibus, prout sicut, quo modo et qualiter et in ea
quantitate et summa quibus deliberatum, provisum, ordinatum seu stantiatum
fuerit per dominos priores Artium et Vexilliferum Iustitie pro tempore existentes,
seu cui vel quibus predicta fieri commis[er]it Et quod ultra dictos famulos teneatur
dictus abbas, monasterium, capitolum et conventus et fideles predicti receptare
quamcumque gentem armigeram dicti Comunis Florentie vel que destinaretur per
dominos priores et Vexilliferum Iustitie seu per dictum offitialem in dictis Abbatia
et fortilitiis antedictis. [. . . . . .]

// fol. 38r // Item quod si contingerit aliquo tempore dictum Comune Florentie assignare episcopatui Aretino fortilitias, possessiones, castra, iurisdictiones
et iura, que dictum Comune Florentie pro tempore teneret in dicta contrata Vallis
Ambre episcopatus Aretii, quod in dicta assignatione debeat semper excipi abbatia predicta et eius possessiones et bona et fideles infrascripti et alii fideles abbatie
predicte, qui sint semper et imperpetuum sub recommendatione et protectione
predictis et prout superius continetur, seu restituatur dicto domino abbati seu
successoribus et capitulo et conventui eiusdem pro tempore existentibus prout
placuerit offitio dominorum priorum Artium et Vexilliferi Iustitie qui pro tempore
fuerint. . . .

Item quod dictum Comune Florentie teneatur et debeat dictum abbatem, mon-
acos, fideles, abbatiam, fortilitias et ipsorum bonorum defendere, protegere, custodire et salvare, ut alios districtuales ipsius Comunis.

[Other paragraphs of the treaty established these conditions: The *fedeles* of the
monastery were to have a six-year tax immunity. During this time, however, they
still had to pay the salaries of the officials sent to them by Florence, to pay the
Florentine salt *gabelles,* and to bear arms with Florence to defend the Val
d'Ambra. After the six years they were to be treated like the other residents of the
Florentine *distretto.* The abbot was obligated to give a five-florin offering to the
city of Florence each year on the feast of Saint John the Baptist. The revenue from
the fines levied by the Florentine officials was to go toward paying the latter's
salaries. The abbot also promised to have the treaty ratified by his subjects within
fifteen days. The treaty was guaranteed by a ten-thousand-florin fine for the
breaking of any of its conditions by either party.]

Document 18 ASF *Provv.,* 37, fols. 82r and v, 25 January 1349 / 1350.
The *Ufficiali delle Castella* are instructed to search for a site in the Val
d'Ambra for the foundation of a town.

Domini priores Artium et Vexillifer Iustitie populi et Comunis Florentie, considerantes quod officium octo offitialium deputatorum, simul cum offitio dominorum

priorum artium et vexiliferi justitie populi et Comunis Florentie, ad providendum circa custodiam, fortificationem et conservationem terrarum, arcium, fortilitiarum seu locorum comitatus seu districtus Florentie expirat circa exitum mensis huius, et quod de aliis in locum seu successores eorum in dicto offitio non fuit hactenus provisum, et quod utile, immo expediens et necessarium est populi et Comuni Florentie quod novi offitiales ad dictum offitium eligantur Habita deliberatione decenti super predictis et infrascriptis omnibus cum offitio duodecim bonorum virorum dicti Comunis et demum inter ipsos omnes dominos priores et Vexilliferum et duodecim bonos viros in sufficienti numero congregatos in palatio populi Florentini, facto misso et obtento diligenti et secreto scruptinio et partito ad fabas nigras et albas secundum formam statutorum, omni iure et modo quibus melius potuerunt, providerunt, ordinaverunt et stantiaverunt quod domini priores Artium et Vexillifer predicti, una cum offitio duodecim bonorum virorum dicti Comunis, possint eisque liceat semel et plures eligere octo cives populares et vere guelfos, homines providos et discretos, in offitiales et pro offitialibus Comunis et pro Comuni Florentie, ad offitium supradictum quod vulgariter appellatur et appellari debet offitium castrorum, pro tempore sex mensium proxime venturorum, incipiendorum die electionis. Qui sic electi et due partes eorum, aliis etiam absentibus et inrequisitis // fol. 82v // vel non acceptantibus vel defuntis habeant et habere intelligantur omnen et totam illam baliam, offitium, autoritatem et potestatem, una cum offitio dominorum priorum Artium et Vexillifferi Iustitie populi et Comunis Florentie, in providendo, faciendo et mandando et exequendo et fieri et exequi faciendo circa fortificationem, fulcimentum, custodiam, recircationem seu conservationem omnium et singularum terrarum, fortilitiarum, castrorum, arcium et locorum comitatus seu districtus Florentie seu que per ipsum vel pro ipso Comuni Florentie tenentur vel custodiuntur vel tenebuntur seu custodientur et alia quelibet que pretextu, causa seu occasione predictorum vel alicuius eorum occurerent, quam et prout hactenus habuerunt dominus Paulus Vettori, Franciscus Benini et alii sex eorum sotii seu college, offitiales ad predicta hactenus deputati simul cum offitio dominorum priorum Artium et Vexilliferi Iustitie populi et Comunis Florentie, vigore electionis eorum seu quarumcumque provisionum vel reformationum dicti populi et Comunis Et cum eisdem modis, formis ac tenoribus, que omnia intelligantur in provisione presenti singulariter repetita. Et spetialiter et nominatim possint, teneatur et debeant providere et ordinare de reponendo et reponi et fieri faciendo unam terram grossam in partibus Vallis Ambre Florentine seu terrarum noviter adquisitarum in partibus supradictis vel in vice comitatu vel in convicinis partibus, ubi, quomodo, quando et prout eis videbitur convenire. Et in predictis et pro predictis omnibus et singulis et quolibet ipsorum pretextu et pro ipsorum observantia et effectu possint ipsi et due partes eorum, ut dictum est, una cum offitio dominorum priorum Artium et Vexilliffer Iustitie populi et Comunis Florentie, semel et plures et quotiens, facere, componere et firmare quecumque ordinamenta provisiones et stantiamenta et omnia que viderint convenire. Et quod quicquid in predictis et circa predicta vel eorum occasione vel causa aut alicuius eorum, ordinaverint, providerint seu fecerint vel mandaverint, semel seu plures et quotiens, scribantur et scribi debeant per scribam reformationum consiliorum populi et Comunis Florentie vel suum coadiutorem. Et sic facta seu provisa et scripta valeant et teneant ac si facta forent per opportuna consilia populi et Comunis Florentie. Et quod quilibet rector et offitialis Comunis Florentie presens et qui pro tempore fuerit, seu qui in civitate, comitatu vel districtu Florentie habet vel habebit aliquod offitium, et quelibet universitas comitatus seu districtus Florentie et quelibet singularis persona teneatur et debeat omnia et singula que per dictos priores Artium et Vexiliffer Iustitite et dictos octo offitiales eligendos, vel duas partes eorum ut dictum est, aut per ipsorum commisarios seu missos vel delegatos predictos vel aliquem ipsorum, provisa, deliberata vel mandata fuerint, exequi et executioni mandare et plenarie observare ad omnem eorum vel alicuius eorum requisitionem, sub pena quingentorum librarum florenorum parvorum cuilibet ipsorum contrafacienti vel non servanti, per dominum potestatem, dominum capitaneum et dominum executorem et ipsorum quemlibet, qui de hoc requireretur secrete seu publice auferenda [in the margin: denegatio expensis]. Salvo quod non possint ipsi domini priores et Vexillifer et octo offitiales, vigore presentis provisionis, expendere nec deliberare quod aliquid expendatur de pecunia Comunis Florentie, nec in aliquo detrahere vel diminuere de jurisdictione, dominio vel iuribus aut imperio Comunis Florentie nec eligere aliquem potestatem, castellanum seu offitialem in aliqua contrata, terra, comitatu sue districtu Florentie, cuius terre potestates et castellani, seu potestates tantum, quando de electione fienda de potestate contingeret tractari, aut castellani tantum quando de electione castellani contingeret tractari, essent imbussulati, et haberi possent vigore imbossulationis euiusdem, secundum formam ordinamentorum hactenus editorum, et ipsa eorum imbossulatione durante. Non obstantibus in predictis vel aliquo predictorum, aliquibus legibus, statutis, ordinamentis, provisionibus vel reformationibus consiliorum populi et Comunis Florentie aut obstaculis quibuscumque, etiam quantumcumque derogatoriis, penalibus vel precisi, vel etiam si de eis vel ipsorum aliquo fieri debuisset vel deberet spetialis mentio et expressa, quibus omnibus intelligatur esse et sit nominatim, expresse et spetialiter ac generaliter derogatum. Et quod pro predictis super in hac presenti provisione contentis etcetera, ut supra in precedenti provisione per omnia continetur.

Document 19   ASF *Uff. Cast.*, *Rocche* 1, fols. 15v – 18r, 19 May (1350). Description of the Giglio Fiorentino project by the *Ufficiali delle Castella* and translation of the document.

Anche i decti uficiali [parve loro che in val dambra=cancelled] provendendo in valdambra dove si fosse luogo piu utile convenevole et soficiente di porre la terra ch'e ordinata e ches si pongha parve loro ches si ponesse la detta terra in valdambra in luogo decto selva piana la quale posono e segnarono e ficharono si ipali e ordinarola in questo modo: cioè che sia di lunghezza di iiii[hundred]lxx braccia e larga braccia ccxlvi. E chè la detta terra abbia quatro porte delle quali l'una raguardi inverso Firenze e chiamisi porta fiorentina, l'altra raquardi inverso Arezo e chiamasi porta san piero, l'altra raquardi verso Siena sichiami porta san quiricho, l'altra ch'era raquardare verso Laterina sichiami porta san giovanni.

[In the margin, opposite the preceding sentence: Le quali porte el comune de Firenze aiuti di fare et paghi el magisterio quanto sara chiarito per l'ofitio d'i signori et de quelli dale castella] E chè la detta terra sia afossata intorno intorno e al presente istecchata e berteschata e a tempo compentente murata

E ala decta terra chiamato il nome didio e della beata virgine Maria e de gloriosi apostoli messer san Piero, e messer san Paolo, beato messer Johani, san Zanobi, santa Reparata e degli atri santi di paradiso. Ad honore et exaltatione et mantenimento del popolo et comune di Firenze e di parte guelfa et ad onore e acrescimento et mantenimento della detta terra puosono nome e che si chiamasse Giglio Fiorentino. E che il segno elarme della detta terra sia il giglio azurro nel campo giallo con rastrello di sopra e daluno de lati del decto giglio sia uno scudicciuolo delarme del popolo di Firenze e nell altro sia unaltro scudicciuolo coll arme del comune di firenze.

E che nel mezzo della decta terra sia una piazza lunga Lxxxx braccia e ampia Lxx E nella decta piazza sia uno pozzo. E allato alla decta piazza dalluna parte sia una chasa del comune con una loggia nella quale stia per lo comune di firenze luficiale della detta terra. // fol. 16r // E dalatra parte allato alla decta piazza dalla parte di sopra sia e facciasi La chiesa della pieve di sampiero. E che sopra il canto della detta terra verso Montuotii si faccia una torre alta xL braccia con ballatoio di pietro intorno sportati dalla parte di sopra e sia sodo sopra terra quatro braccia e abbia la decta torre due volte dentro cioe luna all altezza della dieci braccia e laltra dalla-parte di sopra della decta torre la quale torre sia larga [con le mura=added] verso la lunghezza della terra diece braccia e verso la larghezza della terra largha otto braccia. E abbia uno barbachane intorno intorno e [lat . . . =cancelled]. E muri della torre sieno di grossezza chome sono le mura della torre della recisa de Laterina la quale torre sia affossata e ripata dentro e di fuori della terra con un ponte levatoio e con una porticuiola la quale dea lentrata e luscita nella terra

E che nella detta torre sieno due palchora di legname amatonati sicome si conviene la quale torre sia bene fondata e a piede della decta torre si faccia un pozzo daqua. E ala decta torre si faccia uno procinto di mura largho e spazioso per diece braccia intorno intorno alla decta torre con una porticiuola verso la terra e unaltra dalla parte di fuori. E che fossi della terra sieno dampiezza in boccha di xx braccia e chupi x. E nel fondo i detti fossi sieno larghi diecie *[sic]* braccia.

Nella quale terra sieno nove vie luna sia dentro allato alle mura della terra largha x braccia [sopra . . . =cancelled] lungo a quale via e allato alla decta via sieno chase di larghezza e di lunghezza di x braccia. E poi sia una altra via di larghezza d'otto braccia e allato e insuladetta via sieno chase di lunghezza di braccia xx e larghe dieci. // fol. 16v // E sussequentemente sia unaltra via largha dieci braccia in sulla quale sieno chase lunghe xx braccia e larghe x braccie. E poi sia un altra via largha dieci bracie la quale risponda insulla piazza della terra e insulla decta via sieno le chase lunghe venti otto braccia e larghe x braccie le quali rispondano in sulla via maestra. E sussequentemente si faccia una via maestra che sia larga xiiii braccia e subsequentemente nellaltra parte della terra si facciano chase e vie come e designato e scritto di sopra. * E che la sopradetta via mastra sia per la lunghezza della terra. E un altra via simiglante alla detta via mastra sia e facciasi nel mezzo della decta terra per lo traverso.

E ch in ciascuno chanto della detta terra sia faccia una torre falsa.

E che fuori della decta terra si faccia il mercato il sabato di ciascuna settimana.*
[in the margin, next to the sentences between the asterisks: Si veramente che tutte le case ch riescono insu le vie maestre sieno al meno in -1- palco sfogato e coperte quando fieno compiute a lastre e tegole. E che le mure dinanzi sieno de prieta o de mattoni e siento alte (legion da rectu?) da la terra x braccia]

E che nella decta terra debbano venire ad abitare tutti e singuli huomini e persone degli infrascritti popoli e luoghi con tutte e singule loro famiglie chase masseritie e chose continuamente [sotto=cancelled] diqui a [kalendi agosto=cancelled] set-tembre proximo che viene [in the margin: nota de prirogatione termini] a pena di libri V̊ e cosi comandarono. Cioe gl' uomini e persone di Castiglione Alberti colle sue pertinentie, gl uomini e persone dalla Bad[i]a Agnano con sue pertinentie, gl uomini elle persone dalla Pieve a Prisciano [in the margin: nota de pretio fiendi and nota distibutione soli]

// fol. 17r // E che di qui a per tutto novembre proximo che viene glinfra-scritti huomini e persone vengono simiglantemente ad abitare nella decta terra come decto è alla decta pena ci[o]e

gluomini e persone della villa di Campannole e di San Lorentino
gluomini del comune di Monte Lucci
gluomini del comune di Cacciano
gluomini del comune della Cornia
[in the right-hand margin next to this list: Qui termine per i dominos priores et offitiales castrorum possint semel et plures prorogari]
E chesi disfaccino le chase delle decte ville
E chel campanile della Badia Agnano si dibassi
[The following is an addition in a different hand]

Et chi tornava ad habitare al termine abbia exentione essendo di detti luoghi altri v anni. Et essendo de fuori del contado et destrecto de Firenze abbia la detta exentione tornando etiandio dopo il termene ad habitare nela detta terra III-ʔ-

// fol. 18r // Item quod terrenum dicti castri ematur pro comuni Florentie pretio competenti non excedendo [cclibros = cancelled] c Florenos per officiales predictos vel aliquem eorum aut alia eorum commissarium quod pretium solvatur ut supra

Item quod quilibet [vol . . . = cancelled] hedificanti concedatur in perpetuum locationem pro anno censu unius [denari = cancelled] pullastrium [dando = cancelled] officialium dominorum priorum die vigilie beati Johanis. Et sufficiat quod unus pro aliis presentet quos mictat sine solutionem gabelle

Item quod [domus ante viorum viarum et platee = cancelled] debeant

Item quod qui habebunt facere dictus domos antiores caveant de faciendo usque ad palcum saltem hic ad kalendes Maii pena xxv libros.

Item quod potestas et vicarius vallis arni cum -1- homine pro quolibet dictorum comunium faciant distributionem predictarum casolarium Et quod potestas tuatur predicta facere exequi et punire inobedientes usque in x libri.

"It seems to the said officials — deliberating where in the Valdambra there is a site that would be most useful, appropriate and ample for the placement of the town which has been ordered and which will be founded — that [the town] should be located in the Valdambra in the place that is called Selva piana. They place it, and mark it, and fix the stakes and organize it in this way. It shall have a length of 470 *braccia* and a width of 246 *braccia*; the town shall have four gates of which one will face toward Florence and be called the Porta Fiorentina, another shall face toward Arezzo and be called the Porta San Pietro, another shall face toward Siena and be called the Porta San Quiricho, and another which shall have to face towards Laterina and it shall be called the Porta San Giovanni." [In the margin, opposite the preceding sentence: "The comune of Florence will help to build these gates and the officials of the city will pay that amount which shall be established by the office of the *Signori* and the officers of the *Castella*."] "The town shall be surrounded by ditches and, for the moment, enclosed with palisades. Eventually these shall be replaced with stone walls.

"Having invoked the name of God and of the Blessed Virgin Mary and the glorious apostles Saint Peter and Saint Paul and the blessed John as well as Saint Zenobius, Santa Reparta and the other saints of paradise [the officials] give a name to the said town and for its support it shall be called Giglio Fiorentino in honor and celebration and support of the commune of Florence and the *Parte Guelfa* and their honor and growth. And the device and the arms of the said town shall be a blue lily on a yellow ground with a "rastrello" above and on one side of this lily shall a shield with the arms of the *popolo* of Florence and on the other shall be another shield with the arms of the *comune* of Florence.

"And in the middle of the town shall be a piazza ninety *braccia* long and seventy *braccia* wide. And in this piazza shall be a well. And flanking this piazza, on one side, shall be a house of the commune with a loggia in which the official of the town shall reside for the commune of Florence. And on the other side, flanking this piazza, on the upper side, shall be, and there shall be built, the church of the parish of Saint Peter. Above the corner of the town facing [the castle of] Montuotii a forty-*braccia* tower shall be built. It shall have a projecting stone machicolated gallery at its summit and the tower shall be solid for four *braccia* above the ground and have two vaulted chambers. The first of these vaults shall begin at the level of ten *braccia* and the second shall be above that. The tower shall have a length *including the walls* [added] along the axis of the length of the town of ten *braccia* and along the axis of the width of the town the width of the tower shall be eight *braccia*. The tower shall have a battered base and the thickness of its walls shall be the same as the walls of the tower of the keep at Laterina. The tower shall be surrounded by a ditch and moat inside and outside of the town and it shall have a drawbridge and a small doorway which provide an entrance and an exit to the town.

"Inside the tower there shall be two floors of wood, covered with brick as is appropriate. The tower shall be well founded and at the foot of the tower a well shall be made. A walled enclosure wide and spacious for ten *braccia* in all directions shall be made around the tower with a small gate toward the town and another toward the countryside. The ditches of the town shall be twenty *braccia* wide at their mouth and ten *braccia* deep. And at the bottom the ditches shall be ten *braccia* wide.

"Inside the town there shall be nine streets. One shall be inside and alongside of the walls of the town, ten *braccia* wide. Alongside this street and flanking it shall be houses ten *braccia* wide and deep. Then there shall be another street eight *braccia* wide and alongside and flanking that street shall be houses twenty *braccia* in depth and ten wide. And subsequently there shall be another street ten *braccia* in width on which shall be houses twenty *braccia* deep and ten *braccia* wide. And then there shall be another street, ten *braccia* wide, which runs into the square of the town and on this street shall be houses twenty-eight *braccia* deep and ten *braccia* wide which extend to the main street. And subsequently there shall be made a main street which will be fourteen *braccia* wide and subsequently in the other part of the town houses and streets shall be made just as it is designated and written above. *The main street shall run the length of the town and another street, similar to it, shall be made in the middle of the town across it. And on each corner of this town shall be made a two-sided tower. Every Saturday a market shall be held outside of the town.*" [In the margin, next to the sentences between the asterisks: "It is established that all the houses that front onto the main streets shall have at least one enclosed upper story when they are completed and the front wall (of these houses) shall be of stone or brick and rise ten *braccia* above ground."]

"And all the men and persons of these communities and places must take up permanent residence in the said town with all of their families, houses, equipment and things by" ["the middle of August"=cancelled] "this coming September" [in the margin: "note concerning extension of deadlines"] "or face a fine of five hundred lire; and so [the officials] command. That is: the men and persons of Castiglione Alberti with their possessions; the men and persons from the Badia of Agnano with their possessions; the men and persons from the Pieve a Prisciana" [in the margin: "note about the establishment of prices; note about the distribution of land (lots?)"]

"And by the end of this coming November these men and persons will similarly come to live in the said town, as above and with the same penalties. That is: the men and persons of the village of Campannole and of San Lorentino, the men of the commune of Monte Luci, the men of the commune of Cacciano, the men of the commune of Cornia" [in the right-hand margin next to this list: "this deadline may be extended by the lords priors and the officers of the Castella"]

"And the houses of these villages shall be dismantled.

"And the bell tower of the Badia of Agnano be reduced in height."

[The following is an addition in a different hand]

"Whoever moves into the town within these deadlines, if he is from one of the above places, shall have a (tax) exemption for five years. And if he is from outside the *contado* and *distretto* of Florence he shall have that exemption once he had lived in the town for three years."

[This added on a separate page]

"And the land for this town shall be bought for the commune of Florence for a price not exceeding [two hundred lire=cancelled] one hundred florins by the aforesaid officials or any of them or anyone appointed by them; which price be paid as above.

"And to anyone who receives permission to build [in the town] shall have a perpetual rent of one chicken per year [to be paid] to the officials of the lords priors on the feast of Saint John. And one man may present [the chickens] of all. And he may bring them [into the city] without paying the gate tax.

"And the [houses before the streets and squares=cancelled]

"And those who shall make these front houses must raise them at least one story above ground by the first day of May [1351] or be penalized twenty-five lire.

"And the *podestà* and vicar of the Valdarno with one man from each of the said communes, shall distribute the aforementioned lots. And the *podestà* shall see that this is done and punish offenders [with fines] of up to ten lire."

Document 20   ASF *Cap.*, 4, fols. 63r – 66r, 2 June 1350. Legislation for the foundation of Giglio Fiorentino.

Quedam circa vallem Ambre

In consilio domini Capitanei et populi florentini, mandato nobilium et potentum virorum dominorum priorum Artium et Vexilliferi Justitie populi et Comunis Florentie, ad sonum campane et vocem preconam, ut moris est, convocato, in sufficienti numero congregato in palatio populi florentini. Et die tertia dicti mensis Junii in Consilio domini potestatis et Comunis Florentie, mandato nobilis et potentis militis domini Andriaxii de Rubeis de Parma, civitatis et Comunis Florentie honorabilis potestatis, ad vocem preconam et campane sonitum, ut moris est, convocato et congregato in palatio populi florentini. Et per ipsa iamdicta consilia, ut premictitur, in sufficientibus numeris congregata etcetera, aprobatis etcetera.

[The following appears also in ASF *Provv.*, 38, fols. 51r – 53r, 2 June 1350]

Magnifici et potentes viri, domini priores Artium et Vexillifer Justitie populi et Comunis Florentie, considerantes quasdam provisiones circa infrascripta editas die ultimo menses May proxime preteriti per ipsos dominos priores et Vexilliferum una cum offitio offitialium castrorum Comunis Florentie et eas tamquam utiles volentes effectum mancippari, habita super infrasriptis omnibus et singulis invicem et cum offitio duodecim bonorum virorum Comunis praedicti deliberatione solemni et demum inter ipsos dominos priores et Vexilliferum et duodecim bonos viros in sufficienti numero congregatos in palatio populi florentini, premisso facto et obtento diligenti et secreto scrutineo et partito ad fabas nigras et albas secundum formam statutorum et ordinamentorum dicti Comunis, omni jure et modo quibus melius potuerunt, providerunt, ordinaverunt et stantia verunt.

Imprimis quod turris et fortilitia Giogatoi teneatur, salvetur et custodiatur imperpetuum pro populis et Comune Florentie.

Item quod in partibus vallis Ambre florentine ponatur, edificetur et construatur quedam terra de novo, in quam homines Vallis Ambre praedicte, videlicet de Castilione Alberti
Abbatia Agnani
Plebe Presciani

Cappannole
Sancto Laurentino
Montis lucio
Cacciano et
Cornia

et de curiis seu territoriis dictorum locorum et cuiuslibet seu alicuius eorum redeant et redire teneantur et debeant cum eorum familiis ad habitandum, videlicet homines de Castilione Alberti, de Abbatia Agnani et de Plebe Presciani hinc ad kalendas ottobris venturas, et homines de Cappannole, de Sancto Laurentino de Monteluccii, de Cacciano et de Cornia hinc ad kalendas decembris venturas. Quos terminos domini priores Artium et Vexillifer Justitie dicti populi et Comunis possint una cum offitialibus castrorum dicti Comunis et duabus partibus ipsorum, ut dictum est, semel et pluries et quotiens si et quando eis videbitur prorogare. Que quidem terra ponatur, edificetur et construatur in dictis partibus Vallis Ambre, in loco dicto Selvapiana, et sit et esse debeat per longitudinem seu longitudinis brachiorum quadringentorum septuaginta intra muros, et latitudinis intra muros ducentorum quadraginta sex brachiorum. Et habeat et habere debeat dicta terra quatuor portas seu januas, quarum una, qua respiciatur versus civitatem Florentie nominetur Janua Florentina, et alia qua respiciatur versus civitatem Aretii nominetur porta Sancti Petri, et alia qua respiciatur versus civitatem Senense appelletur porta Sancti Quirici, quarta vero qua respiciatur versus castrum de Laterino nominetur janua Sancti Johannis. Cum platea, viis, stratis, ecclesia, edificiis designatis seu ordinatis per discretos viros Iohannem Gherardi Lanfredini et Pierum Lippi Ilibbrandini, cives honorabiles florentinos, duos ex offitialibus castrorum dicti Comuni vel ipsorum commissione.

Et quod in angulo dicte terre, ex latere versus Castrum Montuozi, fiat et edificetur expensis Comunis Florentie, loco casseri et pro cassero dicti Comunis, quedam turris de lapidibus ad calcinum, altitudinis quadraginta brachiorum, cum ballatorio de lapidibus circum circa, cum duabus voltis labideis, una videlicet per decem brachia supra terram et alia circa summitatem eiusdem turris. Et sit ipsa solida per totum et absque aliquo vacuo quatuor brachiis supra terram et sit latitudinis ex parte exteriori per latus latitudinis dicte terre otto brachiis. Murus autem eius sit eius grossitudinis cuius et prout est et seu erit murus turris que edificatur prope recisam castri de Laterino. Habeat quoque dicta turris circum circa unum barabacane et fossos et ripas, cum pontibus levatoriis et cum uno hostio ex parte anteriori, et inter dictas duas voltas fiendas in ea sint duo palchi. Et insuper habeat procintum muratum circum circa ut conveniet, distans ab ipsa turri undique decem brachiis. Quod procintum habeat duas porticciuolas, unam respicientem interius alteram exterius.

Et insuper quod dicte porte dicti castri fiant et fieri debeant expensis Comunis Florentie et de pecunia dicti Comunis Florentie dumtaxat, quantum capiet salarium magistrorum et manovalium pro muratura portarum predictarum. Lapides autem, calcinam et alia opportuna conferant Comuni et homines dicte vallis.

Item quod fiant circa terram predictam et remote ab ipso loco ubi debebunt esse muri dicti terre per quinque brachia circum circa, fossi boni et sufficientes pro fortitudine dicte terre, videlicet ampli in fundo decem brachiis et in summitate brachiis viginti, profundi vero et cupi brachiis saltem decem. Quos quidem fossos fieri facere teneatur et debeant comunia et universitates Vallis Arni Superioris, que sunt a Sancto Donato in Collina et Sancto Illario inclusive supra, et comunia lige Chianti et universitates et homines dicte lige, prout cuilibet per libras et soldos continget suis sumptibus et expensis. Et ad faciendum id cogi per vicarios dictarum contratarum summarie et de facto.

Stecchatos quoque et bertescas homines dicte vallis eorum sumptibus facere compellantur et manutenere donec terra ipsa murata fuerit circum circa.

Item quod terrenum, super quo fieri debet terra et edificatio supradicta, offitiales castrorum Comunis Florentie seu aliquis ex eis vel alii seu alius, quibus vel cui ipsi offitiales vel due partes ipsorum, ut dictum est, comiserint, emant et emere possint et debeant pro Comuni Florentie et eius vice et nomine, pro eo pretio quo ei seu eis videbitur convenire, non tamen maiore centum florenorum de auro, solvendum de pecunia Comunis eiusdem Florentie, et ipsum terrenum particulariter et divisim per casolaria, plateas sive sola, concedere dare seu locare in feudum seu affictum seu affictum perpetuum seu ad superficiem faciendam, volenti seu volentibus habitationes facere in terra predicta pro annuo afficto seu censu unius pollastri pro quolibet casolari, solo seu platea, solvendo in signum recognitionis dominii dominis Prioribus Artium et Vexillifero Iustitie populi et Comunis Florentie et eisdem dando quolibet anno die vigilie festivitatis beati Johannis Baptiste de mense junii // fol. 64v // in palatio dicti populi florentini.

Dictorum quoque polastrorum dationem et solutionem sufficiat fieri per aliquem de dicta terra pro se et nomine aliorum pro quibus volet solvere, etiam si mandatum non habuerit ab eisdem.

Item quod vicarius Vallis Arni Superioris et potestas seu offitialis dicte Vallis Ambre, cum uno homine de quolibet et pro quolibet dictorum Comunium dicte Vallis per consiliarios dicte Vallis eligendis, habeant baliam et potestatem ac offitium distribuendi semel et pluries et quotiens ipsa casolaria seu plateas inter homines dicte vallis et alios forenses, volentes ibidem edificia fabricare per eum modum et prout eis vel maiori parti ipsorum videbitur convenire. Et quod omnes illi et singuli quibus assignabuntur platee iuxta stratas, quibus directo ibitur ad januas dicte terre, teneantur et debeant facere et edificare domos super ipsis plateis que saltem habeant unum palcum integrum et [a]quarum stillicidia distent a terra saltem per decem brachia. Et quod habeant murellas anteriores de lapidibus seu lateribus et coperturam de lastris tegolis seu docciis. Et satisdare debeant coram offitiales ipsorum de incipiendo et prosequendo dictas domos et perficiendo saltem usque ad palcum inclusive hinc ad kalendas maii secuturas, sub pena xxv librarum florenorum parvorum cuiuslibet ipsorum non servanti, tollenda per ipsum potestem.

Item quod ser Arrigus domini Pauli de Fighino, ad presens potestas et offitialis Comunium et hominum Vallis Ambre Florentine, tanquam benemeritus, redigatur et reafirmetur in offitio et potestaria et in potestatem et offitialem comunium et hominum eorundem, et ex nunc electus et confirmatus esse intelligatur et sit pro sex mensibus futuris, incipidendis immediate post finitos primos sex menses sui offitii supradicti et in electione de eo dudum facte contentos, cum eisdem offitio, familia, salario, modis, conditionibus atque formis, salvo quod infra de iurisditione certorum malefitiorum dicetur. Oui insuper ser Arrigus intelligatur esse et sit durante toto suo offitio supra dicto tam veteri quam novo, superstes ad faciendum fieri et sollicitantum laboreria et fortilitias ac repositionem terre predicte et ad faciendum redire ad habitandum in ea. Et propterea possit facere omnia et singula precepta que eidem videbuntur convenentia pro predictis, et inobbedientem quemlibet et qualibet vice punire et condennare summarie et de facto usque in libris x florenorum parvorum, considerata personarum et negotiorum qualitate. Et ut circa predicta possit intendere diligenter, quod ser Arrigus ipse teneat et tenere debeat continuo durantibus ipsis offitiis in futurum unum equum, et debeat pro offitio superstantarie predicte habere et recipere a Comuni predicto Florentie, pro quolibet mense dicti temporis, libras undecim florenorum parvorum.

Item quod omnia comunia et universitates predicte, omnes et singuli de dicta Valle Ambre Florentine seu de aliquo comunium predictorum qui redibunt ad habitandum in terra predicta secundum dicta ordinamenta habeant, finito tempore quinque annorum quibus // fol. 65r // sunt exenti et immunes et liberi ab oneribus et factionibus Comunis Florentie secundum formam pactorum initorum inter dictum Comune vel alium pro eo, ex una parte, et dicta comunia seu alium vel alios per eis, ex parte altera, omnem illam immunitatem, exemptionem et liberationem per tempus et terminum aliorum quinque annorum, incipiendorum finitis dictis primis quinque annis, quam pro ipsis primis quinque annis habuerunt vigore dictorum pactorum seu quarumcumque provisionum seu reformationum Comunis Florentie, et cum eisdem beneficiis, modis, formis, tenoribus, clausulis atque salvis. Et quod similem per omnia immunitatem et liberationem ac exemtionem habeant et potiantur omnes et singuli alienigene, videlicet de extra comitatum et districtum Florentie, qui redierint ad habitandum et habitaverint in dicta terra, etiam si post dictos terminos assignatos seu assignandos ad redeundum ad habitandum, ut dictum est, venerint ad ibidem habitandum, et duraturum per terminum et tempora supradicta durante ipsius habitatione in terra prefata.

[This is followed by a directive to the "offitiales castrorum" to repair and fortify:

1. the keep at Cassero Cennina, for which forty florins are allotted
2. the defenses at fortilitie Civitelle, for which fifty florins are allotted.

In the version of this document in ASF *Provv.* (fol. 53r) three more projects are named.

3. the defenses at Uzano	two hundred florins
4. the defenses at Lancioline	three hundred florins
5. the walls and towers at Laterina	three hundred florins.

There is no discussion of money for the new town in the Ambra valley except of the one hundred florins for the purchase of the land mentioned in the document.]

Document 21 ASF *SS. Miss.*, 13, fol. 40r, 2 April 1365. Florence gives the Abbey of Agnano permission to build fortifications.

Abbati monasterii de Agnano

Volentes petitioni vestre coram nobis pro parte Reverentie vestre porrecte, de fortificari faciendo vallo et aliis munitionibus vestrum monasterium de Angnano, dyocesis Aretine nostrique districtus, tam pro securitate vestra quam contrate, et ne perversorum studia contra vos vel eos quid noxium valeant machinari in hiis que possumus conplacere, serie presentium vobis permictimus licentiam concedentes quatenus ipsum monasterium foveis et stechatis ac berteschis et aliis quibuscumque guernimentis defendibilibus, quibus emulorum conatibus utilius valeat reparari, fortificari facere valeatis ipsumque custodiri per homines dicti loci et alios, dumtaxat Comunis nostri devotos, quos ad id duxeritis deputandos. Concedentes quibuscumque vestris hominibus et aliis quos habere volueritis, quatenus dictum monasterium fortificare valeant et se in ipso receptare, ipsumque custodire et defendere toto posse iuxta eis et vestris vires Domino permictente concessas. Datum Florentie, die II Aprilis, III indictione.

Document 22 ASF, *Piante dei Capitani di parte,* cartone XVIII, no. 28 (Sixteenth century). Captions of the plan of San Giovanni Valdarno (See Fig. 4).

On left side of sheet (not all visible in Fig. 4):

Note delle misure d[el] chastel Sang[iovane] cioé delle terre di decto chastello e sua mura e strada e fossi cioé come abiamo trovate per la notizia dello epitaffio di pietra che é sotto alla loggia del palazzo del vicario di detto chastello [see chap. 2, n. 10] et ancora oltre a detta nota le habiamo misurato. Tutti braccia, a panno:

La strada del mezzo e largha braccie 19⅔ o insino a braccie 20. La strada lungho le mura di drento largha braccia 16⅔ a panno cioé nella testa del chastello.

Le chase che sono insula strada maestra da ogni lato larghi braccia 38 dala decta strada per insino al chiasso di dreto.

Chiasso di dreto a dette chase largho braccia $3\frac{1}{2}$.

Chase che rispondono in detto chiasso larghe dal peto alla sena braccie $29\frac{1}{3}$.

Vie che si dicano le principale excetto la maestra larghe braccie $15\frac{2}{3}$.

Chase che sono in dette vie dalla parte di verso le mura larghe dal petto alle sene braccia $24\frac{1}{2}$.

Chiasso dreto a dette chase largho braccia $2\frac{1}{2}$.

Chase che rispondono in detto chiasso ed poi in verso le mura largha dal petto alla sena braccia 19.

Via che é lungha le mura dalla parte di levante e di ponente larghe braccia 19. Et dalla parte di verso arezzo braccia 16 et verso feghine braccia 16 a panno.

Mura grosse braccie $1\frac{1}{2}$.

Fossi e via fuora di detta mura a tutto atorno detto chastello larghi detto fosso e via braccia $37\frac{1}{2}$.

La lunghezza del diametro delle chase dalla testa di detto chastello et insino alla via transversale sono braccie 172 a panno, cosi dalla testa diverso feghine come a quella diverso montevarchi.

Le vie transversale sono larghe braccia $9\frac{1}{2}$.

La larghezza del diamitro dellaltre chase da decta via transversale et insino alla piazza braccia 162 a panno.

Piazza largha dalla testa di dette chase et insino alla loggia del palazzo largha braccia $20\frac{2}{3}$ cosi daluno lato come dallaltro.

La larghezza del palazzo, cioé dalla testa diverso feghine a quella diverso montevarchi largha braccia $40\frac{2}{3}$ a panno, cioé col tutto della loggia.

L'altra testa di detto palazzo per el verso della testa che e inverso quella nel verso la madonna lungho braccia $51\frac{1}{2}$ a panno col tutto della loggia.

Noi maestri gentile e batista habiamo fatto le sopra scritte e le sotto scritte misure in detto chastello. Et con la chana a terra di braccia 6 commune. Et si misura la terra et depoi transportato allegato a panno.

Dal mezzo del palazzo del vicario per insino al tutto de' fossi fuora delle mura lungho braccia chane $78 — 0\frac{1}{3}$ a terra che tratto in chane 6 braccia — a terra.

Et sono larghi e fossi e via resta [?] braccia chane 71 braccie $2\frac{1}{3}$ ciascuna meta chome di sopra.

[Continues for ten lines with measurements of the fields and roads outside San Giovanni.]

Document 23 ASF, *Cinque conservatori del Contado*, 258, fol. 602 bis. Report on the flood damage to San Giovanni made 10 March 1553 by Maestro Piero della Zucca. Captions. (See Fig. 5.)

At the top of the sheet: a scale of 80 braccia

In the street at the top of the plan: 14 [braccia, width]

Across the blocks at the top of the plan: 18 via, chase 20, 3, chase 24, via $15\frac{2}{3}$, chase 28, 4, chase 39, maestra 21, chase 39, 4, chase 28, via $15\frac{2}{3}$, chase 24, 3, chase 20, 18

In the cross street: 10 [width]

In the street along the wall on the right of the plan: 18 [width], 200, 10, 170, 18 [width]

Outside the wall on the left of the plan: porta della madonna amezodi

Along the upper border of the piazza: 68, 20, 21, 39, 4, $28\frac{1}{2}$, $15\frac{2}{3}$, 24, 3, 20, 18

In the piazza: piazza diverso la madona braccia 68 et 80, logia 10, palazzo del vicario braccia 39, loggia 10, 20, pozo, piazza largha braccia 80 e lungha 135

Outside the wall on the right of the plan: di tramontana, porta del mulino, Bisogna fare case . . . [?] dellegname, ∇ 15

Across the blocks below the piazza: via $17\frac{7}{8}$, chase 20, chase 24, via $15\frac{2}{3}$, chase $28\frac{1}{2}$, chase 39, via, chase 39, chase $28\frac{1}{2}$, via $15\frac{1}{3}$, chase 24, chase, 20, via, [beyond the wall] questo chastello e largho braccia 328 cholle mura e lungho braccia 790

At the lower cross street: [to the left of the wall] questa torre e rotta e vorebbe si spendere in essa ∇ 8, [in the street] pozo, 10 [width], 10 [width], pozo

In the blocks below the cross street: $17\frac{7}{8}$ via, 20 chase, 3, 24 chase, $15\frac{1}{3}$ via, braccia $28\frac{1}{2}$ chase, 4, braccia 39 case che sono insulla via maestra, 21 via, braccia 39 chase anno tutte dinanzi via et di dietro un chiasolino di br 4, 4, $28\frac{1}{2}$ chase insulla via di mezzo, $15\frac{1}{3}$ via, 24 chase, questo chiasolino e braccia 3 fra le chase, 3, 20 chase, $17\frac{7}{8}$ via, $1\frac{1}{2}$

In the blocks above the lower wall: peraro overo orti, $17\frac{7}{8}$, 20, 3, 24 . . . $15\frac{1}{3}$, 24, 3, 20, $17\frac{7}{8}$

Between the proposed wall (dark) and the site of the ruined wall (light): questa porta e la porta diverso levante e arezzo dove neitto [?] in arno braccia $48\frac{1}{2}$, 14 [width]

below: Perquanto posso vedere[,] la chomunita di Sangiovanni [,] esendo isfaciato il chastello dalla banda di sopra dove e rovinato per lungheza braccia 48 e largha braccia 328 cholle mura[,] disidera di potere curare detta testa chonuno bastione fralle chase e chiassi [e] corti di qualita che predette aperture nonsi possa uscire[,] facendo una porta nel diritto della strada maestra acio che la notte non sia in potesta dogniuna entrare o uscire di detto chastello[;] dove che facendo solo a bocha dele vie sarebbe braccia 121 ma a me pare che starebbe meglio uno bastione fuori delle chase per tuto quanto[.] [T]iene il chastello alto braccia 4 sopra la terra e di fuori li fare la scarpa per infino al piano d['] arno[,] cioe tuta la ripa et chostera almeno ∇ uno il braccia andante che fara ∇ 150 a non lo fare per tuto et ∇ 360 a farlo tutto.

La pianta di questo chastello fu fatta chon bella invenzione benche non sia atta alle moderne guerre. In prima quanto alle site delle chase sono braccia 10 il vano et da ugni banda fra via e via chase 16 et le vie sono di questa misura: la via maestra braccia 21[,] elle dua vie braccia 15⅓[,] et le vie traverse braccia 10[,] et lungho le mura di levante e ponente la via e braccia 14[,] et per tramontana e ½ braccia 17⅞[,] digradando la lunghezza delle chase chome si vede[:] sulla via maestra braccie 39[,] e nell['] altre due vie braccia 28 e 24[,] e quelle di lungho le mura braccia 20[.] [E] il palazzo e nel mezzo fuori della via maestra largho braccia 20 e lungho braccia 39 e piu le loggie cholle due piazze[.] [C]ome si vede fatte chon grande arte.

Document 24 ASF, *Conventi soppresse*, 136, 143 / I no. 23. Captions of the plan of Scarperia from the convent of the Padre di San Firenze, after 1776. (See Fig. 22.)

Title: Pianta di tutti i Beni, che sono nel Castello di Scarperia su le mura, Baluardi, Fossi, e carbonaia del medesimo Castello, di propretà de RR. PP. di S. Firenze. (Not visible in Fig. 22.)

Around the perimeter, from center left: Via Fiorentina, Madonna del Vivaio, Signore Capitano Ciamponi, Signori Conforti, Signori Fabbroni, Via di S. Agata, Signore Consorti, Romagnoli, Via Antica, Via della Capannuccia, Via Bolognese, Via di Poggio di Berghi, stradella, Via Maestra, Via di Ronta, Via del B.S. Lorenzo.

Inside the walls, upper left to lower left, upper right to lower right: Matassi, Porta, Via dell'Oche, Via Bolognese, Piazza, Via de Melai, Via della Torricella, Via del Palagio.

Key (not visible in Fig. 22):

A. Un pezzo di Bastione, con Viti, Frutti, et Gelsi, che teneva Domenico di Michele Matassi, oggi recaduto a detti RR. PP.

B. Un pezzo di Bastione, come il suddetto, che tiene la Signora Ferranti, ne Baccioni.

C. Casa con un pezzo di Bastione come il suddetto che tiene a livello Michele di Giovanni Matassi.

D. Bastioni come i suddetti, oggi recaduti a detti RR. PP.

E. Un pezzo di Fosso con Viti, Frutti, e Gelsi, tiene a livello Signore Capitano Amadis Ciamponi.

F. Terre lavorative ne fossi, allivellate a detto Signore Capitano.

G. Bastione con Viti, Frutti, e Gelsi, allivellato gia a'Signori Zaffiri, oggi affittato a detto Signore Capitano.

H. Un altro pezzo di Bastione, come il suddetto, allivellato a detto Signore Capitano.

I. Fossi, e Carbonaie, gia allivellati a Signori Zaffiri, oggi affittati a detto Signore Capitano.

K. Casa allivellata a Bernardino Ravicciuoli confinata a primo Via Bolognese, a secondo detti RR. "PP." con casa segnata C allivellata a Michele Matassi, a terzo Via dell'Ocche, a quarto detto Bernardo Rovicciuoli.

L. Casa ad uso d'Osteria, con stalla, ed Orto, posto di la da via dell'Oche, come sta'alla medesima, segnata M. Confina primo via Bolognese, secondo signore Bartolommeo Ciamponi, terzo Capella data da Buonomini, quarto mura Castellane, quinto Orto del Palazzo del Pubblico, sesto Chiesino, settimo Via.

N. Casetta, che s'appigiona, confinata primo Via della Torricella, secondo Propositura e Frati di S. Agostino, terzo Signore Ulivi, quarto Signore Termerini.

O. Casetto che s'appigiona, confinata primo Piazzetta, secondo Via de Mellai, terzo Giovanni Fabbrini, quarto Piero Bartoloni.

P. Casamento che s'appigiona ad uso d'Osteria detta della Scala, con Capanna, ed Orto, al medesimo annesso, posto di la dalla via delle Torricella segnata confinata primo Via Bolognese, secondo Signore Cavelliere Ulivi, terzo Signore Dottor Cosimo Ulivi, quarto Signore Capitano Amadis Ciamponi, quinto Piero Bartoloni, sesto Signore Filippo Conforti e Alessandro Pastori.

R. Casetta che s'appigiona confinata primo Via della Torricella, secondo Matteo Romanelli, terzo Signore Bartolommeo Romanelli, anzi Ciamponi, quarto Signori Pinelli e Niccolo Gucci.

S. Casa allivellata al Dottore Omaccini confinata a primo Via del Palagio, secondo Compagnia della SS. Trinita, terzo detti RR. PP. con casa detta il Palagio.

T. Casa che s'appigiona detta il Palagio confinata primo Via del Palagio, secondo Piazza, terzo Via di S. Agostino o delle Cortine, quarto Compagnia della SS. Trinita.

BIBLIOGRAPHY

Angiolini, P. *La fondazione di Alessandria nella tradizione e nella storia*. Alessandria, 1960.

Atlas der historischen Schutzzonen in Österreich. I, *Städte und Märkte*. Graz, 1970.

Bacci, P.D. *Terranuova Bracciolini nella sua storia*. Florence, 1956.

Badellino, O. "Gli statuti di Cherasco e il governo del Comune nel secolo XII." *Bolletino storico bibliografico subalpino* 28 (1926), pp. 45 – 78.

Baldari, E. "San Giovanni Valdarno." *Storia dell'arte italiana*. III, *Inchieste su centri minori*, edited by E. Guidoni. Turin, 1980, II, pp. 135 – 162.

Baldi, E. *L'Oratorio della Madonna delle Grazie in San Giovanni Val d'Arno*. Florence, 1914.

Ballestracci, D. and Piccinni, G. *Siena nel trecento, assetto urbano e strutture edilizie*. Florence, 1977.

Baqué, M.Z. "Des Bordes aux Bastides." *Bulletin de la Société archéologique, historique, littéraire et scientifique du Gers* 40 (1939), pp. 55 – 74, 131 – 150.

Barbieri, G. "Il Mugello, studio geografico umano." *Rivista Geografica Italiana* 60 (1953), pp. 89 – 113, 296 – 378.

Barley, M.W., ed. *European Towns: Their Archeology and Early History*. London, 1977.

Becker, M. "A study in Political Failure. The Florentine Magnates: 1280 – 1343." *Medieval Studies* 27 (1965), pp. 246 – 308.

Becker, M. *Florence in Transition*. Baltimore, 1967.

Beresford, M. *New Towns of the Middle Ages*. London, 1967.

Bernocco, G. *Storia della città e guida degli archivi di Cherasco e dintorni*. Cherasco, 1939.

Bianchi, L.G., and Poleggi, E. *Una città portuale del medioevo, Genova nei secoli X - XVI*. Genoa, 1980.

Biddle, M., and Hill, D. "Late Saxon Planned Towns." *The Antiquaries Journal* 51 (1971), pp. 70 – 85.

Blaschke, K. "Altstadt — Neustadt — Vorstadt, zur Typologie genetischer und topographischer Stadtgeschichtsforschung." *Vierteljahrschrift für Sozial- und Wirtschaftsgeschichte* 57 (1970), pp. 350 – 363.

Blondel, L. "Les Fondations de Villesneuves ou Borg-Neufs aux environs de Genève." *Bulletin de la Société d'Histoire et d'Archéologie de Genève* 9 (1951), pp. 3 – 17.

Bocchi, F. "Centri minori e fonti catastali; strutture sociale e spazio urbano nel territorio bolognese attraverso il catasto Boncompagni (1787): un metodo di analisi." *Storia della Città* 11 (1979), pp. 5 – 42.

Bocchi, F. "Città e campagne nell'Italia centro-settentrionale (secc. XII – XIV)." *Storia della Città* 36 (1986), pp. 101 – 104.

Bocchi, F. "La città e l'organizzazione del territorio in età medievale." *Le città in Italia e in Germania*, edited by R. Elze and G. Fasoli. Bologna, 1981, pp. 51 – 80.

Boheim, H. "Neuere Forschungsergebnisse zur Baugeschichte von Wiener Neustadt." *Blätter des Vereines für Landeskunde von Niederösterreich*, new series 21 (1887), pp. 355 – 379.

Bonasera, F. "Cortemaggiore 'città creata' nella pianura emiliana." *Bolletino Storico Piacentino* 57 (1962), pp. 1 – 9.

Bossini, A. *Storia di Figline e del Valdarno Superiore*. Florence, 1970.

Braunfels, W. *Abendländische Stadtbaukunst, Herrschaftsform und Baugestalt*. Cologne, 1974.

Braunfels, W. *Mittelalterliche Stadtbaukunst in der Toskana*. Berlin, 1953.

Brinckmann, A.E. *Deutsche Stadtbaukunst in der Vergangenheit*. Frankfurt am Main, 1911.

Brinckmann, A.E. *Stadtbaukunst*. Berlin, 1920.

Brocchi, G.M. *Descrizione della provincia del Mugello*. Florence, 1748.

Budelli, G., Camponeschi, C., Fiorentino, F., and Marolda, M.C. "L'Aquila: nota sul rapporto tra castelli e 'locali' nella formazione di una capitale territoriale." *Città contado e feudi nell'urbanistica medievale*, edited by E. Guidoni. Rome, 1974, pp. 181 – 195.

Burke, G.C. *The Making of Dutch Towns*. London, 1956.

Buselli, F. *Pietrasanta e le sue rocche*. Florence, 1970.

Caggese, R., ed. *Statuti della repubblica fiorentina*. Florence, 1901.

Camerani Marri, G., ed. *Statuti di Castelfranco di Sopra, 1394*. Florence, 1963.

Cantini, P. *Vicchio di Mugello, un castello del contado fiorentino dalla fondazione al catasto del 1427*. Florence, 1979.

Carli, G. *Firenzuola: la fortificazione ad opera di Antonio da Sangallo il Vecchio; considerazioni sulla struttura urbana della nuova fondazione fiorentina*. Florence, 1981.

Carmody, F.J. "Florence: Project for a Map, 1250 – 1296." *Speculum* 19 (1914), 39 – 49.

Casalis, G. *Dizionario geografico, storico, statistico, commerciale degli stati di S. M. il Re di Sardegna.* Turin, 1833 – 1856.

Cassan, U. *Neuf Siècles de batisseurs de villes: d'Alphonse de Poitiers à Lyautey.* Paris, 1975.

Cassini, S. *Dizionario biografico geografico storico del comune di Firenzuola.* Florence, 1914.

Castagnoli, F. *Orthogonal Town Planning in Antiquity.* 1963. Reprint. Cambridge, 1972.

Cervi, M.C. "Evoluzione topografica della Piazza Grande di Parma dall'epoca romana alla fine del secolo XIII." *Archivio Storico per le Provincie Parmensi,* fourth series, 14 (1962), pp. 31 – 52.

Cherubini, G., and Francovich, R. "Forme e vicende degli insediamenti nella campagna toscana dei secoli XIII – XV." *Quaderni storici* 24 (1973), pp. 877 – 904.

Chittolini, G. *La formazione dello stato regionale e le istituzioni del contado.* Turin, 1979.

Ciceri, L., ed. *Venzon.* Forty-eighth Congress of the Società Filologica Friulana. Udine, 1971.

Clasen, K.H. "Die ordenspreussische Stadt als Kunstwerk." *Kunstgeschichtliche Studien* (Essays in honor of Dagobert Frey), edited by H. Tintelnot. Breslau, 1943, pp. 9 – 44.

Compagni, Dino. *Dino Compagni e la sua Cronica.* Edited by I. del Lungo. Florence, 1879 – 1887.

Conti, E. *La formazione della struttura agraria moderna nel contado fiorentino.* I. Rome, 1965.

Corsi, D., ed. *Statuti urbanistici medievali di Lucca.* Venice, 1960.

Costa Restagno, J. "La fondazione di Villanuova di Albenga." *Rivista Inguana e Intemelia,* new series, 13 (1958), pp. 135 – 146.

Curies-Seimbres, M.A. *Essai sur les villes fondées dans le sud-ouest de la France aux XIIIe et XIVe siècles sous le nom générique de bastides.* Toulouse, 1880.

Davidsohn, R. *Forschungen zur Geschichte von Florenz.* Berlin, 1896 – 1908.

Davidsohn, R. *Storia di Firenze.* Florence, 1973.

Detti, E. "Urbanistica medievale minore." *Critica d'Arte* 24 (1957), pp. 489 – 504; 25 (1958), pp. 73 – 101.

Detti, E., Di Pietro, G.F., and Fanelli, G. *Città murate e sviluppo contemporaneo; 42 centri della Toscana.* Milan, 1968.

Dickinson, R.E. "Le Développement et la distribution du plan mediéval en èchiquier dans le sud de la France et l'est de l'Allemagne." *La Vie Urbaine* 15 (1938), pp. 271 – 296.

Dickinson, R.E. "The Development and Distribution of the Medieval German Town. I, The West German Lands." *Geography* 27 (March 1942), pp. 9 – 21; "II. The Eastern Lands of German Colonisation." *Geography* 27 (June 1942), pp. 47 – 53.

Dickinson, R.E. "The Morphology of the Medieval German Town." *The Geographical Review* 35 (January 1945), pp. 74 – 97.

Dinelli, P. *Camaiore, dalle origini ai giorni nostri.* Camaiore, 1971.

Dinklage, K. "Kärntner Städtegründungen unter Herzog Bernhard (1202 – 1256)." *Mitteilungen des Institutes für österreichische Geschichtsforschung* 69 (1961), pp. 85 – 96.

Dinklage, K. *Kleine Geschichte von Völkermarkt.* Völkermarkt, 1960.

Dinklage, K. "Völkermarkt zwischen Abt und Herzog. Ein Beitrag zur Gründungsgeschichte mittelalterlicher Städte." *Mitteilungen des Institutes für österreichische Geschichtsforschung* 67 (1959), pp. 278 – 305.

Doñate Sebastia, J.M. *Datos para la historia de Villarreal.* Villarreal, 1973.

Donna, G. *I borghi franchi nella politica e nella economica agraria della repubblica vercellese.* Turin, 1943.

Dupré Theseider, E. "Frederico II, ideatore di castelli e città." *Archivio Storico Pugliese* 26 (1973), pp. 25 – 40.

Egli, E. *Geschichte des Städtebaus.* Erlenbach-Zürich, 1959 – 1962.

Ennen, E. *Die europäische Stadt des Mittelalters.* Göttingen, 1972.

Fanelli, G. *Firenze, architettura e città.* Florence, 1973.

Fasoli, G. "Ricerche sui borghi franchi dell'alta Italia." *Rivista di Storia del Diritto Italiano* 15 (1942), pp. 139 – 214.

Fasoli, G., "Ricerche sulla legislazione antimagnatizia nei comuni dell'alta e media Italia." *Rivista di Storia del Diritto Italiano* 21 (1939), pp. 86 – 133; 21 (1939), pp. 241 – 309.

Ferrandiz e Irles, M. *Fundacion de Villarreal.* Castellon, 1902.

Fiore, F.P. "Fondazione e forma di Cittaducale." *Atti del XIX Congresso di Storia dell'Architettura.* L'Aquila, 1980, II, pp. 475 – 488.

Fisković, I. "Ston u svojem prirodnom i porijesnom prostoru." *Arhitektura* 31 (1977), pp. 22 – 27.

Fiumi, E. "Sui rapporti economici tra città e contado nell'età comunale." *Archivio Storico Italiano* 64 (1956), pp. 18 – 68.

Francovich, R. *I castelli del contado fiorentino nei secoli XII e XIII.* Florence, 1973.

Francovich, R. "Per la storia dell'insediamento mugellano, il castello di Ascianello." *Archeologia Medievale* 1 (1974), pp. 57 – 79.

Frati, E. *Storia documentata di Castel S. Pietro.* Bologna, 1904.

Frey, K. *Die Loggia dei Lanzi zu Florenz.* Berlin, 1885.

Friedman, D. "Le 'terre nuove' fiorentine." *Archeologia Medievale* 1 (1974), pp. 231 – 247.

Friedman, D. "The Porta a Faenza and the Last Circle of the Walls of Florence." *Essays Presented to Myron P. Gilmore*, edited by S. Bertelli and G. Ramakus. Florence, 1978, II, pp. 179 – 192.

Fuhrmann, K.H. "Gründung und Grundriss der Stadt des Deutschen Ritterordens in Preussen." Ph.D. dissertation, Technical University of Dresden, 1932.

Gabotto, F. "Cuneo e le origini comunali in Piemonte." *Bolletino Storico Bibliografico Subalpino* 5 (1900), pp. 19 – 94.

Galantay, E.Y. *New Towns: Antiquity to the Present*. New York, 1975.

Ganshoff, E.L. *Etude sur le developpement des villes entre Loire et Rhin au moyen age*. Paris-Brussels, 1943.

Gantner, J. *Grundformen der europäischen Stadt*. Vienna, 1928.

Gazzola, F. "Breve dissertazione sulle origini di Mondovi." *Bolletino della Società per gli Studi Storici, Archeologici e Artistici nella Provincia di Cuneo*, new series, 44 (1960), pp. 28 – 39.

Gherardi, A., ed. *Le Consulte della repubblica fiorentina, dall'anno MCCLXXX al MCCXCVIII*. Florence, 1896.

Gherardi Dragomanni, F. *Memorie della terra di San Giovanni*. Florence, 1834.

Gizzi, G. "La città dell'Aquila: fondazione e preesistenze." *Storia della Città* 28 (1983), pp. 11 – 42.

Gouron, M. *Les Chartes de franchises de Guienne et Gascogne*. Paris, 1935.

Grote, A. *Das Dombauamt in Florenz, 1285 – 1370. Studien zur Geschichte der Opera di Santa Reparata*. Munich, 1959.

Guidoni, E. *Arte e urbanistica in Toscana, 1000 – 1315*. Rome, 1970.

Guidoni, E. *La città dal medioevo al rinascimento*. Bari, 1981.

Guidoni, E. "La croce di strade. Funzione sacrale ed economica di un modello urbano." *Lotus International* 24 (1979), pp. 115 – 119.

Guidoni, E., ed. *Città contado e feudo nell'urbanistica medievale*. Rome, 1974.

Gutkind, E.A. *International History of Urban Development*. New York, 1964 – 1972.

Haase, C., ed. *Die Stadt des Mittelalters*. Darmstadt, 1969 – 1973.

Hall, T. *Mittelalterliche Stadtgrundrisse, Versuch einer Übersicht der Entwicklung in Deutschland und Frankreich*. Stockholm, 1978.

Hamm, E. *Die Städtegründung der Zähringer in Südwestdeutschland*. Freiburg im Breisgau, 1932.

Hardie, C. "The Origin and Plan of Roman Florentia." *Journal of Roman Studies* 55 (1965), pp. 122 – 140.

Heers, J. "Consorterie familiari alla fine del Medioevo." *La crisi degli ordinamenti comunali e le origini dello stato del rinascimento*, edited by G. Chitolini. Milan-Bologna, 1979, pp. 301 – 321.

Heers, J. *Family Clans in the Middle Ages*. Amsterdam and New York, 1977.

Heers, J. "Urbanisme et structure sociale à Génes au Moyen-Age." *Studi in onore di Ammintore Fanfani*. Milan, 1962, I, pp. 371 – 412.

Herzog, E. *Die ottonische Stadt, die Anfänge der mittelalterlichen Stadtbaukunst in Deutschland.* Berlin, 1964.

Herzog, E. "Problemi urbanistici nell'undicesimo secolo in Germania e Italia." *Critica d'arte* 13 – 14 (1956), pp. 15 – 22.

Hess, W. *Hessische Stadtgründungen der Landgrafen von Thüringen.* Beiträge zur Hessische Geschichte, IV. Marburg/Lahn and Witzenhausen, 1966.

Higounet, C. "Les 'terre nuove' florentines du XIV siecle." *Studi in onore di Ammintore Fanfani.* Milan, 1962, III, pp. 3 – 17.

Higounet, C. *Paysages et villages neufs du Moyen Age.* Bordeaux, 1975.

Hiorns, F.R. *Town-Building in History. An Outline Review of Conditions, Influences, Ideas and Methods affecting Planned Towns through Five Thousand Years.* London, 1956.

Hoenig, A. *Deutscher Städtebau in Böhmen, die mittelalterlichen Stadtgrundrisse Böhmens mit besonderer Berücksichtigung der Hauptstadt Prague.* Berlin, 1921.

Hofer, P. "Die Stadtgründungen des Mittelalters zwischen Genfersee und Rhein," in H. Boesch and P. Hofer, *Flugbild der Schweizer Stadt.* Bern, 1963, pp. 85ff.

Hofer, P. *Die Zähringerstädte, Dokumente zum Städtebau des Hochmittelalters aus 15 Städten Südwestdeutschlands und der Schweiz.* Thun, 1964.

Hoffmann, A. ed. *Österreichisches Städtebuch.* Vienna, 1968 – 1980.

Hyde, J.K. "Medieval Descriptions of Cities." *Bulletin of the John Rylands Library* 48 (1966), pp. 308 – 340.

Keller, H. *Die ostdeutsche Kolonialstadt des 13. Jahrhunderts und ihre südländischen Vorbilder.* Wiesbaden, 1979.

Keller, H. "Oberbayrische Stadtbaukunst des 13. Jahrhunderts." *Lebenskräfte in der Abendländischen Geistesgeschichte. Dank- und Erinnerungsgabe an Walter Goetz.* Marburg/Lahn, 1948, pp. 49 – 124.

Keyser, E. "Der Stadtgrundriss als Geschichtsquelle." *Studium Generale* 16 (1963), pp. 345 – 351.

Keyser, E. *Städtegründung und Städtebau in Nordwestdeutschland im Mittelalter.* Remagen, 1958.

Keyser, E., and Stoob, H., eds. *Deutsches Städtebuch, Handbuch städtischer Geschichte.* Stuttgart, 1939 – 1974.

Klaar, A. "Der gotische Städtebau in Österreich." *Die bildende Kunst in Österreich,* edited by K. Ginhart. Baden-Wien, 1938, II, pp. 13 – 25.

Klaar, A. "Die Siedlungsformen der Österreichischen Donaustädte." *Die Städte Mitteleuropas im 12. und 13. Jahrhundert.* Beiträge zur Geschichte der Städte Mitteleuropas. I, edited by W. Rausch. Linz, 1963, pp. 93 – 115.

Klaar, A. "Die siedlungstechnischen Grundzüge der niederösterreichischen Stadt im Mittelalter." *Jahrbuch fur Landeskunde von Niederösterreich* 29 (1944 – 48), pp. 365 – 385.

Klaar, A. "Strassenplatz und Rechteckplatz." *Unsere Heimat (Monatsblatt der Vereins für Landeskunde und Heimatschutz von Niederösterreich und Wien)*, new series, 4 (1933), pp. 7 – 19.

Klaiber, C. *Die Grundrissbildung der deutschen Stadt im Mittelalter.* Berlin, 1912.

Klapisch-Zuber, C. "Mezzadria e insediamenti rurali alla fine de Medio Evo." *Civiltà ed economia agricola in Toscana nei secoli XIII – XV: Problemi della vita delle campagne nel tardo Medioevo.* Ottavo Convegno Internazionale, Pistoia, 21 – 24 April 1977, Centro Italiano di Studi di Storia e d'Arte, Pistoia, 1981, pp. 149 – 161.

Koepf, H. *Stadtbaukunst in Österreich.* Salzburg, 1972.

Koepf, H. *Stadtbaukunst in Steiermark und Kärnten.* Vienna, 1974.

Kratzsch, K. "Wittelsbachische Gründungen im 13. und 14. Jahrhundert." *Wittelsbach und Bayern. Die Zeit der frühen Herzöge: von Otto I zu Ludwig dem Bayern,* edited by H. Glaser. Munich, 1980, I, pp. 318 – 337.

Lang, S. "Sull'origine della disposizione a scacchiera nelle città medioevali in Inghilterra, Francia e Germania." *Palladio,* new series 5 (1955), pp. 97 – 108.

Lang, S. "The Ideal City from Plato to Howard." *Architectural Review* 112 (1952), pp. 91 – 101.

Lavedan, P. *L'Histoire de l'Urbanisme.* Paris, 1926.

Laveden, P., and Hugueney, J. *L'Urbanisme au Moyen Age.* Geneva, 1974.

Lavisse, E. *La Marche de Brandenbourg.* Paris, 1875.

Leiwehr, E. and Grimm, O. *Marktplätze in Südostbayern.* Passau, 1976.

Leveque, P., and Vidal-Naquet, P. *Clisthène l'Athénien. Annales Littéraires de l'Université de Besançon.* LXV. Paris, 1964.

Liebhart, W. "Die frühen Wittelsbacher als Städte- und Marktgründer in Bayern." *Wittelsbach und Bayern. Die Zeit der frühen Herzöge: von Otto I. zu Ludwig dem Bayern,* edited by H. Glaser. Munich, 1980, I, pp. 307 – 317.

Lillius, H. *Der Pekkatori in Raahe: Studien über einen eckverscholossenen Platz und seine Gebäudetypen.* Helsinki, 1967.

Lisini, A., ed. *Il costituto del comune di Siena volgarizzato nel MCCCIX – MCCCX.* Siena, 1903.

Macci, L., and Orgera, V. "Una lottizzazione dell'ordine camaldolese a Firenze-Oltrearno." *Contributi di metodo per una conoscenza della città.* Florence, 1976.

Maetzke, G. *Florentia.* Rome, 1941.

Magna, L. "Gli Ubaldini del Mugello: una signoria feudale nel contado fiorentino." *Atti del II Convegno del Comitato di Studi sulla Storia dei Ceti Dirigenti in Toscana.* Pisa, 1982, pp. 13 – 65.

Manetti, R. "Gli Ufficiali delle Castella nell'Archivio di Stato fiorentino." *Bolletino Ingegneri* 29 (1981), pp. 15 – 19.

Manetti, R., and Pozzana, M. *Firenze: le porte dell'ultima cerchia di mura.* Florence, 1979.

Mansuelli, G. *Urbanistica e architettura della Cisalpina romana fino al III secolo.* Brussels, 1971.

Marchesi, S. *Compendio storico di Cittaducale (dall'origine al 1592).* Rieti, 1875.

Mariotti, A. "Le terre nuove fiorentine." *Dialettica territoriale fra alta e basso medioevo,* edited by V. Franchetti, A. Mariotti, and G.C. Romby. Florence, 1974.

Martinelli, R., and Nuti, L., eds. *La città di fondazione. Atti del secondo convegno internazionale di storia urbanisitica.* Lucca, 1978.

Maschke, E. "Die deutschen Städte der Stauferzeit." *Die Zeit der Staufer.* Würtembergisches Landesmuseum. Stuttgart, 1977, III, pp. 59 – 73.

Maschke, E., and Sydow J., eds. *Städterweiterung und Vorstadt.* Stuttgart, 1969.

Mazzi, M.S., and Raveggi, S. *Gli uomini e le cose nelle compagne fiorentine del quattrocento.* Florence, 1983.

Meckseper, C. *Kleine Kunstgeschichte der deutschen Stadt im Mittelalter.* Darmstadt, 1982.

Meckseper, C. "Konstanz und die mittelalterliche Stadtbaukunst Italiens." *Konstanz zur Zeit der Staufer.* Constance, 1983, pp. 90 – 109.

Meckseper, C. "Rottweil: Untersuchung zur Stadtbaugeschichte im Hochmittelalter." Ph.D. dissertation, University of Stuttgart, 1969.

Meckseper, C. "Stadtbau." *Die Zeit der Staufer.* Württembergisches Landesmuseum. Stuttgart, 1977, III, pp. 75 – 87.

Mengozzi, G. *La città italiana nell'alto medioevo.* 1931. Reprint, Florence, 1971.

Merlini, A. *Castelfranco di Sopra: arte, storia, e costume.* Florence, 1981.

Michele, U. "Venzone." *Storia dell'arte italiana.* III, *Inchieste su centri minori,* edited by E. Guidoni. Turin, 1980, I, pp. 37 – 68.

Morelli, Giovanni di Pagolo. *Ricordi.* Edited by V. Branca. Florence, 1956.

Moretti, I. *Le "terre nuove" del contado fiorentino.* Florence, 1980.

Morini, M. *Atlante di storia dell'urbanistica dalla preistoria all'inizio del secolo XX.* Milan, 1963.

Moschella, P. "Le Case a 'sporti' in Firenze." *Palladio* 6 (1942), pp. 167 – 173.

Müller, W. *Die heilige Stadt. Roma quadrata, himmlisches Jerusalem, und die Mythe vom Weltnabel.* Stuttgart, 1961.

Münter, G. *Idealstädte.* Berlin, 1957.

Niccolai, F. "I consorzi nobiliari ed il comune nell'alta e media Italia." *Rivista di Storia del Diritto Italiano* 13 (1940), pp. 117 – 127, 292 – 342, 397 – 477.

Niccolai, F. *Mugello e Val di sieve.* Borgo San Lorenzo, 1914.

Nice, B. "I centri abitati della Toscana con pianta regolare." *L'Universo* 27, no.1 (1947), pp. 42ff.

Nigrelli, I. "La 'fondazione' federiciana di Gela ed Augusta." *Siculorum Gymnasium* 6 (1953), pp. 166 – 184.

Noack, W. "Kunstgeschichtliche Probleme der mittelalterlichen Stadtplanung in Deutschland (an Beispielen aus dem Oberrheingebiet)." *Oberrhein-Kunst* 8 (1938), pp. 5 – 18; also *XIV International Congress of the History of Art.* Basel, 1938, II, pp. 129 – 140.

Noack, W. "Stadtbaukunst und geistlich-weltliche Repräsentation im XI. Jahrhundert." *Festschrift Kurt Bauch,* edited by B. Hackelsberger, G. Himmelheber, and M. Meier, Munich, 1957, pp. 29 – 49.

Ottokar, N. "Criteri d'ordine, di regolarità, e d'organizzazione nell'urbanistica ed in genere nella vita fiorentina dei secoli XIII – XIV." *Studi comunali e fiorentini.* Florence, 1948, pp. 143 – 149.

Ottokar, N. *Il comune di Firenze al fine del dugento.* Turin, 1962.

Palumbo, P.F. "La fondazione di Manfredonia." *Contributi alla storia dell'età di Manfredi.* Biblioteca Storica. Rome, 1959, IV, pp. 71 – 107.

Pampaloni, G. *Firenze al tempo di Dante: documenti sull'urbanistica fiorentina.* Rome, 1973.

Pampaloni, G. "I magnati a Firenze alla fine del dugento." *Archivio Storico Italiano* 129 (1971), pp. 387 – 423.

Panero, F. "La genesi e l'assetto distrettuale e urbanistico della villa nuova di Cherasco." *Bolletino della Società per gli Studi Storici, Archeologici e Artistici della Provincia di Cuneo* 74 (1976), pp. 5 – 32.

Paul, J. *Der Palazzo Vecchio in Florenz. Ursprung und Bedeutung.* Florence, 1969.

Paul, J. *Die mittelalterlichen Komunalpaläste in Italien.* Ph.D. dissertation, University of Freiburg im Breisgau, 1963.

Piccinato, L. "Origini dello schema urbano circolare nel medioevo." *Palladio* 5 (1941), pp. 120 – 125.

Pierotti, P. *Lucca, edilizia, urbanistica medievale.* Milan, 1965.

Pierotti, P. *Urbanistica: storia e prassi.* Florence, 1972.

Pirillo, P. "L'organizzazione della difesa: i cantieri della construzione militari nel territorio fiorentino (secc. XIV)." *Convegno Internazionale Castelli, Storia e Archeologia.* Cuneo, 1981.

Pirillo, P. "Un caso di pianificazione territoriale nel contado di Firenze (secc. XII e XIV)." *Studi e Ricerche* 1 (1981), pp. 179 – 200.

Planić-Lončarić, M. *Planirana izgradnja na području Dubrovačke republike.* Zagreb, 1980.

Planić-Lončarić, M. "SOS za baštinu zidine stona." *Arhitektura* 31 (1977), pp. 26 – 36.

Planitz, H. *Die deutsche Stadt im Mittelalter von der Römerzeit bis zu den Zunftkämpfen.* Graz-Cologne, 1954.

Plessner, J. *L'émigration de la campagne à la ville libre de Florence au XIIIe siècle.*
Copenhagen, 1934.

Plessner, J. *Una rivoluzione stradale del Dugento.* Copenhagen, 1938.

Preyer, B. "The 'chasa overo palagio' of Alberto di Zanobio: A Florentine
Palace of about 1400 and Its Later Remodelling." *Art Bulletin* 65 (1983), pp.
387 – 401.

Preyer, B. "Two Cerchi Palaces in Florence." *Renaissance Studies in Honor of
Craig Hugh Smyth* edited by A. Morrogh, F. Superbi Gioffredi, E. Borsook,
and P. Morsellie, Florence, 1985, II, pp. 613 – 630.

Procacci, U. "L'aspetto urbano di Firenze dai tempi di Cacciaguida a quelli di
Dante." *Enciclopedia Dantesca.* Rome, 1970, s.v. *"Firenze."*

Ranalli, F., ed. *Istorie fiorentine di Scipione Ammirato con l'aggiunte di Scipione
Ammirato il Giovane.* Florence, 1847.

Rausch, W., ed. *Beiträge zur Geschichte der Städte Mitteleuropas.* Linz, 1963 – 1974.

Raveggi, S., Tarassi, M., Medici, D., and Parenti, D. *Ghibellini, guelfi, e popolo
grasso. I detentore del potere politico a Firenze nella seconda metà del dugento.*
Florence, 1978.

Recknagel, M. "Die Städte und Märkte des Bayrischen Donaugebiets. Versuch
einer geographischen Übersichtsuntersuchung mit besonderer Berucksichti-
gung der Lage und der Grundrissformen." *Mitteilungen der Geographischen
Gesellschaft in München* 20 (1927), pp. 1 – 118.

Redon, O. "Le Contado de Sienne 1263 – 1270, une frontière mediévale."
Mélanges de l'école française, moyen age – temps modernes 87 (1975), pp. 105 – 139.

Reincke, H. "Über Städtegründung: Betrachtungen und Phantasien." 1957.
Reprinted in *Die Stadt des Mittelalters,* edited by C. Haase. Darmstadt, 1969,
I, pp. 331 – 363.

Reitzenstein, A. Freiherr von. *Die alte bairische Stadt in den Modellen des
Drechslermeisters Jakob Sandtner, gefertigt in den Jahren 1568 – 1574 im Auftrag
Herzog Albrechts V von Bayern.* Munich, 1967.

Repetti, E. *Dizionario geografico fisico storico della Toscana, contenente la descrizione di tutti i luoghi del Granducato, ducato di Lucca, Garfagnana e Lunigiana.*
Florence, 1833 – 1846.

Reynaud, P. "The Role of Design in City Form: Organic and Planned Towns."
Master's thesis, The Massachusetts Institute of Technology, 1980.

Richter, M. "Die 'Terra murata' im florentinischen Gebiet." *Mitteilungen des
kunsthistorischen Institutes in Florenz* 6 (1940), pp. 351 – 386.

Rodolico, F., and Marchini, G. *I palazzi del popolo nei comuni toscani del medio
evo.* Florence, 1962.

Rohault de Fleury, G. *Toscane au Moyen Age: architecture civile et militaire.*
Paris, 1870 – 1873.

Romanini, A.M. "La rielaborazione trecentesca di Pavia romana." *Atti del Convegno di Studio sul centro storico di Pavia.* Pavia, 1968, pp. 123 – 140.

Roncière, C.M. de la. *Florence centre économique régionale au XIVe siècle. Le marché des denrées de première nécessité à Florence et dans sa campagne et les conditions de vie des salariés (1320 – 1380).* Aix-en-Provence, 1976.

Rörig, F. "Die Gründungsunternehmerstädte des 12. Jahrhundert." *Hansische Beiträge zur deutschen Wirtschaftsgeschichte.* Schriften der Baltischen Kommission zu Kiel, IX. Breslau, 1928, pp. 243 – 277.

Rothenfelder, L. "Die Wittelsbacher als Städetgründer in Bayern." *Verhandlungen des historischen Vereines für Niederbayern* 47 (1911), pp. 1 – 106.

Rykwert, J. *The Idea of a Town.* Princeton, 1976.

Saalman, H. *Filippo Brunelleschi; the Cupola of Santa Maria del Fiore.* London, 1980.

Saalman, H. *Medieval Cities.* New York, 1968.

St. Blanquat, O. de. "Comment se sont créés les Bastides du Sud-Ouest de la France?" *Annales* 4 (1949), pp. 278 – 289.

Salvemini, G. *Magnati e popolani in Firenze dal 1280 al 1295.* 1899. Reprint. Milan, 1966.

Santini, P. "Società delle torri in Firenze." *Archivio Storico Italiano,* fourth series, 20 (1887), pp. 25 – 58, 178 – 204.

Scheid, J., and Svenbro, J. "Byrsa. La ruse d'Elissa et la fondation de Carthage." *Annales, Économies, Sociétés, Civilisations* 2 (1985), pp. 329 – 342.

Schultze, J. "Die Stadtviertel, ein stadtgeschichtliches Problem." *Blätter für deutsche Landesgeschichte* 92 (1956), pp. 18 – 39.

Schulz, J. "The Communal Buildings in Parma." *Mitteilungen des Kunsthistorischen Institutes in Florenz* 26 (1982), pp. 277 – 324.

Scoppola, F. "La rocca di Talamone." *Storia della Città* 28 (1983), pp. 43 – 58.

Settimana di studio del centro italiano di studi sull'alto medioevo, 6. *La città nell'alto medioevo.* Spoleto, 1959.

Settimana di studio del centro italiano di studi sull'alto medioevo, 21. *Topografia urbana e vita cittadina nell'alto medioevo in occidente.* 2 vols. Spoleto, 1974.

Severini, G. *Architettura militare di Giuliano da Sangallo.* Pisa, 1970.

Shillaber, C. "Edward I, Builder of Towns." *Speculum* 22 (1947), pp. 297 – 309.

Siedler, E.J. *Märkischer Stadtbau im Mittelalter.* Berlin, 1914.

Spagnesi, G., and Properzi, P. *L'Aquila: problemi di forma e storia della città.* Bari, 1972.

Stahl, B. *Adel und Volk im florentiner Dugento.* Cologne-Graz, 1965.

Stefani, Marchionne di Coppo. *Cronaca fiorentina.* Edited by N. Rodolico. *Rerum Italicarum Scriptores,* XXX, part 1. Città di Castello, 1903.

Sterpos, D. *Communicazioni stradali attraverso i tempi: Bologna-Firenze.* Rome, 1961.

Stoob, H. *Forschungen zum Städtewesen in Europa.* Vienna, 1970.

Sznura, F. *L'espansione urbana di Firenze nel dugento.* Florence, 1975.

Tabanelli, M. *Questo è 'la Massa,' storia e cronache della Massa dei Lombardi dalle origini al 1578.* Faenza, 1972.

Testut, L. *La Bastide de Beaumont en Périgord, 1272 - 1789.* 2 vols. Bordeaux, 1920.

Tout, T.F. "Medieval Town Planning." *Bulletin of the John Rylands Library* 4 (1917 - 18), pp. 26 - 58.

Trabut-Cussac, J.-P. "Bastides ou Forteresses?" *Le Moyen Age* 60 (1954), pp. 81 - 135.

Trachtenberg, M. *The Campanile of Florence Cathedral.* New York, 1971.

Traver Garcia, d.B. *Historia de Villarreal.* Villarreal, 1909.

Trexler, R. *Public Life in Renaissance Florence.* New York, 1980.

Ulbrich, K. "Städte und Märkte in Kärnten." *Mitteilungen des Geographischen Gesellschaft in Wien* 82 (1939), pp. 193 - 222.

Veglia, C. *Fossano, origine storica e profilo odierno.* Cuneo, 1956.

Vigliano, G. *Beni culturali ambientali in Piemonte.* Quaderno del Centro di Studi e Ricerche Economico Sociale, 5. Turin, 1969.

Villani, G. *Cronica di Giovanni Villani a miglior lezione ridotta coll'aiuto de' testi a penna con note filologiche di I. Moutier e con appendici storico-geografiche comp. da Franc. Gherardi-Dragomanni.* Florence, 1844 - 1845.

Villani, M. *Cronica di Matteo Villani a miglior lezione ridotta coll'aiuto de' testi a penna con appendici storico-geografiche compilate da Franc. Gherardi-Dragomanni.* Florence, 1846.

Vinai, C. "Cuneo ed i suoi plani regolatori." *Atti e rassegna tecnica.* Turin, 1951.

Vit, V. de. *Memorie storiche di Borgomanero.* Prato, 1880.

Ward-Perkins, B. *From Classical Antiquity to the Middle Ages: Urban Public Building in Northern and Central Italy, AD 30 - 850.* Oxford, 1984.

Ward-Perkins, J.B. *Cities of Ancient Greece and Italy: Planning in Classical Antiquity.* New York, 1974.

Weissman, R. *Ritual Brotherhood in Renaissance Florence.* New York, 1982.

Weller, K. "Die staufischen Städtegründungen in Schwaben." *Württemburgische Vierteljahreshefte für Landesgeschichte,* new series, 36 (1930), pp. 145 - 268.

Wengert, H. *Die Stadtanlagen in Steiermarkt; ein Beitrag zur Geschichte des deutschen Städtebaus.* Graz, 1932.

Wood-Brown, J. *The Builders of Florence.* London, 1907.

Zdekauer, L., ed. *Il costituto del comune di Siena del'anno 1262.* Milan, 1897.

Zocca, M. "Creazioni urbanistiche del medioevo in Italia." *Palladio* 2 (1938), pp. 161 - 170.

INDEX